D1271916

Why Vietnam Invaded Cambodia

POLITICAL CULTURE AND THE CAUSES OF WAR

Stephen J. Morris

STANFORD UNIVERSITY PRESS
STANFORD, CALIFORNIA
1999

Stanford University Press
Stanford, California

© 1999 by the Board of Trustees of the Leland Stanford Junior University

Printed in the United States of America

CIP data appear at the end of the book

To my mother and
in memory of my father

ACKNOWLEDGMENTS

This study began as work for a doctoral dissertation in political science at Columbia University. A few years later its focus was totally reconceived, and the book was completed after extensive postdoctoral research in Russia and rewriting undertaken mainly at Harvard University. Small but significant revisions were undertaken while I was a fellow at Johns Hopkins University's Paul H. Nitze School of Advanced International Studies.

At Columbia University, thanks go to Professor Thomas P. Bernstein, who as second reader on my dissertation committee agreed to sponsor my dissertation. At Columbia, I also received helpful criticisms from Professor James Morley and other members of my dissertation committee.

Part of the research and all of the writing of my dissertation was made possible by a research grant administered by the University of California, Berkeley, Institute of East Asian Studies. My special thanks for the privilege of working at Berkeley go to the Institute's former director, Professor Robert Scalapino. Then and ever since I have benefited greatly from his personal generosity, diligence, intelligence, and knowledge. My work at Berkeley was also facilitated by Douglas Pike, who made available the Indochina Archive's holdings and work space and was extremely tolerant of my bizarre working hours. My work at the Berkeley Archive, then and later, was also helped by its current guardian, Stephen Denney.

At Harvard University I received a number of postdoctoral fellowships, which funded new research on this and on other related book projects, mostly through the Center for International Affairs, and its John M. Olin Institute for Strategic Studies. My greatest debt there is to Professor Samuel P. Huntington, who welcomed me into an exceptional academic environment. As one of those lucky to have attended his graduate courses during the late 1970s, and lucky to have been affiliated with the Harvard research centers he has directed during the 1990s, I have been inspired and stimulated by Professor Huntington's extraordinary intellectual originality, agility, and open mindedness, and have benefited from his professional support.

The last period of my work at Harvard was made possible by the kind help of Professor Harvey Mansfield, assisted by the fine professional staff of Harvard's Government Department. An important word of thanks goes to Professor Adam Ulam at Harvard. Beginning in 1978, when I was a visiting Columbia graduate student, and later as a Harvard postdoctoral fellow, I was a frequent participant at the Russian Research Center's informal morning coffee hour group discussions, at which many valuable professional and personal ties were established, and where Adam Ulam's brilliant and witty interventions were a source of great enlightenment and entertainment for all. My long association with the Russian Research Center, and thus indirectly my later access to Soviet archives, would not have occurred without Adam Ulam's early professional support and kindness.

Thanks to Professor Karl Jackson and the executive committee of the Foreign Policy Institute at Johns Hopkins University's Paul H. Nitze School of Advanced International Studies, who have provided me with a comfortable and congenial work environment.

My access to the archives of the former Communist Party of the Soviet Union's Central Committee during 1992–93 was facilitated by the Cold War International History Project of the Woodrow Wilson International Center for Scholars. The Project's then director, James Hershberg, and the chairman of its advisory committee, William Taubman, intervened with reluctant Russian bureaucrats on several occasions during the winter of 1992–93 to help provide my access. I was assisted in the archives during 1992–93 by Dimitry Masyakov of the Institute of Oriental Studies in Moscow. My navigation of the archives, then and later when access became highly restricted, was also helped by Mark Kramer. The Institute of Universal History in Moscow helped me with bureaucratic aspects of invitations for several of my visits. Virginie Coulloudon and Jean Christophe Peuch were wonderful friends and wise advisers in Moscow.

My understanding of Vietnam has been facilitated by two visits to the south during the early 1970s and my long association with many Vietnamese over a period of nearly three decades. The late diplomat and intellectual Phung Nhat Minh was my initial guide and friend in South Vietnam and Australia. My conversations over the years in Saigon, Hue, Paris, Cambridge, and

Washington with numerous Vietnamese intellectuals, and with two more recent defectors from communism, Truong Nhu Tang and Colonel Bui Tin, have informed me in many ways. Finally, my long friendship with the irrepressible and witty iconoclast Doan Van Toai, who has survived both communist prisons and an anticommunist assassin's bullets, has included countless hours of always fascinating and sometimes hilarious conversation amounting to a special education on contemporary Vietnam.

In the case of Cambodia, my education was hindered by the limited amount of credible Western scholarship, but was helped by my visit to the border areas during 1983 as a freelance television correspondent for CBS News. I also made private visits there again in 1984 and 1985, and to Phnom Penh in 1996 and Kratie in 1998. Thanks are especially due to Cambodia's current King Norodom Sihanouk, who honored me with a ninety-minute private interview in 1985; and also to Prince Norodom Ranariddh; His Excellency Son Sann; Thailand's former U.N. Ambassador H. E. Birabongse Kasemsiri; his then deputy Kobsak Chutikul; and to many other Thai and Cambodian officials. Narankiri Tith provided me with his personal recollections of the Khmers Rouges leaders as students and with a mimeograph of then Prince Sihanouk's unexpurgated and still unpublished memoir *La Calice Jusqu'a La Lie*. Stephen Heder kindly provided me with a copy of the transcripts of his 1980 interviews with former Khmers Rouges cadres and guided me to other sources. He also loaned me copies of photographs of the Khmers Rouges from the Toul Sleng archives. Two years of work among the Cambodian community in the United States during 1989–91, in support of a democratic and peaceful future for their homeland, provided another dimension of my education in the values and political thinking of Cambodians.

My understanding of the nature of revolutionary communist states began with my informal education in Australia by the brilliant, now late, Czech-Australian intellectual and academic psychologist, Dr. Frank (Franta) Knopfelmacher. Franta introduced me to the classical German sociologists, especially Max Weber, and much more. My development as a writer has been helped by my friendships with several clever and decent people from Australia—notably my former philosophy teacher, Professor David Armstrong, my former fellow student and now law professor Martin Krygier, and my former senior academic colleague and later editor, Owen Harries.

The eminent historian of Vietnam Professor William Duiker, as well as another, anonymous reviewer, made helpful criticisms of an earlier version of the entire book manuscript. Martin Krygier read and criticized an earlier draft of the introduction, and Stephen Heder read and criticized excerpts of an earlier version of the sections on Cambodia. Though the criticisms of all of the above have prompted revisions to the manuscript, responsibility for this final version is mine alone. Jim Gerrand, Julio Jeldres, and Narankiri Tith kindly provided me with photographs from their personal collections.

Thanks to my editors at Stanford University Press, Muriel Bell, Stacey Lynn, and Mike Walker. Although they were prepared to publish my manuscript in an earlier form, they endured my laborious efforts to revise the manuscript to my own ultimate satisfaction.

Funding for my work on this and other book projects has been provided by the Lynde and Harry Bradley Foundation, the Smith Richardson Foundation, the John M. Olin Foundation, and the Carthage Foundation, under the auspices of Harvard University's Faculty of Arts and Sciences. Final revisions were undertaken with funding for work on several related projects provided by the William H. Donner Foundation and the Sarah Scaife Foundation, under the auspices of Johns Hopkins University's Paul H. Nitze School of Advanced International Studies. I thank them all for their generous support.

I owe a special debt of thanks to my mother and my late father for their extraordinary patience and support.

S.J.M.

CONTENTS

Abbreviations   xiii

Preface   1

Introduction: International Relations, Rationality,
and Marxist-Leninist Political Cultures   5

PART ONE
The Local Genesis of the Conflict

1. Roots of a Conflict: The Vietnamese Communists and the
   Cambodians, 1930–70   23

2. The Public Rise and Secret Fall of "Militant Solidarity":
   Vietnamese and Cambodian Communists, 1970–75   47

3. The Foreign Policy of Democratic Kampuchea, 1975–78   69

4. The Public Disintegration of "Militant Solidarity" in
   Indochina: Vietnam and Cambodia, 1975–78   88

PART TWO
The Internationalization of a Conflict

5. Vietnam and the Communist World, 1930–68   119

6. North Vietnam's Tilt Toward the Soviet Union,
   1968–75   143

7. The Collapse of Vietnamese-Chinese Relations   167

8. The Emergence of the Soviet-Vietnamese Alliance   197

9. The Consequences of the Vietnamese Invasion   219

Conclusion: History and Theory   229

Notes   245

Bibliography   289

Index   305

Photographs follow page 115

ASEAN	Association of Southeast Asian Nations
COSVN	Central Office for South Vietnam
CCP	Chinese Communist Party
CGDK	Coalition Government of Democratic Kampuchea
Comecon	Council for Mutual Economic Assistance
CPT	Communist Party of Thailand
CPV	Communist Party of Vietnam
CPSU	Communist Party of the Soviet Union
DRV	Democratic Republic of Vietnam
DK	Democratic Kampuchea
FUNK	National United Front
GRUNK	Royal United National Government of Kampuchea
ICP	Indochinese Communist Party
KCP	Kampuchean Communist Party
KPRP	Kampuchean People's Revolutionary Party
KPNLF	Khmer People's National Liberation Front
KPRP	Khmer People's Revolutionary Party
LPRP	Lao People's Revolutionary Party
NLFSV	National Liberation Front of South Vietnam
PRC	People's Republic of China
PRK	People's Republic of Kampuchea
PRGSV	Provisional Revolutionary Government of South Vietnam
PSB	Vietnam's Public Security Bureau (Cong An)
SOC	State of Cambodia
SRV	Socialist Republic of Vietnam
SEATO	Southeast Asia Treaty Organization
VCP	Vietnamese Communist Party
VWP	Vietnamese Workers' Party
VCP	Vietnamese Communist Party

Why Vietnam Invaded Cambodia

POLITICAL CULTURE AND THE CAUSES OF WAR

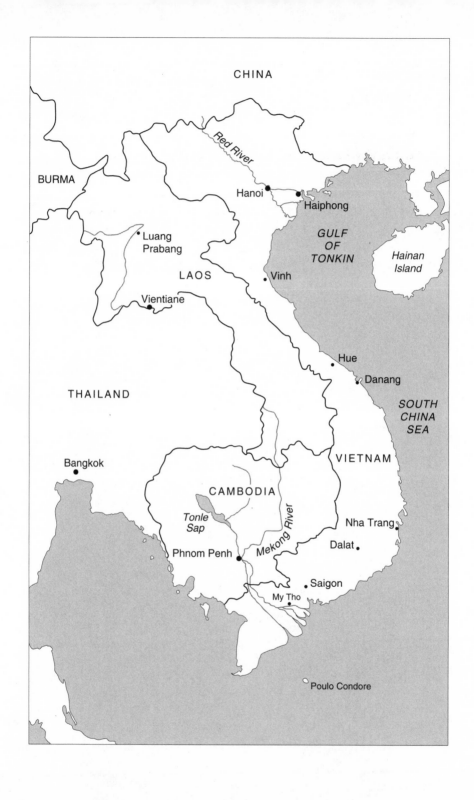

THAILAND

LAOS

104°

106°

14°

14°

SIEM REAP
ODDAR
MEANCHEY

Phnom
Thbeng
Meanchey

STUNG TRENG

RATANAKIRI

PREAH VIHEAR

Stung Treng

Lomphat

• Siem Reap

BATTAMBANG

• Battambang

Tonle

Sap

KOMPONG THOM

KRATIE

MONDOLKIRI

• Kompong
Thom

Senmonorem

• Pursat

PURSAT

Kompong Chhnang

• Kratie

KOMPONG
CHHNANG

KOMPONG CHAM

12°

• Kompong Cham

12°

KOMPONG
SPEU

Phnom Penh

VIETNAM

• Krong
Koh Kong

Kompong
Speu

Takhmau

• Prey
Veng

SVAY RIENG

KOH KONG

PREY
VENG

• Svay Rieng

TAKEO

Takeo •

Ho Chi Minh
City

KAMPOT

• Kampot

Kompong Som
(Sihanoukville)

Mekong

10°

GULF OF
THAILAND

10°

SOUTH
CHINA
SEA

CAMBODIA

International boundary

Province boundary

National capital

• Province capital

0   50 Kilometers

0   50 Miles

104°

106°

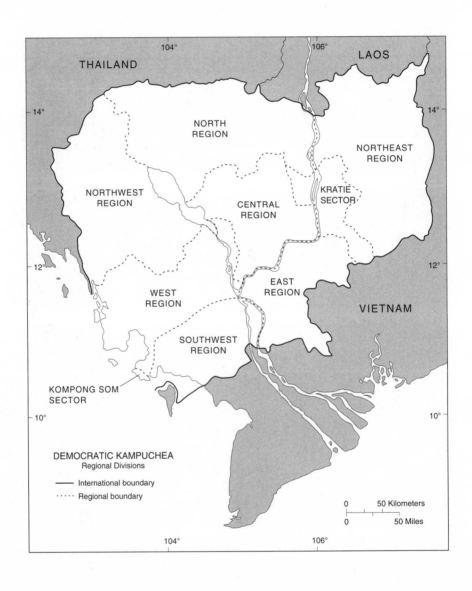

THAILAND

LAOS

104°

106°

14°

14°

NORTH
REGION

NORTHEAST
REGION

NORTHWEST
REGION

CENTRAL
REGION

KRATIE
SECTOR

12°

12°

WEST
REGION

EAST
REGION

VIETNAM

SOUTHWEST
REGION

KOMPONG SOM
SECTOR

10°

10°

DEMOCRATIC KAMPUCHEA
Regional Divisions

International boundary

Regional boundary

0   50 Kilometers

0   50 Miles

104°

106°

This book is a work of both political science and history. It is the only scholarly study to date of the causes of Vietnam's decision to invade Cambodia in
1978. As a work of political science it is concerned to show how and explain
why some weaker states provoke conflict with stronger neighboring states
while apparently disregarding their objectively perilous power situation. In
this effort it goes beyond the established realist tradition and offers primarily political culture explanations of the foreign policy decision making of
both primary belligerents. Most important, and perhaps unique, in this regard is the study's emphasis on specific features of a chiliastic regime—its
ideology and its paranoia in—explaining certain irrational state behaviors
that have contributed to the outbreak of war. In developing its distinctive
perspective, this book brings history and the insights of sociology and psychology to bear in a critical way on some of the concepts and prototheories
that dominate the academic study of international relations.

What is also novel about this book is that it presents together for the first
time two separate but complexly intertwined histories: one of Vietnam's relations with Cambodia and the other of Vietnam's relations with the Soviet
Union and China. Moreover, it does so making extensive use of the archives
of the former Communist Party of the Soviet Union, located in Moscow.

Until the collapse of the Soviet Union in 1991, most studies of the foreign
policies of communist states rested almost entirely on the interpretation of
official public statements and actions. The motives of policymakers had to
be inferred from these publicly observed events. Inevitably much was speculative, and rarely was there solid ground for analytical certainty. The partial
opening of Communist Party archives in Russia during the early 1990s provided the opportunity for a qualitative leap forward in our understanding of
how and why various communist political elites made policy, not only in the

Soviet Union itself but also in the many other areas of the world where that state was directly involved.

The Soviet Union was a long-time sponsor and ally of the Vietnamese communists. Documents that I have found in the Russian archives include reports by the Soviet ambassador in Hanoi of his conversations with Vietnamese leaders, Soviet analyses of the political and military intentions and capabilities of the Vietnamese, and evaluations of Vietnamese-Chinese relations. Most important, I have discovered translations of top secret Vietnamese Communist Party Politburo reports, covertly acquired by Hanoi-based Soviet intelligence operatives. No documents of this level of political sensitivity were ever acquired by the French or American governments during their military involvements in Indochina.

The Russian sources used in the book are restricted to those held in the archives of the former Soviet party's Central Committee. While Soviet Politburo documents—kept in the Russian Presidential Archive—have been selectively declassified by the Russian government, the Presidential Archive itself has always been off limits to all but a tiny, select handful of Russians. This means that whereas documentary records of conversations of top Vietnamese leaders with the Soviet ambassador in Hanoi were available, conversations of the same Vietnamese leaders with Soviet leaders in Moscow were not. I was therefore unable to have access to such important records as the accounts of the important secret meetings of the Vietnamese and Soviet leaders held in Moscow in June and November 1978. Nevertheless, so long as the Vietnamese Communist Party's own archives and similarly those of the Chinese Communist Party remain closed to scholars, the Russian documents cited in this study will remain the most valuable sources on Vietnamese foreign policy ever revealed.

Unfortunately, the liberal political spirit that prevailed in Russia in 1991–92 has subsequently diminished, and this has led to a gradual closing down of access to important Russian archival sources on the history of international affairs. Further research of the kind that is embodied in this book will not be possible unless the current trend is reversed.

In the case of Cambodia, some of the important written primary sources are compromised. Most of the documentation left behind by the Khmers Rouges when they fled Phnom Penh in 1979 was captured by their Vietnamese communist enemies. Thus the only documents on Cambodian Communist Party decision making made available have not come from free scholarly access to open archives but were released after careful scrutiny by Vietnamese communist leaders, who have a vital interest in the kind of history that will be written. I have tried to take this into account when deciding which of the published internal documents of the Khmers Rouges to use, by comparing them carefully with other relevant public sources.

Other valuable sources on Southeast Asian history—the Archives d'Outre Mer located in Aix-En-Provence, France, and the University of California's Indochina Archive located in Berkeley, California—have also been used. I have also interviewed former policymakers and policy advisers, including most notably then Prince (now King) Sihanouk of Cambodia, and several Vietnamese, Cambodians, and Russians.

Despite the profound American presence in Indochina during some of the years examined, the role of the United States figures only marginally in this study. All of the available evidence suggests that United States' behavior, other than its withdrawal from the region in 1973–75, played no role in the Vietnamese decision to invade Cambodia.

Introduction: International Relations, Rationality, and Marxist-Leninist Political Cultures

On December 25, 1978, the armed forces of communist Vietnam began a full-scale invasion of communist Cambodia (Democratic Kampuchea). The invasion was significant for several related reasons. In the century that has seen the birth and demise of communism, it marked the beginning of the first and only extended war ever fought between two communist regimes. Moreover that war was made possible by the material sustenance of the two smaller belligerents by the two largest communist states—the Soviet Union and the People's Republic of China. Finally, that war generated a second, briefer war between communist states—the border war between Vietnam and China in February 1979.

THE PROBLEM

The genesis of the Vietnamese invasion poses a puzzle because it was a weak local power (Cambodia) that initiated armed conflict against an incomparably more powerful local opponent (Vietnam). Moreover China, the main external ally of that weak local power, was much weaker militarily than the Soviet Union, the main external ally of the stronger local power. Thus the weak initiator of armed conflict could not have imagined that its existing alliance system would balance the power of its adversary and its adversary's existing alliance system. Furthermore, as we will see, there is no evidence that in initiating armed conflict the weaker local power was contemplating expanding its range of allies, nor even contemplating utilizing the power of its existing allies. Instead, the weaker power was anticipating that it could either intimidate its more powerful neighbor or else win any full-scale war alone. This puzzling behavior is only the most bizarre in a series of puzzling events that affected the Vietnamese decision to invade Cambodia.

The causes of the Vietnamese invasion were multiple and complex in their interconnection. The background cause was the imperial ambition of Vietnam's leadership, which had always wished to dominate the entire region of what was formerly French Indochina. The immediate or triggering cause, without which the invasion was unlikely to have taken place, was the provocative military attacks upon the communist Vietnamese by the communist Cambodians. These attacks occurred intermittently over a five-year period, peaking in 1977–78.

Among the secondary factors relevant to the outbreak of the war was North Vietnam's foreign policy behavior during the previous decade. By aligning itself with the Soviet Union, in a process that began in the late 1960s at the height of China's conflict with the Soviet Union, North Vietnam had needlessly antagonized China. Vietnam's subsequent decisions to purge and begin to expel its ethnic Chinese minority population and to join the Council for Mutual Economic Assistance (Comecon), the Soviet-dominated economic bloc, further antagonized China. This spiral of Vietnamese alienation from China and into alignment with the Soviet Union "globalized" a regional struggle for power in Cambodia, because this realignment convinced Beijing that Hanoi's actions in Cambodia were in Moscow's interests, at Moscow's behest, and threatening to Chinese security.

It will be seen that Hanoi's decision to begin to align itself with Moscow *preceded* its recognition of the problem posed for it by the Khmers Rouges (Red Khmers) when the latter was still only an insurgency movement. Moreover Hanoi needed aid from both the Soviet Union and China in its war against the United States and South Vietnam, and later in its postwar domestic reconstruction. Thus Hanoi's decision to align—although only partially at first—rather than to remain neutral between the Soviet Union and China, poses another puzzle.

A final puzzle is the fact that the Vietnamese communist leaders failed to inform the Soviet Union in advance of their intention to invade and occupy Cambodia. This deceit was perpetrated despite the fact that during the six months between the decision to invade and the actual invasion, Hanoi had already fully aligned itself with Moscow, who as Hanoi's patron stood to suffer from any international condemnation of or reaction against the invasion. Moreover, Moscow was Hanoi's only protector against China, and Moscow's military and diplomatic support would be essential for a successful Vietnamese conquest of Cambodia.

The various puzzles exist as puzzles only insofar as one accepts certain basic assumptions of contemporary academic theorizing about the nature of international relations. These assumptions, which have been articulated by the dominant realist school and modified by their mainstream critics, are first, that states tend to focus their foreign policy upon the pursuit of state power, with preservation of national autonomy and security as a minimum goal and extension of national power as a maximum goal.[1] Liberal critics of realism tend to emphasize the importance of economic prosperity as a goal of state policy. Most academic theorists ignore any state motive other than the pursuit of power or wealth.[2] Second, states tend to base their judgments about the appropriate policy to pursue on the basis of the incentives and constraints of the "international system," which realists define as the international power configuration of states. Thus, for realism, a state's judgments about its actual or potential power resources, either alone or in coalition with others, compared with the power resources of adversaries, will determine what policies the state will feel able to pursue.[3] For most critics of realism, the "international system" is conceived to include more than just "the power configuration of states." International and transnational institutions are also said to be relevant. But the idea that the "international system," however defined, constrains the behavior of states, is not challenged. In other words, a form of environmental or situational determinism is built into contemporary international relations theory. The third assumption is that states act rationally in the pursuit of their goals. That is, it is assumed that decision makers make judgments about what policies to pursue only after calculating the likely impact of external constraints and the resources available for action upon the policy's attainability, as well as the expected costs of such action. This proposition may be called *instrumental rationality* or the *rationality of means*. It is a theoretical assumption shared by both realists and their mainstream critics.

These assumptions dominate theoretical discussions and guide analysis in Western academic studies of international relations, and percolate down to influence the thinking of Western journalists, diplomats, and foreign policy analysts. This theorizing is founded upon an image of states as rational, calculating maximizers of material self-interest.

Recently a challenge to parts of this established image has been mounted by a small number of scholars. The most significant challenge has come from Samuel Huntington, who gives major weight to nonmaterial, "civilizational" values as the goals of state power in the post–Cold War era.[4]

But the image of states as rational, calculating maximizers of material self-interest remains an assumption of most academic writing on international relations. The rationalistic and materialistic bias of academic theory leaves no place for concepts such as resentment, envy, rage, hubris, arrogance, or contempt as causes of action. These latter motivations provide examples of the ideal type, which Max Weber categorized as *emotional* action. Academic theory also ignores what Weber defined as *value-rational* action:

> the actions of persons who, regardless of possible cost to themselves, act to put into practice their convictions of what seems to them to be required by duty, honor, the pursuit of beauty, a religious call, personal loyalty, or the importance of some "cause" no matter in what it consists.[5]

By contrast with the sociological insights of Weber, contemporary academic theorizing about international relations rests upon an assumption of a *universal* human nature that transcends cultures over space and time. We will see, after examining the events that led to the Vietnamese decision to invade Cambodia, that the behavior of the local belligerents cannot be explained in terms of any assumption about a universal human nature. This study supports the view that specific cultural outlooks have influenced the foreign policy behavior of communist regimes.

POLITICAL CULTURE AND FOREIGN POLICY

My analysis begins with the following axiomatic propositions: 1) the causes of wars are to be found in the policies of states; 2) the policies of states are determined by the values, attitudes, perceptions, and judgments of a state's political decision makers, acting in an environment of domestic and international pressures and opportunities; 3) the values, attitudes, perceptions, and judgments of a state's political decision makers are to some extent the product of a cultural predisposition; and 4) this cultural predisposition, which we will call a political culture, does not necessarily determine political decisions, but it influences them to some degree.

The concept of culture is one of the central concepts of the social sciences. Culture may be defined as a recurring pattern of cognitive and evaluative orientations toward social objects. Following Clifford Geertz, we can differentiate the cognitive and evaluative aspects of a culture by the terms *worldview* and *ethos*.[6] Culture is action practiced by individuals insofar as they are members of a group—be that group a family, a friendship circle, a neighborhood, or else an ethnic, religious, regional, national, or transnational association. Culture is observed when it is manifested in human behavior; but culture is only fully understood by means of introspection and empathy.[7]

When we refer to the political culture of a nation's foreign policy decision makers, we are referring to a very discriminate subcategory of culture. We are not referring to mass culture—that is, the culture of the general population—political or otherwise. We are referring to *political elite* political culture. In all political systems, political elites make foreign policy decisions, and it is their political culture that is of interest to this study. This is not to deny that aspects of mass culture may provide a component of political elite political culture. But they are not necessarily identical.

Another potentially important distinction for our purposes is between a *traditional* and a *nontraditional* political culture. The traditional political culture (of a political elite or of a general population) is the customary pattern of interpreting the world and the nation's role in it, as has been practiced since time immemorial and passed on from generation to generation. The nontraditional political culture comprises any novel or even aberrant political outlook and ethos. It may be, but is not identical with, a modern political culture, which is defined by some writers as one that is oriented toward instrumentally rational behavior. Nontraditional political culture may derive from a drastic change in the nation's relative material status (e.g., as has been the case of the United States in the second half of the twentieth century, which led the traditionally dominant isolationist political culture to be overshadowed by a newly emergent and powerful internationalist political culture).

Alternatively, a nontraditional political culture may derive from the emergence of new types of political elites, especially, but not only, those who are bearers of revolutionary ideologies (as was the case of France in the 1790s, Russia after 1917, and Iran after 1978). In the latter cases, the subtype of nontraditional political culture is *revolutionary millenarian* or *chiliastic*.

A state's political elite may possess elements of traditional and nontraditional political cultures, expressed either in the form of different political factions or in different tendencies in the mind of one individual leader. For this and other reasons, empirical application of the distinction between traditional and nontraditional political cultures may be difficult to make in some instances. But it is not necessarily always difficult.

The approach sketched here assumes that political actors interpret their external environment and interact with it in the light of their subjective interpretations. Of course, not all political actors' interpretations are manifestations of culture. Each individual is unique and possesses individual intellectual qualities. This suggests that the study of individual leadership personality is also very relevant to the study of foreign policy decision making.

This work is primarily an analytical history based upon original primary research. But it is also interwoven with theoretical observations demonstrating how political culture has affected the foreign policy of certain Marxist-Leninist states. The study gives traditional political culture some weight in the analysis. We may crudely summarize the salient aspects of traditional Vietnamese and Cambodian cultures, with regard to their mutual political relations, by stating that Vietnamese political elites have always despised all Cambodians, and Cambodian political elites have always deeply resented all Vietnamese. This broad-brush summary of attitudes will be elaborated on throughout the book, most especially with general historical illustrations in the next chapter. But since the study argues further that the foreign policies of these states were also deeply influenced by a transnational revolutionary political culture, whose features are often misunderstood, let us next consider the salient aspects of that culture in some detail.

THE REVOLUTIONARY POLITICAL CULTURE OF
MARXIST-LENINIST REGIMES: IDEOLOGY

Marxist-Leninist regimes are contemporary examples of a more general political type known as the chiliastic or revolutionary millenarian regime. One writer on chiliastic movements of Europe in the Middle Ages, Norman Cohn, has captured their essential qualities:

> It is characteristic of this kind of movement that its aims and premises are boundless. A social struggle is seen not as a struggle for specific, limited objectives, but as an event of unique importance, different in kind from all other struggles known to history, a cataclysm from which the world is to emerge totally transformed and redeemed.[8]

Much has been written about how the domestic policies of Marxist-Leninist regimes emanate from their revolutionary millenarian political culture. In all cases, after seizing power, Marxist-Leninist regimes have instituted revolutionary changes in the structure of their nation's polity, economy, and society. In each case the scope of party-state control was expanded dramatically to encompass every aspect of the individual's social existence. This new system of political domination came to be referred to by Western analysts as the totalitarian state.[9] The regimes themselves rejected such a term as a self-reference. But they explained and justified their revolutions in millenarian terms, as attempts to create a "new socialist man."

But no conceptually sophisticated attempt has been made to explain the foreign policies of these regimes in terms of their chiliastic political culture.[10] Most academic country specialists analyze the foreign policy of a Marxist-Leninist state toward a specific region and, lacking real theoretical concerns, have tended to rest rather sloppily upon the ubiquitous intellectual crutch of "national interest," which is rarely defined, let alone intellectually defended. Yet we must ask one basic question: If it is reasonable to argue that a chiliastic political culture has had some impact upon the domestic policies of Marxist-Leninist regimes, why should we not suspect that such a political culture has had an impact upon their foreign policies?

Marxist-Leninist regimes have all had a common core of what Alexander George calls "philosophical beliefs." Most important for our purposes are the beliefs in the inevitability of historical progress, culminating in the triumph of communism; the moral superiority of even the supposedly "transitional" socialist form of socioeconomic organization over the capitalist form; the inherent mutual hostility of the "capitalist world" and the "socialist world"; and the inevitability of conflict between imperialism (the "highest stage of capitalism") and socialism. The nations ruled by Marxist-Leninist "vanguard" communist parties describe this conflict as the international "class struggle." Marxist-Leninists, as adherents to the doctrine that there are laws of history, reject the notion that major historical changes can be determined by "accidental" events. Marxist-Leninist ideology is also universally characterized by an optimistic vision of the ultimate outcome of the struggle.[11]

Nevertheless, there have been some important variations in the explicit content of the ideology of Marxist-Leninist regimes. For example, Stalin's regime was more deferential toward the role of formal education, expertise, and technology as tools of historical change than was Mao Zedong's regime. Mao, disdainful of these factors, had great faith in the role of human will in affecting history.[12] The Vietnamese communists were closer to the Stalinist than to the Maoist position on this question. But the Cambodian communists adopted Mao's idiosyncratic deviation from Marxist orthodoxy enthusiastically. These explicit assumptions affected the notion of what was "objectively possible," in choosing means toward politically desired ends. Belief in the importance of human will relative to the "objective" factors of material force (military or economic), made Mao and his disciples less cautious than Stalin and his successors in their choice of military strategies and tactics.[13] This also affected their ability to realistically gauge their prospects of success.

We have already proposed several analytical distinctions within the concept of political culture. Most important have been the distinctions between the cognitive and evaluative dimensions of culture, between political elite and mass culture, and between traditional and nontraditional culture. These distinctions are not mutually exclusive. And there is probably one more distinction worth making. For it would be a serious mistake to reduce the political culture of Marxist-Leninist regimes to the explicit content of their ideology. The political culture of Marxist-Leninist regimes may be analyzed in terms of two distinct elements: the *formal* content, which is contained in the explicit concepts and prescriptions of its ideology; and the *informal* content, which is the more implicit pattern of thinking about politics.

THE REVOLUTIONARY POLITICAL CULTURE OF
MARXIST-LENINIST REGIMES: PARANOIA

The most pervasive informal dimension of Marxist-Leninist political culture is its paranoid tendencies. All chiliastic regimes provide collective examples of what is known in the psychiatric profession as the Paranoid Personality Disorder, defined as "a pattern of pervasive distrust and suspiciousness of others such that their motives are interpreted as malevolent."[14] The Communist Party, especially and in some instances only at the higher echelons, provides a paranoid political culture.[15]

The paranoid tendencies of Marxist-Leninist regimes, most pronounced in those led by first generation revolutionaries, are clearly manifested in their domestic policies. All such regimes have created a huge secret police apparatus, the purpose of which has been the permanent surveillance of all aspects of their citizens' lives. They have also periodically waged massive campaigns of terror and violence against all or segments of their populations. In every one of these mass terror campaigns, internal "reactionaries," actually innocent of any oppositional activity, were falsely accused of trying to sabotage the revolution, often in conspiracy with foreign enemies. The regimes' propaganda organs insisted that "the enemy" was still concealed and had to be discovered, "unmasked," and destroyed, no matter how well hidden. These terror campaigns resulted in the deaths of millions in the Soviet Union and China, and hundreds of thousands in Vietnam and Cambodia. (The victims of these terror campaigns have often been military officers, political cadres, and others with skills necessary to defend the state against its real enemies.) The guilt and fear induced by such massive bloodletting further exacerbated the paranoid vision of the ruling elite, which now saw the world as embroiled in an unceasing struggle between the Revolution and its foreign and domestic enemies.

This view finds some support in the work of Robert C. Tucker, a biographer of Stalin, who argues that an understanding of the paranoid personalities of Stalin and Hitler is crucial to an understanding of the behavior of their regimes.[16] Tucker argues that the paranoid personalities of these two leaders influenced not only domestic but foreign policy.[17] Tucker's psychological analysis is supported by Hitler biographers.[18]

Although the events we are considering do not involve the regimes of Stalin or Hitler directly, they do involve the very similar personal tyrannies of Mao Zedong and Pol Pot.[19] But does this interpretation apply to the more oligarchic communist regimes of the post-Stalin Soviet Union, post-Mao China, and Vietnam, which are the other key actors in this case? Insofar as these ruling groups share key elements of the Stalinist or Maoist belief system, it does. Tucker appears to have wrongly assumed that the paranoid personality factor is confined to personal dictatorships. In fact, while "cult of personality" regimes may be more paranoid than their oligarchic alternatives, in all chiliastic regimes the paranoid personality disorder is characteristic of the ruling elite as a whole. Consider the way in which in all of these regimes have consistently interpreted any important conflict between themselves and other communist regimes in apocalyptic terms. Consider the examples of Stalin's reaction to Tito's demand for organizational independence from the Soviet Union, Mao's reaction to Khrushchev's "détente" policies, and Brezhnev and Mao's interpretations of each other's domestic and foreign policies. So, too, the Vietnamese conflicts with the Chinese and Cambodians were also interpreted by each party in apocalyptic terms. These conflicts were considered by the participants not as reasonable disagreements of interest between states led by political comrades, but as Manichaean life-and-death struggles against "international reactionaries" and "agents of imperialism."

In reality, despite sincerely expressed pro forma deference to Karl Marx, all of these Marxist-Leninist regimes seem to share a view of conflict in history not as the outcome of "impersonal historical forces," as Marx would have it, but rather as the outcome of deliberate conspiracy, as Lenin himself practiced it.

The key implication of this interpretation of chiliastic regimes is that because the paranoid cognition of the leadership influences decision making, these regimes are often functioning with a crippled grasp of their real political environment, at home and abroad. Often crippled does not mean always so. But just once can be fatal.

Several points of amplification and clarification need to be made at this stage. The first is that chiliastic regimes are not the only regimes led by paranoid leaders. World history is replete with important examples from ancient times until the present day. Even democracies have been led by people suffering from mild symptoms of paranoid personality disorder.[20] But throughout history most paranoid leaders have not also been ideologues in the strict sense. It is the potent combination of ideology and paranoia that distinguishes chiliastic regimes and makes them less prone to analysis in terms of the preservation or enhancement of power or economic well-being as their sole interest.

Second, the paranoid personality is characterized not only by delusions of persecution but also by delusions of grandeur.[21] This explains why the chiliastic regime is generally optimistic about its prospects of victory against objectively overwhelming odds. The element of "subjectivism" as Marxist-Leninists describe it, so highly pronounced in the cases of Hitler, Mao, and Pol Pot, is present to some degree in all chiliastic regimes. Its prevalence explains why the rational cost-benefit calculations that characterize the foreign policy of some regimes do not always bear upon the foreign policies of chiliastic regimes.

This psychological dimension of delusions of grandeur is connected with the explicit content of the chiliastic ideology, which proclaims the inevitable victory of the true believers and their just cause. Thus some justification for the boundless optimism of the paranoid leadership can be found in the optimistic strand of the ideology's content. This does not necessarily imply a causal connection in either direction, but it certainly entails a mutually reinforcing relationship between the formal aspect of the culture, contained in the explicit precepts of the ideology, and the informal aspect, which is the elite's pattern of cognitive and evaluative thinking.

It is characteristic of any individual paranoid condition that the person feels that his or her autonomy is gravely threatened. The person "is constantly preoccupied with issues of control and domination."[22] This is also true of chiliastic regimes, as their domestic policies and institutions demonstrate.

Another important aspect of the paranoid thought process is construction of the "paranoid pseudocommunity." As the paranoid individual's delusions evolve, they become systematized. The ideas of persecution by separate individuals or groups become organized in such a way that the person eventually feels that all of the persecutors are actually unified in a single group plotting against the individual.[23] This "paranoid pseudocommunity" construction is also characteristic of chiliastic regimes. We should recall how each such regime's internal political dissidents, and even the nondissident "enemy" social classes targeted by the regime, are always falsely perceived as agents of hostile foreign powers.[24] As we will see, the "paranoid pseudocommunity" construction is also a feature of Marxist-Leninist regime thinking about external enemies. Conspiracy is often imagined where none exists. When this occurs it will cripple the regime's ability to defend itself by compromising with one enemy at the expense of another. Moreover, instead of preventing an alliance of enemies, the "victim's" hostile acts can create such an alliance.

We should note, however, that paranoia is a variable condition that takes different forms. It can be found, in varying degrees, sometimes in otherwise normally functioning personalities as well as sometimes in highly disordered personalities.[25] In the cases provided by the leaders of chiliastic regimes, the paranoid beliefs are held by otherwise normally functioning personalities. That is, the paranoid actors are oriented toward and effectively interact with their real social environment most of the time. In some instances they demonstrate real political brilliance, as the well-documented rise to power of both Hitler and Stalin shows. It is intriguing that the same person can be frequently socially competent and occasionally politically brilliant, but on other occasions manifest profoundly devastating political and military irrationality. One purpose of this study is to hypothesize about the conditions under which this paradoxical irrationality may occur.

SUMMARY OF THE ARGUMENT

Vietnam's decision to invade and occupy Cambodia in December 1978 was not inevitable in any objective sense. Other choices were available. But the decision was prompted by the perceptions and anxieties of both local regimes' leaders, in the context of the values and aspirations of these regimes and the international alignments they had chosen.

The background cause was the imperial ambition of Vietnam's communist leadership, which had always wished to dominate the entire region of what was formerly French Indochina. That imperial ambition flowed in large part from the traditional political culture of Vietnamese political elites. It was reinforced by the revolutionary internationalist ideology and organizational structures of the Communist International, an institution in which the founders of the Vietnamese communist movement were politically educated. Yet this background cause, while a manifestation of political culture, did not provide an example of irrationality. For the latter, we must look at other causes of the war.

The immediate or triggering cause was the provocative military attacks on Vietnam by the communist Cambodians. Given the massively disproportionate military weakness of Cambodia relative to Vietnam, and given Cambodia's inability to mobilize allies more powerful than those available to Vietnam, the behavior of Cambodia's leaders makes no sense from the perspective of any theory that incorporates a "rational actor" assumption. This irrational behavior by Khmers Rouges leaders was compounded by their bloody purges of the regime's own ranks during 1978. Those purges sapped Democratic Kampuchea's limited military strength, provided politically useful defectors to its enemies, and encouraged the Vietnamese to believe that they could prevail easily by military means.

The intermediate cause was North Vietnam's alignment with the Soviet Union, in the context of the international political conflict between the Soviet Union and China. By aligning itself with the Soviets, in a process that began in the late 1960s at the height of China's conflict with the Soviet Union, North Vietnam had needlessly antagonised China when it needed Chinese aid to prosecute its war against South Vietnam and the United States. Vietnam's post-1975 decisions first to discriminate against, then to purge, and finally to begin to expel its ethnic Chinese minority population, followed by a decision to join Comecon, further antagonized China. Vietnam's moves deepened Chinese hostility at a time when Vietnam was faced with a small but persistent military challenge from China-aligned Cambodia—a challenge that Vietnam might have dealt with more effectively by enlisting the politically neutral mediation of China. Instead, this spiral of Vietnamese alienation from China and into alignment with the Soviet Union convinced Beijing that Hanoi's actions in Cambodia were in Moscow's interests, at Moscow's behest, and threatening to Chinese security. Hanoi's actions thereby inflamed the paranoid tendencies of Beijing's leaders and focused the preexisting Chinese anxiety about Soviet expansionism upon Indochina.

Though China had misperceived the role of Moscow in Hanoi's decision making, its *response* to this misperception, and to its accurate perception of Vietnam's imperial ambition in Cambodia, was rational. China marshaled its material resources, both economic and military, to try to pressure a change in Vietnamese behavior. The Chinese, like the Soviet leaders, were often misled by the paranoid styles of thinking they shared with their clients. But this did not cause them to act irrationally toward their clients' enemies. Irrationality was a feature of Cambodia's policy toward Vietnam and Vietnam's policy toward China.

This book argues that all of these puzzlingly self-damaging actions by the local powers can be explained, but only with reference to their political culture.

Khmers Rouges political culture consisted of the leadership's traditional cultural values and perceptions, its revolutionary ideology, and its paranoid delusional thought patterns. Among the range of traditional Cambodian values and perceptions, the ones relevant to the Khmers Rouges were a sense of inferiority and a deep resentment toward their more powerful neighbors, especially the Vietnamese, which led to a desire to "prove" themselves superior to their neighbors. This passionate desire to alleviate the traditional sense of inferiority and resentment was transmuted by adherence to a revolutionary ideology, which I have labeled "hyperMaoism." Just as hyperMaoism provided the inspiration in Khmers Rouges domestic policy for a fanatical campaign of bloodletting and rapid socioeconomic communalization, so in foreign policy it led the Khmers Rouges leaders to try to prove themselves more ideologically "advanced" and powerful than the Vietnamese, and to believe that they could defeat an enemy whose armed forces possessed overwhelmingly superior numbers and firepower. Subsequent failure generated paranoid delusions, whereby these same leaders concluded that their truly desperate situation was a product of betrayal by internal enemies, who had to be destroyed.

Traditional Vietnamese culture has always included a profound contempt for the culture of Cambodia. This attitude has persisted to the present day, even within the Vietnamese Communist Party elite. Vietnamese disdain has reopened the festering wounds left in Cambodian culture by the past two centuries of Vietnamese military invasions and occupation. Thus, the Vietnamese communists' traditional cultural attitudes have contributed to breaking the bonds of revolutionary solidarity that had earlier tied most Cambodian communist leaders to their Vietnamese tutors.

In its global orientation, Vietnamese communism has been more in the mainstream of Marxist-Leninist political culture. Vietnam's leaders pursued ideological orthodoxy in domestic and foreign affairs—but as followers, not as leaders. This quest for orthodoxy made Hanoi uncomfortable with polycentrism in the communist world and impelled it to take a stand in support of the "international line" of one of the communist powers. For a majority of Vietnamese communist leaders, the simple Soviet line seemed closer to Marxist-Leninist orthodoxy than the complex Chinese position. Mao's domestic and foreign policy "leftism," especially during the Great Leap Forward and the Great Proletarian Cultural Revolution, alienated key figures in Hanoi and reinforced North Vietnam's inclination toward the Soviet Union. Following Hanoi's initial tilt toward Moscow in 1968–70, Beijing's lurch from radicalism to rapprochement with the West, especially with the United States in 1971–72, convinced Hanoi that Beijing had further betrayed genuine "proletarian internationalism" and could not be trusted.

Distrust eventually snowballed into paranoia. This condition later led to Hanoi's false belief that Beijing was instigating Khmers Rouges attacks upon it, and then to an unfounded fear that Beijing would use Vietnam's ethnic Chinese minority to subvert Vietnamese power. Thus, it is argued, a combination of ideological orthodoxy and spiraling paranoia explain why Vietnam's communist leaders became increasingly hostile toward their former ally.

This study demonstrates that in the events leading to the Vietnamese invasion of Cambodia—in which actions of the Vietnamese, Cambodian, Chinese, and Soviet leaders were contributing factors—ideological and paranoia-induced misperception characterized all parties. Even so, there is an unexpected pattern to Cambodian and Vietnamese behavior. It was the weaker regime that behaved irrationally toward the stronger, not the stronger toward the weaker. Prevailing academic theories, and even mere common sense, suggest that it is the stronger who have the luxury of being able to act provocatively, not the other way around. Thus, Cambodian communist behavior toward Vietnam and Vietnamese communist behavior toward China provide a puzzle that only an uncommon cultural sense can solve. Namely, a combination of anxiousness and powerlessness, in the context of a dispute between regimes possessing faith in their own ideological virtue, led Hanoi's and Phnom Penh's leaders to act in such a way as to provoke hostility from more powerful neighbors.

PART ONE

The Local Genesis of the Conflict

Roots of a Conflict: The Vietnamese Communists and the Cambodians, 1930–70

For more than three decades the Vietnamese communists have successfully propagated the image of their nation's history as a perennial metaphor of the biblical legend of David engaged in a heroic struggle with foreign Goliaths—the Chinese, French, and the Americans. Whatever the truth of this image, it can be at best only a half-truth. For it conceals another very different dimension of Vietnamese history—that of the dynamic Sinicized settler civilization engaged in a perpetual march to the south and west, conquering its smaller and weaker neighbors and destroying their cultures in the course of colonizing them.

TRADITIONAL VIETNAMESE FOREIGN POLICY TOWARD CAMBODIA

Vietnamese civilization began in what is now the Red River delta of Vietnam in the half millennium B.C. The expansion of Vietnamese civilization was first at the expense of the Chams, an Indianized Hindu people whose kingdom of Champa once flourished in what is now central Vietnam. After centuries of intermittent warfare with Vietnamese dynasties to their north, much of Champa was destroyed in the second half of the fifteenth century. The remnant Cham settlements were finally overcome at the end of the seventeenth century. Large-scale massacres of Chams were conducted, and the royal survivors, together with 5,000 refugees, made their way to Cambodia where they were given refuge in 1692.[1] Some Chams did remain in what is now Vietnam, but by 1960 the total number was only 28,000 individuals as compared with 30,000 families in the eleventh century.[2]

The Khmer, who constitute the dominant ethnic group of the Cambodian nation-state, were the second major civilization to be diminished at the hands of the Vietnamese. The Khmer civilization created at Angkor had reached its peak in the thirteenth century. It began to decline over subsequent centuries, suffering military defeats at first mainly at the hands of the Siamese. Khmer settlements were created in what is now southern Vietnam prior to the arrival of Vietnamese settlers during the seventeenth century. But Cambodian political sovereignty there was gradually ceded to the Vietnamese emperors. By the end of the eighteenth century, Cambodia had shrunk even further.

Vietnamese culture and institutions were overwhelmingly the product of adopted Chinese models. The Vietnamese likewise adopted the Chinese worldview.[3] For example, the Vietnamese emperor conceived of his throne as the product of the "mandate of heaven." Therefore he expected the deference of foreigners. Following the model of the Chinese imperial court, this entailed the creation of a system of international relations in which the Vietnamese court was the focus of a tributary system of dependent nations. Vietnam's neighbors were expected to send the Vietnamese emperor "periodic envoys and gifts in acknowledgement of their cultural homage."[4]

The Vietnamese court mimicked the Chinese in its condescending attitude toward its neighbors. For example, the Vietnamese referred to Cambodia's civilization as that of "border barbarians," borrowing the term that the Chinese had used to describe their non-Chinese minorities during the Ch'ing period. The Cambodian nation was called "the country of the upper barbarians."[5]

However, the attempts of the Vietnamese court to duplicate the Chinese system of international relations were stymied by one basic geopolitical reality: China was a huge nation whose cultural and economic power could not be challenged by any of its neighbors in East and Southeast Asia; Vietnam, by contrast, was a middle-ranking regional power whose strength was no greater than that of several of its rival neighbors, most notably Siam and Burma. Thus the very hierarchical conception of international politics favored by the Chinese and Vietnamese made sense given the realities of China's relative regional power, but made no sense for Vietnam's approach to many of its neighbors, and was continually challenged by the most important of these, the Siamese. During the first half of the nineteenth century, the only neighbors of Vietnam who regularly behaved as vassals to the Vietnamese court were the courts of Luang Prabang and Vientiane (both towns in what is now Laos), and the court of Phnom Penh (now the capital of Cambodia).[6]

The Vietnamese emperors had begun interfering in the internal politics of

Cambodia long before the unification of Vietnam in 1802. On several occasions throughout the eighteenth century, the Vietnamese responded, usually with military force, to the call of one contending indigenous faction for the Cambodian throne against another that was supported by Siam. But for the most part, the Vietnamese emperors preferred to rule indirectly.[7]

In the early nineteenth century, having already absorbed large tracts of what is now southern Vietnam from Cambodia, the Vietnamese role inside its shrunken neighbor was enhanced. Having participated in the enthronement of Nak Ong Chan in 1813, the Vietnamese turned Cambodia into a protectorate. But after Nak Ong Chan's death at the end of 1834, the emperor in Hue instituted direct rule and turned Cambodia into a Vietnamese province. Along with new Vietnamese administrators, ethnic Chinese who had migrated to Vietnam were encouraged to move to Cambodia.[8]

Throughout their period of colonization in the 1830s, the Vietnamese tried to impose their own culture upon the Cambodians. Not only did they dispatch their own administrators, but they attempted to change Cambodian clothing, language, and agriculture. The Vietnamese even hoped that their Sino-Vietnamese Mahayana forms of Buddhist worship would permeate the Cambodians' Theravada form of Buddhism.[9] This cultural arrogance differentiated Vietnamese imperialism from Siamese imperialism and was most profoundly felt by ordinary Cambodian people. In this way the Vietnamese emperors established themselves as hereditary enemies in the eyes of Cambodians until the present day.

TRADITIONAL CAMBODIAN FOREIGN POLICY TOWARD VIETNAM

For most of the two centuries prior to the coming of the French colonialists in the middle of the nineteenth century, Cambodian statecraft toward Vietnam was shaped merely by considerations of the power struggle among contending members of the Cambodian royal family. The Vietnamese emperors in Hue were often called upon by one contender for the Cambodian throne to provide armed forces to assist in the overthrow of his Cambodian rivals. Malays, Chams, and Siamese were often called upon by other Cambodians for the same purpose. But by the early eighteenth century, the rival Siamese and Vietnamese had become the most powerful factors in Cambodia's internal power struggles.[10]

By the eighteenth century Cambodia's foreign relations were little more than those of a tributary state. Whoever ruled the nation did so with the support of either Siam or Vietnam. The kings of either of these countries were rewarded for their support by major territorial concessions on the part of Cambodia. Both larger neighbors also required continuing signs of subservience in the forms of material and symbolic tribute.

It was not until the beginning of the nineteenth century that Vietnam was unified. Vietnam's unification made it an overwhelmingly powerful neighbor and an ominous threat to the very survival of Cambodia.

Throughout the nineteenth century Cambodia's relations with its main neighbors went through several phases. From 1794 until 1806, which Vietnam spent mostly in the final throes of civil war, Cambodia was mainly under the influence of the Thai kings of Siam. From 1806 until 1814 Cambodia was in the first phase of dual allegiance to Siam and Vietnam, with the former dominant. From 1814 until 1830 the dual allegiance continued with the Vietnamese now more important. After 1830, Vietnamese influence increased, culminating in a policy of partial annexation of Cambodia between 1835 and 1845. Cambodia, having lost its independence, had withered to the status of a "protectorate" of its eastern neighbor.[11]

During all these years there were sporadic popular uprisings against the Siamese and especially the Vietnamese. There were occasional military confrontations with the armed forces of one or the other neighbor inside occupied Cambodia by rival Cambodian forces. But there was never an attack against the established territory of the neighbor itself. And no Cambodian leader—certainly no Cambodian king—ever confronted both of his neighbors at the same time. It was always understood that victory against one enemy neighbor required the acquiescence, if not the overt support, of the other. Thus, although the Cambodian leaders could be faulted for the efficiency of their alliances, they only pursued a policy of military confrontation with a more powerful neighbor through the logic of balancing external alliances. They were imperfectly but recognizably realists.

VIETNAMESE COMMUNISM AND COMINTERN REVOLUTIONARY CULTURE

Vietnamese communist ambition in Laos and Cambodia was not only a product of traditional political cultural attitudes and patterns of behavior. It was also given justification by the newer conceptions of the Soviet-controlled Communist International (Comintern), of which the Vietnamese communist movement's founder, Nguyen Ai Quoc (later known by his final alias, Ho Chi Minh), was an active functionary.

Nguyen Ai Quoc had been a founding member of the French Communist Party, which split from the French Socialists in 1920 over the issue of loyalty to the Comintern. In 1923 he left France secretly at the invitation of the Comintern leadership for a brief apprenticeship at the Comintern's Eastern Bureau. He studied at the Communist University for the Toilers of the East in Moscow and was eventually assigned to work with the Comintern office in China.[12] For at least sixteen years, from July 1923 to July 1939 (and perhaps longer), Quoc was a full-time functionary of the Comintern, working in the USSR, western Europe, China, Hong Kong, Siam, and Malaya. Vietnam and the other states of French Indochina, although important parts of his work assignment and important to him personally, were not his only areas of political concern.

In recent years the Vietnamese communists have begun to openly celebrate their genesis in the Comintern. As the official monthly *Vietnam Courier* wrote in 1984:

> The Comintern gave guidance to the Indochinese revolution through its assessment of the international situation and its overall decisions on the political line and the organization of colonized peoples in struggle against imperialism; and through its assessment of the situation in Indochina and concrete decisions on it.[13]

The idea of a federation of the disparate peoples of what the French had named Indochina followed from Comintern notions of what future Soviet republics would look like around the world after communist revolutionaries had seized power. Lenin wrote in 1920:

> Federation is a transitional form to the complete unity of the working people of different nations.
>
> The feasibility of federation has already been demonstrated in practice both by the relations between the R.S.F.S.R. [Russian Soviet Federated Socialist Republic] and other Soviet Republics (the Hungarian, Finnish, and Latvian in the past, and the Azerbaijan and Ukrainian at present), and by the relations within the R.S.F.S.R. in respect of nationalities which formerly enjoyed neither statehood nor autonomy. . . . In this respect, it is the task of the Communist International to further develop and also to study and test by experience these new

federations, which are arising on the basis of the Soviet system and the Soviet movement.[14]

According to subsequent Comintern literature, prior to the attainment of "the dictatorship of the world proletariat," the future communist bloc was to be a network combining individual nation-states and "federated unions."[15] In a paternalistic letter written by the Central Committee of the Chinese Communist Party to the Central Committee of the Indochinese Communist Party in April 1934, all of this was made very explicit:

> Comrades, follow our path and the path of the Soviet Union. It is the sure, infallible, proven path to victory. . . . Hand in hand with the communists of France, hand in hand with the communists of China, Japan, India, and Indonesia, the bolsheviks of Indochina will rouse the oppressed masses for the victorious assault against imperialism. The frontier between Kuomintang China and French Indochina will cease separating our peoples; Soviet Indochina and Soviet China will be unified in the midst of the World Federation of Soviet Republics.[16]

Comintern theory was recommending the universalization of the Soviet experience. In the Indochinese case this meant that the Vietnamese, because of overwhelming numerical superiority, would perform the same historical role vis-à-vis the Cambodians and Laotians as Russians played vis-à-vis the non-Russian nationalities of the Soviet Union. It should be noted in this context that the Soviet Russians always paid lip service to the idea of the right of national minorities to national self-determination. But any attempt by Soviet republican governments to test such promises were met with massive repression.[17]

THE INDOCHINESE COMMUNIST PARTY IN LAOS AND CAMBODIA, 1930–45

Under Comintern influence, the Vietnamese communist leaders formally staked a claim to the political future of Laos and Cambodia in the very year that their party was founded. In Hong Kong on January 6, 1930, the Comintern emissary Nguyen Ai Quoc united two rival Marxist groups into a single Vietnamese Communist Party.[18] Initially a section of the Communist Party of France, it declared itself an independent party, though a loyal member of the Comintern, a month later. But Quoc had ignored the content of the protocol of the Comintern's Executive Committee, dated November 28,

1929, which had called for the unification of all parties into an Indochinese Communist Party.[19] Later in 1930, after the Comintern had reviewed the intramural controversy over the party's name, it issued instructions that the name should be changed to the Indochinese Communist Party (ICP). The Comintern argued that the party's name was the "point of attraction of all the communist elements of Indochina, as the party of all the proletarians—Annamite [Vietnamese], Cambodian, Laotian, etc." Moreover: "Not only does Indochina have a geographic, economic, and political unity, but above all we have a need for unity of struggle, for a unique direction of all of the Indochinese proletariat opposed to all of the forces of reaction in Indochina, to the policy of division of French imperialism."[20]

A plenary session of the VCP provisional committee was held in October 1930. In accordance with the resolutions of the Comintern, the party's name was changed to the Indochinese Communist Party.[21]

As it happened there were no real revolutionary movements in either Cambodia or Laos at this time. And of the 211 founding members of the party, not a single one was from Cambodia or Laos.[22] Yet according to a recent Vietnamese communist analysis: "The 1930 political platform of the party charted the course for the revolution of each country."[23] The Comintern's intention was clear: Emancipation of the three different nations of French Indochina was to be carried out not by the independent efforts of each of the three peoples, but rather under Vietnamese communist tutelage. Prior to World War II, these ideas were purely speculative, as there were no revolutionary possibilities in either Laos or Cambodia. But they did provide a legitimizing doctrine for the Vietnamese, and a conceptual framework for their and our understanding of political developments that would eventuate.

During the 1930s the ICP was engaged in an intense struggle for preeminence within Vietnam against rival political groups. The Indochinese Communist Party was never able to dominate the anti-French resistance in Vietnam until after World War II. Prior to World War II, the ICP was simply one anticolonial movement among many.[24] In April 1938 it had fewer than two thousand members, the overwhelming majority of whom operated illegally.[25]

But it was in a better position than were communists in Laos and Cambodia. Prior to World War II, there was no substantial communist movement in either of these two neighboring countries. And the secret internal documents of the ICP show that the organization that existed was overwhelmingly dominated by ethnic minorities—Chinese and Vietnamese. For example, in his correspondence with Moscow dated September 1930, Nguyen Ai Quoc claimed to have in Cambodia a party membership of 124, of which 120 were Chinese and 4 were "Annamites" (Vietnamese). The party-controlled labor union consisted of 300 ethnic Chinese.[26] In 1934 a Comintern official complained, "In Cambodia and in Laos it is necessary to make the indigenes participate in the Party apparatus."[27]

By March 1935, in the wake of the French suppression of the party, there were only 9 party members in Cambodia, with no communist youth movement and only a 4-man trade union and a 50-member peasant union under party control. In Laos, with a population a third of Cambodia's, the ICP had 32 members, a 25-member youth movement, 55 members of a trade union, and 69 members of a League against Imperialism.[28] A year later, in July 1936, party membership in Laos had dropped to 28, and in Cambodia there was only one party cell, which was in any case cut off from the Vietnamese party leadership.[29] In April 1938 the Cambodian branch of the ICP had a mere 16 members, all of them ethnic Chinese, and the party controlled only a 100-man trade union.[30]

Still, these membership figures, while demonstrating the weakness of the ICP in Cambodia and Laos, need to be put in some perspective. First, by the mid-1930s the ICP structure throughout most regions of Vietnam itself had also been weakened by French repressions. By 1935, with the exception of eastern Cochinchina, the northern Annam province of Nghe An, and some sparsely populated mountainous provinces of northern Tonkin, the party was almost nonexistent. The city of Hanoi, for example, had only 30 party members. Second, despite the numerical weakness of the ICP organizations in Laos and Cambodia, their token role in the party was taken seriously. Before the Party Congress of March 1935, the party organizations of Cambodia, Cochinchina, and southern Annam were unified under the guidance of the stronger Cochinchinese organization. And the 13 delegates to the Party Congress of 1935 included 1 from Laos and 3 representing the newly combined organizations of Cochinchina, southern Annam, and Cambodia.[31] Indochina as a whole was indeed the ICP's political and geographical frame of reference.

In 1940 the party instigated uprisings against French colonial rule. As in 1930–31 the uprisings were met by firm repression. The party ranks were devastated. Most ICP leaders were arrested and executed. Fortunately for the communist cause, Nguyen Ai Quoc and some top cadres were safely ensconced in areas of China controlled by Mao's Red Army. They were to return to Vietnamese soil in 1941.

In the wake of the failed rebellion of 1940, the ICP's first task was to rebuild a significant political movement in Vietnam. In May 1941 Nguyen Ai Quoc founded the Viet Nam Doc Lap Dong Minh Hoi (Vietnam Independence League), or Viet Minh, an ostensibly noncommunist nationalist organization, actually controlled by ICP cadres.[32] Its purpose was mobilization of mass support for an eventual ICP seizure of power.[33] Nguyen Ai Quoc, in an attempt to cover his Comintern tracks, soon took on the pseudonym Ho Chi Minh. Although Ho's name was unknown to most Vietnamese before 1945, by then he had built a small political organization that operated in remote base areas.

The Japanese coup d'état against the French Vichy colonial regimes in March 1945 was to prove as important psychologically in Laos and Cambodia as in Vietnam. It delegitimized French colonial authority in the eyes of many who had previously regarded the French as invincible. Thus, when the Japanese surrendered in August 1945, indigenous movements sprung up to fill the power vacuum. The most striking uprising was the so-called August Revolution (in fact a Bolshevik-type coup d'état), which gained Ho's Viet Minh prestige throughout Vietnam. But Ho's fifteen-month attempt to negotiate independence from France was unsuccessful. War broke out in December 1946.

After World War II communism still influenced the Laotian and Cambodian anticolonial resistance only by way of the Vietnamese.[34] Following the outbreak of war between the Viet Minh and France, most Viet Minh military operations were carried out in Vietnam itself. But Laos and Cambodia saw some Viet Minh activity, and provided important base areas, as they would continue to do for thirty years.

ICP OPERATIONS IN CAMBODIA, 1946–54

In Cambodia armed resistance against the French had broken out in 1946, as was the case in Vietnam. The resistance was known as the Khmer Issarak (KI), or Free Cambodians. It was in fact a diverse collection of armed groups under different leaders, only some of whom were influenced by the Viet Minh. Strong barriers to Vietnamese influence over the Cambodian people still persisted, even within the anticolonial resistance. Memories of precolonial Vietnamese imperial dismemberment and conquest of former Cambodian territories were deeply etched into Cambodian national consciousness.

French colonial administrative decisions also exacerbated Cambodian resentment against the Vietnamese. Upon acquiring full control of Indochina in the second half of the nineteenth century, French colonial administrators redrew the borders between Cambodia and its neighbors. Concerning Cambodia's western border with what is now Thailand, this was in Cambodia's favor: Several Cambodian provinces that the state of Siam had occupied militarily were restored to the Cambodian crown. But in the east of the country, between 1870 and 1914, several Cambodian regions were handed over to the colonial administrative entities into which Vietnam had been divided. In some cases, such as that of the current Vietnamese province of Tay Ninh, these were areas that were almost totally populated by Cambodians and administered by Cambodians. This amputation of territory was formally recognized by a series of treaties signed by the French without the consent of the Cambodian king. The integration of the French colonial entity named Cochinchina—in fact, the Saigon region and the Mekong delta region of what was formerly southern Cambodia—into the territory of Vietnam was formally legalized by the French in the Along Bay agreement of June 5, 1948.[35]

Furthermore, as in Laos, Vietnamese had returned to Cambodia under French protection to serve as administrators for the colonial regime. The French had given preference to Vietnamese as workers in the rubber plantations and in the service sector.[36] Vietnamese also came as immigrants to Cambodia, taking over much of the commerce of the country in conjunction with the Chinese. At the end of World War II, the Cambodian capital, Phnom Penh, was primarily a non-Khmer city. Of the officially estimated population of 110,639 in 1946, 33,005 (30 percent) were Chinese and 29,294 (26 percent) were other Indochinese, overwhelmingly Vietnamese.[37] In the rural areas, patterns of migration and settlement showed a marked distinction between Chinese and Vietnamese. While the Chinese migrants to Cambodian rural areas were predominantly males who often married Khmer women, the Vietnamese migrants to rural communities were usually family units and remained culturally unassimilated and quite distinct from their Khmer neighbors.[38]

For all these reasons, even under French colonial rule Cambodian anti-French sentiment was partly deflected toward the Vietnamese, who continued to be perceived as the real exploiters. This meant that Vietnamese communist political activities among the Khmer were not only difficult, but often had to be carried out by individuals of mixed Vietnamese-Khmer ethnic backgrounds. For example, two of the ICP's most prominent members working in Cambodia were Sieu Heng and Son Ngoc Minh, both of mixed Vietnamese-Khmer ethnicity.[39]

By 1946 there was evidence of ICP-controlled armed forces in Cambodia. A Viet Minh unit was located in the Battambang province of western Cambodia. There, according to a French intelligence report of August 1946, the Viet Minh had organized nearly all the "Annamites" of the province, and maintained a camp with a unit of two hundred men armed with nonautomatic weapons provided by the Japanese. The Viet Minh were less numerous but better armed than the noncommunist Khmer Issarak forces supported by the Siamese.[40] Revolutionary committees were established at the end of 1946 in provinces of Cambodia adjacent to southern Vietnam, notably those of Takeo, Prey Veng, and southern Kandal. These committees were soon integrated into a front organization, officially recognized by the Viet Minh in March 1947, called Lien Doan Viet Kieu Cuu Quoc Cao Mien, or the League of Vietnamese Émigrés in Cambodia for National Salvation.

At the end of 1947, the Committee of Liberation of the People of Southeast Cambodia was created to develop a revolutionary movement among the Khmer people.[41] Khmer Issarak Liberation Committees were established at the end of 1948 to undertake politico-military action among the Khmers. Agitation and organization of workers on the rubber plantations of eastern Cambodia was also undertaken by the Viet Minh. These workers were predominantly ethnic Vietnamese. But the role of Vietnamese commissars in controlling the Khmer Issarak rebels led to tensions between KI and Viet Minh troops and even defections by Khmer rebels.[42]

As late as 1948 there was still no communist party section in either Cambodia or Laos. An ICP Central Executive Committee report at the beginning of 1949 called for the establishment of such sections. It stated that conditions for choosing new party members in these countries would be "less strict," but after their organization it would be necessary "to think about causing them and educating them to raise their political level."[43]

In 1949 the Vietnamese communists created the Canvassing Committee for the Creation of a Revolutionary Cambodian People's Party. According to Bernard Fall, this Committee was "almost entirely composed of carefully selected Vietnamese with considerable experience in Khmer affairs."[44] Shortly thereafter, special Vietnamese armed units, known as Vietnam Troops to Help Cambodia, were created to provide a military shield for Vietnamese communist political operations inside Cambodia. The headquarters for Viet Minh military and political operations in South Vietnam were transferred to Prey Veng province of Cambodia. From there were established in 1950 a network of "cadre committees," though once again these party organizations were overwhelmingly staffed by ethnic Vietnamese.[45]

In March 1950 a preparatory meeting of Viet Minh and Khmer Issarak leaders was held at Ha Tien in southern Vietnam, in the presence of Vietnamese communist leader Le Duc Tho. There, Nguyen Thanh Son, chief of the Viet Minh's committee for foreign affairs in southern Vietnam, spoke favorably of the role of the Vietnamese émigré population in Cambodia, whom he claimed constituted a "driving force destined to start off the Revolutionary Movement in Cambodia." Later in his speech Son seemed to be complaining when he spoke of the fact that although the "Party of the Proletariat" (the ICP) had been able to guide the Movement, it was composed of mostly Vietnamese and did not yet have "deep roots among the Khmer people." But the role of the ICP was vital, according to Son, because "as Cambodia finds itself on the Indochinese chessboard, the Khmer Revolution must be placed under the guidance of the Indochinese proletariat."[46]

In April 1950 a meeting of Viet Minh and Khmer Issarak leaders took place, entitled the First National Congress of the Khmer Resistance. At that meeting a Unified Issarak Front and a Provisional Central Committee of Liberation of the Cambodian People were established, led by the ICP's Son Ngoc Minh and under the control of ICP members.[47]

All of these organizational efforts were to pave the way for the emergence of a new Cambodian political party under Vietnamese control. In February 1951 the old ICP officially resurfaced under a new name—Dang Lao Dong Viet Nam (the Vietnamese Workers' Party), or Lao Dong.[48] Although the new name suggested it had formally renounced its claim to authority over all the revolutionary movements of Indochina, it simultaneously announced the creation of two fraternal parties: a Lao Independence Party, staffed almost entirely by Vietnamese, and a Revolutionary Cambodian People's Party. According to Fall, the new Cambodian party "was not only entirely created by the Lao Dong, but its very name and statutes had to be translated from Vietnamese into Cambodian." Ethnic Vietnamese dominated the leadership of this party.[49] During 1951 the Vietnamese communists spoke several times of the idea of a federation of the three states of Vietnam, Cambodia, and Laos, and the eventual reunification of the revolutionary parties of the three countries.[50]

According to French intelligence reports of the time, until August 1951 only a tiny number of Cambodians were admitted into the party. A Cambodian communist party history secretly circulated in the early 1970s gave some statistics on early party membership. It claimed that in 1951 the first Cambodian communists consisted of about forty trained by the ICP, ten trained by the French Communist Party, and three or four trained by the Thai Communist Party.[51] In spite of a formal directive from the Central Committee at the time encouraging rectification of this situation, the French report of December 1952 noted: "The recruitment and the formation of Cambodian cadres turned out nevertheless difficult, the candidates showing themselves at the time to be not very understanding, and to be nonchalant and undisciplined."[52]

Not to be discouraged by this fact, the Viet Minh leaders continued recruitment and training of a certain number of Cambodians. Initially these recruits were sent for training to South Vietnam, but in June 1952 it was decided to establish in each zone of Cambodia a political-military school led by Vietnamese and a Committee of Vietnamese Advisers.[53]

Over the next three years Vietnamese cadres continued the difficult task of trying to recruit ethnic Khmer into both the political and military organizations they controlled. They still achieved only limited success in this venture. For example, according to a French intelligence analysis of March 1952 (based upon important captured Viet Minh documents and informants), the cell secretariat or section bureau of Phnom Penh had a permanent staff of thirty-four, of whom twenty-seven were Vietnamese, three were Chinese, and only four were Cambodians.[54]

French political concessions to the royal government of King Norodom Sihanouk, and Sihanouk's own personal political prestige, had made the task of any armed anti-French resistance more difficult than in Vietnam. But the profound enmity that existed between Khmer and Vietnamese ensured that the Vietnamese-run party and its anticolonial fronts would gain little popular support inside Cambodia.[55]

In accordance with the Geneva agreements signed by the French and the Viet Minh in 1954, all Vietnamese communist forces were withdrawn from Cambodia. The royal government of Sihanouk was given full independence and international recognition in November 1953. But with the retreating Vietnamese went some five thousand Khmer communist cadres, soldiers, and their families, referred to by most noncommunists as "Khmer Viet Minh."[56] They were to be given further training in Hanoi, and kept there in reserve, waiting until history would provide an opportune moment.

THE ORIGINS OF THE KHMERS ROUGES

The withdrawal to Hanoi in 1954 of half of the small number of pro-Vietnamese Khmer communists left a near vacuum on the Cambodian left. A front party called the Pracheachon (People's) Party was formed to engage in legal politics, while the real communist party operated clandestinely. In the 1955 elections, won overwhelmingly by Sihanouk's Sangkum Reastr Niyum (People's Socialist Community) with 630,625 votes, or 83 percent of the total, Pracheachon fared badly. This pro-Hanoi party won only 29,509 votes, which was 4 percent of the total.[57] However, the election was anything but fairly run, so it is impossible to know how much popular support the Pracheachon really had.[58]

The political near-vacuum on the left was rapidly filled by a group of younger communists, many of whom had returned from France in the 1950s. In France they had studied on educational scholarships provided by the French government. Some of them, including Khieu Samphan, Hu Nim, and Hou Yuon, had received advanced degrees (two from prestigious French universities). Others, like Saloth Sar (later known as Pol Pot), failed to complete their studies.[59] But while they were not all introduced to Marxism in France, they did all attend the "popular university" run by the French Communist Party.[60]

According to noncommunist Cambodian classmates of the Khmer radicals, during their stay in France the Cambodian Marxists manifested no signs of hostility toward the Vietnamese. On the contrary, it was these young radicals, not the more conservative Cambodians, who fraternized with the Vietnamese students at Montpelier. The radical Cambodian students also criticized the use by other Cambodians of the common pejorative term *youn* to refer to the Vietnamese.[61]

In 1953 Pol Pot and other Cambodians in the first wave of French-trained radical students returned to Cambodia. They joined the Vietnamese-controlled segment of the anti-French resistance, the Issarak Front, led by Son Ngoc

Minh, in the last days of the anticolonial war. Pol Pot also joined the Vietnamese-sponsored protocommunist Khmer People's Revolutionary Party (KPRP).[62] This suggests that in those formative years, revolutionary values were more important than traditional values in shaping Khmers Rouges attitudes toward the Vietnamese.

It would be a mistake to place too much emphasis on the French experience in forming the Khmers Rouges leadership, for some key members of Pol Pot's subsequent inner circle—notably Nuon Chea and Ta Mok—never went to France. (Mok had never been outside Cambodia prior to 1979.)[63] However, the contingent that returned from France did make an important impact in Phnom Penh, where many of them became teachers in the city's private schools during the late 1950s. Through their teaching positions they strongly influenced many young students, some of whom were later to follow them into the jungle.[64] And from behind their legitimate professions in Phnom Penh, they were also able to gradually gain control of that city's underground communist network at a time when the small rural cells were in the process of disintegration. The rural cells had suffered from the betrayal of the party by its leader, Sieu Heng, who had turned government informer.[65] That is why, operating from their Phnom Penh urban base, the returnees from France were able to seize important leading positions within the Khmer People's Revolutionary Party in 1960.[66]

That year the party's name was changed to Kampuchean Workers' Party, in line with the title of the Vietnamese party. The date of the 1960 conference is now celebrated as the date of the founding of the Kampuchean Communist Party (KCP),[67] although it only assumed that title in 1966.[68] It should also be noted that the 1960 date only became official within the party during the late 1970s, probably in 1977. We know from one defector that prior to that time the party was said to have been founded in 1951, an obvious claim of direct lineage from the KPRP.[69] The discrepancy between founding dates is significant, as it indicates Khmers Rouges desire either to defer to or to assert an identity independent of the Vietnamese communists.[70]

In 1963 Pol Pot was made general secretary. That same year most of the Central Committee of the KCP, under pressure from Sihanouk's police, fled Phnom Penh for the countryside. (Those fleeing included Pol Pot, Ieng Sary, Son Sen, and Nuon Chea. Other prominent KCP leaders Khieu Samphan, Hu Nim, and Hou Yuon stayed behind and engaged in legal politics.) In the country, the KCP members began organizing the rural population for an

eventual guerrilla insurgency against Sihanouk's government. Their main social base at this time were the ethnic minorities of the hill regions of both
the northeast and the southwest.[71] These hill people had long resented the
lowland Khmer attitudes of cultural superiority toward them. Later, during
the 1970–75 war against the republican government led by Lon Nol, the
Khmers Rouges also recruited heavily among illiterate ethnic Khmer from
the hinterlands of Kampot and Kompong Chhnang, and from the mountainous confines near Pailin.[72] The alienation of these culturally marginal-
ized segments from mainstream Khmer society made them initially the ideal
source of mass support for the revolutionary plans of the Khmer communist
intelligentsia.

But it is important to note that the early political organizing of the Khmers
Rouges was undertaken in the shadow of the Vietnamese communist forces,
which from 1965 on were using the eastern zones of Cambodia as a sanctuary, rest, and resupply zone. There is no evidence that at this time the Vietnamese communists and Khmers Rouges were in any open conflict. It is inconceivable that the tiny Khmers Rouges forces could have functioned in
such circumstances. Nor is there any evidence that the Khmers Rouges leaders were frightened of the Vietnamese at this time. If the Khmers Rouges
were fearful, they could have retreated to other remote parts of Cambodia,
such as the northwest, where there were no Vietnamese forces.[73]

On the contrary, there is strong evidence that Pol Pot and his group of
Cambodian communists were still deferential toward Vietnam in the 1960s.
For example, in July 1965 Pol Pot visited Hanoi and discussed with the Vietnamese communist Politburo the appropriate strategy for the Cambodian
communist movement. Though there were differences in their outlook and
political priorities, which we will discuss, the Vietnamese and Cambodian
leaders discussed strategy from the perspective of comrades.[74] Pol Pot returned to Hanoi for political discussions in November 1969.[75] It is likely that
the hatreds that were later to be so intensely manifest had not yet surfaced.
For the Khmers Rouges leaders during the 1960s, revolutionary values were
still more important than traditional Cambodian values of ethnic hostility
toward the Vietnamese.

It is not clear exactly when the Cambodian communists developed their
attachment to Maoism. The Vietnamese communists claim that Pol Pot and
Ieng Sary already "worshipped Mao and admired Mao's thought" when
they were still in France.[76] The Vietnamese also claim that Pol Pot first met

Mao in 1960.[77] But Sihanouk claims that it was not until after their return to Cambodia that these young communists came under the influence of Maoism through the Chinese embassy in Phnom Penh. Sihanouk also claims that during the 1950s and 1960s, some made secret visits to China.[78] These claims are either false or misleading.

The imbibing of Maoist ideology by the Khmers Rouges appears to have been quite gradual. And the Vietnamese communists themselves must have played some direct role in assisting that process since they had been under Chinese communist influence during the years 1950–56 and 1963–64 (see Chapter 5) when, as we have just seen, Vietnamese communist influence over many Cambodian communists was still significant. Pol Pot made his first trip to China in late 1965 through early 1966. The Kampuchean Communist Party platform of the early 1960s, which Pol Pot presented to the Vietnamese in June 1965, makes no direct reference to Mao. But an October 1967 letter from Pol Pot to the Chinese Communist Party does.[79] Pol Pot's 1965–66 and 1970 visits to China did not initiate, but most likely further intensified, Maoist ideological influence upon the Khmer Rouges.

PRINCE SIHANOUK'S POLICY TOWARD VIETNAM

Prince Sihanouk was fearful, as Cambodians have been since the early nineteenth century, of the ambitions of the Vietnamese. He wrote in January 1963: "Whether he is called Gia Long, Ho Chi Minh, or Ngo Dinh Diem, no Annamite [or Vietnamese] will sleep peacefully until he has succeeded in pushing Cambodia toward annihilation, having made it first go through the stages of slavery."[80] Sihanouk reiterated the same fears nearly twenty years later:

> The Khmer people have serious reasons not to like the Vietnamese. Our neighbors in the east have, in effect, in the course of the centuries, "swallowed" territories which had always belonged to Cambodia and have colonized them, leaving to the local population only the choice between submission and flight.[81]

Sihanouk recognized that many Cambodians hated the Vietnamese so much that they dreamed of reconquering some lost territories. But he took a different approach:

> In my relations with Vietnam, I have always adopted a realist attitude. Heaven has made it our neighbor for eternity and it was numbering in the [1960s], in

the north and the south, nearly fifty million inhabitants, about eight times more than Cambodia then. "Red" or "blue" it was a very dangerous neighbor, to be handled with care.[82]

A second thrust of Sihanouk's strategic thinking was that the United States would not remain forever in Southeast Asia, while the communist powers would. Therefore, he concluded, he had to make an accommodation with China and North Vietnam.[83]

At the outset of his rule, Prince Sihanouk espoused a policy of neutrality between East and West, officially declared on December 23, 1954, by Premier Penn Nouth.[84] It was a policy pursued by Sihanouk at the 1955 Bandung conference of the nonaligned nations, and in his rejection of American overtures to join the Southeast Asia Treaty Organization (SEATO) in 1956.[85]

In the wake of the Geneva agreement of June 1962, in which the major powers declared that Laos would remain a neutral country, Sihanouk was convinced that Laos would inevitably become communist. He was fearful, too, that this fate would befall his own country, especially if the Laotian conflict were to spill over into Cambodian territory. Unimpressed by the irresolution of the United States regarding the fate of Laos, he decided that his nation's security would be best protected by a tilt toward the communist bloc, and in particular toward China. Sihanouk hoped that friendship with China might provide some kind of insurance for his country against the ambitions of North Vietnam.[86] He knew already that the North Vietnamese were using his country's territory for the Ho Chi Minh Trail, their supply route to the war in South Vietnam.

By the early 1960s Sihanouk's foreign policy was also being increasingly influenced by his anger toward the hostile policies of the United States and the pro-U.S. governments in Thailand and South Vietnam. The Khmer Serei (Free Khmer) guerrillas, whom he believed correctly were backed by the U.S. Central Intelligence Agency (and who were led by Sihanouk's long-standing political rival Son Ngoc Thanh), were broadcasting anti-Sihanouk propaganda from Thailand and South Vietnam.[87] In August 1963 Sihanouk broke diplomatic relations with South Vietnam.[88] In November of that year he terminated all U.S. military assistance programs in Cambodia.[89] In December 1963 Sihanouk signed the country's first military assistance agreement with China. On May 3, 1965, Sihanouk broke diplomatic relations with the United States.[90]

From 1965 on, the Chinese, Russians, and Czechs were allowed use of the port of Sihanoukville to supply the Vietnamese communist troops in South Vietnam, and the North Vietnamese and Viet Cong were allowed use of eastern Cambodian provinces as a sanctuary in their fight against "U.S. imperialism."[91] Sihanouk continued to build his ties to the PRC, and the Chinese recognized value in having Sihanouk as an ally. In October 1965 the Chinese invited Sihanouk to Beijing to preside as guest of honor at national day celebrations.[92]

Throughout 1966 and 1967 Sihanouk issued statements supporting Hanoi's stand on preconditions for negotiations, and recognizing the legitimacy of the Hanoi-controlled National Liberation Front of South Vietnam (NLFSV) as "the sole legal representative of the South Vietnamese people."[93] For example, according to Hanoi radio, in March 1967 Prince Sihanouk sent a message to the secretariat of the Tricontinental Conference in Havana "strongly condemning the U.S. aggressive war in Vietnam and voicing Cambodia's full support for the Vietnamese people's struggle against U.S. aggression and for national salvation."[94] In April 1966 Sihanouk raised the status of the Trade Mission of the Democratic Republic of Vietnam [North Vietnam], or DRV, which had been established in July 1962, to that of Representation of the DRV Government.[95] On June 8, 1967, the DRV issued a declaration: "It recognizes and undertakes to respect the territorial integrity of Cambodia within her present borders."[96] Shortly after this declaration, which followed one week after a similar one by the NLFSV Central Committee, Sihanouk sent letters to Nguyen Huu Tho, the chairman of the NLFSV Central Committee Presidium, and to Pham Van Dong, the DRV premier, proposing the raising of diplomatic relations between each of their political entities and the royal government of Cambodia.[97] Then on June 24, 1967, a communiqué issued in Hanoi announced the establishment of diplomatic relations between the DRV and Cambodia.[98] Sihanouk's foreign policy now tilted strongly toward North Vietnam.

NORTH VIETNAM VERSUS THE KHMERS ROUGES
OVER SIHANOUK

The Vietnamese communists had a markedly different attitude toward the government of Sihanouk from that of the Khmers Rouges. At the time of the Geneva Accords in 1954, they had recognized the political weakness of their position within Cambodia, which is why they agreed to withdraw all their

armed forces from that country. The Vietnamese communists' main immediate concern was to gain control over South Vietnam. Cambodia was seen
in terms of how it could assist in that objective.

By contrast, the KCP leaders, under pressure from Sihanouk's police and
army, were implacably opposed to his "feudal regime." From 1960–67 they
had accommodated themselves to the Vietnamese strategy by waging political but not armed struggle against the royal government of Cambodia. But
in 1967 they saw Sihanouk turn against their legal political activities. That
year they began to actively prepare for an imminent guerrilla insurgency
against the prince's government.

In April 1967 peasant disturbances erupted in the Samlaut region of Battambang province, in western Cambodia.[99] There were genuine local grievances underlying the rioting, which the Cambodian government decisively
crushed.[100] The Khmers Rouges played no role in this rebellion, though the
revolutionaries later attempted to take some credit for it, and were encouraged by it to attempt to foment the same elsewhere.[101]

In January 1968 the KCP began to lead an open rebellion against the government of Cambodia, with KCP forces concentrated among the ethnic minority hill dwellers, the Khmer Loeu (Khmer Highlanders), in the northeast.
It was met by determined government suppression, though it managed to
continue at a diminished level for two years.[102] By early 1970 the KCP had
several thousand trained guerrillas operating in several different parts of the
country, though most of them were located in the northeastern highland
provinces of Ratanakiri and Mondolkiri, near where the Vietnamese communist troops protecting the Ho Chi Minh Trail might have appeared to be
providing a military shield.[103]

Although they had captured many of their arms from those government
forces they had defeated, the Khmers Rouges were also receiving some limited assistance from the Vietnamese communists. But they did not receive
all the assistance that they wanted. According to one former Vietnamese
communist cadre, the Khmers Rouges had asked North Vietnam for arms
to use in a general insurrection against Sihanouk's government. But Hanoi
had refused, thinking that the Khmers Rouges forces were too weak, were
unpopular among the people, and would be smashed immediately if they
rose up. More important perhaps in Hanoi's reasoning, Sihanouk's government was advantageous to the Vietnamese communist armies, in that it
allowed them to use Cambodian territory to attack South Vietnam.[104] As

a result of the limited support they were receiving from the Vietnamese communists, many in the Khmers Rouges felt that Hanoi had abandoned them.[105]

THE CHANGE IN SIHANOUK'S POLICY TOWARD
NORTH VIETNAM

Eventually, Prince Sihanouk's attitude toward the Vietnamese communists was altered by domestic politics. Many members of the Cambodian government and military felt increasing resentment over continuing Vietnamese encroachments upon Cambodian territory. According to Sihanouk, many army officers had resented his decision to cut off relations—especially military ties—with the United States. They and other elite figures like his cousin Prince Sisowath Sirik Matak wanted Cambodia to be more closely aligned with the United States and to join it in fighting the Vietnamese communists. Sihanouk himself did not want to antagonize the Vietnamese communists, but he also wanted to respond to pressures from his government and army.[106]

In late 1967 the prince began to return to a more genuinely neutral stance between the United States and North Vietnam. He was partly reacting to the Battambang uprisings, endorsed by the Khmers Rouges, which he mistakenly saw as an instrument of China and perhaps North Vietnam.[107] He was also reacting to the activities of the "legal" Khmers Rouges politicians— Hou Yuon, Hu Nim, and Khieu Samphan—who were using the Sino-Khmer Friendship Association to spread Maoist and anti-government propaganda. But he was also reacting to the widely publicized appearance of powerful evidence of Vietnamese communist sanctuaries on his territory. On November 9, 1967, the Western journalists George McArthur and Horst Faas discovered an abandoned NLFSV (or Viet Cong) camp four miles inside Cambodia.[108] On December 4, 1967, the United States issued a protest note to Cambodia expressing concern over the use of Cambodian territory by the North Vietnamese and Viet Cong.[109] In late December the United States began a diplomatic campaign to win international support for proposals to strengthen international supervision of Cambodia's neutrality.[110]

In an interview with the American journalist Stanley Karnow, Sihanouk indicated that his government would do nothing if the United States attacked Vietnamese communist bases in remote areas of the country. He would only retaliate, perhaps by calling for Chinese, North Korean, or Cuban help, if the victims were Cambodians or Vietnamese legal residents of Cambodia.[111] The same message was repeated to U.S. government envoy Chester Bowles in Phnom Penh in January 1968.[112]

During 1968 Sihanouk publicly denounced the Khmers Rouges for wanting to "open the doors of Cambodia to their masters, the Viet Minh."[113] In 1969 Sihanouk began to publicly criticize the activities of the North Vietnamese and Viet Cong inside Cambodia. At a Phnom Penh press conference on May 17 he stated: "I regret that our Viet Cong and Viet Minh friends, who have proclaimed respect for our neutrality, independence, and territorial integrity within our frontiers and have recognized these frontiers, are also aiding and training the Khmer Reds."[114]

In May Sihanouk restored diplomatic relations with the United States. But the following month he also raised the representation of the National Liberation Front of South Vietnam to ambassadorial level. He was under continuing pressure from within his own government to try to remove Vietnamese forces completely from Cambodian soil. These pressures led to his fateful trip abroad in January 1970, ostensibly for medical treatment in Paris.

On March 8 and 11, violent demonstrations against the Vietnamese communists and local Vietnamese civilian residents broke out in the eastern province of Svay Rieng.[115] On March 11, large street demonstrations against the Vietnamese communists took place in Phnom Penh. The embassies of North Vietnam and the Provisional Revolutionary Government of South Vietnam (PRGSV) were sacked, as was the office of the Vietnam News Agency.[116] Many correspondents claimed government sponsorship of these demonstrations.[117]

Prince Sihanouk left Paris for Moscow and Beijing on March 13, 1970, not only to request further aid for Cambodia, but also to try to persuade Hanoi's patrons to influence their client.[118] Sihanouk later stated that his request for pressure on Hanoi was rebuffed by Soviet leaders.[119]

On the same day that Sihanouk arrived in Moscow, the Cambodian government, now being run by Lon Nol, prime minister and army chief of staff, asked the DRV and the PRGSV to remove their armed forces from Cambodian territory by dawn on March 15.[120] On March 18, 1970, while Sihanouk was still in Moscow, Lon Nol led a bloodless palace coup. Cambodia was now on the brink of a full confrontation with the Vietnamese communists.

CONCLUSIONS

The Vietnamese communist attitude toward Cambodia, and toward Cambodia's communist movement in particular, was partly a reflection of traditional Vietnamese attitudes toward their western neighbors. The Vietnamese communist attitude had also been partly formed in the 1930s by the Comintern directive to have a federation of states ruled by an Indochinese Communist Party. The Comintern directive was important at that time in that it gave a degree of Marxist political legitimacy, via the concept of "proletarian internationalism," to an ambition that could otherwise have been interpreted unambiguously as mere Vietnamese imperialism. At the time that the directive was issued, the communist world was a monolith, and the geographical expansion of Vietnamese communist power could be portrayed to other comrades as simply the expansion of the "socialist camp."

But after 1960, with the rapid breakdown of unity within the "socialist camp," national political self-determination emerged as a new legitimizing concept in evaluating political relations between Marxist-Leninist states and revolutionary movements. Khrushchev's wooing of Yugoslavia with talk of "different paths to socialism" had started the rot. China's defiance of the Soviet Union after 1960 had provided a second model for others. In the particular case of Indochina, it provided a model for the Cambodian communists. As a corollary, the Comintern ethos, in which the Vietnamese communists had been ideologically nurtured, no longer carried the same ideological weight in the communist world. Vietnamese communist ambitions toward Cambodia, and the Kampuchean Communist Party, were not going to be accepted automatically by their comrades elsewhere.

In 1975, given the evolution of the communist world, the concept of an Indochinese Federation would be replaced in formal pronouncements by the Vietnamese communists with the concept of a "special relationship" between themselves and their Cambodian and Laotian neighbors. But this change of language, of political concept, and, to an insignificant extent, of attitude, would be gradual. And as we will see, it would not greatly alter the unequal power relations among the Indochinese nations—an inequality that the Comintern had originally legitimized.

The policy of the Cambodian leader Prince Sihanouk toward the temporarily divided Vietnamese was consistent with that of most traditional Cambodian rulers prior to the nation's colonization by France. On the one hand he sought not to antagonize his nation's more powerful eastern neighbors, North and South Vietnam. At the same time he sought the insurance of foreign protection from the Vietnamese. First he adopted a policy of neutrality between East and West. Then in 1963, when he felt that his rule was being challenged by the pro-American government in South Vietnam, he shifted his alignment to the Chinese and North Vietnamese. In 1967, when he felt the ideological and chauvinist pressures of China at the height of the Cultural Revolution, he tilted back toward neutrality. This behavior was, as he himself has stated, in conformity with a realist approach to politics. Finally, the pressures of domestic politics, particularly the discontent of his own political elites, eventually pushed Sihanouk even further into a pro-Western position in 1969–70, and ultimately led to his removal from power.

Note that there was an old tradition of statecraft in Cambodia that attempted to protect the nation from its many competing and more powerful neighbors by a subtle and flexible policy of balancing alliances. Sihanouk's foreign policy was partly guided by that political tradition.

Sihanouk's realism contrasted vividly with the foreign policy orientation that would emerge when the Cambodian communists conquered power in April 1975. But a foretaste of the subsequent untraditional foreign policy orientation was to be found in the bizarre behavior of the Khmers Rouges toward their allies during the insurgency years of 1970 through 1975—that is, even before they had conquered state power.

The Public Rise and Secret Fall of "Militant Solidarity": Vietnamese and Cambodian Communists, 1970–75

On the eve of the Lon Nol coup d'état in March 1970, achieving hegemony in Cambodia still seemed a long-term consideration to the Vietnamese communists. Their short-term objective was to win a victory over the United States and South Vietnam. For North Vietnam, Cambodia was a geopolitical problem whose only immediate significance was its role in the struggle for South Vietnam. Up until March 1970 it was a problem the Hanoi leaders had managed to their own great military advantage. As long as Sihanouk was in power, and continued to allow the Vietnamese communist armies use of Cambodian territory as a sanctuary and a logistical supply route, then Hanoi had no reason to want to overthrow him. On the contrary, Sihanouk's survival—or at least the survival of his policies towards Hanoi, Saigon, and Washington—was, in the short-term, a strategic necessity for the Vietnamese communists.

The Khmers Rouges had held a very different view of Sihanouk. They wanted to overthrow his "feudal regime" and to establish their own dictatorship in its place. Inspired by Mao Zedong's defiance of Soviet authority, these Cambodian revolutionaries were willing to accept short-term political and military assistance from the Vietnamese. But they rejected a relationship of *total* dependency upon Vietnamese communist political guidance and military assistance for achieving their revolutionary goals.

Though in early 1970 the Hanoi leaders did not know of the antipathy of the Khmers Rouges leaders toward them, they did know that the Khmers Rouges were not under their direct control. But given the military and political situation throughout Indochina at that moment, there was no reason for Hanoi to doubt that eventually this discrepancy would be rectified by tried and proven methods: the threatened or actual exercise of military power by the People's Army of Vietnam, and the dispatch of Hanoi's loyal political agents—in this case the Khmer Viet Minh—in its wake.

The bloodless palace coup engineered within Sihanouk's own government rearranged some of Indochina's political alliances. The coup also unleashed political and military events that none of the contending armed political forces, communist and noncommunist, could have predicted or controlled. But it also revealed, to those who were paying close attention, the bizarre outlook of the Khmers Rouges, particularly their disregard of any constraints imposed by the fact of their relative political and military weakness.

The events of 1970–75 set the stage for the Third Indochina War, which in a sense took an embryonic form even before the Second Indochina War had concluded.

THE CAMBODIAN INSURGENCY UNDER HANOI'S PATRONAGE: APRIL 1970–MARCH 1972

The Lon Nol coup appeared to take everyone, including the United States government, by surprise.[1] The conclusion of William Shawcross, one of the most prominent writers critical of the Nixon Administration's policy, after examining government records acquired through the U.S. Freedom of Information Act, was: "No direct link between the United States government and Sihanouk's usurpers before the coup has been established."[2]

The replacement of Sihanouk by a regime determined to rid Cambodian soil of any Vietnamese communist presence changed the political relationship between the Vietnamese communists and the Khmers Rouges. Hanoi needed its Cambodian sanctuaries in order to prosecute its war against the United States and South Vietnam. As a senior Vietnamese communist official, Hoang Anh, stated in a secret report to a plenary session of his party's Central Committee nine months after the coup:

> We must devote considerable attention to Cambodia since our successes in South Vietnam will very much depend upon how effectively we will operate in Cambodia. . . . The matter of Cambodia is very important. For its successful resolution we must enhance our military efforts there and materially aid the local patriotic forces.[3]

After the March 1970 coup, Hanoi shared with the Khmers Rouges the basic short-term objective of toppling the government of Cambodia. The militarily necessary political realignment soon expressed itself on the diplomatic level. On March 21, the North Vietnamese government (DRV) denounced the Lon Nol coup as the work of the United States and quickly pledged its support to Prince Sihanouk, who was to become the nominal leader of an anti-government coalition.[4] On May 26, Sihanouk was received as an official visitor to North Vietnam.[5] The coalition political organization that Sihanouk nominally headed was commonly known by its French acronym FUNK (Front Uni National du Kampuchea, or National United Front of Cambodia). The government that ostensibly represented the people in FUNK-controlled areas (though most of its ministers were based in Beijing) was called the Royal United National Government of Kampuchea, usually referred to again by its French acronym, GRUNK.

The political realignment quickly expressed itself also on a military level. At the end of March, the North Vietnamese and Viet Cong forces moved out of their border sanctuaries and began major attacks against the army and towns of the Khmer Republic.[6] At the same time, approximately one thousand of the Khmer Viet Minh, who had been trained in Hanoi, were reinfiltrated back into Cambodia.[7] Their assigned task was to help supervise the areas that would be captured by Vietnamese communist armies.

On April 30, 1970, exactly six weeks after the Lon Nol coup, troops of the United States and South Vietnam launched a major attack on the border sanctuaries inside Cambodia. The Vietnamese communists, anticipating the attack, fled in advance of the allied sweep. Although the Vietnamese communist forces had been at war with the new Cambodian government's forces for several weeks, public protests and congressional opposition within the United States precluded the extended American military operations inside Cambodia that any successful pursuit of the communist armies would have required. Thus, when American forces withdrew from the border areas after only two months, they had successfully cleared most of the base areas that threatened the Mekong delta region of South Vietnam.[8] But they had hardly diminished the communist manpower available inside Cambodia as a whole. In the first four months of fighting the Vietnamese communists had seized control of half the territory of Cambodia.[9] In spite of continued American bombing attacks upon them, North Vietnam's battle-hardened veterans remained in a good position to deal with the highly motivated, but poorly trained and equipped army of the Khmer Republic.[10]

For the next two years of the struggle for Cambodia, it would be Hanoi that would determine the outcome of military events. By the end of 1970, there were four North Vietnamese combat divisions in Cambodia, with some ten thousand of these troops targeting the republican army, and others protecting the Ho Chi Minh Trail supply line to the South Vietnam battlefield.[11] Some of these forces had been transferred there from Laos after the American incursion into Cambodia. And Hanoi's plan was to transfer more in order to bring the total number of Vietnamese communist troops in Cambodia to 70,000. Hanoi also anticipated that indigenous Cambodian recruitment would raise total anti-government strength to 140,000, a number considered sufficient to defeat the "not much more than 100,000 man army of Lon Nol."[12] In fact, these goals for recruitment of Cambodians would not be realized until near the war's end, by which time Hanoi had lost control of the insurgency.

At the beginning of the war it was obvious to both the Vietnamese communist leaders and the Khmers Rouges that the latter were not yet strong enough to seize Phnom Penh on their own. If Cambodia was to have a communist government, then the North Vietnamese and Viet Cong armies would have to play a role. But even granted this objective military reality, the Vietnamese communists' political attitudes toward the Khmers Rouges can only be considered as highly patronizing. An illustration is provided in a Vietnamese communist document of April 1970:

> Although the Cambodian revolutionaries are enthusiastic, they are incapable. We have come to their help in time and have provided them with quick assistance. We have helped them to systematize their doctrine, map out their policy lines, set up their organization, and draw up their plans of action. They have agreed totally to everything we suggested to them.
>
> We should display a narrow feeling in our relationship and make them realize that their existence depends on ours. Our helping them is one of our international obligations. On the other hand, Cambodia is our staging area. The Cambodian Revolution is weak and its organization loose. We have to strengthen it.[13]

The Vietnamese communist leaders in Hanoi made explicit in their secret meetings that their party's policy was to "strengthen the revolutionary base in Cambodia and lead the country along the path to socialism."[14] And despite their dismay with the general capabilities of the Cambodian insurgents, the Vietnamese were optimistic about the prospects of a communist victory in Cambodia. As one captured communist document summarized the Hanoi view: "The Cambodian Revolution is entering a new phase. . . . From a vacillating neutralist regime, Cambodia now can follow a steady policy. When the enemy is defeated, she will become a democratic and independent country and proceed toward socialism."[15]

Thus it was clear that although the Vietnamese communists' primary concern with Cambodia related to its significance for the military situation in South Vietnam, there were other important policy objectives involved. In a report to Moscow written in May 1971, the Soviet ambassador to North Vietnam mentioned in passing that "the Vietnamese comrades" had in the past year raised "in a cautious manner" the issue of "a socialist federation of Indochina." This, the ambassador noted, "is an extremely delicate question," but he went on to suggest that the matter could be used "in the general interests of socialism."[16] At the same time the Soviets recognized a problem in Vietnamese self-centerdness and condescension toward their Indochinese dependents. In his report, Ambassador Shcherbakov noted that Hanoi was the coordination center for activities of the "liberation fronts of Vietnam, Laos, and Cambodia," and recognized that the Laotians and Cambodians accepted Vietnamese leadership and depended upon it. But he was also concerned with the Vietnamese approach to the relationship:

> Nevertheless, at times the narrowly nationalistic approach of the Vietnamese comrades to the solution of the problems of Indochina is too obvious, and the noticeable attempts by them of subordination of the problems of Laos and Cambodia to the interests of Vietnam results in the concealed discontent of the Laotian and Cambodian friends.[17]

The Soviet embassy had already recognized the seeds of a problem that would subsequently become the dominant one in the region for nearly two decades. Still, the only obstacle to its long-term goals that Hanoi perceived at this time was not the Khmers Rouges but the United States.

KHMERS ROUGES VERSUS CHINA AND NORTH VIETNAM
OVER SIHANOUK

Between April 1970 and March 1972, the Vietnamese and Cambodian communist forces, after seizing control of an area, set up a political administration controlled by the National United Front (FUNK) and nominally under the authority of Prince Sihanouk's Royal Government (GRUNK), which was based in exile in Beijing. FUNK propaganda initially exploited Sihanouk's authority in its recruiting appeals for the insurgency. A leaflet in Cambodian distributed in mid-1970 provides an illustration:

To All Our Fellow Countrymen

Our people enjoyed peace for almost fifteen years, during which time the
people of our neighboring countries suffered endlessly from the war brought
about by the American imperialists and their lackeys. Cambodia was in such a
peaceful and prosperous condition that it used to be the Island of Peace of Indochina. This peace, prosperity, and well-being were due to the leadership of
Prince Norodom Sihanouk. But at present, Cambodia is endangered because of
the deposition of Prince Sihanouk from his position of Chief of State by the
clique of Lon Nol, Sirik Matak, and Cheng Heng, the faithful servants of the
American imperialists. . . . Dear people! All the people of Cambodia have now
risen, following the appeal of Samdech [Sihanouk], Chief of State.[18]

Propaganda appeals emphasizing Sihanouk's leadership role in the insurgency were important in the first year of the war, and reflected the influence
of the North Vietnamese upon Cambodian insurgent propaganda. But according to one Vietnamese communist cadre who defected, the Khmers
Rouges thought the use of Sihanouk, against whom they had been fighting
for three years, was a deliberate attempt by North Vietnam to create difficulties for the Khmers Rouges.[19] This defector's report is partly corroborated
by documentary evidence that shows that, within a year, as direct Vietnamese control at the unit level diminished, Sihanouk's role began to be down-
played by the Cambodian communists. For example, a FUNK pamphlet of
March 19, 1971, distributed to guide celebrations of the first anniversary of
the Front's formation, contained the following instructions to cadres:

With regard to Samdech Sihanouk, he should be known as the Chairman of
the National United Front of Cambodia. It is not necessary to display his picture. . . . All achievements have been gained by our people's armed forces, not
by Sihanouk. We should not deny his contribution flatly, but should tactfully
explain to the people that the success is not due to Sihanouk, but it is due to
our Party.[20]

Sihanouk recalls an incident in Beijing, which probably took place in
1970, that gives additional evidence of the basic split between the Vietnamese and Chinese, on the one hand, and the Khmers Rouges on the other, over
the use of Sihanouk's name and popularity as an instrument of political mobilization within Cambodia:

One day, the Hanoi government sent me a message requesting me to make up
some badges, the first model of which must consist of my portrait, and the second of the royal coat of arms adopted by GRUNK. According to my North
Vietnamese "friends," the Khmer people remained very Sihanoukist and very

royalist. . . . In order to win them to our just cause and in order to arouse them to enlist with the FUNK troops, it would be good to distribute these badges to them. The Chinese government, informed of this matter by me, made no objection to it. It promptly produced several thousand copies of these badges in a qualified factory. At the moment of sending these badges in question to Hanoi to be dispatched to Cambodia, Messrs. Ieng Sary, Thiounn Mumm, etc., created an obstruction. The young Khmer communists, freshly arrived from the USSR, Czechoslovakia, East Germany, France, etc., launched extremely virulent and injurious diatribes against Sihanouk and the Khmer monarchy, whose "State Legitimacy" the K.R., in order to serve their own interests, exploited shamelessly. . . . The badges did not leave for Kampuchea. They were thrown into the garbage can.[21]

Sometime in the middle of 1971, as the Khmers Rouges leaders began to consolidate their control within FUNK, they began a process of removing the pro-Sihanouk elements from positions of power in insurgent-controlled areas. This coincided with the beginning of a process of radicalization of the revolutionary regime in areas FUNK controlled. Two years later the Khmers Rouges began an intensive propaganda campaign to discredit the Prince in the eyes of the Cambodian peasants.[22]

But the Vietnamese communists, on the other hand, continued to emphasize a political role for Prince Sihanouk. This did not mean that Hanoi wanted Sihanouk to return to real power. Henry Kissinger noticed the condescending, cynical attitude of Le Duc Tho, the Hanoi politburo's expert on the other countries of Indochina, toward the Prince. According to Kissinger, Tho made fun of the Prince's recent visit to Hanoi and the Prince's love of luxury. Tho also showed Kissinger a propaganda film about Sihanouk's visit to Cambodian territory controlled by the Khmers Rouges. The American secretary of state saw the clear implication that "Sihanouk was there on the sufferance of the Khmers Rouges." Kissinger added, "The primary use that Le Duc Tho seemed to see in Sihanouk was as a means to demoralize and undermine the Lon Nol government."[23]

This difference between the Vietnamese and Cambodian communists over the use of Sihanouk is interesting for two reasons. First, it demonstrates the political sophistication of the Vietnamese, revealing their understanding of the mentality of the Cambodian peasants, and their patient and careful approach to mobilizing the Cambodians for their own purposes. This calculating attitude of Hanoi's leaders is especially notable given Sihanouk's close identification with the Chinese, a point to which we shall return later.

Second, it demonstrates the lack of political sophistication of the Khmers Rouges. In their desire to minimize even the appearance of a political role for Sihanouk, the Khmers Rouges were manifesting impatience with "united front" tactics in general. They were displaying what Lenin called an "infantile leftist" approach to the pursuit of power. That is, they were reluctant to compromise any political values, even temporarily, as a tactic for attaining power.

HANOI'S INSTRUMENTS FOR CONTROL OF THE INSURGENCY

The Vietnamese communists began with two political instruments for establishing their political control over the Cambodian insurgency: the "Khmer Viet Minh" Cambodian communists who had been trained in North Vietnam since 1954, and the liaison committees that were created immediately after the Lon Nol coup. Both of these political instruments depended for their survival upon the presence in Cambodia of the military units of North Vietnam and the South Vietnamese National Liberation Front, or Viet Cong. Yet even such awesome protection was politically insufficient for the task at hand.

The Cambodian insurgency consisted of three distinct political tendencies: the Sihanoukists, the Khmer Viet Minh, and the Khmers Rouges. Some of the cadres and fighters for FUNK were royalist supporters of Prince Sihanouk (Khmer Rumdoah). But the Sihanoukists never held real power. Political power within FUNK was in the hands of Cambodian communists. However, none of these communist power wielders were the Khmer Viet Minh returnees from North Vietnam. All the top political and military posts within FUNK and its armed forces were held by the Maoist nationalists, who formally identified themselves as members of Angka Padevat (the Revolutionary Organization)—as the KCP was publicly called—but whom Sihanouk had dubbed the Khmers Rouges (in English, Khmer Reds; in Khmer, Khmer Krahom). The Hanoi-trained communists never attained leadership positions in the Cambodian Revolutionary Organization itself, although during 1970 and 1971, in some areas under Vietnamese military control they held positions of state power from the village to the tambon (sector) level.[24] There is evidence that upon their return to Cambodia, the Khmer Viet Minh military cadres were given low-ranking positions within the Cambodian insurgency's armed forces, usually involving demotion from the rank they had attained in North Vietnam.[25] Eventually they, together with the political cadres, would be liquidated by Pol Pot's security forces. Thus at the outset, Pol Pot and his circle had retained party and military structures independent of the Vietnamese. Hanoi's Trojan Horse method of controlling the Cambodian communist revolution had been countered.

Immediately after the overthrow of Sihanouk, the Vietnamese communists formed liaison committees for handling relations between the North Vietnamese and Viet Cong troops on the one hand, and the Khmer communists on the other. The liaison committees had two primary tasks, both covert. The first was to inform the Khmer communists of the Vietnamese communist party's policies, particularly those involving how the Vietnamese thought the anti-U.S. struggle should be undertaken. The other primary task was to assist the Khmers by providing them with experts in the military, economic, security, and medical fields. The secondary, *overt* task of the committees was to solve disputes between the Khmer and Vietnamese communist troops.[26] The liaison committees have been referred to by another Vietnamese communist defector as advisory committees.[27]

The liaison committees were organized in a vertical system, starting with a central liaison committee, followed by regional liaison committees, and below them, zone liaison committees. This hierarchy was structured to parallel the organization of the Khmer communists.[28] But the liaison committees only had a role so long as there were Vietnamese communist troops directly supporting the Cambodian insurgency. That situation would only pertain until 1973.

FIRST CONFRONTATIONS BETWEEN VIETNAMESE AND CAMBODIAN COMMUNIST TROOPS

During the two years after the Lon Nol coup, in spite of Hanoi's careful attempts to guide the Cambodian insurgency, as the size of the Cambodian guerrilla forces expanded rapidly there were frequent clashes between Vietnamese communists and the Khmers Rouges.[29] Even before 1970 the top leadership of the Kampuchean Communist Party had concluded that Vietnam was not a reliable ally. When the KCP had decided to launch an armed uprising against the Sihanouk government in 1968, the Vietnamese communists had refused to support the action.[30] But although the Lon Nol coup of 1970 had changed Hanoi's political objectives in Cambodia so that Vietnamese and Cambodian communists had a common enemy, the blatancy of

Hanoi's desire to control the Cambodian insurgency seems to have turned the KCP leaders against the Vietnamese communists. At a Party Congress held in September 1971, the KCP leaders resolved that Vietnam was the long term 'acute enemy' of Kampuchea.[31] A decision was made to try to expel all the Vietnamese communist troops and cadres. In considering the rationality of this KCP decision, it must be noted that at the time the decision was made the Cambodian government forces still outnumbered the communist troops in Cambodia, and three-quarters of those communist troops were Vietnamese.[32]

Interestingly, the Vietnamese communists were at that time unaware of the KCP policy. A document from the South Vietnamese People's Liberation Army Political Staff Department, which was disseminated to all Vietnamese communist units operating inside Cambodia in October 1971, drew attention to these conflicts between "friendly forces and ours." It spoke of the need to correct "shortcomings that unfavorably affect the friendship of the two Parties and countries." But the document did not suggest that conflict was a product of deliberate policy by the Khmers Rouges leaders, and it did urge a conciliatory attitude on the part of Vietnamese cadres and soldiers:

> How do we properly solve frequent conflicts between both sides? With a large combat strength operating in the Khmer Republic, frictions between both sides are unavoidable. There is an essential difference in the two peoples. We must make positive efforts to minimize these conflicts and properly solve them, for they concern the two Parties and the peoples of the two nations.
> We must be calm and objective to carefully determine whether the friction is caused by our personnel, the Khmers, or by the enemy. We must realize that the responsibility of our Party is to promote the solidarity among the Khmer and Vietnamese Parties, to defeat the common enemy.[33]

In the first months after the KCP leaders' expulsion decision not only were the Vietnamese communists unaware of it. Some Cambodian insurgent leaders were too. In early 1972, when most main force units of the North Vietnamese army had voluntarily been withdrawn from Cambodia for the Easter offensive against South Vietnam, some cadres of the Cambodian front FUNK were still being instructed to exercise restraint in their relations with the Vietnamese. As a circular from the FUNK Committee in the 25th Sector (Kandal province) urged:

> When checking the travel passes of Vietnamese cadre and soldiers, the Khmer cadre, soldiers, guerrillas, and militiamen should display a spirit of internation-

alism, respect each other in the sense of equality, and forgive every small mistake and unkindness displayed by the travellers. Any Vietnamese cadre or soldier operating in the 25th Sector, who travels without a pass, is to be sent back to his parent unit's installation. . . . If the passless traveller is from outside the 25th Sector, however, he is to be kept for investigation. In this case, the detainee should be treated with politeness. Such bad manners as boasts, threats, or vengeance are to be avoided.[34]

Nevertheless, many Khmers Rouges units were carrying out kidnapping and assassinations of Viet Cong cadres already in late 1971.[35] Some Khmer communist leaders (possibly the returnees from Hanoi who were excluded from the Pol Pot led KCP) were initially explaining these incidents to their Vietnamese allies as the work of enemy agents. For example, a letter from the secretary of a Khmer communist regional party committee to the chief of the Vietnamese Liaison Section stated it this way:

> Dear Comrade Ba Hai
> . . . Due to the close cooperation between the Communist Parties of the two countries, the Khmer Revolutionary forces have liberated half of K. But, besides military achievements, friction has developed between Khmer and friendly units resulting in the death of a number of Vietnamese cadre and soldiers, especially since the beginning of 1971 to date. The cause of these incidents was not known until recently when we discovered that enemy sabotage agents had been planted in friendly units and agencies to carry out sabotage activities and create dissension between friends.

The Khmer leader went on to describe concrete instances of murder and looting of "Vietnamese comrades" that had already taken place. He claimed also: "Under these circumstances, I urgently ordered my men to arrest the murderers and sentenced a number of them to death." But more telling signs of the seriousness of the problem were found in the Khmers Rouges officer's concluding sentences:

> I would like to explain to you that whenever a similar incident occurs, it is better for the Vietnamese cadre concerned to report it to our higher headquarters for settlement in lieu of remaining silent and seeking ways for vengeance. Such action only contributes to our disunity. I do not think it is right for your men to use military force against our men and, consequently, impair our sovereignty.
> Finally, to maintain the friendship between the Khmers and Vietnamese, may I suggest that you notify me of every incident that occurs. I pledge to seriously punish those at fault.[36]

DISAGREEMENTS OVER THE VIETNAMESE
NEGOTIATION STRATEGY

Though it was not the cause of their falling out, differences between the Khmers Rouges and the Vietnamese over negotiations as a political tactic came to the fore during the final negotiations of the Paris peace agreements, in October 1972. The Vietnamese communists wanted the Khmers Rouges to follow their example and negotiate with the United States and the republican government. By 1973 negotiation was also the preferred policy of China—a nation that the Khmers Rouges leaders considered a friend. But the Khmers Rouges resisted all Vietnamese and Chinese attempts to initiate a negotiating strategy. The position of the Khmers Rouges, as stated by both Khieu Samphan and Hu Nim, was that there should be no negotiations and no "ceasefire on the spot," only a fight to the finish.[37]

But apparently Sihanouk, under the influence of both Zhou Enlai and Pham Van Dong, did not share the Khmers Rouges' unequivocal repudiation of negotiation and compromise. After the signing of the Vietnam peace agreement in Paris in January 1973, Sihanouk visited North Vietnam as part of a delegation that included Khmers Rouges leaders Ieng Sary and Keat Chhon.[38] At a luncheon in Hanoi on January 30, 1973, Sihanouk announced that the policy of FUNK, which he was the chairman of, had been revised in the light of the Vietnam ceasefire. According to two Agence France-Presse correspondents at the luncheon, Sihanouk stated that his new policy included "an overture to the United States, a decrease of the military activities of the Cambodian resistance fighters, and provision for general amnesty in Cambodia." Sihanouk was also quoted as saying that "If the United States is willing to play the game of friendship with an independent and nonaligned Cambodia, we will be able to arrive at a quick reconciliation with the Washington government." But Sihanouk added that Lon Nol and "his clique of traitors" must be retired if there was to be a settlement. Finally, and most important, Sihanouk claimed that the new policy had been given full support by China's Premier Zhou Enlai and North Vietnam's Prime Minister Pham Van Dong.[39] But it had not been given the green light by the leaders of the "domestic resistance," that is by the Khmers Rouges. Shortly thereafter, it seems, the Khmers Rouges leadership said no. On February 1, North Vietnam indicated that it was adhering, publicly at least, to the rigid no compromise position enunciated by Sihanouk in March 1970.[40]

The Khmers Rouges had rejected Sihanouk's advocacy of a political road to power, in defiance of the preferences of both North Vietnam and China. In their Black Paper published in September 1978—to present their side of their dispute with the Vietnamese—the Khmers Rouges claim that the Vietnamese tried to pressure them throughout 1972, but especially in January 1973, to negotiate a peace agreement in Cambodia.[41] As we will see, the Vietnamese had good reason to have wanted a negotiated settlement in Cambodia.

The disagreements between the Khmers Rouges on the one hand, and the North Vietnamese and Chinese on the other, over negotiation strategy, does not explain the strange military strategy of the Khmers Rouges in mid-1973. The signing of the Paris agreements on Vietnam in January 1973 had diverted most U.S. bombing capability to Cambodia. But on June 30, the president of the United States was forced by Congressional pressure to sign a law barring all funding of American combat operations throughout Indochina by August 15. This meant an end to American bombing by that date. Yet instead of waiting until the August 15 deadline to undertake a major military offensive, the KCP launched their attack on Phnom Penh in July, directly in the face of massive American bombardments.

Not only did the Khmers Rouges offensive fail, but it incurred massive losses. Why did the KCP leaders not postpone their offensive until after August 15? There is evidence that they had instructed their forward commanders to capture Phnom Penh before August in order to "prove to the world that they could humble the U.S."[42] This suggests that the Khmers Rouges decision was not motivated by any military rationality, but rather by a fanatical ideological zeal, whereby they imagined that they would be proving the virtue of Khmer communism and their ability to outshine the Vietnamese communists. If so, this decision puts the September 1971 decision to expel the Vietnamese troops and advisers in a more clearly ideological light.

THE KHMERS ROUGES CAMPAIGN TO EXPEL THE VIETNAMESE

When the high-level KCP decision of September 1971 to expel the Vietnamese from Cambodia was finally put fully into practice in 1972, the procedure often adopted was for the KCP "domestic" cadres (i.e., those not trained in Hanoi), especially those at regional and sector levels, to open negotiations with Vietnamese troop commanders and Party cadres, calling upon them to leave Cambodia. If the Vietnamese refused, "popular demonstrations" against them would be organized by the KCP "domestic" cadres. If the Vietnamese still refused to leave, the KCP "domestic"-led armed forces would attack the Vietnamese. Fighting occurred mostly in late 1972 and mid-1973.[43]

Beginning in late 1971, but continuing through 1974, Pol Pot also conducted a secret purge of the Hanoi-trained Khmer Viet Minh communists.[44] Nothing was ever publicly announced. The victims were simply lured away by some pretext—usually meetings, study sessions, or celebrations—and secretly executed. The task of identifying and liquidating pro-Vietnamese communists was undertaken by the Nokorbal (State Security) branch of the KCP.[45]

Although the actual purges of pro-Hanoi cadres were carried out discreetly, the attitudes that motivated them were already apparent to other Cambodian insurgents. According to Ith Sarin, a noncommunist Cambodian who spent 1972 with the Khmers Rouges:

> Vis-à-vis North Vietnam, the PKK [Kampuchean Communist Party] is in close
> cooperation, but less favorable than with Red China. There is also distrust
> of North Vietnamese unstated intentions. Hou Yuon said that the PKK has
> foreseen all in preparing for danger from the VC/NVA. . . . The PKK tends to
> sympathize more with Red China. It sees there a constant support, efficacious
> and disinterested. It has modelled its leadership after the Chinese. It should like-
> wise be noted that most of the higher cadres of the Party are pro-Chinese social-
> ists. The Party also sees in China a counterweight to the Vietnamese danger.[46]

The initial public discretion of the Khmers Rouges leaders had been effective. The Vietnamese leaders had not immediately recognized the hostility of Pol Pot's KCP leadership. In November 1971 a FUNK delegation was received in Hanoi by Party Secretary Le Duan, who expressed "elation" at FUNK military victories.[47] At the official banquet, delegation leader Ieng Sary stated that the two parties had "identical conceptions and stands" on conduct of the war.[48]

According to a former high official of the Viet Cong's Provisional Revolutionary Government,[49] it was not until 1972 that the Vietnamese communist leaders became aware of the profound antagonisms that existed at the highest level of the KCP. That is because it was only then, after most of the Vietnamese communist forces had left Cambodia in order to take part in the Easter offensive against South Vietnam, that the Kampuchean Communist Party leaders felt secure enough to launch systematic harassment against those Vietnamese military units and the liaison committees that still remained.

Though the evidence is imprecise, it is clear that by 1972 the Khmers Rouges had grown to a sizeable military force. According to the Khmer Republic's intelligence service, by the end of 1970, FUNK's main forces numbered between 12,000 and 15,000 men. By November 1971 their numbers had increased to between 18,000 and 25,000. It was estimated that by May 1972, the numbers had reached between 35,000 and 40,000. Khmers Rouges growth continued in 1973.[50]

With the signing of the Paris peace agreement in January 1973, most main unit Vietnamese communist forces were withdrawn from most of Cambodia. According to the United States Embassy in Phnom Penh 42,000 North Vietnamese troops remained in Cambodia, but 35,000 of these were servicing Hanoi's supply system into South Vietnam. Only 7,000 were combat troops, half of which were aiding the Khmers Rouges.[51]

This Vietnamese withdrawal left Pol Pot's Revolutionary Army of Democratic Kampuchea the dominant military factor on the anti-government side. The FUNK administration was by this time being treated as an independent authority by the North Vietnamese and Viet Cong. Soldiers and cadres of the Vietnamese communist forces who needed to travel through zones controlled by the Khmers Rouges, or needed to buy rice from the Cambodian population in these zones, had to get written permits from FUNK authorities. Reflecting the increasing difficulties in relations, Hanoi's Central Office for South Vietnam (COSVN)—North Vietnam's political and military field headquarters for South Vietnam—established a "K-Operation" section, which provided a small number of soldiers to protect the liaison committee units. But Khmers Rouges pressures became so intense that these lightly protected units had to shift their zone of activities, eventually to the border area of South Vietnam. According to one Vietnamese communist defector, in early 1974 the soldiers and cadres of one unit were forced to retreat to South Vietnam proper, but even then were ambushed en route by the Khmers Rouges.[52]

Other political activities by the Vietnamese communists also came under considerable pressure. The General Association of Patriotic Vietnamese Residents in Cambodia was an organization established and controlled by COSVN for the purpose of maintaining Viet Cong control over the Vietnamese residents in Cambodia and enlisting their support for the Viet Cong. As the war in Cambodia dragged on and Khmers Rouges control over the insurgency became consolidated, the association began making considerable efforts to encourage Vietnamese residents to endure the Khmers Rouges authority and not to depart for South Vietnam. In all likelihood the Vietnamese communists wanted to have a social base for future political involvement in Cambodia. But these efforts were not very successful. The association showed itself impotent in the face of draconian Khmers Rouges policies directed against the Vietnamese residents. In early 1973 the armed units that the association had organised to protect the Vietnamese settlements were disbanded at Khmers Rouges insistence. At the same time the Khmers Rouges began to relocate the Vietnamese residents by force from lowland areas to forested and mountainous areas. The ostensible reason was to protect them from the Cambodian government's armed forces. But the Vietnamese residents—who were forced to abandon their property and lost the ability to earn a good income from fishing and trading as a result of the relocation—regarded this as a means whereby the Khmers Rouges could rob them of their property and exploit their labor. They then came to resent the association and the Viet Cong for failing to protect them from Khmers Rouges oppression.[53]

During this period after the signing of the Paris agreement, KCP purges of Cambodian communists suspected of being pro-Vietnamese continued.[54]

HANOI'S RESTRAINED REACTION TO KHMERS ROUGES ATTACKS

By February 1973 the Vietnamese communist leaders knew that the demonstrations and armed attacks against their forces were deliberate and that the Khmers Rouges leaders were now conspiring to seize Vietnamese communist weapons and materials and to drive all Vietnamese forces out of Cambodia.[55]

But the Vietnamese command of the C-50 Military Region (eastern Cambodia), under instructions from the Central Office for South Vietnam (COSVN), ordered its troops and agencies to avoid all clashes with the Khmers Rouges and act with restraint toward them. The NLF troops in the C-50 Military Region were upset by this and urged either retaliation against the Khmers Rouges or withdrawal to South Vietnam.[56] But it was reported by one defecting North Vietnamese cadre that in the middle of 1973 the COSVN Party Military Commission issued the following directive:

> If the Red Khmers want to violate our sanctuaries, to kill our troops, we must adequately react for self-defense; but we must not open fire first. We only need to threaten the friendly troops. Limit the damages to the minimum.[57]

Why did the Hanoi leaders behave with such restraint and even maintain the appearance of friendly indifference in the face of such provocative acts by their purported allies?

By mid-1973 only 2,000 to 3,000 North Vietnamese and Viet Cong combat troops, along with 2,000 political cadres, remained engaged in the war in Cambodia (although between 18,000 and 27,000 more troops were protecting the Ho Chi Minh Trail to support the war in South Vietnam).[58] To have engaged in a serious military confrontation with the Khmers Rouges would have required the transfer of troops needed in North or South Vietnam, thereby strengthening the military position of Hanoi's main enemy, the government of South Vietnam. Furthermore, if Hanoi's military retaliation was to serve any meaningful deterrent purpose it would also have to have resulted in a weakening of the Khmers Rouges and thus a strengthening of the position of the pro-U.S. Lon Nol government in Phnom Penh. The Hanoi leaders must have realized that such a weakening of "revolutionary solidarity," regardless of who was responsible, could only serve the interests of the Vietnamese communist party's principle enemies, and create greater difficulties for Hanoi's attainment of its immediate goal—the conquest of South Vietnam. Dealing with Khmers Rouges hostility would have to be postponed until after victory in South Vietnam. In any case, in the short-term, the Hanoi leaders had other cards to deal against the Khmers Rouges—most notably, the withholding of Chinese supplies.

The Khmers Rouges were totally dependent upon North Vietnam allowing Chinese military and economic supplies to be transported to them down the Ho Chi Minh Trail. The Vietnamese government could decide how much aid, if any, got through to the Cambodian guerrillas. In September 1973, Sihanouk told the Agence France-Presse in Beijing that after the Paris peace agreement was signed, Hanoi cut off the supply of ammunition to the Khmers Rouges. It was turned back on briefly for the August–September seige of Kompong Cham, but then cut off again. According to Sihanouk, lack of ammunition caused the "popular forces" to evacuate Kompong Cham after they had taken three-quarters of the city.[59] In an interview with the *Far Eastern Economic Review* three months later, Sihanouk reiterated the charge that his forces were short of ammunition, laying the blame upon Hanoi. He explained Hanoi's motives:

> The Democratic Republic of Vietnam and the PRG of South Vietnam no
> longer need Phnom Penh or the harbor of Sihanoukville for the needs of

national liberation in South Vietnam. Besides, Nixon's America would not fail to hold responsible—and to punish in several ways—the DRVN and the PRG if the military situation were to become catastrophic for Lon Nol's regime. The U.S. Government on many occasions has let it be known to the DRVN that American aid for reconstruction would be cut off and that the U.S. Air Force would intervene again against North Vietnam if the military situation in Cambodia were to change sharply in favour of GRUNK.[60]

No doubt there is some plausibility in Sihanouk's explanation of Hanoi's behavior. But we have seen that the Vietnamese communists had other reasons not to welcome a Khmers Rouges victory in Phnom Penh.

On the other hand, we must note that during 1973, North Vietnam did provide some important military assistance to the Khmers Rouges in the form of heavy weapons units, which assisted in the August–September siege of Kompong Cham.[61] North Vietnam did help transport aid from China, across Vietnamese territory, and down the Ho Chi Minh Trail to the Khmers Rouges forces inside Cambodia. And GRUNK leaders continued to be received in Hanoi. For example, Sihanouk visited Hanoi for one week at the end of January 1973. According to the Hanoi press agency, on the occasion of the conclusion of the Paris agreement on ending the war and restoring peace in Vietnam, Sihanouk sent a congratulatory telegram to the Vietnamese leaders.[62]

After his visit to the "liberated zones" of Cambodia in March 1973, Sihanouk was again received in Hanoi, this time in the company of Special Envoy Ieng Sary. The speeches on this occasion once again asserted "the fraternal friendship and militant solidarity binding the peoples of Vietnam, Cambodia, and Laos."[63]

The Vietnamese communist leaders also continued to receive Khmers Rouges leaders as heads of delegations without their being accompanied by Sihanouk. For example, Pham Van Dong received a FUNK/GRUNK delegation led by Ieng Sary in Hanoi in November 1973.[64] In March 1974 another FUNK/GRUNK delegation led by Khieu Samphan and Ieng Sary was welcomed in Hanoi by top Vietnamese party leaders, including Truong Chinh and Le Duc Tho.[65] That delegation was again received in Hanoi at the end of May, on its return from an international trip. According to the joint communique issued at the end of the visit, the Khmers Rouges delegation had received "a warm welcome permeated with the militant solidarity and fraternal friendship between the two peoples." Premier Pham Van Dong reaffirmed "the Vietnamese people's" support for "the just and certainly victorious struggle of the Cambodian people."[66]

In spite of all of these declarations—which spoke of support from "people" to "people," not party to party—relations were severely strained. But they were far from the breaking point. The Khmers Rouges leaders, in their more rational moments, recognized the need to have some relationship with Hanoi if they were to win. The Vietnamese communists had a more complex position. They did not want a decisive Khmers Rouges victory. But they could not afford the consolidation of the pro-American Cambodian government of Lon Nol. For Hanoi, the optimum outcome was a continuation of the Cambodian civil war, which is why it kept turning the flow of supplies to the Khmers Rouges on and off intermittently. Hanoi was waiting until a North Vietnamese victory in South Vietnam could allow it to turn its full attention to Cambodia.

But Hanoi was to be disappointed. Despite its ascendant position it could not micromanage the course of history throughout Indochina. The Khmers Rouges conquest of Phnom Penh on April 17 preceded Hanoi's conquest of Saigon by two weeks. Khmers Rouges authority throughout Cambodia had become a fait accompli without massive direct Vietnamese communist military intervention.

THE FATE OF THE INDOCHINA FEDERATION

As we have discussed earlier, traditional Vietnamese imperial ambitions in Indochina had been given a veneer of Marxist-Leninist legitimacy through the concept of an Indochinese federation, formulated by the Comintern in 1930 at the time of the founding of the ICP. The idea of a federation was taken up again by the Vietnamese communist leadership during the Viet Minh war against the French. But by 1970 the Hanoi leaders, although still in favor of a federation in principle, had become much more reticent about publicly proposing such a political formation. By 1975 they had undertaken a tactical retreat. There were two reasons for this.

The first was Hanoi's relations with Beijing. Vietnam's great neighbor and patron had always laid claim to a role in determining the future of Indochina. Beijing's close material and ideological support for the Khmers Rouges insurgency, as well as for the insurgency's nominal head of state, Prince Sihanouk, confirmed China's commitment to Cambodian independence. That is why, as the Soviet embassy in Hanoi pointed out in 1971, the Vietnamese comrades were "in no hurry" to organize the liberation forces of its neighbors in the framework of a united front of struggle. Instead, the Vietnamese were said to be satisfied having their relations with "the Cambodian and Laotian friends" conducted on a bilateral party basis, and with the "leading position they have succeeded to occupy in the Indochinese liberation movement."[67]

The "facts on the ground" were the second reason why by 1975 Hanoi was forced to put the idea of an Indochina federation on hold. Hanoi had always understood that its ability to realize the Indochina Federation depended upon its control of the political and military situation in each country. Pol Pot's purges of the Khmer Viet Minh during the early 1970s had diminished the prospects of Hanoi directing the Cambodian revolution from within. The Khmers Rouges conquest of Cambodia two weeks before Hanoi conquered South Vietnam had precluded Hanoi reasserting political control by means of a "fraternal" Vietnamese military intervention, ostensibly to assist Cambodia's "liberation."

But this did not mean that Hanoi had abandoned entirely its desire for an Indochinese federation. In February 1973 the Soviet ambassador to North Vietnam spelled out what he believed to be Hanoi's goals.

> The program of the Vietnamese comrades for Indochina is to replace the reactionary regimes in Saigon, Vientiane, and Phnom Penh with progressive ones, and later when all Vietnam, and also Laos and Cambodia, start on the road to socialism, to move toward the establishment of a Federation of the Indochinese countries. This course of the VWP [Vietnam Workers' Party] flows from the program of the former Communist party of Indochina.[68]

By 1975 Hanoi was still hoping for a resurgence of pro-Vietnamese elements within the Cambodian party leadership to restore its influence. But as we will see, its hopes were built on sand.

CONCLUSIONS

The ultimate outcome of the 1970–75 war in Cambodia—the victory of the Khmers Rouges—was not the preferred choice of any of the actors involved other than the Khmers Rouges, and possibly the radical faction (the so-called "Gang of Four") temporarily ascendant in Beijing from September 1973 until Mao's death in September 1976.

The Vietnamese communists preferred a Cambodian communist government under its control, dominated by its trained agents, the so-called Khmer Viet Minh. Their initial attempts to realize that goal, by devastating the army of the Cambodian government and helping build up a guerrilla insurgency, could not be followed up with maximum direct military intervention. These limited Vietnamese political and military actions resulted instead in the ascendancy of the Khmers Rouges. The Vietnamese communists were aware of the Khmers Rouges leaders' hostility toward them only in mid-1972, but by then they could do little to affect events. They could not crush the Khmers Rouges without risking sabotage of their primary immediate goal, which was conquering South Vietnam. The Vietnamese could only impede the Khmers Rouges victory, hoping thereby to be able first to subjugate South Vietnam, and then be in a position to come to the "fraternal assistance" of the Cambodian comrades, on the model of the Soviet Union in Eastern Europe in 1944–45, and "help" them to win the final victory.

But Hanoi failed to realize even this solution, because of the premature collapse of the Lon Nol government. In the aftermath of the independent victory of the Khmers Rouges, which had bestowed international legitimacy upon the new Cambodian regime, Hanoi was forced to wait and try other methods.

On a broader level, the events that took place during the years 1970–75 demonstrated a profound difference between the outlooks of the Vietnamese communists and the Khmers Rouges on their general attitudes toward politics and war, particularly in their attitudes toward the relationship between means and ends.

Consider their different perspectives on the role of Sihanouk in the insurgency. The Vietnamese communists, like the Chinese, recognized Sihanouk's popularity among the peasants and sought to use this in propaganda activities in order to recruit voluntary peasant support for their insurgency. The Khmers Rouges, by contrast, were fearful of Sihanouk's popularity, and were psychologically incapable of taking a purely instrumental and exploitative attitude toward it. Instead they attempted to sabotage Chinese and Vietnamese endorsed propaganda efforts in this direction. Eventually the Khmers Rouges discarded such persuasive techniques of political recruitment and relied instead upon the coercion of the population.

Even more bizarre was the behavior of the Khmers Rouges toward the Vietnamese themselves. As we have seen, between 1970 and 1972 the Khmers

Rouges had depended upon the Vietnamese communist defeat of the Cambodian army for their initial successes in expanding their "liberated zones." Moreover, they were almost totally dependent upon the goodwill of the Vietnamese communists for their military supplies from China, which had to traverse North Vietnam in order to reach Cambodia. In spite of all of these facts, the Khmers Rouges chose to confront and attack their Vietnamese communist allies long before they had vanquished their principal enemy—the American-backed republican government in Phnom Penh. In so doing, the Khmers Rouges were imposing upon themselves a more difficult and uncertain path to the seizure of state power.

These actions parallel the bizarre quality of the Khmers Rouges leaders' decision to undertake a major military offensive against Phnom Penh during mid-1973 in the face of massive U.S. air attacks. Given the fact that the U.S. government was already publicly committed to ending all of its bombing sorties by August 15, the failed offensive cost the Khmers Rouges thousands of soldiers and cadres unnecessarily.

All of this behavior indicates a pattern of unrealistic thinking on the part of the Khmers Rouges leadership about the relative capabilities and weaknesses of themselves and their enemies. Moreover, this behavior indicated a rigid inflexibility on the part of the Khmers Rouges leadership as to the choice of means to be used in the pursuit of their objectives. The Khmers Rouges leaders seemed unable to distinguish between those goals that were of immediate priority and those goals that were less pressing, and could be temporarily sacrificed to be pursued later.

This pattern of irrational thinking and behavior was to be manifested repeatedly over the next few years. It had not proved fatal to the Khmers Rouges so long as Hanoi had its hands tied by its need to deal with more powerful enemies in South Vietnam. But after April 30, 1975, Hanoi had its hands free, and those hands had become very powerful indeed.

CHAPTER THREE

The Foreign Policy of Democratic Kampuchea, 1975–78

In order to understand fully the evolution of Vietnamese-Cambodian relations after 1975, and particularly Vietnam's decision to invade Cambodia, we must first examine the broader pattern of Khmers Rouges foreign policy.

From its inception in 1975, the Cambodian communist regime, which officially called itself Democratic Kampuchea, had assumed that the Vietnamese communist state was its main enemy. Given that judgment (the underpinnings and consequences of which we will examine in the next chapter), it would have seemed logical for the Khmers Rouges regime to follow the traditional realist pattern of Cambodian statecraft and try to ensure its own survival by enlisting the support of Cambodia's other powerful immediate neighbor in the west, Thailand (which historically had also distrusted Vietnam). But the Khmers Rouges did not even attempt to do this. On the contrary, while it was confronting Vietnam in the east, the Khmers Rouges regime initiated armed attacks against Thailand in the west.

Cambodian foreign policy from 1975 to 1978 was not completely confrontational. It also included some normal diplomatic relations. But the unusual aspects of Cambodian foreign policy make no sense without reference to the revolutionary political culture of the Khmers Rouges.

REVOLUTIONARY POLITICAL CULTURE AND KHMERS ROUGES POLICY

Immediately upon their seizure of power in April 1975, the Khmers Rouges began the most radical and violent revolution in the radical and violent history of communist states. The Khmers Rouges immediately emptied all of the cities and towns of Cambodia. Their former residents were forced at gunpoint to march into the countryside to take up new lives as malnourished peasant slaves. At the same time the Cambodian communists gathered together all of those Cambodians whom they could identify as soldiers and government officials of the former regime, and took them away to be executed en masse. In the case of former military officers, their entire families, including infants, were also executed.

The regime banned all religious worship, destroyed Buddhist temples, and forced monks to become peasant laborers. The Chams, an ethnic and religious minority, were especially persecuted by being geographically scattered and forced to change their style of dress and dietary habits. Within the next year the regime began to seek out all of those who were educated at the high school level or beyond. Depending upon the geographical region, these people were subject to special internment camps or to outright execution.

Most economic activity was undertaken in agricultural communes. The regime undermined family life by physically separating the sexes at work and rest, and by imposing communal eating.[1] From the age of six onward, children were separated from their parents for work and sleep.[2] Premarital and extramarital sex was banned under sanction of death. Money was abolished. Cambodia had become a slave society in which people worked from ten to fourteen hours a day on a dangerously inadequate diet.[3]

In their domestic policies the Khmers Rouges leaders were inspired by the domestic policies of Mao Zedong in China. We should recall the response of the Khmers Rouges leaders to the death of Mao Zedong in 1976. On September 18, 1976, a rally was held in Phnom Penh to mourn the Chinese leader's passing.[4] At the rally Pol Pot read a eulogy emphasizing Mao's material and moral support for the Cambodian revolution.[5] At a Peking banquet on September 28, 1977, Pol Pot spoke of Mao Zedong Thought as the inspiration behind his regime's policies.[6] Even as late as 1983, after the Khmers Rouges had publicly renounced purported "errors" committed during their revolutionary transformation, and after they had dropped all Marxist policies from their statements of future intent, a top KR leader, Ieng Sary, openly expressed his admiration for Mao Zedong.[7]

The programs of Chairman Mao that most strongly influenced the Khmers Rouges were the Great Leap Forward and the Great Proletarian Cultural Revolution. Sihanouk believes that Mao's Cultural Revolution had a special influence on the entire Khmers Rouges leadership.[8] As for the influence of the Great Leap Forward, we have the Kampuchean Communist Party's own testimony: "We believe that we can build up the country quickly. . . . We have

only to organize the strategy and tactics to strike in whatever way is necessary. This is the Super Great Leap Forward. The Super Great Leap Forward
has concrete meaning."[9]

In this excerpt from an internal party document, we see more than
the Khmers Rouges being inspired by Maoist programs. We also see that
the Khmers Rouges were motivated by the desire to *outdo* Mao Zedong
and the Chinese communists in the radicalism of their revolution. As another internal party document stated: "Our socialism is characterized by its
speed. . . . Compared to other countries, in terms of method we are extremely fast."[10]

The forced evacuation of the cities; the execution of former government
officials, military officers, and the educated; the rapid creation of communes; and the frontal assault upon religion and individualism constituted
an application and extension of Maoist ideology to the most extreme degree.
In this sense it is fruitful to consider the Khmers Rouges political culture as
"hyperMaoist."

For the first two and a half years in power, the Cambodian communists
attempted to conceal, from both their own people and the outside world, the
fact that they were communists. This political strategy of deception has almost always characterized communist revolutionary movements prior to
their seizure of state power. But the continuation of this strategy by the
Khmers Rouges even after their conquest of the Cambodian nation evinced
an especially manic conspiratorial approach to political life. One internal
party document illustrates such forms of thinking on this matter: "The situation inside the country and outside the country is sufficient to allow the
Party to emerge. Friendly Parties have requested our Party to emerge. They
see the situation as one when we ought to emerge. Moreover, they need our
support."

Given the fact that the "friendly parties" referred to are almost certainly
the Chinese and North Koreans, the Khmers Rouges' claim that the more
powerful parties needed Cambodian support suggests a certain delusion of
grandeur. The same document also reveals the leaders' fear of unidentified
enemies: "Enemies also want us to emerge so they can observe us clearly,
and so they can proceed to accomplish their long-term objectives."[11]

Then suddenly on September 27, 1977, the regime announced that the
ruling Angka Padevatt (Revolutionary Organization) was in fact the Kampuchean Communist Party (KCP).[12] The announcement, which immediately

preceded Pol Pot's first public official visits to China and North Korea, indicated a new self-confidence on the part of the Cambodian communist leaders. It anticipated their impending, clear public alignment with powerful Asian friends.

In their internal party documents, the Cambodian communists seemed at times confident of their hold on power. A certain degree of confidence resulted from the fact that the party had executed or imprisoned virtually all former leaders of precommunist Cambodian society and maintained a terroristic hold over the Cambodian people.[13] Yet in spite of their ostensible self-confidence, the Khmers Rouges revealed two continuing fears, which were interconnected.

The first fear was of Cambodia's neighbors to the west and the east, Thailand and Vietnam. In a document from August 1976, Pol Pot asserted that these neighbors were attacking and tormenting Cambodia. That allegedly explained the speed of the socialist revolution, which Pol Pot claimed would make Cambodia stronger:

> Why must we move so swiftly? Because enemies attack and torment us. From the east and the west they persist in pounding and worrying us; this is their strategy. . . . If we are slow and weak, the contemptible people to the west will mistreat us also. If, on the other hand, we are strong and courageous for one, two, three, or four years, the contemptible people to the east and the contemptible people to the west will be unable to do anything to us.[14]

Note Pol Pot's political judgment that building socialism quickly—which had already involved massacring hundreds of thousands of people, destroying their traditional culture and institutions, and creating second-class citizens out of the "new people"—would make Cambodia internally stronger and better able to deal with its external enemies. This judgment suggests a total disconnection from reality, which is clearly the product of paranoia and misguided ideological assumptions.

Furthermore, Pol Pot asserts that the Vietnamese and the Thais were actively attacking and tormenting the Cambodians. Yet, while the Thais and the Vietnamese were hostile to the Democratic Kampuchean regime, the charge that they were attacking Cambodia has little independent evidence to support it. Given that fact, and Pol Pot's lack of any details, his claim was almost certainly a delusion.

Of course, the Khmers Rouges did have good reason to distrust their erstwhile comrades to the east. As we have discussed earlier, the Vietnamese had devised a strategy for controlling their smaller Indochinese neighbors. It included infiltrating the communist parties of its neighbors with people it had trained and indoctrinated. In the case of Cambodia, this involved the so-called Khmer Viet Minh, whom Hanoi assumed would act as its agents. So the Khmers Rouges leaders did face a legitimate threat to their autonomy from Vietnam. But Pol Pot and his supporters had anticipated the Vietnamese strategy, and had preempted it when they arrested all of the Khmer Viet Minh soon after they returned from Hanoi with the North Vietnamese army in the early 1970s, and again after the victory of 1975. Still, Pol Pot and his circle seemed unconvinced of their own success. They feared that some agents of Hanoi might still be hidden within the party.

This was the second great anxiety of the party leaders—a diffuse fear of internal enemies. In a document from December 1976, a party leader speaks incessantly of this worry. For example: "In addition we should ask: are there still treacherous secret elements buried inside the Party, or are they gone? According to our observations over the last ten years, it's clear they're not gone at all. . . . From every direction traitors continue their activities."[15]

The report went on to warn that "microbes" had hidden inside the party in the years of the "people's" and "democratic" revolutions of the 1960s and early 1970s. However, the party leadership was confident that as the socialist revolution advanced the party would be able to "locate the ugly microbes. They will be pushed out by the true nature of socialist revolution."[16]

The Khmers Rouges leaders had begun to expand their internal purges in late 1976 and 1977. Reports began to appear of purges within the Kampuchean Communist Party leadership. Four province chiefs from Cambodia's western region were reported to have been executed during the first two months of 1977. Their assistants were all taken away to unknown destinations.[17] A senior Thai military figure later claimed that these purges had been in response to an attempted coup in the respective northwestern provinces.[18]

One available, though partial, index of the acceleration of that terror was the number of people taken each year to the Tuol Sleng interrogation, torture, and execution center in Phnom Penh. It represented only a fraction of the executions carried out by the regime, but it offers some insight into the extent of Pol Pot's terror directed against the regime itself. In 1975, 200 prisoners were registered; in 1976, 2,250; in 1977, more than 6,000; and in 1978 the number was almost 10,000.[19] All were denounced as enemies and tortured into writing confessions of treason against either the party or the state.

As in earlier communist regimes, most notably Stalin's Soviet Union and Mao's China, some of the victims were former top party leaders and even personal friends of Pol Pot. And, as in the Soviet and Chinese examples, almost none of the thousands of Cambodian victims appear to have been guilty of any of the crimes to which they were forced to confess. For by 1977 prisoners were confessing to involvement in elaborate and implausible conspiracies on behalf of both the Vietnamese and the C.I.A.![20] According to the internal reports of Democratic Kampuchea's security forces, conspiracies against the Cambodian revolution involved the Soviets, the Americans, the Thais, and the Vietnamese operating in collusion.[21]

This fantastic plot, which envisioned profoundly hostile forces cooperating with each other for the first time, solely in order to destroy Democratic Kampuchea, is a classic example of the "paranoid pseudocommunity" construction.

Khmers Rouges thinking about foreign policy was influenced partly, but not only, by its leaders' paranoia. In part it was also influenced by formal ideological beliefs. As we have seen, in their domestic policy the Khmers Rouges implemented an extreme extension and application of Mao Zedong's ideology. In their foreign policy utterances, the Khmers Rouges embraced two Maoist ideological precepts. The first was the doctrine of self-reliance. Contrasting Democratic Kampuchea with its predecessor regime, Phnom Penh radio stated: "No one can be as contemptible as the Lon Nol clique . . . which ignominiously lived by begging. . . . Entirely different from the traitorous republic, the new Cambodia is now capable of providing everything for itself."[22]

This precept was also embraced in internal party documents:

> We have no assistance from outside for industry or agriculture. . . . Broadly speaking, other [socialist] countries were greatly assisted by foreign capital after liberation. For us, at present, there is some Chinese aid, but there isn't very much compared with other countries. This is our Party's policy. If we go and beg for help we would certainly obtain some, but this would affect our political line.[23]

The second Maoist precept was the primacy of the subjective factors of human will and ideological purity in triumphing over objective material factors. Publicly, the Khmers Rouges stated: "The great victory of the Cambodian revolution, based as it is on the stand of political conscience and revolutionary morals, is irrefutable proof that the human factor is the key and that the material factor is only secondary."[24]

This conception of the importance of subjective factors in political or military strength and success was also expressed in internal party documents. For example in mid-1976 it was stated: "[T]echnology is not the decisive factor; the determining factors of a revolution are politics, revolutionary people, and revolutionary methods."[25]

Again, in the party journal *Tung Padevat* (Revolutionary Flags) of June 1976, a discussion of the continuing struggle between revolution and counterevolution contained the following analysis:

> Are they strong or not? This problem does not depend on them. It depends on us. If we continuously make absolute measures, the enemies will only retreat. They will be continually scattered and smashed to bits. When we are strong they are weak, when we are weak they are strong. Our being strong means that we have correct concepts, and take correct political and military measures.[26]

APPLYING "SELF-RELIANCE": DIPLOMACY
AND FOREIGN TRADE

In the general pattern of its diplomatic relations, it seems that the foreign policy of Democratic Kampuchea was initially inspired by the xenophobic example of Mao's Cultural Revolution. For immediately after the Khmer Rouge seized power they expelled all westerners and almost all foreign diplomats.[27] By early 1978 only the Chinese, North Koreans, Albanians, Yugoslavs, Laotians and Egyptians retained embassies in Phnom Penh.[28] Apart from maverick Romania, no Warsaw Pact country was recognized by the new regime. This was in spite of the fact that the Soviet Union had attempted to create normal state-to-state relations with the DK leadership. For example, Soviet Foreign Minister Andre Gromyko had congratulated Ieng Sary on the latter's appointment as Foreign Affairs Minister. The message was broadcast on Phnom Penh radio.[29]

The foreign diplomats stationed in Phnom Penh led a closely guarded existence, allowed little contact with each other and no contact at all with the Cambodian population. They lived in an almost hermetically sealed country.[30]

For a year and a half after its seizure of power the DK government undertook no foreign trade, except perhaps with China and North Korea (although the details of this are secret). The KCP leadership referred to this as a policy of "self-reliance."

In early 1976 the Khmers Rouges leaders began to expand their diplomatic relations with the noncommunist developing world. Diplomatic relations were formally established with nonaligned Peru on April 23 and with prowestern Malaysia on April 28.[31] By the middle of May, all of the members of the Association of Southeast Asian Nations (ASEAN) except for Indonesia had established diplomatic relations with Democratic Kampuchea. The Indonesian exception was probably related to Indonesia's continuing suspicion of China, with which Democratic Kampuchea was closely aligned. Undoubtedly even more important was DK political support for the Timorese guerrilla organization Fretilin, which was resisting Indonesia's takeover of the former Portugese colony, and DK recognition of its Democratic Republic of East Timor.[32]

It is clear that although the Khmers Rouges leaders wanted to keep their *people* physically isolated from the rest of the world, they were engaged in a desperate quest for recognition of their *regime* by foreign, especially Third World, states. Their motive was clearly political support in their increasingly difficult, albeit still partially concealed, conflict with communist Vietnam.

On January 3, 1977, it was announced that Democratic Kampuchea and the Netherlands were establishing diplomatic relations.[33] In late January a Yugoslav economic delegation visited Cambodia. The two countries signed an economic and trade cooperation agreement, and announced that Yugoslavia had provided economic aid to DK in the form of farm equipment.[34] In February Foreign Minister Ieng Sary led a delegation to Burma.[35] Later in the month Sary visited Malaysia, where discussions focused on future economic relations between the two countries. The Malaysian foreign minister pledged his country's support for Cambodia's reconstruction.[36]

The emergence of a foreign trade policy reflected the trend away from the ideal of "self-reliance." In October 1976 the government of Democratic Kampuchea established a trading house called Ren Fung Company, Ltd., in Hong Kong. Its purpose was to expand the country's foreign trade.[37] The imports from Japan included some 10,000 tons of steel, textiles, vehicles, chemical products, and construction equipment.[38] From Hong Kong the DK was importing millions of dollars worth of goods, in particular chemicals, textiles, iron and steel, medical and pharmaceutical products, insecticides, petroleum products, and transport equipment. The DK was believed to be paying off its debt to China partly by exporting an unknown amount of rice, rubber, and pepper to China, North Korea, and Laos. But its imports from Japan and Hong Kong were paid for by China, possibly out of a $20 million grant from China offered in 1975.[39] The extent of this foreign trade was relatively tiny. Thus, by developing a partial dependence on Chinese economic assistance and imports of equipment and medicine, Democratic Kampuchea was not practicing complete autarky; however, it was also not building a trade-oriented economy.

Moreover, the expansion of diplomatic and foreign economic relations during the three and a half years of Khmers Rouges authority in Phnom Penh never included the United States. An overture made by the new Carter administration on March 14, 1977, via its Peking-based liaison office, was vigorously rebuffed by the Foreign Ministry of Democratic Kampuchea.[40]

CENTRAL ALLIES: CHINA AND NORTH KOREA

Despite its proclamations of "self-reliance," the key element of DK foreign policy remained its close alliance with the People's Republic of China. Pol Pot, Ieng Sary, and other Khmers Rouges leaders had made many clandestine visits to China during Mao's lifetime. But only in September 1977, one year after Mao's death, did Pol Pot make his first publicly announced visit to the PRC. The visit followed by one day the public announcement of the existence of the Kampuchean Communist Party.[41]

The Khmers Rouges delegation—which consisted of Pol Pot, Ieng Sary, Vorn Vet, and Thiounn Thioeunn—was greeted at the airport by Prime Minister and Party Chairman Hua Guofeng, who later hosted a dinner in the Great Hall of the People attended by the Chinese Communist Party's four deputy chairmen.[42] This constituted a singular honor for a foreign visitor. Pol Pot was also reportedly greeted by 100,000 cheering Chinese citizens as he drove through Tiananmen Square in the heart of the city.[43]

At the conclusion of the China visit, the DK delegation proceeded to North Korea, where it received an equally enthusiastic reception during its five-day stay. According to the official communiqué, talks held between Comrade Kim Il-song and Comrade Pol Pot "proceeded in an atmosphere of militant friendship and comradely trust."[44] The title Hero of the Democratic People's Republic of Korea (DPRK) was conferred on Pol Pot at a public ceremony, attended by Kim Il-song, in Pyongyang on October 7.[45] Clearly, the government of the DPRK was the second most important friend of the government of Democratic Kampuchea. In November a DPRK civil aviation delegation visited Cambodia, and a trade protocol between the DK and the DPRK was signed in Phnom Penh.[46]

CREATING A SECOND FRONT: DEMOCRATIC KAMPUCHEA
  AND THAILAND

Given Pol Pot's stated concern for the security threat from Vietnam, it is difficult to understand the behavior of the Khmers Rouges toward their other
main neighbor, Thailand. During 1977 many attacks were made by Khmers
Rouges soldiers on Thai villages just across the border.

In late January, two hundred Khmers Rouges soldiers attacked four Thai
villages, killing twenty-nine Thai civilians and one Thai policeman.[47] The
Khmers Rouges later admitted to perpetrating the atrocity, but justified it by
claiming that the villages were part of Cambodian, not Thai, territory.[48]
Khmers Rouges attacks on Thai villages in the border provinces occurred
in February and April.[49] In June, five Thai marines were killed and several
others wounded after a Khmers Rouges ambush.[50] In July, three hundred
Khmers Rouges soldiers fought a running battle with Thai forces, killing
seventeen. The clash involved tanks, armored personnel carriers, and air
strikes by the Thais.[51] At the beginning of August, two hundred Khmers
Rouges troops crossed the Thai border to attack three Thai hamlets, killing
thirty-one civilians.[52] Afterward, the Thai prime minister warned that Thailand would take military action against Cambodia if Khmers Rouges attacks
continued.[53] In October Khmers Rouges attacked three villages in the
Aranyaprathet district.[54] Then on November 2, Khmers Rouges forces
launched simultaneous attacks on more than ten Thai villages along a forty-
mile stretch of the border.[55]

These unprovoked attacks on Thai villages made no sense given the
Phnom Penh regime's difficulties with its eastern neighbor, and its ostensible
desire for economic relations and diplomatic support from the rest of the
outside world. Some Thai leaders claimed at the time that the Democratic
Kampuchean High Command was not behind these attacks, which they believed were instigated by local Khmers Rouges soldiers without the knowledge of the central authorities in Phnom Penh.[56] Phnom Penh radio claimed
that the Thais had instigated the attacks, and called for talks to resolve the
dispute.[57] But on December 15, over two hundred Khmers Rouges troops,
supported by Thai insurgents, attacked two Thai border villages, reportedly
killing sixteen Thais.[58] The Thai government decided not to protest because
of, as Thai Foreign Minister Uppadit put it, a desire to "build a good atmosphere" and not to interfere with the process of establishing normal diplo-

matic relations with Cambodia.⁵⁹ Despite Thai government attempts to appease them, the next day Khmers Rouges troops launched four apparently coordinated attacks on Thai villages and border outposts.⁶⁰

EXPANDING TIES IN SOUTHEAST ASIA

In spite of their unresolved conflict with Thailand, the Khmers Rouges continued to expand their diplomatic efforts with other nations in Southeast Asia. In late November 1977 the DK government hosted a three-day visit by Burma's President Ne Win—the first ever visit by a foreign head of state to Democratic Kampuchea.⁶¹

On December 3, Chinese politburo member Chen Yonggui arrived in Phnom Penh, leading a delegation consisting of two aides from the Central Committee's International Liaison Department and one from the Foreign Ministry.⁶² The Chinese visitors were taken on a tour of the countryside. But the nature of the delegation (one politburo member and three foreign policy specialists, and the absence of experts on agriculture or the economy) suggests that the probable purpose of the visit was to discuss Democratic Kampuchea's precarious relations with its immediate neighbors.

On December 6, before the Chinese delegation had left, a Malaysian Government delegation, led by Foreign Minister Rithaudeen, arrived in Cambodia. In spite of the troubles being experienced by Thailand, its neighbor and fellow member of the Association of Southeast Asian Nations (ASEAN), Malaysia offered development assistance to Democratic Kampuchea.⁶³ Malaysia also announced that the government of Cambodia had expressed a desire to expand economic and trade relations with Malaysia.⁶⁴

Possessing the enthusiastic support of China and North Korea, friendly relations with Burma and Malaysia, and a trade outlet to Japan and Hong Kong, the government of Democratic Kampuchea was not isolated in the Asian region. Yet its troops continued to attack neighboring Thailand, whose leaders clearly desired friendly ties.

THE ENIGMA: DEMOCRATIC KAMPUCHEA'S UNREMITTING CONFLICT WITH THAILAND

In late December 1977 the Swedish ambassador to Thailand, Jean-Christophe Oberg, entered Cambodia on a two-day visit reported by the Thai press as an attempt at mediation between Thailand and Cambodia.[65] By mid-January 1978 Democratic Kampuchea had broken diplomatic relations with the Socialist Republic of Vietnam (SRV), and was engaged in an escalating military conflict with Vietnam on its eastern border. The *New York Times* reported "substantial progress" had been achieved by Thailand in trying to bring the Cambodian leaders to the negotiating table.[66] But Cambodian attacks on Thai border villages and military outposts were continuing.[67] On January 20, 1978, the Thai military disclosed publicly what had been indicated privately for some time: that the Khmers Rouges were supporting Thai communist guerrillas with training and arms, and were even accompanying them in attacks on Thai military outposts.[68]

These revelations did not deter the Thai leaders in Bangkok. At the end of January, Thai Foreign Minister Uppadit Pachariyangkun undertook a four-day visit to Phnom Penh. At a banquet there he attributed the Cambodian attacks to an unnamed "third party."[69] On his return to Bangkok, Uppadit announced that Thailand and Cambodia had agreed to restore friendly relations and to exchange ambassadors as soon as possible. He also announced that both countries had agreed to an immediate resumption of economic and trade relations.[70]

Barely four days had passed before another Khmers Rouges attack upon a Thai border patrol police base was reported, with civilian villages nearby being put to the torch.[71] Three days later, on February 9, a combined force of three hundred Khmer communist soldiers and Thai communist guerrillas attacked Paet Um village in Nam Yun district, retreating with several hundred Thai villagers abducted into Cambodia. A second attack on the same village took place on February 12. During that same period Cambodian attacks upon Thai soldiers were reported in two other provinces along the border.[72] On February 15, a Cambodian army force seized fifty Thai villagers in Buriram province, and abducted them into Cambodia.[73] The Thai foreign minister stated that he could not understand the motive behind the attack, in the light of the agreements he had reached with the DK foreign minister to halt such border skirmishes.[74] An official note sent by Uppadit to Ieng Sary on February 17, urged that he help stop the skirmishes.[75] Three days later a band of sixteen Khmer Rouge and Thai guerrillas raided another Thai village, and abducted six villagers, five of whom managed to escape.[76] On February 24, the Cambodian government responded to the Thai note concerning the border incidents, blaming "forces from the Thai side" for starting the incidents.[77]

In trying to explain the behavior of their neighbor, the two most important Thai government leaders refused to attribute blame to the DK leadership in Phnom Penh. On February 16, Foreign Minister Uppadit claimed that he still believed in the sincerity of the Khmers Rouges leaders, particularly Foreign Minister Ieng Sary. Uppadit said that "the border attacks might be a result of poor communications in Cambodia or lack of discipline by Cambodian field commanders."[78] On March 3, Thai Prime Minister Kriangsak suggested that Thai communists were responsible for the attacks and that "small bands of Cambodian soldiers had unintentionally trespassed into Thai territory from time to time."[79]

Attacks on Thai border villages, involving the abduction of hundreds of Thai civilians, continued throughout March 1978. The attacks occurred not just in one region, but in many different provinces along the entire Thai-Cambodian border. Interviews with those who had managed to escape indicated what the purpose of the attacks and kidnappings were: the Thai Communist Party, aided by the Khmers Rouges, was trying to forcibly recruit Thai civilians in the border area to join their guerrilla forces for future attacks on Thai government troops.[80]

On April 1, 1978, Cambodian gunners for the first time pounded the Thai town of Aranyaprathet with long-range Chinese rockets.[81] On April 9 Thai communists and Khmers Rouges attacked another Thai village in Buriram province, killing seventeen people, burning down seventy houses, and making off with a tractor and four trucks, as well as goods from the local market.[82] Only after this attack did the Thai prime minister warn of retaliation by his country's armed forces.[83] Yet at the end of April another series of grenade and rocket attacks against Thai border villages and the town of Aranyaprathet took place.[84] Clearly, the Khmers Rouges were interested in more than just helping the Thai communists forcibly recruit guerrillas. Defecting Thai communist guerrillas, who had been abducted, indoctrinated, and given military training inside Cambodia, reported that their ultimate mission was to create a "liberated zone" for the Thai communists inside Thailand.[85]

Could this have been going on, as the Thai prime minister had once suggested, at the initiative of local Khmers Rouges, without the knowledge or approval of the central leadership of Democratic Kampuchea? There is evidence that there were some variations in the way Khmers Rouges *domestic* policy was applied throughout different regions of Cambodia. But these variations were matters of degree, not of kind. The sponsorship of the Thai communists was a matter of the type of policy, not a question of degree of application. It is unlikely that local commanders all along the border could have been carrying out such a policy without approval from Phnom Penh. This is especially unlikely when we recall that Pol Pot had carried out a purge of Khmers Rouges leaders in the northwestern region of the country during 1977.

One conclusion seems inescapable: At the same time that it was engaged in confronting its powerful neighbor to the east, the government of Democratic Kampuchea was also sponsoring an insurgency against its western neighbor.

One should recall the evidence of internal Cambodian communist party documents in which Pol Pot told his inner circle during August 1976 that "enemies attack and torment us." These enemies were said to be both in the east (Vietnam) and the west (Thailand). He claimed that these enemies were persisting in "pounding and worrying us."[86] There is no independent evidence to support this claim. And we have seen that during and after the Cambodian attacks upon Thailand in 1977 and 1978, the Thai leaders were going out of their way to appease the Khmers Rouges. Thus the statement almost certainly expresses a paranoid fantasy on the part of Pol Pot. His paranoid delusions about the Thais might explain the Khmers Rouges attacks.

It was China's intervention that partially tempered Khmers Rouges policy. Thailand had been beseeching the Cambodian leaders to negotiate their differences with Thailand. Thai requests had remained unanswered until China intervened in the middle of June 1978. As a result, a train of events was set in motion, culminating in Ieng Sary's arrival in Thailand on July 14, 1978.[87]

Ieng Sary's visit to Thailand did not result in a joint communique. Instead, the foreign minister of Democratic Kampuchea, in a notable breach of etiquette, used his press conference at the end of his visit as a platform to virulently denounce Vietnam. Sary thereby embarrassed his hosts, for Thailand had already exchanged ambassadors with Vietnam, and was trying to establish normal relations with that country.[88]

Nevertheless the Ieng Sary visit did presage an improvement in relations between Democratic Kampuchea and Thailand. There were only minor skirmishes between Thai soldiers and the Khmers Rouges during July and August.

On September 14, 1978, Ieng Sary informed the Thai Foreign Ministry that his country was ready to designate an ambassador to Bangkok.[89] Two days later Thai Foreign Ministry officials arrived in Phnom Penh to prepare the opening of the embassy of the Royal Thai Kingdom.[90] They were given a friendly reception by Ieng Sary.[91] It seemed that the low-level conflict between the two countries was finally over.

In the wake of a tacit peace agreement with Thailand, Democratic Kampuchea began a diplomatic offensive in the Southeast Asian region. The DK motive was a need to compete with a similar move already underway by the Vietnamese. Both Indochinese communist leaderships saw the diplomatic support of ASEAN as an important factor given an impending conflagration.

On August 6, 1978, Phnom Penh radio announced that the Government of Democratic Kampuchea and the Government of the Republic of Indonesia had agreed to establish diplomatic relations at the ambassadorial level as of August 7.[92] This belated recognition (two years after DK had established relations with all the other members of ASEAN), meant that the Khmers Rouges leaders had now established relations with the most anti-Chinese government in Asia, and one that was battling a guerrilla insurgency in East Timor that DK had supported in the past.

On October 17 Ieng Sary arrived in the Philippines on the first leg of a three-nation diplomatic visit. The Khmers Rouges leader's three-day visit, which came hard on the heels of one by Vietnam's Prime Minister Pham Van Dong, was to the soil of the most pro-American nation in Southeast Asia, the only one still hosting American military bases. It was also a nation whose government was battling Maoist guerrillas of the New People's Army, a movement that the Khmers Rouges must surely have considered fraternal. But there was an obvious reason for these ideological compromises. At a press conference Sary stated that his visit there and to other ASEAN countries could be considered a success if it elicited sympathy and moral support for his country, which was in great danger of being "swallowed" by Vietnam.[93]

From the Philippines, the Cambodian leader traveled to Djakarta, where he held meetings with top Indonesian officials, including President Suharto.[94] The Indonesians made no public statement of their views. But for Indonesia to have received an official from Democratic Kampuchea was itself a diplomatic breakthrough for the Khmers Rouges. It also represented a drastic change in the Khmers Rouges conception of foreign policy—a move away from ideology-based xenophobia to more conventional diplomacy based on normal state-to-state relations. The change in conception probably reflected PRC tutoring. But PRC tutoring was only brought to bear upon minds that had recently been concentrated wonderfully by the threat of a hanging (to paraphrase Samuel Johnson).

CHINA'S INFLUENCE UPON KHMERS ROUGES
FOREIGN POLICY

The Khmers Rouges were influenced by China but they were not puppets of China. There were two sources of Chinese influence on the Khmers Rouges. The first was China's material support for the regime. But the Khmers Rouges liked to attribute their purported successes to their own efforts and to their political independence from their aid-giving foreign friends. In January 1978, while Deng Yingchao, Zhou Enlai's widow, was in Cambodia in a fruitless attempt to urge Phnom Penh to negotiate with Hanoi, Phnom Penh radio stated:

> We distinguish between good and bad friends. We respect and love friends who are good to us, who respect the independence, sovereignty, and territorial integrity of Cambodia, and who deal with us on equal footing. But our friend-making criterion is not based on whether this or that friend can provide material aid. It is based on the principles of equality, mutual respect, and mutual benefit, on sentiments of solidarity in accordance with the principle of respecting and protecting the right of each country, be it large or small, to manage its own destiny.[95]

That the distinguished Chinese emissary was having trouble in her dealings with the Khmers Rouges leaders was made more evident by the DK refusal to grant her request to see Prince Sihanouk, then under house arrest in Phnom Penh.[96]

The second source of Chinese influence on the Khmers Rouges was Mao Zedong's ideology. But this was of declining relevance for the Chinese leadership after Mao's death in September 1976. Even before the death of Mao Zedong, Khmers Rouges foreign policy had little in common with the increasingly pragmatic, realpolitik approach to the world being fostered by Zhou Enlai. With Mao's decline during his final years, the only support KCP policy radicalism could have had in China was from the so-called Gang of Four, who were arrested in October 1976.

Evidence of Chinese dissatisfaction with Khmers Rouges domestic radicalism, which had foreign policy implications, is to be found in the January 1979 secret report of Chinese politburo member Geng Biao. After noting that the Cambodian insurgent army, upon its victory in 1975, was divided into factions, the Chinese leader proceeded to criticize the Khmers Rouges leadership for its response to that factionalism: "If these three factions were properly handled when the Kampuchean army began to consolidate its ranks in 1976, the situation could have been better. But the Kampuchean Communist Party did not follow the correct approach in handling them, thus leading to an expansion of mutual contradictions."[97]

The eyewitness account of Laurence Picq (a French woman who was married to a senior Khmers Rouges foreign ministry official and who worked inside the DK Foreign Ministry in Phnom Penh), provides direct evidence that the Khmers Rouges were suspicious of China and resistant to Chinese attempts to control their regime. For example in January 1976, elder foreign ministry cadres stated: "We have to watch out for China. . . . We certainly owe China a lot and it is a great country, but it wants to make us its satellite."[98]

In mid-1977 during one of the criticism and self-criticism sessions that foreign ministry cadres had to endure, one of the criticisms Picq recalls being hurled against her was: "You like China and don't hide it. But China is not a real friend, she wants to colonize us."[99]

Picq also recounts a seminar for foreign ministry workers held in July 1978, at which Ieng Sary lectured on the international situation. Sary reportedly stated that "Russia was plunging into an inextricable quagmire, with China following the same path."[100]

By mid-1978 China seemed to be attempting to exercise a moderating influence upon the radical foreign policy of Democratic Kampuchea. China needed an independent Cambodia for geostrategic reasons, to prevent encirclement by the Soviet Union. This does not mean that it endorsed the foreign or domestic policies of the Khmers Rouges. On the contrary, especially after the death of Mao Zedong, China probably saw Khmers Rouges domestic policies as dangerously self-destructive, considering the fact that the Phnom Penh regime was facing an imperial neighbor to the east, and might ultimately need to mobilize the entire population to resist invasion. China also probably saw Khmers Rouges foreign policies as dangerously provocative, especially given the disproportion of forces on Hanoi's side, and the Vietnamese communists' ready predisposition to use military power for political gains. After Mao's death, China's attitude towards the Khmers Rouges was one of strict realpolitik, which found the radicalism of its clients an embarrassment and an impediment to its broader strategic goals.

CONCLUSIONS: EXPLAINING KHMERS ROUGES FOREIGN POLICY

The primary puzzle of Khmers Rouges foreign policy is their decision to confront Vietnam (discussed in the next chapter). The secondary puzzle, the solving of which has some bearing on solving the primary question, is the Khmers Rouges confrontation with Thailand.

That the leadership of Democratic Kampuchea regarded the government of capitalist Thailand as their ideological enemy is no mystery. But Thailand was not a security threat. What needs to be explained is why the Cambodian communist leadership pursued a military struggle against Thailand, even at a low level, when their nation, according to their own judgment, faced a mortal threat from its other immediate neighbor. The attacks upon Thailand were not at the urging of their external patron, China.

The weight of evidence suggests that Khmers Rouges radicalism, in foreign policy as well as in domestic affairs, was the result of decisions freely arrived at by the Khmers Rouges leaders. To the extent that the Chinese government was able to exercise influence, it was in moderating the most extreme aspects of Khmers Rouges domestic and foreign policy and in pointing the regime in the direction of a more traditional realpolitik foreign policy. However, from the perspective of the objective security interests of China and the Khmers Rouges, such a moderating influence may have been too little and certainly was too late.

Support for Thai communist revolutionaries was in part an ideological imperative. It is not surprising that a regime so fanatical in its pursuit of ideological "purity" at home would undertake a fanatical pursuit of ideological objectives abroad.

But Khmers Rouges behavior can also be explained by their paranoid belief that Thailand was "attacking and tormenting" Cambodia and threatened to dominate it. Pol Pot apparently believed that only by demonstrating strength could the "contemptible enemy to the west" be thwarted. Moreover, the Khmers Rouges were inspired by Maoist ideology to believe that they could defeat a more powerful neighbor. For although the Khmers Rouges never fully adhered to the Maoist precept of "self-reliance," they did act in accordance with the Maoist precept of the primacy of subjective over material forces.

It is worth noting the analogy with Chinese foreign policy during the 1960s. Between 1963 and 1969, Mao Zedong embraced a policy of confronting both superpowers. Mao treated both the United States and the Soviet Union as equally dangerous enemies. Only after the Soviet invasion of Czechoslovakia in August 1968, and especially after the Soviet threat of 1969 to launch a military strike against Chinese nuclear weapons installations, did Mao revise his strategic outlook and move toward rapprochement with the West. Thus Maoist China's 1963–69 "two front" strategic posture anticipated the 1975–78 strategic posture of Pol Pot's Cambodia.

CHAPTER FOUR

The Public Disintegration of "Militant Solidarity" in Indochina:
Vietnam and Cambodia, 1975–78

Even before the collapse of the pro-American governments in South Vietnam and Cambodia, fundamental realignments of Indochina's revolutionary forces had already taken place.

The Vietnamese communists had demonstrated an affinity for the Soviet Union and the Cambodian communists for China, which placed them in rival global-strategic camps. Not that their alignments were equally firm. After all, the Vietnamese still maintained cordial relations with the Chinese, while the Khmers Rouges, by contrast, had no diplomatic relations with, and had engaged in hostile acts against, the Soviet Union. (The Laotian communists were, as always, firmly under the control of the Vietnamese.)

But in spite of the replication of the Sino-Soviet dispute among the communist parties of Indochina, there was nothing inevitable about the outbreak of war. Other developments were possible. One could think of several reasons why neither of the rival local communist parties would have wanted their relations to deteriorate to the stage where war would even be a likely option.

In the case of the Vietnamese communists, their chances of reconstructing their country after thirty years of war depended upon a peaceful environment in which military expenditures could be reduced, and foreign aid and trade could be attracted. Vietnam's reconstruction and economic development certainly would have been greatly facilitated by the continuation of the flow of Chinese technical personnel, equipment, and financial aid. Given the political, military, and economic support of the Chinese government for the Khmers Rouges, any Vietnamese military moves against the new Cambodian regime would endanger continued Chinese economic aid to Vietnam, and perhaps result in even more severe retaliation.[1]

But on the other hand, the objective of controlling Cambodia was one that the Vietnamese communist leaders had pursued for several decades. If political penetration of the Kampuchean Communist Party leadership, on the Laotian model, had failed—and by April 1975 the prospects for that strategy must have been seen as uncertain at best—then a military solution would be the only way of realizing the objective. Yet the question remained for the Vietnamese leaders of whether such an action was worth the cost of China's likely economic and perhaps even military retaliation.

For the Cambodian communists by contrast, whose Maoist ideology of "self-reliance" precluded the kind of international economic help the Vietnamese were looking for, there were still good reasons why they should have avoided conflict with the Vietnamese. The most obvious one was the disparity of military force between themselves and their neighbor. Vietnam's armed forces were not only better equipped than Democratic Kampuchea's, there were also almost ten times as many of them. Furthermore, given the drastic nature of the revolutionary upheaval they were imposing upon their own people, the Khmers Rouges should not have expected their physically enfeebled and depleted population to have been enthusiatic supporters of their cause. Of all the actors in the Indochina conflict, it was the Khmers Rouges for whom war, by any objective evaluation of its situation, made least sense.

In spite of the strong case that could be made that neither the Vietnamese nor the Cambodian communists should have wanted war with each other, total war did break out. War broke out between the Indochinese communists not because of the machinations of external powers, as both the Cambodian communists and the Vietnamese communists have continually claimed. It broke out because of the incompatible political objectives of the two victorious communist parties, and because the weaker of these two contending parties, the Khmers Rouges, had a very poor grasp of the actual, objective social, political, and military conditions under which it operated.

We have already considered the role of Khmers Rouges political culture in Cambodian foreign policy. Let us now briefly examine the relevance of Vietnam's domestic structure and political culture.

THE DOMESTIC CONTEXT OF VIETNAMESE FOREIGN POLICY

Upon seizing control of South Vietnam at the end of April 1975, the Vietnamese communists had many problems to cope with. Dealing with the surrender of an enemy armed force of one million soldiers, and taking control of a society of over twenty million people, most of whom were unsympathetic to communism, and some of whom were politically organized, was an enormous undertaking.

In the aftermath of their acquisition of state power following their victory over the French in 1954, the Vietnamese communists had undertaken several bloody reprisal and terror campaigns—against their former enemies, against the better-off peasants, and against the intellectuals of North Vietnam. These campaigns, the most important of which were called the Campaign Against Counterrevolutionaries and the Land Reform campaign, were not only modeled on programs already conducted in China. They were actually carried out under the supervision of Chinese communist cadres. Tens of thousands of Vietnamese were executed during these campaigns.[2]

Over the next two decades, the influence of the "Chinese model of socialist construction" upon Vietnamese domestic politics fluctuated. But by 1975, Chinese communist influence over the Vietnamese communists, though not totally absent, was at its historic nadir. Now more susceptible to the influence of the Soviet Union, and to some extent sensitive to the opinions of the international political community, the Vietnamese leaders chose programs of repression less bloody than those of the 1950s.[3]

The Hanoi leaders lured almost two hundred thousand former military officers and government officials of the defeated Republic of Vietnam into incarceration in forced labor camps for an imprisonment that would last many years.[4] Next, the Hanoi leaders dissolved all of the newly conquered South Vietnam's independent social organizations, including schools, sports associations, and religious charities, and brought the entire society under the direction of party-controlled organizations. Those who protested these changes were arrested and denounced as agents of the CIA.[5] Those Vietnamese arrested for political dissidence were accused by their interrogators and by the state-controlled media of being "agents of imperialism" and, in particular, "agents of the CIA."

In these policies we can see the influence of both Marxist-Leninist ideology and a certain paranoid interpretation of political life. But the Vietnamese communist approach to politics, though ideological and paranoid, was a measured and calculating one. It was by 1975 unaccompanied by the periodic hysterical and violent campaigns that had characterized the political reigns of the Vietnamese communists' original political mentors, Joseph Stalin and Mao Zedong, and which the Vietnamese had emulated briefly during the 1950s.[6] The Vietnamese approach was also less fanatical and violent than that of their younger Cambodian comrades.

A DASH ACROSS THE BRINK: RELATIONS BETWEEN THE SOCIALIST REPUBLIC OF VIETNAM AND DEMOCRATIC KAMPUCHEA, APRIL–AUGUST 1975

When Phnom Penh surrendered to insurgent forces on April 17, 1975, the Khmers Rouges victors were enthusiastically congratulated by the Vietnamese communists. By the time the North Vietnamese army had marched into Saigon some two weeks later, Phnom Penh and most of the major towns of Cambodia had been emptied of their former inhabitants. Cambodia, now renamed Democratic Kampuchea, had begun its long march toward the Maoist Utopia. But in spite of the real differences between the Vietnamese and Cambodian approaches to revolution, there were few public signs of Vietnamese communist dissatisfaction with their neighbor's new social experiment.

The new rulers of Democratic Kampuchea were intoxicated by their success in winning a military victory over the republican government. They even insisted that they had fought without foreign help and that they alone had "defeated U.S. imperialism."

Democratic Kampuchea engaged in limited international diplomacy prior to September 1977. Its main foreign friends were China and North Korea. Still, on the few international matters in which they were involved, such as their armed clash with the United States after their seizure of the American ship *Mayaguez*, the Cambodian rulers received diplomatic support from Hanoi.

But concealed from international view, the tensions that had surfaced during the war years not only had not abated, they had been exacerbated. The ostensible issue of the conflict was a dispute over the border between Vietnam and Cambodia. As we have mentioned already (in Chapter 1), between 1870 and 1914 the French colonial administration had redrawn the borders between Cambodia and Vietnam by amputating large chunks of formerly Cambodian territory and making them administratively part of their Vietnamese colonial entities. In June 1948, in the Along Bay agreement, the French formally recognized their then colony of Cochinchina—what had once been southern Cambodia (to the Khmers Rouges, Kampuchea Krom)—as part of Vietnam.[7]

The resentment felt by most Cambodians at this humiliation, combined with the spirit of triumphalism that permeated the Khmers Rouges, fed into an ambition for the forceful recovery of lost territories. Sihanouk reports that in 1975 the Khmers Rouges told him "we are going to recover Kampuchea Krom."[8] Yet such ambition should have been tempered by the limits imposed upon it by military realities.

At the time of their victory in April 1975, the Khmers Rouges army had 230 battalions, mostly understrength, with the main force units estimated at between 55,000 and 60,000 troops.[9] The North Vietnamese army was 685,000 strong, supported by a 3,000-man navy and 12,000-man air force flying 268 combat aircraft, including 1 light bomber squadron and 6 fighter-bomber squadrons.[10]

Nevertheless, in early May the Khmers Rouges attacked Vietnamese-controlled islands in the Gulf of Thailand, claiming the islands that the French had reassigned to their former Vietnamese colony, and which had been inherited by South Vietnam. The Vietnamese communists, though surprised, responded decisively. By the end of May they had recaptured the islands by force, taking 300 prisoners. In early June the Vietnamese retaliated further by attacking and occupying the Cambodian island of Puolo Wai.[11] These actions seemed to restrain for a time Khmers Rouges enthusiasm for further military challenges to the Vietnamese.

According to the Vietnamese, on June 2, 1975, Pol Pot received Nguyen Van Linh, representing the Vietnam Workers' Party (as the VCP was then named). Pol Pot told Linh that the fighting was due to the "ignorance of local geography" of the Kampuchean troops.[12] In June 1975 Pol Pot, Nuon Chea, and Ieng Sary led a KCP delegation that secretly traveled to Hanoi for negotiations.[13] In July 1975 a high-powered delegation from Vietnam, led by Communist Party First Secretary Le Duan, paid what was described as a "friendly" visit to Cambodia. The actual purpose of the visit, not revealed at the time, is now believed to have centered on the border and territorial dispute between the two countries. (The Cambodian island that Vietnam had occupied was returned in August.)[14]

Publicly the Vietnamese communists gave no hint of any problems. The official Hanoi monthly *Vietnam Courier* spoke of the talks being held in "a cordial atmosphere full of brotherly spirit. Complete unanimity was reached on the problems discussed." The brief article went further. In spite of differences in the two regimes' approaches to "socialist construction," the Vietnamese publication praised the Khmers Rouges for depopulating the cities. It praised Cambodia's new social order without qualification: "Liberated Cambodia is living in a new and healthy atmosphere."[15]

CREATING OVERTLY NORMAL RELATIONS,
AUGUST 1975–DECEMBER 1976

The Vietnamese had retained some of their military forces on Cambodian soil after the joint communist victories of 1975.[16] It took some political effort by the Chinese to convince the Hanoi leaders that the troops should be returned to Vietnam. We can only assume that the Vietnamese had regarded these armed forces as a potential device to promote some future political objective inside Cambodia. Yet, while the political direction Cambodia would take was of some concern to the Hanoi leaders, influencing that direction was a long-term, not an immediate consideration.

Throughout 1976 there were public greetings exchanged on special occasions. The promulgation of a constitution by the Cambodians was hailed by the Vietnamese in January 1976. An editorial in *Nhan Dan*, the official party daily, claimed that the constitution was "unanimously adopted" by the Third National Congress of People's Representatives of Kampuchea "following wide and democratic debates among broad masses of the people throughout the country." The newspaper expressed a positive attitude toward its neighbor's achievements: "In spite of the numerous difficulties encountered, the revolution of Kampuchea continues to move forward."[17]

In April 1976 the first anniversary of the Khmers Rouges victory was hailed by Vietnamese Party and government leaders. Le Duan, Ton Duc Thang, Truong Chinh, and Pham Van Dong sent a message congratulating Khieu Samphan, Nuon Chea, and Pol Pot on their respective "elections" as president of the Presidium of Democratic Kampuchea, president of the Assembly of People's Representatives, and premier of the government. The message referred to the "great victory of the resistance against the U.S. imperialists and their lackeys, for the complete liberation of the country."[18]

The Vietnamese media spoke glowingly of the "achievements" of the "Cambodian workers, peasants, and revolutionary army." They also denounced the alleged bombing of Siem Reap in February 1976 by U.S. aircraft, thus repeating an unsubstantiated Khmers Rouges claim. Hanoi Radio made further charges in defense of the Khmers Rouges:

> The U.S. imperialists have aided and abetted the Thai reactionaries in conduct-
> ing many provocations and violations of the Cambodian border by sending
> war vessels into Cambodia's sea areas, abducting innocent fishermen, inciting a
> number of people to flee their country into Thailand, and slandering the new
> regime in Cambodia.[19]

In June 1976, on the seventh anniversary of the founding of the Provisional
Revolutionary Government of the Republic of South Vietnam (PRGRSV)—
the ostensibly separate governing structure of the Vietnamese communists in
South Vietnam—the Khmers Rouges leaders sent messages of congratulation.
This was warmly responded to by PRGRSV leaders.[20] One month later, on
the occasion of the formal reunification of Vietnam as the Socialist Republic
of Vietnam (SRV), Phnom Penh Radio broadcast a commentary entitled
"Militant Solidarity and Friendship Between Peoples of Democratic Cambodia and the SRV Grow Constantly Greener and Sturdier."[21]

Various official delegations from Vietnam visited Cambodia during 1976.
In July a press delegation from Vietnam was received. In the farewell speech,
broadcast over Phnom Penh Radio, the head of the delegation praised "the
comprehensive achievements of the Cambodian people and revolution," and
spoke of "the heroic Cambodian people, under the clear-sighted leadership
of the revolutionary organization." The delegation head thanked the "comrade leaders of the Cambodian revolution."[22]

In July an agreement was signed by representatives of the two governments to open an air route between Hanoi and Phnom Penh.[23] But during
that same month the first public hint of tensions between the two neighbors
came to the fore. In an interview with the leader of a Vietnamese newspaper
and television delegation visiting Cambodia, Pol Pot spoke of Cambodian-
Vietnamese friendship and unity as "a strategic question and a sacred sentiment. . . . Only when this friendship and solidarity is strong can the revolution in our two countries develop satisfactorily." He conceded that "obstacles and difficulties" may arise. Nevertheless, Cambodia would "stand firmly
on this position."[24]

On September 21, 1976, the air service between Hanoi and Phnom Penh,
via Saigon, was actually begun.[25] A Cambodian women's delegation visited
Vietnam in August and September 1976. Then in December 1976, the Revolutionary Organization, as the KCP was still publicly referring to itself,
sent greetings to the Vietnam Workers' Party on the occasion of its Fourth
Congress.

Thus, by the end of 1976, the outward signs still suggested close ties between the communist parties and governments of Vietnam and Cambodia. Yet these outward signs concealed the real feelings of both parties. The Vietnamese leaders were hoping that some pro-Vietnamese elements would eventually emerge within the leadership of the Kampuchean Communist Party. At the same time the rulers of Democratic Kampuchea were possessed by a seething hatred and fear of the rulers of Vietnam—a hatred and fear that threatened to boil over into armed confrontation.

CAMBODIA IN THE CONTEXT OF HANOI'S GENERAL STRATEGIC OUTLOOK

As we have already seen, the Vietnamese communist leaders had originally hoped that the Cambodian communist movement—which they had founded and sponsored for several decades—would upon seizing state power adopt a pro-Vietnamese policy along the lines embraced by the victorious Laotian communists. Yet the hopes of the Hanoi leaders had been dashed. From as early as 1973 until 1975 the Vietnamese were the objects of armed attacks by the Khmers Rouges army, mainly inside Cambodian territory, although at war's end also on Vietnamese territory. Only a decisive Vietnamese counterattack against Cambodian occupied islands in the Gulf of Thailand during May and June 1975 subdued Khmers Rouges military offensives against their erstwhile allies.

In spite of their weak political position inside Cambodia, the Vietnamese leaders still harbored hopes for a restoration of their influence within the Khmers Rouges leadership. Interestingly, the resignation of Pol Pot from the prime ministership, publicly announced by Phnom Penh Radio in September 1976, was taken seriously by both Pham Van Dong and Le Duan.

In a conversation with the Soviet ambassador to Vietnam on November 6, 1976, Pham Van Dong characterized the situation in Kampuchea as complex, which is why "it is difficult to say anything definite." Dong suggested that perhaps Pol Pot was actually sick. He emphasized that for the Hanoi leaders the resignation of Pol Pot's brother-in-law, Foreign Minister Ieng Sary, was unexpected. It is well known, said Pham Van Dong, that Ieng Sary is pro-Chinese. With Nuon Chea, the new premier of Kampuchea, "we are able to work better, we know him better than other leaders of Kampuchea."[26]

Meeting with the Soviet ambassador on November 16, 1976, Le Duan speculated that "apparently" Pol Pot and Ieng Sary had been removed from the leadership. This was welcomed by the Vietnamese leader because these two Khmers were said to constitute a "pro-Chinese sect conducting a crude and severe policy." He added that "these are bad people." Le Duan asserted, however, that Nuon Chea, a member of the KCP Standing Committee and Secretariat, who had replaced Pol Pot as prime minister of Democratic Kampuchea in September, was a person of pro-Vietnamese orientation. Le Duan added that "he is our man and my personal friend."[27]

In expressing these opinions of Pol Pot's deputy Nuon Chea, both the Vietnamese communist leaders proved to be badly mistaken. But this misjudgment was not a whim of the moment. As we will see, Le Duan was to reiterate this opinion over the next two years.

Le Duan also expressed his confidence that in spite of current obstacles, the relationship would develop in a way that he favored: " I can promise that with Kampuchea all will be in order. Sooner or later it will be with Vietnam; the Khmers do not have another way out. We know how to work with them and know where to display decisiveness and where to display flexibility."[28] Le Duan stated that in relations toward Cambodia the Vietnamese leaders acted in coordination with the Laotians. Kaysone Phomvihan, the general secretary of the Lao People's Revolutionary Party (LPRP), was described as "a very good person" who stood for "friendship with Vietnam and the Soviet Union."[29]

But Hanoi's relationship with Laos was not only relevant to Cambodia. In evaluating the situation in Thailand, Le Duan spoke of his disappointment with the role of the Communist Party of Thailand (CPT). Although there was a revolutionary movement in Thailand, the CPT was unable to lead this movement. Le Duan attributed this to the fact that the CPT was under the influence of Beijing. But he emphasized that the Vietnamese Workers' Party was taking measures to strengthen its influence with the CPT. He thought that the fact that one of the CPT Politburo members was Vietnamese and that the general secretary was half-Vietnamese would help. But Vietnamese communist activities were hampered by the fact that Thailand is geographically separated from Vietnam. That is why the Vietnamese had to act largely through Laos, through the LPRP. Using the Laotians as an intermediary was potentially beneficial given that, according to Le Duan, ten million people of Lao descent were living in Thailand.[30]

This conversation between Le Duan and the Soviet ambassador gives us a sense of the broader strategic interests of the Vietnamese communist leadership in the region. Regardless of the behavior of the Khmers Rouges, the Vietnamese looked to establish their influence over the communist movement of Thailand, which was not a neighbor of Vietnam. In so doing they acted in competition with the Chinese. But this competition was by no means a strategy of realpolitik, which might have propelled Hanoi into supporting the government of Thailand (as the Soviets had done there and in other Southeast Asian nations where the anticommunist state was challenged by a Maoist insurgency). The Vietnamese leaders also acted in accordance with an ideological imperative. For in choosing to try and establish their influence over the CPT and ultimately the Thai "revolutionary movement," as well as over Laos and Cambodia, the Vietnamese leaders were acting as if Hanoi was a patron for "genuine" Marxist-Leninist revolutions in Southeast Asia.

KHMERS ROUGES PARANOIA: FROM DOMESTIC TERROR
TO EXTERNAL WAR

As our previous discussions suggest, the Cambodian communists had good reason to fear Vietnamese ambitions toward Cambodia in the long term. But the question arises of how imminent a danger to the power of the Khmers Rouges was posed by Vietnamese ambitions during the mid-1970s. Was Pol Pot's estimation of Hanoi's immediate intentions and plans realistic, exaggerated, or unfounded?

As we have discussed earlier, the Vietnamese had devised a strategy for controlling the communist movements in Laos and Cambodia. A key element of this strategy involved infiltrating the communist parties of its neighbors with people it had trained and indoctrinated. In the case of Cambodia, Hanoi trained and supported the so-called Khmer Viet Minh, whom it assumed would act as its agents. So the Khmers Rouges leaders did have real enemies in Hanoi. But Pol Pot and his supporters had anticipated the Vietnamese strategy, and had preempted it by arresting all of the Khmer Viet Minh soon after they returned from Hanoi with the North Vietnamese army in the early 1970s, and again after the victory of 1975. Nevertheless, Pol Pot and his circle continued to fear that agents of Hanoi might still be hidden within the party. In a speech delivered on September 27, 1977, Pol Pot publicly suggested a link between his "vigilant" foreign policy and his internal terror: "in our new Cambodian society, life-and-death conflicts still exist, as enemies in the form of various spy rings working for imperialism and international reactionaries are still planted among us to carry out subversive activities against our revolution."[31]

Behind the scenes, Pol Pot was carrying out another purge of his party and administration to eliminate what he believed were Soviet or Vietnamese agents plotting a coup d'état.[32] If in fact there was an internal conspiracy directed from abroad, then it was natural to regard any responsible external power as an active enemy. And given the spirit of triumphalism that pervaded Khmers Rouges thinking after their victory of 1975, it was natural that they should consider dealing with the problem of the enemy conspiracy not only internally, but also at its external source. After all, the Khmers Rouges leaders believed, and publicly reiterated many times, that in 1975 the Kampuchean revolutionary army *alone* had "defeated the American imperialists." And their current enemy—Vietnam—was not as strong as the United States.

In April 1977, on the occasion of the second anniversary of the "liberation" of Phnom Penh, the government and government-controlled media in Hanoi offered congratulations and praise for the Democratic Kampuchean regime. In its public gestures, the Vietnamese government showed no signs of tension or animosity toward its neighbor. *Nhan Dan* published a glowing account of a Vietnamese women's delegation that had recently returned from Cambodia. It stated: "The Cambodian people were enthusiastically embarking on irrigation work . . . women are vigorously surging forward and joining men to become owners of the country."[33] And Vietnamese party and state leaders sent a message congratulating their counterparts on the anniversary of their victory.[34] But this goodwill gesture reaped no beneficial consequences for Vietnam. The Khmers Rouges deliberately chose the second anniversary of the Vietnamese communist conquest of South Vietnam to leave a truly bloody calling card. On April 30, 1977, Khmers Rouges units attacked several villages and towns in An Giang and Chau Doc provinces of southern Vietnam, burning houses and killing hundreds of civilians.[35] The Vietnamese leaders were shocked by this unprovoked attack and could not understand any strategic rationale behind it.[36] Nevertheless, they decided upon military retaliation.[37]

According to the deputy military commander of Vietnam's Tay Ninh province, during April and May 1977 the Khmers Rouges forces had carried out systematic attacks upon Vietnamese border villages, making it impossible for Vietnamese peasants to work there. The Vietnamese side claimed that it then offered to settle the border question peacefully with the Khmer Rouges but the offer was refused. According to the Vietnamese, the Khmers Rouges then concentrated up to two divisions on the border adjacent to Tay Ninh, and in the middle of May these forces undertook massive attacks upon Vietnamese territory.[38]

Reports of larger clashes between the rival communist armies took several months to appear in the West.[39] In late June Radio Djakarta reported that armed clashes had taken place in two Vietnamese provinces.[40] At the end of July, Phnom Penh Radio began hinting at border clashes.[41] A few days later what would become a recurring motif—the danger of Cambodia being "swallowed" by an unnamed external force—was heard for the first time over Phnom Penh Radio.[42]

During late August 1977 Phnom Penh Radio began praising the "high revolutionary vigilance" of the Revolutionary Army in the northeast region, as manifested in its successful defense of the borders. Other reports indicated that Cambodia and Vietnam were now fighting on several fronts along their border. Regular forces in formations as large as 4,000 to 5,000 on both sides were said to be involved.[43] Phnom Penh Radio, while extolling the army's sacrifices, suggested it faced a complex array of enemies. Not only the "U.S. imperialists, their lackeys, and the traitorous clique," but also "enemies of all stripes" and "enemies, near or far, big or small." The broadcast continued:

> Our country is small and has few people. The geographical position and political regime of our Democratic Cambodia do not permit us to commit aggression against any country. A small and weak country cannot swallow a big country. . . . However, the Cambodian people and Revolutionary Army are determined to defend our independence, sovereignty, and territorial integrity within our present borders.[44]

Yet when on September 27, 1977, Pol Pot openly declared the existence of the Kampuchean Communist Party, the Central Committee of the Vietnamese party sent a message of congratulations, publicly expressing its joy.[45] Interestingly, this message was sent after hundreds of Vietnamese civilians had been massacred in Khmers Rouges raids on September 24. The background to this strangely inappropriate message is worth considering.

Local Vietnamese commanders had invited the Hungarian journalist Kandor Dura to witness the evidence of atrocities committed by the Khmers

Rouges during this attack. He was taken to Tay Ninh province accompanied by workers from the department of agitation and propaganda of the Ho Chi Minh City committee of the Vietnamese Communist Party (VCP) and a strong armed guard. In Tay Ninh, Dura witnessed ruined buildings and many dead and burned people, mainly women and children. He was briefed on the military situation along an extensive border region, including alleged attacks upon 737 Vietnamese border posts, the destruction of several villages, and civilian casualties running into the hundreds. Dura witnessed the evacuation of the Vietnamese population away from the border that took place at this time.[46]

The Hungarian journalist was asked by the local Vietnamese officials to write about these events, indicating that at any moment a broad propaganda campaign against the Khmers Rouges might be unfolded. In this context the Vietnamese referred to the holding of a special meeting of the Politburo of the VCP in Saigon on September 30, under the leadership of Le Duan. Many of the local officials meeting with Dura openly abused the Chinese, but others were more cautious, noting only that a certain unnamed great power is "interfering in their internal affairs and is complicating the situation extraordinarily." One Vietnamese agit-prop official even claimed that Vietnam had taken several Chinese prisoners during the battles with the Khmers Rouges in April and May.[47]

Yet on October 1 the situation totally changed. The Vietnamese demanded that Dura hand over all of his materials (photos, notebooks) and requested that he not discuss what he had seen and heard with anyone. He was told that this matter had been decided in Hanoi at the highest level. The conversation was repeated immediately upon Dura's disembarkation at Hanoi's Xia Lam airport.[48] The Hanoi leaders suppressed the evidence until the end of 1977, when the journalist's notes, films, and other materials were returned.[49]

It seems that the Hanoi leaders were under pressure from local authorities to respond to Khmers Rouges attacks. But in September they still hoped that the conflict could be resolved without resort to all-out war. They were preoccupied with internal problems, and were hesitant to break openly with Phnom Penh, because of the likely repercussions in Hanoi's relations with Beijing.[50]

In a conversation with the Soviet ambassador in Hanoi that took place on October 6, 1977, Le Duan struggled to provide a coherent explanation for the behavior of the Khmers Rouges. He described the leadership of Cambodia as "strongly nationalistic and under the strong influence of Peking." But in characterizing individual leaders, the Vietnamese party secretary stated that Pol Pot "always was Trotskyist," while Ieng Sary is "a fierce nationalist and pro-Chinese." Turning to other leaders of the KCP, Le Duan expressed his view that Nuon Chea and Son Sen "have a positive attitude toward Vietnam." They were said to be the only people of pro-Vietnamese tendency who had survived Pol Pot's terror, since the majority of skilled workers, who had expressed themselves in favor of friendship with the SRV, had been annihilated. Nuon Chea and Son Sen had only survived, according to Le Duan, because of their "high authority in the country."[51]

After noting the massacres of Vietnamese women and children by the Khmers Rouges, Le Duan noted that the Vietnamese army had the capability to rout the Kampuchean army quickly. But the leadership of Kampuchea was said to be striving to draw the SRV into a serious conflict in order to inflame nationalistic and anti-Vietnamese attitudes inside Cambodia. Vietnam's response, according to Le Duan, was to display patience and to attempt to find a peaceful resolution of all questions with Kampuchea. The Vietnamese leader felt that if it had not been for Pol Pot and Ieng Sary, Kampuchea would have been friendly toward Vietnam.[52]

In October the Vietnamese began to try to recruit an army and political front from among Cambodian refugees in southern Vietnam and overseas. The purpose was to remove Pol Pot from power.[53] It seems that Hanoi was preparing to resume its strategy of the early phases of its war against the former Republic of (South) Vietnam—building a guerrilla force that would be commanded and supported logistically by the resources of the Vietnamese communist state.

In November a top-level Vietnamese Party delegation, led by Le Duan, visited Beijing. The subject of their discussions was not announced. Perhaps anticipating that the visit would help the position of Democratic Kampuchea, Phnom Penh Radio noted the visit in nondescript but friendly terms.[54] But according to the secret Vietnamese account, neither side at the meeting raised the issue of the Vietnamese-Cambodian conflict (see Chapter 7).

In December 1977 the border fighting between Vietnam and Cambodia intensified even further. Hanoi used warplanes, artillery, and around 20,000 men in a major thrust into the "Parrot's Beak" province of Svay Rieng, Cambodia, only 55 miles from Ho Chi Minh City.[55] But the Vietnamese attempted to downplay the significance of the fighting. Apparently they believed that a display of strength would bring the militarily inferior Cambodians to negotiate. Instead the KCP attitude hardened. The stage was set for an open break between the governments of Vietnam and Cambodia.

DEMOCRATIC KAMPUCHEA'S CHALLENGE TO VIETNAM

On December 31, 1977, the government of Democratic Kampuchea announced that it was "temporarily" severing diplomatic relations with the Socialist Republic of Vietnam, pending the withdrawal of the "aggressor forces" of the SRV from the "sacred territory of Democratic Kampuchea" and the restoration of the "friendly atmosphere between the two countries"[56] Khieu Samphan, on behalf of the Cambodian government, read a speech at this time on Vietnamese "aggression." He explained Vietnam's behavior in terms of two motives: The immediate motive was said to be the desire to plunder rice and livestock from the Cambodians in order to help solve Vietnam's hunger problem; but the basic cause was said to be the SRV's longstanding desire to include Cambodia as a member of a Vietnamese-dominated Indochina Federation.[57]

In its first reply to the Cambodians, the Vietnamese government confirmed that there was a territorial and border dispute between the two countries. But it accused the Cambodians of having introduced force into the dispute in May 1975, and of having made incursions into Vietnamese territory on many occasions. The SRV claimed to have made many attempts to negotiate the dispute, but said it had faced repeated rebuffs.[58] In going public the Hanoi leaders had decided that there was little chance of reconciliation between themselves and their former allies.

The decisive military penetration of the Parrot's Beak region of Cambodia by the Vietnamese army was initially halted short of the city of Svay Rieng after the Vietnamese had inflicted a major defeat upon their enemies.[59] In early January 1978, the Vietnamese withdrew from Cambodia, taking with them thousands of prisoners as well as civilian refugees.[60] With their forces only twenty-four miles from Phnom Penh, the Vietnamese could have easily captured the capital city and occupied all of Cambodia. But as they explained to a Bulgarian journalist later, this was impossible for them politically.[61] The purpose of their offensive seems to have been to inflict damage upon and thus temper Khmers Rouges aggression. It had no such effect. Instead, the leaders of Democratic Kampuchea proclaimed the Vietnamese withdrawal a major victory for the Kampuchean revolution, equal in historical significance to its "defeat of U.S. imperialism" on April 17, 1975. The leadership claimed: "Our 6 January victory over the annexationist, expansionist, Vietnamese aggressor enemy has given all of us greater confidence in the forces of our people and nation, in our KCP and our Cambodian Revolutionary Army, and in our Party's line of people's war."[62] Unresponsive to Vietnamese demands for negotiations, the Khmers Rouges persisted in launching attacks inside Vietnamese territory.[63]

There were certain objective military facts that should have been strongly influencing the decisions of the leaders of both sides. First was the huge disparity in *size* of the armed forces of each side. In 1977 the armed forces of Democratic Kampuchea were estimated to total 70,000. The armed forces of the Socialist Republic of Vietnam were estimated to total 615,000. Second was the disparity in *quality of weaponry* of each side. The armed forces of DK constituted a light infantry: It included a few light tanks, some 200 armored personnel carriers, and virtually no air force. By contrast, the armed forces of the SRV included some 900 medium and light tanks, and a 12,000 person airforce with 300 combat aircraft, including one light bomber squadron and 8 fighter ground attack squadrons of 150 aircraft.[64] The third military factor was the disparity in *size of population* bases: The DK relied upon a population of less than 7 million while the SRV relied upon a population of nearly 50 million. The final critical factor was the difference in the *condition of the population* of each side: Most of the Vietnamese, though poor, were in reasonable physical condition, whereas half the Cambodian population was in a state of total physical and mental exhaustion as a result of hunger and disease.

Yet the leadership of Democratic Kampuchea acted as if these objective material and human disadvantages either did not exist or else did not matter. Moreover, in the best Orwellian tradition, they continued to describe the Vietnamese withdrawal from Cambodian territory, after having inflicted savage losses upon Khmers Rouges forces, as a Cambodian victory. Their only question was why the Cambodians had been "victorious." An answer was provided in the party's propaganda broadcast on Phnom Penh Radio:

> On this question the entire party, army, and people share the reason that the reason we triumphed over the Vietnamese was because we had earlier defeated the U.S. imperialists, and the Vietnamese were not as powerful as the U.S. imperialists. Even with this in mind, there were still some who maintained that

Vietnam was a large country with a population of 50 million. And how could Kampuchea, with its population of only 8 million people, defeat Vietnam? . . . We defeated them because we had to defeat them. This is the main point.[65]

In other words, in military matters as in domestic politics, will can overcome an objectively unfavorable balance of material forces. All that is required is to devise the appropriate methods.

We were small in number and we had to attack a larger force. Therefore we had to preserve our forces to the maximum. and try to kill as many of the enemy as possible. This was our slogan. In terms of numbers, one of us had to kill 30 Vietnamese. If we could implement that plan, we would certainly win. We would defeat Vietnam, regardless of its size. . . . So far, we have succeeded in implementing this slogan of 1 against 30. . . . our losses are one-thirtieth of those of the Vietnamese.

This claim of already having achieved only one-thirtieth of the losses of the Vietnamese was pure fiction. But according to the logic of the now official formula, Democratic Kampuchea's prospects were bright in any future armed conflict with Vietnam:

Using these figures, 1 Kampuchean soldier is equal to 30 Vietnamese soldiers. . . . If we have 2 million troops, there should be 60 million Vietnamese. For this reason, 2 million troops should be more than enough to fight the Vietnamese, because Vietnam only has 50 million inhabitants. We do not need 8 million people. We need only 2 million troops to crush the 50 million Vietnamese; and we still would have 6 million people left. We must formulate our combat line in this manner in order to achieve victory.[66]

Here we see one fantasy compounded upon another: that the Cambodian army had actually routed the Vietnamese, that they had inflicted and would continue to inflict 30 times as many losses on their enemy as they had suffered themselves, and that they could raise an army of 2 million from their own depleted and enfeebled population of (allegedly) 8 million to "crush" 50 million Vietnamese.

In discerning the motivation of the Khmers Rouges' irrational military actions against Vietnam—the faith of the Khmers Rouges leaders in the superiority of their own objectively weaker forces—we are rediscovering a mystical faith typical of millenarian movements. Cambodia itself experienced such movements during the last century. Take, for example, the anti-Vietnamese uprising of 1820 led by a Buddhist monk named Kai. It is chronicled in a narrative poem of 1869, which contains the following passage:

When he heard of the expedition against him, elderly Kai washed the heads of his soldiers, reciting sutras to give them strength, and shaking drops of water onto them to keep the Vietnamese from dispersing them in battle. If the Vietnamese fired guns, the power of the Khmer would keep the bullets from going far or coming close to them. When Kai's blessings were over, his soldiers lost their apathy, and went out to battle the Vietnamese.[67]

Here we have a precedent for the Khmers Rouges injunction to their soldiers to kill 30 Vietnamese for every Cambodian killed. But instead of the magical power of water and blessings, we now have the magical power of pure Marxism-Leninism and Mao Zedong Thought, and the Khmer Revolutionary Army fighting an authentic "people's war" against a corrupt "revisionist" foreign invader. The "hyperMaoist" ideology of the Khmers Rouges justified and rationalized undertaking what on any objective evaluation of real material forces would have seemed, and in fact was, an impossible task.

VIETNAM'S ATTEMPT TO PROMOTE A CAMBODIAN UPRISING

Following the break in diplomatic relations with Democratic Kampuchea, the Vietnamese began a propaganda campaign against the domestic terror of the Cambodian communists. Between January and April 1978, Hanoi gradually shifted its appellation from "the Kampuchean authorities" to "the Phnom Penh authorities." By June it had become "the Pol Pot–Ieng Sary clique." According to *Nhan Dan*:

> The Pol Pot–Ieng Sary clique have proved themselves to be the most disgusting murderers in the latter half of this century. Who are behind these hangmen whose hands are smeared with the blood of the Kampuchean people, including the Cham, who have been almost wiped out as an ethnic group, the Viet, and the Hoa? This is no mystery to the world. The Pol Pot–Ieng Sary clique are only a cheap instrument of the bitterest enemy of peace and mankind. Their actions are leading to national suicide. This is genocide of a special type. Let us stop this self-genocide! Let us stop genocide at the hands of the Pol Pot–Ieng Sary clique![68]

The call to save the Kampuchean people from genocide was not merely rhetorical. It was, in the context of the broader international propaganda campaign Hanoi was waging, an attempt to legitimize its impending overthrow of the Cambodian communist regime. The question was no longer if, but when and how.

Within the first four months of 1978, the Vietnamese had created a secret network of camps for the purpose of building a "liberation army" of Cambodians from among refugees and other civilians brought from Cambodia to Vietnam.[69]

Pol Pot had assisted the formation of this "liberation army" by expanding his domestic terror in the Eastern Zone of Cambodia in 1978. Unable to otherwise explain the successes of the Vietnamese army at the expense of his own—given his earlier promulgation of the magic slogan of thirty dead Vietnamese for every one dead Khmers Rouges soldier—Pol Pot concluded that the Eastern Zone was a nest of traitors. Thus soldiers from the Southwestern Zone, together with forces of the internal security apparatus, moved into the Eastern Zone to locate and eliminate the "hidden traitors."

There is no evidence that the people whom Pol Pot's emissaries attempted to kill were agents of Vietnam. Of course, Hanoi itself soon publicly endorsed Pol Pot's harsh judgment, because it served Hanoi's political purposes to have the world believe that *its* new Khmers Rouges allies were always good anti–Pol Pot revolutionaries. On the contrary, the people Pol Pot was now attempting to kill had loyally carried out orders from the Khmers Rouges leadership for the previous three years. These orders had involved them attacking Vietnamese and ethnic Cambodian civilian targets inside Vietnam and bearing the brunt of Vietnamese retaliation. One of the eventual victims of Pol Pot's purge of "traitors," Sao Pheum (who suicided), was secretary of the Eastern Zone of the KCP and a member of the KCP Politburo Standing Committee. He had been one of the most staunch advocates of attacking the Vietnamese.[70]

The Vietnamese leaders felt that they could very easily solve their problems with Democratic Kampuchea by liquidating the Khmers Rouges regime within twenty-four hours of introducing their forces into Cambodia. But Hanoi had developed both a theoretical and a political justification for pursuing another course. Discussing the Vietnamese position in March 1978, Tran Quyen, a member of the VCP Central Committee, provided some insight into Vietnamese communist thinking. He contrasted Cambodia in 1978 with Czechoslovakia in 1968. In Czechoslovakia, counterrevolutionaries had overthrown the revolutionary power, and that is why bringing in outside forces was necessary. In Cambodia, by contrast, in the years since the victory of the revolution [in 1975] power had not been changed.[71] By implication, for Hanoi the KCP was an inherently "healthy" force, corrupted only by the political control of Pol Pot and Ieng Sary.

But there was also a political justification for not invading. Since 1975 the Chinese had accused Vietnam of expansionism and hegemonism. They had already used the previous entry of Vietnamese forces into Cambodia to the detriment of the SRV's authority, especially in Southeast Asia and in the revolutionary movements in the region. If the SRV were to invade Cambodia, that action might "frighten Laos," which was not in Vietnam's interest. Besides that, in the view of Tran Quyen, "the Chinese might occupy Laos."[72]

At the same time, Tran Quyen noted that "the ultimate goal of the SRV is the establishment of friendly relations with Kampuchea." However he did not see this being realized by peaceful negotiations in the foreseeable future. There had to be "favorable changes" in Cambodia and these would take time. The harsh dictatorial policies of the Pol Pot regime, placed the population in an extremely difficult situation. Le Duan had called the existing system in Cambodia "slaveholding communism." But although internal opposition to the regime existed, it lacked an organized character.[73]

Thus a Vietnamese policy of sponsoring and helping organize revolutionary insurrection within Cambodia made political sense. And the view that there were some elements within the Khmers Rouges leadership who were secretly friendly toward Vietnam gave Hanoi grounds for hoping that there could ultimately be a restoration of pro-Vietnamese communist leadership in Cambodia. But the question remained: Would this strategy of sponsoring "people's war" succeed?

By late May 1978 fighting was taking place on both sides of the border.[74] The introduction of air power by the Vietnamese in June, with almost thirty bombing missions daily, meant that the Khmers Rouges were suffering heavy casualties.[75] By the middle of the year, the leadership of the Cambodian "liberation army" was in the hands of former KCP cadres of the 203rd (Eastern) Region, some of whom had participated in the April and May uprisings, and all of whom had fled to Vietnam to avoid execution in Pol Pot's purges.

THE VIETNAMESE DECISION TO INVADE CAMBODIA

Sometime in the middle of 1978, the Vietnamese leaders realized that an insurgency modeled upon previously successful Vietnamese adaptations of Maoist "people's war" would not succeed. Pol Pot's loyalist military units and police apparatus were simply too powerful. The only solution was to launch a conventional invasion, as the Soviet Union had undertaken against Czechoslovakia in 1968.

On June 15 the Vietnamese Communist Party Politburo transmitted a request to the Soviet Union for a visit by a VCP delegation led by General Secretary Le Duan to Moscow, beginning on June 21 and lasting seven to nine days. The purpose was said to be to meet with Leonid Brezhnev and other Soviet leaders in order to exchange opinions about the situation in Vietnam and a series of important international questions. The bearer of the VCP Politburo's request, Foreign Minister Nguyen Duy Trinh, stated that the situation in Vietnam was being determined in many aspects by "the war of Kampuchea against the SRV," and by questions of the attitudes of the Chinese nationalities living in Vietnam, problems that the Hanoi leaders believed were closely connected. The VCP predicted the further aggravation of the situation, which explained "the urgent necessity of carrying out timely consultations with the Soviet comrades." Trinh stated that Le Duan intended "to express several requests to the leadership of the CPSU [Communist Party of the Soviet Union] in Moscow." The Vietnamese foreign minister expressed his side's opinion that the visit must be undertaken secretly.[76]

Unfortunately we have no record of the minutes of those secret meetings in Moscow. But a former senior Vietnamese official has stated that in June 1978, Vietnamese communist political cadres were advised that an invasion of Cambodia was in preparation.[77] Though not openly discussed, one purpose of the meeting was for the Vietnamese to insure Soviet political and military backing in any future escalation, or at least to provide a Soviet insurance policy against possible Chinese military retaliation. The Soviets had no intention of going to war with China over Vietnam and Cambodia, but naturally did not reveal that view. But a Treaty of Friendship and Cooperation would be publicly signed in Moscow in November (see Chapter 8).[78]

In a briefing on July 25, 1978, a Vietnamese foreign ministry official told the Soviet charge d'affaires in Hanoi that the Khmers Rouges had concentrated fourteen of the seventeen regular divisions of the Kampuchean army, and 16 regiments of local armed formations, on the Vietnamese border.[79]

In a meeting with the Soviet ambassador in Hanoi in early September 1978, Le Duan stated that the Vietnamese Communist Party Politburo had set as its goal "to solve fully this question [of Kampuchea] by the beginning of 1979." He indicated that Vietnamese calculations about the possible reaction of China had now changed.

Le Duan stated that if China wanted to prevent changes inside Kampuchea that were unfavorable to it, it would have to transfer ten divisions there. But he calculated that China would be unable to do this because the transfer of troops by sea to Kampuchea is "a very difficult matter." An offensive by land from the north is very complex, and the Chinese "haven't managed to do anything so far." In addition, Le Duan emphasized that it was impossible for Vietnam to wait until Beijing "consolidates itself in Kampuchea."[80]

Le Duan also spoke of the efforts that Vietnam had undertaken in promoting a Cambodian resistance. He claimed that there were nine batallions of Khmers, trained by the Vietnamese, operating at that time. There were also said to be twenty leaders of provincial districts "coming out against the Phnom Penh regime and sympathizing with Vietnam." Le Duan claimed that the Vietnamese were trying to establish contacts with Sao Pheum (Souvanna). The Vietnamese leader stated that "he is our man," and that Hanoi wanted Sao Pheum to "take over the leadership of the movement inside Kampuchea." Again Le Duan restated his belief of previous years that Nuon Chea, a member of the Khmers Rouges top leadership, "is a person who feels sympathy for Vietnam." As for Nuon Chea's trip to China where he delivered an anti-Vietnamese political speech, Le Duan claimed that this was "not characteristic of his political views." Rather, insisted Le Duan, the Phnom Penh authorities forced Nuon Chea to do this, "but we understand well his situation."[81]

The common characteristic uniting all of those Cambodian communists of whose pro-Vietnamese sympathies Le Duan seemed strongly convinced was their former membership in the Indochinese Communist Party. This fact, along with Vietnamese ethnic identity, was considered a sound basis for identifying those individuals who would be favorably disposed to Vietnamese communist political influence. Yet Le Duan's political judgment has been proved totally wrong by the subsequent behavior of Nuon Chea and Son Sen. Both Khmers Rouges leaders remained loyal to Pol Pot. Son Sen only came into conflict with Pol Pot in June 1997 as the Khmers Rouges movements began to disintegrate. Similarly, only after even Ieng Sary had defected and Pol Pot had lost control of his movement and was arrested by some of his former hard-core comrades did Nuon Chea cease being a Pol Pot loyalist.[82] These historical facts must also lead us to question Le Duan's evaluation of Eastern Zone leader Sao Pheum. This is especially so given the fact that at the time Le Duan claimed that the VCP was trying to establish contact with Sao Pheum, that person had already been dead for three months.[83]

Could these errors by Le Duan simply have been a result of his trying to impress his Soviet interlocutor with his political optimism? Possibly. But the gross error involved in claiming that Vietnam's prospects were partly tied to making contact with a man who had been dead for three months was so serious as to be very embarrassing if revealed. Thus one has to conclude a degree of genuine ignorance on the part of Le Duan. The Vietnamese leader was simply leaping to unwarranted conclusions about the political views of Cambodian leaders on the basis of irrelevant factors.

In October Vietnamese radio began broadcasting a series of Vietnamese newspaper accounts of a purported uprising in Kampuchea, allegedly in response to purges of the Kampuchean Communist Party and its cadres in the armed forces.[84] It also broadcast appeals by Cambodians, who claimed to be former members of the army and communist party of Kampuchea, calling for the people either to "rise up against the traitorous Pol Pot-Ieng Sary clique" or else to "desert your ranks" and live with the people in the jungle or "make your way to Vietnam."[85] All of this was political preparation for Vietnam's military "final offensive" against the Democratic Kampuchean regime. Agence France-Presse reported that the Soviet Union was delivering "sizeable" quantities of tanks, aircraft, missiles, and munitions to Vietnamese ports.[86]

On December 3, Hanoi Radio announced the formation of a Kampuchean United Front for National Salvation in what it called the "liberated zone" of Kampuchea. It was said that the Front had been formed at a conference of "200 representatives of the Kampuchean people from all walks of life." No date for the conference was given, but it was said to have elected a fourteen-member Central Committee with Heng Samrin as its president. Heng Samrin was described as a former party member from the Eastern Region's political organization, and formerly a political commissar and commander of the 4th Division. According to Hanoi's broadcast:

> The conference also unanimously adopted the front's 11-point statement on the tasks and goals of the Kampuchean revolution and called on the entire Kampuchean people to rise up to struggle for the overthrow of the nepotist Pol Pot-Ieng Sary clique and to build a peaceful, independent, democratic, neutral and nonaligned Kampuchea in advance to socialism.[87]

The Vietnamese had created the basis of a puppet government, which it intended to install in Phnom Penh. This would provide a kind of political fig leaf for its invasion.

In the first two weeks of December, parts of two Vietnamese divisions moved cautiously into the Eastern Region of Cambodia, reaching seventy miles into the southeastern part of the country.[88] Then, on December 25, Hanoi launched an all-out offensive, using thirteen divisions, and over 150,000 troops. That force captured Phnom Penh on January 7, 1979.[89] The People's Republic of Kampuchea was created shortly thereafter with Heng Samrin as chief of state, and Pen Sovan as secretary-general of the Kampuchean People's Revolutionary Party (KPRP). (Pen Sovan and Heng Samrin were both purged in later years.) The KPRP bore the name of the party that Hanoi had created in September 1951 to be the Cambodian component successor to the Indochinese Communist Party.

The Khmers Rouges leadership, with more than half its army destroyed, fled to the western region of the country. Initially they attempted to confront the Vietnamese army head-on with main force units. This fanatical strategy cost them enormous numbers of men. Subsequently, the Khmers Rouges reverted to a guerrilla war.

CONCLUSIONS

The Vietnamese decision to counter militarily the attacks upon its territory and citizens by the army of Democratic Kampuchea is perfectly understandable. Of course, the Vietnamese communists had been responsible for much of the enmity of many Cambodians toward them by virtue of their aborted attempts to establish control over the Cambodian communist movement during several decades of revolution and war. But Vietnam's direct efforts at subversion appear to have been abandoned after 1975. In fact, until early 1978 it seems that the Vietnamese leaders were responding to Cambodian attacks defensively and with some sense of political and military proportionality. Even Vietnam's decision to support an internal rebellion against the Democratic Kampuchean regime could not be considered extreme or unusual given Democratic Kampuchea's continuing attacks upon Vietnam. This decision reflected a compromise between Vietnam's defensive national security needs vis-à-vis Cambodia and its prudent desire not to upset China.

But the eventual decision of the Vietnamese leaders to undertake a full-scale invasion and occupation was a choice, not a necessity. The Vietnamese could have continued their punishing attacks upon the Cambodians inside Cambodian territory with devastating results. The overwhelming Vietnamese superiority in manpower and firepower would have ensured the drastic weakening of their enemy's military capacity over the long-term, and made Cambodia ripe for collapse at the hands of Vietnamese-armed rebels. But this strategy provided no guarantee that any ensuing regime, though likely deferential to Vietnam, would be under Vietnamese control. Only a direct Vietnamese invasion could ensure the latter outcome. And thus we return to the factor of Vietnamese imperial ambition. Such ambition is, as we have seen, a deeply-rooted element of Vietnamese elite political culture. It is this ultimate value that goes a long way toward explaining the political choice that was eventually made.

The other dimension of the explanation lies in Vietnam's peculiar relationship with China, and the way that Hanoi's paranoid thinking about Chinese-Cambodian relations distorted its evaluation of the problem posed by the Khmers Rouges. During the years 1975–77, Vietnamese responses to Khmers Rouges provocations were extremely measured, even restrained. But by 1978 what one might call a "paranoid spiral" in Vietnamese-Chinese relations (discussed in Chapter 7), compounded by the bizarrely aggressive behavior of the Cambodian regime, led the Vietnamese communists to conclude that Khmers Rouges behavior was at the behest of China. Thus a calm and calculating approach to what had earlier seemed a manageable problem took on an emotional and apocalyptic quality as Hanoi came to see Cambodia as a Chinese dagger pointed at Vietnam. The Vietnamese leaders could not wait for the "Pol Pot-Ieng Sary genocidal clique" to be subverted by a combination of massive Vietnamese conventional military counterattacks and Vietnamese-sponsored guerrilla insurrection. The Khmers Rouges leadership and army had to be rapidly and completely destroyed. For the ethnic Chinese "fifth column" in Vietnam was perceived by Hanoi as a second, interconnected dimension of the Chinese attempt to weaken Vietnam and to prevent its development as a strong socialist state.

Yet although in this instance the paranoid thinking of the Vietnamese communist leaders caused them to exaggerate the scope of the threat posed to them by the Khmers Rouges and caused them to choose a policy of invasion and occupation in pursuit of the total destruction of the Khmers

Rouges, paranoia did not also result in the Vietnamese acting irrationally in their choice of means. By choosing to tighten their relationship with the Soviet Union (see Chapter 8), and guarantee its logistical support, if not its direct intervention, the Vietnamese leaders were taking militarily necessary steps in pursuit of an attainable, although not guaranteed, political outcome. And although their decision to invade may also have been affected by flawed information about the political situation in Cambodia (e.g., that Nuon Chea, Son Sen, and other top Khmers Rouges were sympathetic to Vietnam), this did not mean that their thinking about and behavior toward Cambodia was irrational.

The same cannot be said about the Khmers Rouges' decision to confront Vietnam militarily. It makes no sense from any perspective that assumes the universality of rational, calculating behavior by states, especially with regard to questions of war and peace.

Certainly history has provided all Cambodians with a deep and genuine basis for grievance against the Vietnamese nation. The territorial exactions that Vietnamese rulers have realized over the past two centuries—either through their own efforts or through the capricious decisions of French colonial administrators—have diminished greatly the geographical size, economic resources, and national esteem of the Cambodian nation. Moreover, the communist leaders who ruled Cambodia from April 17, 1975, had their own specific reasons, well-founded in their own more recent historical experience, for distrusting Vietnamese communist intentions toward their control over the Cambodian nation.

But whereas the Cambodian communist leaders had legitimate grievances against and bases for distrust of the Vietnamese communist leaders, in 1975–77 they had no good reason to believe that Cambodia was in imminent danger of succumbing to Vietnamese domination. For at that time Vietnam's leaders were preoccupied with their own internal developments, and in any case were concerned not to antagonize the Chinese more than they already had.

Nor was there any wisdom, from the Khmers Rouges leadership's own political perspective, in choosing to redress their grievances and allay their anxieties by use of military force against an incomparably more powerful enemy. For, as we have seen, Khmers Rouges actions incited and encouraged the Vietnamese to do what the Khmers Rouges feared—invade and overthrow their regime.

How then do we explain both these unfounded beliefs and these irrational acts? The answer lies in the distorted worldview of Khmers Rouges leaders.

The belief of Pol Pot and his circle after 1975 that they faced an *imminent* danger of domination by Vietnam was a delusion, equivalent to their belief that the regime was in imminent danger of internal subversion. Hanoi's actual internal penetration strategy had been countered by Pol Pot's internal purges of 1973–75. Internal subversion was now imagined as resulting from the regime having been penetrated by "enemies of all stripes." Yet the delusional nature of these fears is suggested by the fact that the purge victims of 1977–78 included old comrades of Pol Pot himself, by the fact that the only evidence against the victims consisted of confessions extracted by torture, and most of all by the bizarre allegations leveled against them—that they were agents of the Vietnamese, the KGB, and the CIA acting in coalition. Clearly, in constructing in their own minds this example of a "paranoid pseudocommunity," the inner circle of the Khmers Rouges leadership was demonstrating how it was saturated with a culture of paranoia.[90]

Parallel to this delusional thinking about internal subversion, we found delusional thinking in the "hyperMaoist" domestic ideology of the leaders of Democratic Kampuchea. The Khmers Rouges boasted of going faster and further in the extent of their "construction of socialism" than any other socialist state (including states with which they were friendly). They believed that more socialism and collectivism and less capitalism and individualism, together with more terror against the "class enemy," would unify the Cambodian people. The Khmers Rouges leaders believed that rapid socialist transformation of Cambodia's social and economic structure would strengthen Cambodia against threats from Vietnam.

In reality, rapid "socialist transformation" made the Cambodian population physically degenerate. Together with the terror, it made many people normally predisposed against Cambodia's hereditary enemy now unwilling to support their government in its ultimate struggle. Thus this delusional thinking about Cambodia's domestic revolution, rooted in Khmers Rouges ideology, contributed to the destruction of the Khmers Rouges state called Democratic Kampuchea.

Finally, in discerning the motivation of the Khmers Rouges' irrational military actions against Vietnam—the faith of the Khmers Rouges leaders in the superiority of their own objectively weaker forces—we are rediscovering a mystical faith typical of millenarian movements.

As we have seen, the paranoid and mystical ideological tendencies in Khmers Rouges behavior toward the Vietnamese were to be found in the whole range of their foreign policy. It is these factors, rather than the urgings of their Chinese patrons, that explain Khmers Rouges behavior.

Comintern functionary Nguyen Ai Quoc (Ho Chi Minh) in Moscow, 1935.
Comintern Archives, Moscow

(*Opposite, above*) General Secretary of the Vietnamese Communist Party
Le Duan, Hanoi, 1980. *Photograph courtesy James Gerrand.*

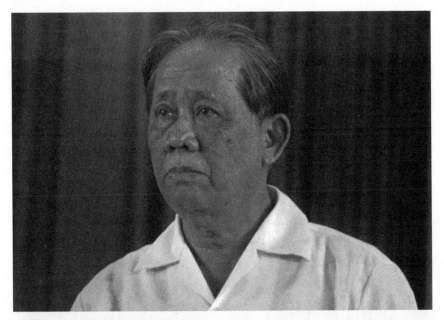

(*Below, left*) Le Duc Tho, Vietnamese Communist party politburo member, Paris, 1973. *White House photograph.*

(*Below, right*) Xuan Thuy, member of the Vietnamese Communist Party secretariat, 1973. *White House photograph.*

Prince Sihanouk with Liu Shaochi (*left*) and Zhou Enlai (*right*) on an official visit to the People's Republic of China, Beijing, 1955. *Photograph courtesy of Narankiri Tith.*

(*Above*) Prince Sihanouk with Soviet Premier Bulganin on an official visit to the Soviet Union, Moscow, 1955. *Photograph courtesy of Narankiri Tith.*

(*Below*) Prince Sihanouk with President Eisenhower, Washington, 1958. *Photograph courtesy of Julio Jeldres.*

(*Above*) Pol Pot

(*Below, left*) Ieng Sary, former Foreign Minister of Democratic Kampuchea and former brother-in-law of Pol Pot, 1981. *Photograph courtesy of James Gerrand.*

(*Below, right*) Son Sen, former Defense Minister of Democratic Kampuchea, 1981, murdered on orders of Pol Pot in 1997. *Photograph courtesy of James Gerrand.*

(*Above*) Khmers Rouges leaders, including Pol Pot and Nuon Chea (*first and second from left*), Cambodia, late 1970s.

(*Below*) Pol Pot with Zhou Enlai's widow, Deng Yingchao, and Khmers Rouges leaders Nuon Chea and Ieng Sary, at Phnom Penh airport, January 1978 (see p. 84). *Photograph courtesy AP/Wide World Photos.*

(*Above*) Ho Chi Minh meeting Chinese Communist Party chairman Mao Zedong, Beijing, 1958. *Vietnam News Agency photograph.*

(*Below*) Ho Chi Minh being farewelled by Deng Xiaoping and other Chinese leaders, Beijing, 1965. *Xinhua News Agency photograph.*

(*Above*) Ho Chi Minh meeting with Soviet communist leaders Mikhail Suslov and Leonid Brezhnev in the Soviet Union, 1959. *Novosti Agency photograph.*

(*Below*) Pham Van Dong meeting with Soviet Premier Alexei Kosygin in Moscow, 1969. *Novosti Agency photograph.*

PART TWO

The Internationalization of a Conflict

CHAPTER FIVE

Vietnam and the Communist World, 1930–68

The decision of the Vietnamese communists in the period of Sino-Soviet enmity to align themselves with the Soviet Union, and thus antagonize China,
was causally relevant to the outbreak of the Third Indochina War. It made
Vietnam's conflict with Cambodia an issue in the Sino-Soviet conflict. Western analysts have explained Vietnam's alignment with the Soviet Union by
referring to national security concerns or the concept of nationalism, in both
cases, justified by a perceived need to protect Vietnam's independence from
its hereditary enemy, China. But such explanations are divorced from the
historical behavior patterns of both traditional and revolutionary Vietnamese elites.

In the premodern era—that is, in the millenium between liberation from
Chinese rule and the arrival of French colonialists—the Vietnamese emperors traditionally deferred to China.[1] In the twentieth century all Vietnamese
political elites, communist and noncommunist, continued the traditional pattern of deference to China. In order to understand why the communists who
ruled North Vietnam from 1954 on broke with that pattern after 1968, one
has to understand their complex political culture. This requires an outline of
the history before 1968 of Vietnamese communist relations with the communist world.

IN THE ERA OF INTERNATIONALIST UNITY

As we have discussed already in the context of Vietnamese-Cambodian relations (see Chapter 1), Vietnamese communism was created by a Vietnamese functionary of the Commmunist International, Nguyen Ai Quoc (born
Nguyen Sinh Cung), who much later adopted the alias of Ho Chi Minh.
Quoc, who left French-colonized Vietnam before World War I, arrived in

Paris at war's end. During 1919 he became active in the French socialist movement. In 1920 Quoc joined the breakaway group that founded the French Communist Party.

The Comintern Origins of Vietnamese Communism

By 1923 Nguyen Ai Quoc had caught the attention of the Comintern. He was invited to Moscow to work at Comintern headquarters and to undertake political education at the Kommunisticheskii Universitet Trudyashchiksia Vostoka (KUTV) (Communist University for Toilers from the East).[2] Quoc also sat on the executive body of the newly-formed Krestintern (Peasant International) during the organization's brief existence. He was a delegate to the Comintern's Fifth Congress in Moscow in 1924.[3]

The main purpose of Nguyen Ai Quoc's sojourn in Moscow was to prepare him for his role as a full-time functionary of the Comintern in the Far East. At the end of 1924 he was posted to Canton to work as an interpreter on the staff of Mikhail Borodin, the Comintern's representative in South China. Quoc had two functions in Canton: First, to act as a liaison between the Comintern's Far East Bureau and the emerging communist movements in Southeast Asia; second, to help establish a communist organization in Vietnam.[4]

Nguyen Ai Quoc created for Vietnam an organization with ostensibly nationalist goals, through which Marxist ideas could be gradually introduced. That organization was called the Viet Nam Thanh Nien Kach Menh Hoi (Vietnamese Revolutionary Youth Association), or simply Thanh Nien.[5] Though the ideology of Thanh Nien was anticolonialist, it was also explicitly internationalist.[6] Thanh Nien propounded the virtues of internationalism not just because of political advantage to Vietnamese anticolonialists. The organization's doctrine also proclaimed internationalism to be a virtuous end in itself for all revolutionaries. The motto of Thanh Nien was: "First make a national revolution; then make a world revolution." Vietnamese revolutionaries should not be satisfied with making a revolution in their own country:

> After the political and social revolution, there will still remain oppressed peoples. There will still be differences between nations. It is then necessary to have a world revolution. After that the peoples of the four corners of the earth will befriend one another. It will be the age of world fraternity.[7]

In February 1930 a meeting was held in Hong Kong with representatives of three communist factions and Nguyen Ai Quoc representing the Comintern. There the differences between the factions were ironed out and a new party, the Vietnamese Communist Party (VCP), was formed. Appointed secretary-general was Tran Phu, a former schoolteacher and Thanh Nien member, recently returned from political training in Moscow. He drafted a party program and regulations, which were adopted at a plenary meeting of the first (temporary) Central Committee, held in Hong Kong in October 1930. At that meeting, in response to a directive from the Comintern, the name of the party was changed to the Indochinese Communist Party (Dan Cong San Dong Duong).[8]

The ICP As Comintern Section

In the late 1920s the Comintern subordinated all Southeast Asian communist parties to a secretariat of the League of Oppressed Peoples of Asia. That secretariat was in turn subordinated to the Central Committee of the Chinese Communist Party in Shanghai.[9] The process was a formalization of what had been a close informal relationship between Vietnamese and Chinese communists in the 1920s.[10] Contacts with the Chinese Communist Party (CCP) became difficult after 1931, when the Chinese party apparatus in Shanghai was devastated by Kuomintang (KMT) arrests.[11] On April 11, 1931, the Executive Committee of the Comintern recognized the Indochinese Communist Party as an independent section of the Comintern.[12]

The suppression of the communist-led Vietnamese peasant revolts of 1930–31 by the French in early 1931 was massive and extensive, devastating the ICP organization inside Vietnam. But the Comintern connection saved the party. The strategy of sending promising young Vietnamese to Moscow for political training meant that there was always a pool of newly trained recruits who could return from abroad to take over party activities from those imprisoned or killed. From 1931 to 1935 the party was directed inside Vietnam predominantly by those trained in Moscow.[13] But the internal leadership was subject to the authority of an External Directing Bureau in southern China. This External Bureau received its instructions from the Comintern via the Central Committee of the CCP in Shanghai and the Far Eastern Bureau of the Comintern located in the Soviet consulate in the same city.[14]

During this period, in conformity with the radical "class against class" line of the Comintern, nationalism came under especially severe attack within party journals.[15] Party statutes revealed that the ICP Central Committee was under the authority of the External Directing Bureau, which itself was under the authority of the Comintern. A majority of the Directing Bureau and its permanent committee were chosen from delegates selected by the Comintern.[16] Throughout the Comintern's remaining years, the ICP closely adhered to every twist and turn of Comintern policy.

There is another historical aspect of the Vietnamese communist relationship with the Stalinist Soviet Union that bears reflecting upon. As already noted, since the late 1920s there was always a pool of Vietnamese recruits studying at the KUTV in Moscow. Nguyen Ai Quoc spent the years 1933–38 in Moscow, during the *Yezhovshchina* (the terror named for Stalin's notorious commissar for internal security, Nikolai Yezhov). The terror struck not only Soviet citizens, but also foreign communists residing there. Foreign communist party leaders and Comintern functionaries were liable to be arrested and executed.[17] This happened on a massive scale, and the Polish and Korean parties exiled in the Soviet Union were actually dissolved.[18] By contrast, there is no record of any Vietnamese being arrested during the terror. This is strange when one realizes that Nguyen Ai Quoc was in some disfavor, and politically inactive, until 1938.[19] Quoc was not only a member of a foreign communist party, but also had been a member of the Comintern apparatus.

In spite of Quoc's tribulations, and direct experience with Stalin's terror, the Vietnamese party continued to express reverence for Stalin long after the Soviet dictator's death. In its major foreign policy proclamation of the early 1960s, the Vietnamese party appraisal was on balance a defense of Stalin. Its mild criticism did not mention Stalin's foreign policy or his liquidation of foreign communists, only his domestic policies.[20] In commemorating the ninetieth and centenary anniversaries of Stalin's birth, the Vietnamese made no mention of the terror of the late 1930s. Yet since 1956 even the Soviets have criticized this.[21]

The Vietnamese communists have consistently defended Stalin's foreign policy. For example, on the centenary anniversary of Stalin's birth, the Vietnamese communist party newspaper wrote:

> Regarding the international communist and workers' movement and the national liberation movement in the world, Stalin, together with the other Soviet leaders, contributed a great deal to their varied activities. In conjunction with other party leaders, Stalin waged a struggle against all expressions of opportunism—Trotskyism, rightist opportunism, bourgeois nationalism—in defense of the purity of Marxism-Leninism.[22]

This opinion, expressed in 1979, was not the price of membership in the Soviet bloc. The Hungarian communists, who were also members of the Soviet bloc, and who, unlike the Vietnamese, lived under the shadow of the Soviet army, wrote on the same occasion of how "Stalin had caused great difficulties and grievous losses to the international communist movement." The Hungarian communists wrote of Stalin's "sectarian views that hampered the antifascist collaboration of communists, socialists, and other democratic forces." The Hungarians also denounced the development of Stalin's "personality cult" and the subsequent trials that "took place on the basis of false charges and the spreading of unfounded accusations, which had many victims among political emigrants."[23]

To have survived that bloody period as a witness to the murder of old comrades, and still be deferential to the memory of Stalin, is strange to say the least. It suggests that Ho and his disciples—unlike the Hungarians, not to mention the Yugoslavs—had permanently internalized the political values of that era. This would imply, among other things, an authentic commitment to some general vision of Stalinist virtue and, in particular, to the Stalinist concept of international communist unity.

The Chinese Connection

From their very beginning the Vietnamese communists relied upon access to the territory of China as a sanctuary from which to direct activities inside French-controlled Indochina. As we have also noted, the link between the ICP and the Comintern was partly through the Central Committee of the CCP. This entailed some direct liaison between the top personnel of the two parties. In the late 1920s, during the years of the KMT-CCP alliance, Nguyen Ai Quoc was training young Vietnamese sailors, workers, and students in Canton at a Special Political Training Class. Mao Zedong's Peasant Seminar was being held nearby, and apparently maintained close contact with the training class. The Chinese Communist Party was also providing financial aid for the training class.[24] The break between the KMT and the CCP in 1927 temporarily ended this cooperation.

In the fall of 1938, Nguyen Ai Quoc went from the Soviet Union to China, where he joined the communist Eighth Route Army.[25] He was the only leading ICP figure with the CCP at the time. His ostensible function was as a journalist for the Eighth Route Army.[26] Given his previous condition of disfavor in Moscow, and his begging for a political assignment, he probably would have had to report back to Moscow, probably to the People's Commissariat of Internal Affairs (NKVD).[27] In June 1940 he was joined by Pham Van Dong and Vo Nguyen Giap, who were to attend the CCP party school in Yenan. These plans were scrapped after the fall of Paris to the Nazis threatened to change the situation in Indochina drastically.[28] But the new CCP-ICP connection remained and during the 1940s the Chinese provided military advisers and training.[29]

Quoc returned to Vietnam in 1941. In May of that year he formed the Viet Nam Doc Lap Dong Minh (Vietnam Independence League), or Viet Minh as it was popularly known. Most Viet Minh bases were located in areas contiguous to the Chinese border. But there was little substantial cooperation between the Vietnamese and Chinese communists until late 1946. At that time a CCP provincial commissioner was sent to the Vietnamese border area to help train Viet Minh cadres. In August 1947, Chinese forces in the Hundred Thousand Hills border area were commanded to operate in cooperation with the Viet Minh. And in September the Viet Minh purchased twelve million piasters worth of equipment from the Chinese, which was sent to northern Vietnam before the French fall offensive began.[30] Though the bulk of the Chinese communist forces were dispersed elsewhere, there was nevertheless a close cooperation between Chinese and Vietnamese communist forces along their common border.

But it was the military victories of the Chinese communists over the Kuomintang armies in 1949 that changed the fortunes of the Vietnamese communists. Former Politburo member Hoang Van Hoan, writing after his defection to China in August 1979, confirms the claim made by the French high commissioner in Saigon at the time, that early in 1950 Ho Chi Minh made a secret visit to China and asked for Chinese help.[31] In April 1950, agreements were signed whereby the Central Military Committee of the CCP ordered the PLA's Second, Third, and Fourth Field Armies to provide advisers at batallion, regiment, and division levels for a Vietnamese division. A Chinese Military Advisory Group (CMAG) was organized by the Chinese Third Field Army and a military school was set up by the Fourth Field Army.[32] Chinese military and political advisers began to arrive in Viet Minh zones in the summer. China supplied the Viet Minh with a considerable number of weapons and ammunition. Between April and September 1950 the Chinese delivered military materiel to equip 16,000 soldiers.[33] In the 1950s China helped train five Viet Minh divisions and assisted in the reorganization of Giap's military forces. The Chinese were also involved in the opening of more military schools and the establishment of a political commissar system.[34] The CMAG, which was composed of seventy-nine experienced PLA officers, arrived in Vietnam in early August. With this new Chinese support, in September 1950 the Viet Minh launched a successful military campaign against French forces in the border towns.[35]

Chinese aid and training continued, and increased to a sufficient degree that it gave the Viet Minh an offensive capacity that it would not otherwise have had. The amount of Chinese aid is estimated to have risen from between ten and twenty tons a month in 1951 to four thousand tons a month in the spring of 1954. Chinese advisers played a role in planning every major campaign of the war.[36]

In 1951 the CMAG offered a plan to the Viet Minh leaders for streamlining their military command structure and for training and reorganizing their troops. Ho and the Vietnamese leaders agreed and CMAG played a crucial role in the reorganization and training.[37]

Chinese sources claim that in 1952 the Vietnamese leaders, through the medium of CMAG, had even asked for the intervention of Chinese troops into the battles for northwestern Vietnam, but that the CCP Central Committee had rejected the request on principle.[38]

Especially important was the Chinese role in the battle for Dien Bien Phu. From the time the battle for the French base was underway in March 1954, the Viet Minh army was under the direction of Chinese advisers operating at various levels, including one Chinese general, Wei Guoqing, at Giap's headquarters. According to official Chinese sources, for this particular battle China supplied the Viet Minh with more than 200 trucks, 10,000 barrels of oil, 100 cannons, 3,000 guns of various kinds, 2.4 million bullets, 60,000 artillery shells, and approximately 1,700 tons of grain. The Chinese also provided important road construction and an anti-aircraft regiment, and drove the 1,000 trucks that brought supplies in.[39] With Chinese anti-aircraft defenses protecting the long-range artillery, the Viet Minh gunners were able to direct devastating firepower on the French positions. Viet Minh success at Dien Bien Phu would not have been possible without Chinese assistance.

Some scholars have tended to assume differences of ambition between the Vietnamese and the Chinese at the Geneva Conference of 1954, which negotiated a political settlement in Indochina. China was willing to accept the need for a Viet Minh military withdrawal from Cambodia and Laos, while the Vietnamese communists were allegedly wanting to maintain their forces in these countries. These scholars have suggested that China pressured the Vietnamese into accepting the agreement, and that these differences were at least a cause of the antipathy which surfaced during the 1970s.[40] But the evidence of Vietnamese resentment in 1954 is weak, based largely on polemics that were written after the Vietnamese-Chinese dispute became public in 1978. On the other hand, there is solid evidence of the exhaustion of the Viet Minh after the siege of Dien Bien Phu.[41] This meant that political concessions by the Vietnamese communists in Laos and Cambodia might well have seemed reasonable even to them at the time. Moreover, as these scholars concede, Chinese policy was also Soviet policy. Yet Soviet advocacy of Vietnamese withdrawal in 1954 did not cause antipathy toward the Soviets to surface in the 1970s.

Thus we should not conclude that negotiations at the 1954 Geneva Conference were important in affecting later deterioration of relations between the Vietnamese and Chinese communists. In fact, the Vietnamese-Chinese relationship continued to be very close for two more years after Geneva.

The Chinese Model of "Socialist Construction"

The Vietnamese communists not only depended upon the Chinese communists materially. They were also under Chinese influence in their approach to consolidating and developing their political, economic, and social power. From 1950 until 1957 almost every major policy and every institution introduced in the zones controlled by the Vietnamese communists was a replica of something that had already been developed by the Chinese. Ho Chi Minh explained why:

> Marx, Engels, Lenin, and Stalin are the common teachers for the world revolution. Comrade Mao Tse-tung has skilfully "Sinicized" the ideology of Marx, Engels, Lenin, and Stalin. . . .
> Owing to geographical, historical, economic, and cultural conditions, the Chinese revolution exerted a great influence on the Vietnamese revolution, which had to learn and indeed has learned many experiences from it.
> Thanks to the experience of the Chinese Revolution and to Mao Tse-tung's thoughts, we have further understood the ideology of Marx, Engels, Lenin, and Stalin and consequently scored many successes. This the Vietnamese revolutionaries must engrave on their minds and be grateful for.[42]

In late 1950 the Vietnamese communists began a campaign to study the Chinese communist experience. Writings by Mao Zedong, Liu Shaoqi, and

Zhu De were translated into Vietnamese and distributed to almost every Viet Minh civilian and military unit. For several years all Vietnamese cadres were compelled to discuss and draw lessons from the Chinese writings.[43]

Specific Chinese communist mass campaigns were copied by the Vietnamese. First there was the Patriotic Emulation campaign to increase performance in industry, agriculture, and the military. It was followed by a rectification campaign within the party in 1952–53, in accordance with which 15,800 cadres are said to have undergone "thought reform." The Chinese Three Anti campaign of 1951, intended to "cleanse" party and government agencies, was introduced by the Viet Minh in 1953.[44] But the two most important imitations of Chinese campaigns undertaken by the Vietnamese were the Land Reform campaign of 1953–56 and the Hundred Flowers campaign of 1956, in which Mao urged the masses to voice constructive criticism of the party.[45] Finally, the crackdown which followed the Hundred Flowers liberalization was similiar to the Anti-Rightist campaign that had begun in China several months earlier.

The pattern of Vietnamese communist imitation of Chinese communist campaigns ended in 1958, when Mao initiated his Great Leap Forward. The Vietnamese collectivization campaign, which had begun with the formation of mutual-aid teams and low-level cooperatives in 1955, and proceeded into the phase of high-level cooperatives in 1961, never developed into the phase of massive communes, such as had been created in China during 1958–59. It seems that the Vietnamese leaders regarded the Maoist leap into communes as a break with Marxist-Leninist orthodoxy.

Nevertheless, the Chinese model continued to play a role in the establishment of the Vietnamese communist society. The idea of applying "study sessions" and "criticism and self-criticism" to individuals in the mass organizations, rather than just to the party members, was a method of social control borrowed by the Vietnamese from the Chinese.[46] The use of thought reform programs, reform through labor, and reeducation camps, emphasizing psychological transformation as well as physical forms of punishment, were also variations on the Soviet model that the Vietnamese borrowed from Mao's China.

Solidarity with the Soviet Bloc

It is not necessary for our purposes to review the history of Vietnamese communist stands on foreign policy issues between World War II and the outbreak of Sino-Soviet hostility. But during this period, on three major issues of relations between communist parties, the Vietnamese support for the Soviet Union's position indicated a deep commitment to solidarity with the Soviet bloc.

The first issue was the conflict between Stalin and Tito, which led to Yugoslavia's expulsion from the Cominform and the Soviet branding of Tito as an imperialist agent. Though the Vietnamese communists were far removed geographically from this conflict, and preoccupied with a difficult military struggle against France to which the Soviets could offer little help at that time, they still followed the Soviet line and denounced Tito as an enemy. In 1950, when the DRV was searching desperately for international diplomatic recognition, the Yugoslav offer of that was rejected and Tito was denounced as, among other things, "a spy for American imperialism."[47]

The second issue was the Eastern European crisis of 1956, and in particular the Soviet invasion of Hungary. Hanoi's mass media endorsed the crushing of the Hungarian revolution by the Soviet army, an action that it described as a "glorious success of the valiant Hungarian people."[48]

The third issue, equally important as an indicator of Hanoi's fidelity to the Soviet line, was its reconciliation with Yugoslavia in 1957. Khrushchev had initiated a Soviet-bloc reconciliation with the Yugoslavs in 1955. This rapprochement continued (with a brief cooling in late 1956 in the light of the Hungarian events) until late 1957.[49] In spite of what had transpired before, and what would transpire in the future in Vietnamese-Yugoslav relations, Hanoi established diplomatic relations with Belgrade in March 1957. In the summer of that year, Ho Chi Minh visited Yugoslavia. Subsequently Pham Van Dong and other Vietnamese officials described Yugoslavia as a "socialist country."[50] This was the last time such ideological deference towards the Yugoslavs was to emanate from the Vietnamese.

IN THE ERA OF POLYCENTRISM

The factors underlying the breakdown of relations between the Soviet Union and the People's Republic of China emerged in 1956, with Khrushchev's speech to the Twentieth Party Congress of the CPSU. Khrushchev asserted several new doctrinal stands at this congress, which became matters of contention between the Soviet Union and China: 1) In the conflict between "imperialism" and the "socialist camp," war was no longer inevitable and the avoidance of nuclear war was desirable; 2) the expansion of socialism could take place without the resort to revolutionary war, and in the west could take place by communists following the "parliamentary road" to power; 3) the "class struggle" need not continue under a socialist state, which in the Soviet case was now defined as a "state of all the people" instead of as a "dictatorship of the proletariat"; 4) Stalin's historical role had to be reevaluated in the light of his crimes and errors in domestic and foreign policy.

The new positions enunciated at the Twentieth Party Congress of the CPSU came shortly after the Soviet leaders had undertaken a rapprochement with Yugoslavia, expelled from the Soviet bloc by Stalin in 1948. The attempt to woo Yugoslavia back into the "socialist camp" in 1955 had been undertaken with the promulgation of the doctrine of "different roads to socialism," which was an attempt to broaden the limits of variation in the methods of "socialist construction," and to reject the notion that every variation from the Soviet model amounted to heresy. The combination of the Twentieth Party Congress doctrinal changes, together with the new political relationship of the Soviet Union and Yugoslavia, created shock waves throughout the "socialist camp," especially in Eastern Europe. Ultimately it led to political disorder in Poland and a breakdown of Soviet authority in Hungary in October 1956. This greatly disturbed the Chinese, and caused them to reevaluate the CPSU's leadership within the communist world.

Subsequently, other differences arose between the Soviets and Chinese that had more of a "national security" aspect to them. They emanated from China's policy toward Taiwan, China's border conflict with India in 1959, China's desire to acquire nuclear weapons, and the Soviet desire to establish a "joint command" over China's naval forces as the price of its assistance. But throughout the 1950s the Soviets and Chinese publicly managed to maintain a facade of unity to the outside world.

First Vietnamese Responses to the Sino-Soviet Dispute

At the same time as international solidarity was breaking down, the Vietnamese communist leadership made its decision to launch an armed uprising against the government of South Vietnam. That decision was taken at a plenum of the Central Committee of the Lao Dong (Vietnamese Workers' Party) in May 1959.[51] Hanoi anticipated that the United States might intervene directly to prevent the victory of the communist forces in South Vietnam, but thought it unlikely.[52] Yet the Hanoi leaders took their decision, and even committed their own forces to the battle, without the absolute certainty of all-out Soviet and Chinese support. Attempting to ensure Soviet and Chinese support for the war in South Vietnam, and later to ensure protection of North Vietnam, became the most important foreign policy issue for the Vietnamese communists.

It is not clear that promoting internationalist solidarity between the Soviet Union and China was the best guarantee of aid from both Moscow and Beijing. The separate testimonies of two former "insiders"—a Hungarian and a Polish diplomat who both dealt with Vietnamese affairs—suggest that national competition was what eventually accelerated Soviet and Chinese aid to Hanoi.[53] But promoting "internationalist solidarity" was the path first chosen by the Hanoi leaders, reflecting both ideology and their past experiences of success.

The Sino-Soviet conflict did not become a major issue to the other communist parties until 1960. In November and December of that year, a meeting of eighty-one communist and workers' parties took place in Moscow. Great difficulties emerged in the attempt to formulate a final declaration acceptable to all parties, in particular to both the Soviets and the Chinese. At first the Chinese refused to sign the declaration. According to Khrushchev, at the conference Ho Chi Minh attempted to mediate between the Soviets and Chinese. Khrushchev quotes Ho as saying to him: "Comrade Khrushchev, China is a very big country with a very big Party. You can't permit a schism in the movement. You must make sure that the Chinese sign this declaration along with the rest of us. Only if it is unanimously endorsed will this document have great international importance."[54]

Vietnamese mediation seems to have had some effect, because the Chinese eventually did sign the final document. It is important to recognize this early example of the Vietnamese communists' continuing concern for political unity in the "socialist camp." Similar concern could be seen in their response to the Soviet-Albanian confrontations of 1961. Albania's leadership, dominated by party secretary Enver Hoxha, was modeled upon that of Stalin, and shared the Maoist Chinese revulsion at Khrushchev's doctrinal changes at the CPSU's Twentieth Party Congress of 1956. Furthermore, the Albanians had long been embroiled in an ideological and power struggle with Tito's Yugoslavia, a country that Khrushchev had now restored friendly relations with. For these reasons Albania became a militant ally of China and a thorn in the side of the Soviet Union.[55] For a brief period, it was more appropriate for the Soviets to direct their ire at the Albanians rather than directly confront the more significant Chinese.

At the Twenty-second Congress of the CPSU in October 1961, Nikita Khrushchev launched an attack upon Stalin and upon the Albanian communist leaders. The Chinese delegation, led by Zhou Enlai, walked out of the Congress early and returned to Beijing. The Vietnamese delegation left the Congress, but did not return to Hanoi. Instead they went on a tour of the western Soviet Union. In other words, the Vietnamese were expressing their dissent from the Soviet position, without expressing the same defiance as the Chinese.[56] Two months after the CPSU Congress, the Soviet Union broke diplomatic relations with Albania. The Vietnamese did not follow the Soviets, but continued a friendly, in fact "comradely" relationship with the Albanians. Unlike the Soviets, the Vietnamese continued to refer to Albania as a member of the "socialist camp." But at the same time, the Vietnamese also insisted upon the leadership of the USSR within that camp. The Vietnamese party expressed its position in an article published in the party journal *Hoc Tap* on the twentieth anniversary of the founding of the Albanian party in November 1961.[57]

The Vietnamese were not yet taking sides, but rather still attempting to reassert the unity of the "socialist camp." During 1962 and early 1963, the Vietnamese communists attempted to mediate between the Soviet Union and China and to dampen their dispute. In January 1962, it was subsequently revealed, the Central Committee of the Lao Dong sent letters to other parties suggesting that an international meeting of communist and workers' parties be held, and that until that meeting took place there should be a moratorium on public polemics between parties.[58]

Then in February 1963 the Politburo of the Lao Dong issued a public statement, revealing that it had sent the letters in January 1962, and once again appealing for unity between parties. This public statement called for an end to public criticism of each other by all parties, called for an international meeting of parties to discuss divergences of views, and stated that the Soviet and Chinese parties should take the major responsibility for preparing that meeting.[59] This was to be the last occasion in which the Vietnamese would attempt to mediate publicly between the Soviet Union and China. Hanoi had already abandoned its own recommendations for a moratorium on parties publicly criticizing each other by publishing attacks on Yugoslavia.[60] In March 1963 it began its public shift toward the Chinese position.

The Tilt Toward China

Khrushchev had never shown a great interest in events in Vietnam. The former Hungarian diplomat Janos Radvanyi has reported the different responses of the Chinese and Soviet leaders to the situation in Vietnam in May 1959. After a visit to Hanoi that month, a Hungarian delegation stopped over in Beijing, where the Chinese leaders were keen to hear of the situation in Vietnam and seemed aware that the North Vietnamese leaders were about to begin their armed struggle. But during the Hungarians' next stop in Moscow, Khrushchev, who was interested in discussing a range of issues with them, showed no interest whatsoever either in Vietnam or in the Hungarians' recent visit to Hanoi.[61] At the same time, the Soviet Union was giving aid to North Vietnam.

But the Soviet attitude toward Vietnam was always dictated by the attitude the Soviet Union was taking toward both China and the Western powers. After the Cuban missile crisis of October 1962, Khrushchev decided not to become involved in a military situation where the Soviet Union could directly confront the United States again, and more especially one where the Soviet Union was at a major military disadvantage.

On March 13, 1963, a *Nhan Dan* editorial for the first time denounced "modern revisionism"—a Chinese code word for both Yugoslavia and Khrushchev's doctrines. It suggested that Yugoslavia represented the worst, but not the only form of this deviation. In April the Chinese media published a speech by Le Duan denouncing Yugoslav revisionism, especially on the issues of revolutionary change, class struggle, and proletarian dictatorship.[62]

More significant politically was the joint statement of Vietnamese President Ho Chi Minh and Chinese Chairman Liu Shaoqi at the end of the latter's visit to Vietnam in May 1963. The statement carefully distinguished the views of each. For example, from the Vietnamese alone: "President Ho Chi Minh stresses . . . that the unity of the Communist Parties of the Soviet Union and China is the pillar of the unity of the socialist camp and the international communist movement."[63]

The communiqué also expressed views common to the Chinese and Vietnamese. But while expressing the desire for unity, Ho agreed with Liu that the Yugoslavs were not a part of the international communist movement and were a danger to it.[64] This anti-Yugoslav statement amounted to a particular slap in the face to the Soviets because only six months earlier, in December

1962, the Soviet Union had begun a new rapprochement with the Yugoslavs. There was more to come.

In July 1963 the United States, Great Britain, and the Soviet Union signed a treaty banning the testing of nuclear weapons in the atmosphere, outer space, and underwater. On July 31 the Chinese government, which was developing its own nuclear weapons, issued a statement opposing the treaty. It called instead for the total prohibition and destruction of nuclear weapons. It also denounced the Soviet Union for "capitulation to U.S. imperialism."

On August 6 and 9, 1963, *Nhan Dan* published editorials supporting the Chinese stand on the treaty. Then in the September issue of *Hoc Tap*, Hanoi openly criticized the Soviet Union for the first time:

> The treaty was signed as the result of a deal struck by the leaders of the nuclear powers. . . . It therefore runs counter to the peace-loving peoples of the world. . . . Compared with the demand of the people of the world and with the previous stand of the Soviet government on the prohibition of nuclear weapons, the treaty signed recently is a step backward. . . . The Chinese Government proposals are fully correct and reasonable, and fully reflect the demand and aspiration of peace-loving people throughout the world.[65]

Why would Hanoi have taken such a position in support of China's stand on the test-ban treaty? It cannot have been simply because of the intrinsic merits of the issue, which did not bear upon the short-term, or even long-term national security or power aspirations of North Vietnam. North Vietnam was not planning to become a nuclear power. (By contrast, China's opposition to the treaty could be understood simply in terms of her own real capacity and desire to acquire nuclear weapons, which would soon require atmospheric testing.) Obviously, the issue had great symbolic significance for the Vietnamese communists. At a time when the dispute between the Soviet and Chinese parties had become public, the stand was demonstrating a more general alignment with the Chinese and against the Soviets.

Khrushchev recognized this. In an analysis written in late 1969 or 1970 he stated:

> When the rupture between the Communist Party of the Soviet Union and the Communist Party of China came out into the open, China began to lead the Vietnamese Laborer's Party around by a halter. A large segment of the population in Vietnam—and therefore of the Party—is Chinese. China began to use its considerable influence to start quarrels between Vietnam and the Soviet Union and to turn the Vietnamese Party against us. Some of the key positions

in the leadership of the Vietnamese Party are now held by pro-Chinese comrades. At a time when we have been doing everything we could to help Vietnam, the pro-Chinese elements in Vietnam have been doing everything they could to please China. In other words, they have been working not only against us, but against Vietnam's own best interests. It's a great pity.[66]

Leaving aside the secondary question of the "ethnic Chinese" explanation of Vietnamese communist behavior Khrushchev offers, it is clear that the Vietnamese stand was recognized by the Soviet leaders as part of a general pro-Chinese alignment, and must surely have been intended as such by the Vietnamese.

In December 1963 the Ninth Conference of the Vietnamese Workers' Party Central Executive Committee issued an important resolution, titled "World Situation and Our Party's International Mission." The resolution expounded the foreign policy of the Vietnamese communists at that time. It summarized the basic ideological outlook of the Vietnamese party leaders and presented its views on what it perceived to be the major problems of the international communist movement. The central concern of the Vietnamese was the "fierce struggle between the two lines: the Marxist-Leninist line and the modern revisionist line."[67] According to the Vietnamese, revisionist ideas manifested themselves on several different issues: the problem of international war and peace; the struggle of national liberation movements against colonialism; the problem of transition to socialism and proletarian dictatorship; and the problem of constructing socialism and communism. But the attitude of revisionists to war and peace was of greatest concern.[68] The Vietnamese communists viewed a correct Marxist-Leninist stand as requiring a militant policy. The resolution stated: "Revolutionary struggle is not contradictory to the struggle for protecting peace. Separating these two struggles, laying emphasis only on the problems of peace, race, general disarmament, and so forth is creating illusions among the people and increasing the danger of war."[69]

Who were the revisionists? According to the Vietnamese there were two different groups of revisionists: the "Tito clique" in Yugoslavia, which Hanoi regarded as not a socialist country, and the revisionists within "fraternal socialist parties." There was said to be a close political as well as ideological connection between the two.[70]

The revisionists in "fraternal socialist parties" were clearly Nikita Khrushchev and his supporters in the Soviet Union and Eastern Europe. Although the Vietnamese did not name Khrushchev directly, the content of their criticisms indicated that it was his political and ideological viewpoint that was of concern to them.

Throughout most of 1964, at least until the fall of Khrushchev in October, the Vietnamese media kept up its attacks upon Soviet foreign policy positions, though without ever naming the Soviet Communist Party or Khrushchev directly. This distinguished the Vietnamese criticisms from those of the Chinese. Hanoi's attacks were always directed against "modern revisionists." This, plus the fact that the Vietnamese communists still regarded the CPSU as a fraternal party, suggested that they thought that there were "genuine Marxist-Leninists" within the CPSU who might eventually regain power from the "revisionists." The disagreements between the Vietnamese and Soviet parties lacked the nationalist element that was one factor in the Sino-Soviet conflict. The key to the Vietnamese attitude toward the CPSU was the latter's general viewpoint on relations with the West ("imperialism"). At the same time, one cannot ignore the fact that at this time the Soviet attitude toward "imperialism" was correlated with the Soviet attitude toward the war in South Vietnam.

The Vietnamese alignment with China and against the Soviet Union was not only expressed through the veiled terminology contained in public statements. It was also expressed in the diplomatic relations between the Vietnamese and the Soviet-bloc countries. One former Polish official reports numerous displays of rudeness by Vietnamese officials, including by Prime Minister Pham Van Dong, toward the Soviet ambassador and East European emissaries at diplomatic receptions in Hanoi in 1963 and 1964.[71]

The Vietnamese alignment with China also expressed itself in the form of purges of the political and military elite. Perhaps the most famous was the case of Hoang Minh Chinh. One of Hanoi's leading ideological cadres, he had been given advanced training in Moscow in the late 1950s and returned to North Vietnam in 1961 to head the party school's philosophy department. After the split within the communist movement in the early 1960s, Chinh was asked by Politburo member Truong Chinh to help formulate the party line on the ideological questions dividing the international communist movement. But after the Ninth Plenum, he was denounced as a revisionist, expelled from the party, and sent to a reeducation camp.

A similar fate befell four of the principal military aides to Defense Minister Vo Nguyen Giap. Although Giap himself was considered revisionist by Party Secretary Le Duan, he was under the protection of Party Chairman

Ho Chi Minh. But the four highly regarded aides—chief of military intelligence for the general staff, Colonel Nguyen Minh Nghia; chief of operations, Colonel Do Duc Kien; Giap's chief of cabinet, Colonel Le Minh Nghia; and head of the training department, Colonel Nguyen Hieu—were all sent to prison for holding revisionist views. Two of the party's leading cadres, Le Vinh Quoc and Van Doan, who were then in training in the Soviet Union, decided not to return to Vietnam.[72] Hundreds of Vietnamese military officers who had been trained in Soviet military academies in the 1950s and early 1960s found themselves demoted or reassigned to positions of no significance.[73]

These purges were taking place at a time when Hanoi was in the process of escalating its armed struggle against the government of South Vietnam. The Vietnamese communist leaders were thereby depriving themselves of some of their skilled military cadres and officers—resources that were critically important for what was then the leadership's major political objective. The purges indicate that ideology played a crucial role in the party elite's thinking. The purges also suggest that the elite profoundly distrusted those it considered to have been contaminated by exposure to ideologically incorrect training.

The event that signaled a change in the Vietnamese communist position was the fall of Khrushchev. That event was reported without comment in the Hanoi media. Shortly after Khrushchev's fall a provocative article in *Hoc Tap* was first modified and then withdrawn from circulation. The article had not only strongly denounced revisionist positions but had gone further by distinguishing between modern revisionists and "true communists" in the Soviet Union, thus publicizing Vietnamese communist views on internal Soviet Party affairs. Following the withdrawal of the *Hoc Tap* article, the Vietnamese media ceased engaging in any polemics that had a bearing on the Sino-Soviet dispute.

The Vietnamese communists still maintained friendly relations with the Albanians. But their position on the Sino-Soviet conflict suddenly became one of cautious neutrality.[74]

Neutrality in the Sino-Soviet Dispute

According to the former Hungarian diplomat Janos Radvanyi, the new Soviet leaders, Leonid Brezhnev and Aleksei Kosygin, believed that Khrushchev had neglected the Vietnamese and Korean communists and were determined to restore a closer relationship. Prime Minister Kosygin was sent on a diplomatic mission to Pyongyang and Hanoi in February 1965, the purpose of which was to reestablish close cooperation with the two Asian parties.[75] During his visit to Hanoi, Kosygin learned of the Vietnamese communist need for protection against U.S. air attacks. The Soviet leader promised the Vietnamese more sophisticated anti-aircraft missiles and MIG fighters, and the necessary training to use them. Vietnamese requests for more economic and political support were also agreed to.[76]

During April 1965 Le Duan visited both Moscow and Beijing, and in both capitals he was offered the possibility of "volunteers" being sent from each country to assist Vietnam. In the Chinese case it was made explicit that such "volunteers" would be sent in order to fight. Although the Chinese had earlier threatened to prevent Soviet supplies for North Vietnam from being transported across Chinese territory, the Vietnamese leaders were able to arrange an agreement between Moscow and Beijing facilitating this traffic.[77] The arrival of the first shipments of new Soviet surface-to-air missiles and other equipment that month, and the expectation of more, boosted the confidence of the Vietnamese leaders in their ability to step up the war in South Vietnam.[78]

Though Chinese influence in Hanoi was still strong, and remained so for the time being, China's status as a center of influence within the international communist movement was gravely set back by events in Indonesia in September 1965. The Indonesian Communist Party (Partai Komunis Indonesia, or PKI) was then the largest nonruling communist party in the world, and exercised considerable influence over the radical nationalist government of President Sukarno. China's close relations with Indonesia were referred to as the "Beijing-Djakarta axis," a radical alliance within which Beijing sought to include Pyongyang and Hanoi. But on September 30, military units sympathetic to, and probably directed by, the PKI attempted to assassinate the anticommunist generals who commanded the Indonesian armed forces. The ultimate purpose seems to have been a coup d'état.[79] The attempt failed, and in their counteroffensive the Indonesian army massacred most of the PKI leaders and crushed their organization, thereby destroying the PKI as a political force for the indefinite future. Sukarno was eventually forced to resign and Indonesia's new leadership became a bitter enemy of China and turned toward the West. Mao's claim that Beijing was replacing Moscow as the new center of world revolution was thus severely discredited.

Although it was claimed at the time that the Soviets, unlike the Chinese, were trying to urge the Vietnamese communists to negotiate a political settlement of the war with the United States,[80] there is no solid evidence that this was so. On the contrary, the account of former Hungarian diplomat Radvanyi, based upon reports from the Hungarian embassy in Hanoi at that time, indicates that the Soviets' main concern was to strengthen their influence with the Vietnamese. Their main instrument in this quest was stepped-up military assistance. For example, the Soviet Politburo's emissary to Hanoi in January 1966, Alexander Shelepin, made no attempt to modify the Vietnamese refusal to negotiate unconditionally. Instead he signed a new agreement promising additional weapons, invited the Vietnamese party to send a delegation to the Twenty-third Congress of the CPSU in March 1966, and offered to send Soviet special rocket troops to back up the Soviet missiles. The Vietnamese leaders gladly signed the agreement and agreed to send Le Duan to the Soviet party congress, but according to Radvanyi they turned down the offer of Soviet military personnel, apparently so as not to be in the position of also having to accept Chinese ground forces in Vietnam.[81]

Hanoi's gratitude continued to be spread in equal amounts to the Soviets and Chinese. But Soviet influence was clearly improving. The combination of increased Soviet aid, especially the air defense system necessary to defend North Vietnam against the United States Air Force, and the political setback suffered by China in Indonesia, had so far improved Moscow's influence in Hanoi. But a third factor would reinforce this trend. It was the outbreak of the Great Proletarian Cultural Revolution in China.

As we have noted earlier, the Vietnamese communists had copied not only Chinese communist political institutions but also almost every major Chinese communist political campaign between 1950 and 1957. This came to an end with Mao's launching of the ultra-radical Great Leap Forward in 1958. The Vietnamese communists seemed to share the Soviet view that the Great Leap was a leftist deviation from Marxist-Leninist orthodoxy. Their disdain for Maoist ultra-leftism was now heightened by two aspects of the Cultural Revolution: the "personality cult" of Mao Zedong and the party-destroying activities of the Red Guards.

Ho Chi Minh's authority within the Vietnamese communist party was not based upon fear, but rather upon a genuine respect for his political wisdom and experience, which had brought the party so many unanticipated successes since 1930. Ho Chi Minh's "personality cult" existed, but not to the same degree as that of Stalin or Mao. During China's Cultural Revolution, Vietnamese party theoreticians pointed to this distinction, though without naming Stalin or Mao.[82]

In his report to party cadres in 1968, the party ideologist, Truong Chinh, made the same point indirectly against the Maoist approach to revolutionary power: "[I]t is necessary to struggle against officialdom and commandism, the system of family organization under one head of the family, and a personal cult, because they, too, are against the spirit of socialist democracy and cause serious consequences to the state."[83]

The Vietnamese were possibly initially disturbed with the situation in China for very practical reasons. The chaos in China threatened to disrupt the shipment of war-related supplies. The Chinese had allegedly been interfering with the transportation of Soviet aid to North Vietnam coming overland through China. But that charge was always publicly denied by the Vietnamese communist leaders. And any problems that might have existed apparently were resolved by the agreement of the Chinese and Soviets in early 1967 to allow the North Vietnamese to play a major role in transporting Soviet supplies across China.[84]

But the basic concern that the Vietnamese had with the Cultural Revolution was the one stated in their veiled criticisms—that it constituted a break with Marxist-Leninist orthodoxy. For the Vietnamese communists not only was the "personality cult" an un-Leninist phenomenon, so too was the army-backed Red Guard assault upon the party. All Vietnamese communist writings emphasize the leading role of the party, both in the seizure of power and in socialist construction.[85]

Yet, whatever the reservations the Vietnamese had about the Cultural Revolution, they never criticized it explicitly. And although their statements on the Cultural Revolution lacked the enthusiasm found in statements by the Korean communists, the Vietnamese leaders did at least make some pro forma statements of support for it.[86]

In their doctrinal statements about the problems within the international communist movement, the Vietnamese emphasized the dangers of "revisionism," more than of leftist "dogmatism."[87]

The Chinese leaders were initially opposed to Hanoi's decision, announced on April 3, 1968, to enter into negotiations with the United States.[88] This opposition was confirmed by former Politburo member Hoang Van Hoan in

December 1979, shortly after his defection to China.[89] But the Chinese deny the Vietnamese charge that they drastically reduced aid to North Vietnam in 1969 and 1970 in response to the Vietnamese decision to enter negotiations.[90] However, on this issue, Beijing was taking a more militant stand than Hanoi vis-à-vis the United States. It is clear that at this stage Beijing could not have been accused of wanting to abandon the Vietnamese communists in return for rapprochement with Washington.

One Hungarian diplomat who visited Hanoi in 1966 reported to his colleagues that the Vietnamese communist leaders tried not to discuss the Sino-Soviet conflict with him, but when pressed they described the whole thing as merely a "difference of opinion."[91] This remarkable statement was not mere diplomatic circumlocution. For in 1968 the Vietnamese leaders were still publicly referring to the differences between the Soviet Union and China as the product of "imperialist schemes" and speaking optimistically of restoring international communist unity.[92]

CONCLUSIONS

Throughout the entire period of international communist unity (which somewhat incongruously includes the period of Yugoslavia's expulsion from the bloc), Vietnamese communism was never a maverick "national communist" movement on the Titoist model. It was, rather, an integral part of an international movement that was headed by the Soviet Union. At no time prior to 1960 did the Vietnamese communist leaders question the authority of Moscow or its general line for the rest of the "socialist camp."

During this period under review, the Vietnamese communist movement also maintained close ties with the Chinese Communist Party. The Vietnamese communists had depended upon Chinese aid from 1950 to 1954 for their military and therefore political success. Furthermore, for decades Chinese communism had provided training, political and cultural advisers, and a model for the phase of "socialist construction" in North Vietnam. Thus, whatever tactical disagreements might have existed between the Chinese and Vietnamese parties in their foreign relations, and whatever ideological reservations the Vietnamese might have had about Mao's domestic radicalism during the Great Leap Forward and the Great Proletarian Cultural Revolution, the overriding pattern of their relationship before 1968 was one of Chinese economic and military aid, political tutelage, and psychological inspiration for the Vietnamese. Thus until 1968, the relationship between China and Vietnam was consistent with the traditional suzerain pattern of the previous millenium.

In the light of these basic patterns of Vietnamese communist international political solidarity with the Soviet Union and China, it is difficult to be skeptical of the claim of the Vietnamese communist leadership that "proletarian internationalism" has been one of their deeply held values. The Vietnamese Communist Party had been nurtured on its solidarity with the Communist Party of the Soviet Union and the Chinese Communist Party. "Proletarian internationalism"—the unshakeable solidarity of Marxist-Leninist parties in the common struggle against "imperialism"—was part of the formative Comintern political culture of Vietnamese communism. And proletarian internationalism had helped the Vietnamese communists to achieve political power in the northern half of Vietnam. On the basis of their past experience, they concluded that it would be the proletarian internationalist outlooks of the Soviet Union and China that would enable them to achieve victory in South Vietnam.

That is why the break between the two "fraternal parties," far from being relished by the Vietnamese communists, was not something they were happy with or wished to encourage. Fundamental political antagonism between Marxist-Leninist parties was not a phenomenon that the Vietnamese communists were capable of understanding fully.

Up until 1968 the Vietnamese Communist Party's advocacy of proletarian internationalism could not be separated easily from the party's quest for political power as an explanation of its alignment in the Sino-Soviet conflict. The imperatives of the quest for power required that they maintain good relations with anyone who might willingly provide them with the economic and military aid that could sustain their ultimate victory. Hanoi's tilt to China in 1963–64 could be interpreted as a reaction against Khrushchev's abandonment of the Vietnamese communist cause, although it was also a valid critique from a Marxist-Leninist perspective of his general compromise of the worldwide struggle against imperialism.

Similarly, the VCP's shift to neutrality in 1965 followed immediately after the new interest shown by the Soviets in the Vietnamese issue, and the new Soviet aid offers that accompanied it. During this period there is no way of distinguishing the Vietnamese alignment in terms of the ideological commitment to anti-imperialist struggle rather than in terms of Hanoi's power-based orientation toward maximizing external aid. Self-interest and ideological values were again in harmony.

But there are certain distinctive patterns of thought and attitude manifested in the Vietnamese communist political stands. They included a rigidly Manicheaen view of the world that followed the Stalinist doctrine that the world was divided into two camps: the "camp of peace and socialism" and "the camp of war and imperialism." Those who attempted to challenge that crude bipolar view from within the international communist movement— such as Tito in Yugoslavia—were denounced as agents of imperialism. Moreover, once Vietnam had decided to identify itself with the Chinese line and against the Soviet line on international affairs, those within the party who had been associated with the Soviet Union were purged and sent to prison as "revisionists." This was in spite of the fact, especially in the case of General Giap's aides, that they had long been valuable members and servants of the party. More important, it was in spite of the fact that all of the purged military officers would otherwise have been considered crucial resources for Hanoi's impending escalation of the military struggle in South Vietnam.

This behavior on the part of the Vietnamese leaders suggests that a highly ideological and paranoid thinking about political life is at the core of Vietnamese communist politcal culture. Their thinking and approach to political life was less extreme in degree, but not in kind, from the thinking and political approaches of Stalin and Mao.

In the bigger picture, the Vietnamese choice of allies and adversaries in international affairs was a product of their political values; it was not reducible to any simple evaluation of how alliances within the international or regional balance of power would affect their national security. Moreover, their choice of how to deal with serious political conflicts among their allies reflected their political culture's value of "proletarian internationalist" unity among Marxist-Leninist states, not any Realist judgment of how exploitation of differences among allies might enhance their national security or power.

CHAPTER SIX

North Vietnam's Tilt Toward the Soviet Union, 1968–75

In November 1978 the Soviet Union and the Socialist Republic of Vietnam signed a Treaty of Friendship and Cooperation. Following upon a series of events, especially the admission of Vietnam into Comecon the previous June, this treaty was the culmination of the gradual integration of Vietnam into the Soviet bloc. Yet prior to 1978 no Western academic specialist had perceived any Vietnamese communist alignment with the Soviet Union.[1]

The failure of the Western experts to detect a shift in the Vietnamese position and their complacent reiteration of a view of Hanoi's foreign policy as equidistant between Moscow and Beijing reflect a failure to carefully examine and interpret all of the relevant evidence. In this case the relevant evidence is the record of where the Vietnamese communists have stood on the issues that have divided the Soviet Union and China.

I have chosen to look at such issues from the years 1968–75. They are policy issues of contention between the USSR and the PRC in which neither the national security nor the economic well-being of the Vietnamese communist state were affected by the outcome. A communist party's stand on any single issue alone does not provide evidence of alignment in the Sino-Soviet dispute. Only a *sequence* of stands indicates either alignment or independence. The issues discussed are ones about which the VCP and mass media of the Democratic Republic of Vietnam made public statements of attitude. The phrase "statements of attitude" is crucial, because on many issues of contention between the Soviet Union and China, third communist parties have utilized one of their alternative options: mere factual reporting of events, reporting the views of both sides, or reporting nothing. On many issues of contention between the USSR and the PRC, the national security interests and economic well-being of third parties were not at stake. This is why these options have always been salient ones for communist parties wishing to preserve their political independence.

The issues chosen for examination are: the Soviet invasion of Czechoslovakia (1968), the Soviet-West German détente (1970), the attempted coup d'état in the Sudan (1971), the military coup and political revolution in Portugal (1974–75), and the civil war in Angola (1975). On all of these issues, the Vietnamese took the Soviet line. I will then identify briefly the important international issues on which Hanoi did not take a stand. I will also consider the temporary interruption of this tilt caused by President Nixon's visit to Moscow in 1972. Finally, I will try to explain the Vietnamese communist decision to tilt to the Soviet Union, after conducting a critical evaluation of possible alternative explanations.

EVIDENCE OF NORTH VIETNAM'S TILT TOWARD THE SOVIET UNION

The Soviet Invasion of Czechoslovakia, 1968

The Soviet Union's invasion of Czechoslovakia in August 1968 was a landmark event in international relations, and particularly in international communist relations.[2] Almost a decade after the Chinese had begun their challenge to Soviet authority within the communist world, it provided a clear demonstration of Soviet willingness to use military force to defend its imperial authority. The Czechoslovakian Communist Party in January 1968 had begun a reform program that involved dismantling some of the Soviet-type political and social institutions that had existed since 1948. But at no time did the Czechoslovakian leaders suggest that they might withdraw from the Warsaw Pact.[3] Thus their liberal reforms were not a military problem but rather an ideological challenge to the legitimacy of the Soviet Leninist political model.

To the Chinese communists the Soviet action was the behavior of a "gang of social imperialists and social fascists."[4] But China was not the only communist state to denounce the Soviet-led invasion. So too did China's ally, Albania, and the genuinely independent communist states of Romania and Yugoslavia.

But not North Vietnam. Throughout the pre-invasion crisis the Hanoi media had not reported Soviet-Czechoslovak tensions. Their first admission of such came the day after the invasion began:

Since January of this year the reactionary forces in Czechoslovakia have increased their antisocialist activities, seriously threatening the fruit of the revolution in Czechoslovakia and creating a danger for the regime and state structures of the Socialist Republic of Czecholovakia, a success of the socialist camp. . . .

Recently, these counterrevolutionary and antisocialist elements in Czechoslovakia have continued to increase their hostile actions, thereby making the faithful and firm members of the Czech Communist Party and political workers of the Socialist Republic of Czechoslovakia adopt countermeasures by requesting the armed forces of the USSR and allies to help protect their socialist regime and state.

To this noble end, on the morning of 21 August, 1968, the fighters of the armed forces of the USSR and its allies Bulgaria, Hungary, GDR, and Poland moved into Czech territory.[5]

On the following day both Hanoi dailies, *Nhan Dan* and *Quan Doi Nhan Dan*, reproduced on their front pages the Soviet news agency TASS statement preceded by the introduction quoted above.[6] On August 26 the newspapers of the DRV published the text of a *Pravda* article titled "The Defense of Socialism, the Supreme Internationalist Duty."[7]

The Soviet-German Détente, 1970

The treaty signed by the Soviet Union and the Federal Republic of Germany (FRG) on August 12, 1970, was the first manifestation of a purported détente between the Soviet Union and the West. Though the culmination of a series of steps undertaken by the FRG under the rubric of *Ostpolitik*, it was also the beginning of a series of initiatives undertaken by the Soviet Union. The treaty included recognition of the inviolability of all borders of the then current states of Europe, East and West; agreement that both sides would settle future disputes by peaceful means; and a resolution to improve and extend economic and scientific cooperation.[8]

The Soviet Union publicly interpreted the treaty as deriving from a Leninist view of international affairs and from a belief in peaceful coexistence between communist and noncommunist states.[9] The Soviets also spoke of the goodwill of the European states.[10]

The Chinese response to the treaty came in the *People's Daily*:

It is a monstrous fraud to cover up the aggressive features of Soviet revisionist social-imperialism and West German militarism with the cloak of "peace." It is also a component part of the monstrous "global Munich" scheme which

Soviet revisionism and U.S. imperialism, collaborating and contending with each other, are energetically putting into effect to divide the spheres of influence in Europe.[11]

Although European political events have no direct bearing on Vietnam's security, the Vietnamese communists have not hesitated to express their views on such events. In early 1970 Hanoi began denouncing *Ostpolitik* as an illusionary attempt to seduce Eastern Europe into accepting West German domination.[12] Hanoi considered *Ostpolitik* as part of the "global strategy of the US imperialists," which was doomed to fail.

This Vietnamese analysis of *Ostpolitik* would appear to have more in common with the Chinese than the Soviet position. Though the Vietnamese did not regard the Soviet Union as a "social imperialist aggressor," their view of the western democracies was as jaundiced as China's at that time. Yet the Vietnamese chose to express support for the Treaty with little delay. *Nhan Dan* wrote:

> But in view of the deep changes favorable to the revolution that have occurred in the world balance of forces . . . in view of the continuous growth of the Soviet Union and the other socialist countries, the all-round development of the German Democratic Republic and its ever-higher international position, in view of the solidarity of the socialist country members of the Warsaw Treaty, and also as a result of the failure of the Kiesinger government's new *Ostpolitik*, the Willy Brandt administration has had to sign the . . . treaty.
>
> This is a blow dealt at the ambitions of the bellicose and revanchist forces in West Germany.[13]

Note that the affirmation of the treaty by the Vietnamese was from a different perspective from that of the Soviets. Hanoi made no reference to the "Leninist principle of peaceful coexistence," but instead saw the Treaty as the outcome of a struggle in which the *Ostpolitik* of West Germany had failed. No reference was made to any mutual benefits of the Treaty, nor to the goodwill of FRG leaders. On the contrary, Hanoi's view of the FRG was laced with suspicion.[14] It implied here that the Soviet Union shared its suspicion of German motives. But the Soviets' public utterances did not indicate any concern for German deception. Rather, they praised West German leaders for their "common sense" and "realism." It appears that Hanoi was supporting the Soviet position in spite of its own ideological instincts on this issue.

The Attempted Communist Coup in the Sudan, 1971

The Sudan, a former British colony, had been ruled by a group of radical military officers, led by Colonel Ja'afar el-Nimeiri, since May 1969. Nimeiri made a deal with Sudan's Communist Party, offering its members positions of power in exchange for their support.[15] The communists took advantage of this to penetrate trade unions, universities, and the armed forces. But in late 1970 Nimeiri turned against them.[16] The communists reacted. On July 19, rebel troops and Sudanese communist leaders seized power in a coup. However, three days later Nimeiri was back in a countercoup. The coup ringleaders were arrested and many were executed. The pro-Moscow Sudanese Communist Party was severely set back.

The Soviet Union had been an important patron of the Sudanese government, especially during Nimeiri's rule. But immediately after the coup, TASS summarized the putschists' statements and reported public elation with the new regime.[17] The next day TASS reported an article expressing sympathy for the coup.[18] On July 22 TASS reported the countercoup by pro-Nimeiri army units.[19] Subsequently, Moscow campaigned against the executions of Sudanese communists.[20] The Soviets stopped all aid and most of its commercial dealings. It halted delivery of spare parts for the Sudan's Soviet-made military equipment.[21] But by mid-August, desiring to mend relations, Moscow slowed its propaganda campaign.

The Chinese government had maintained good relations with all the post-independence Sudanese governments.[22] For days after the coup, China's media said nothing. Only five days after Nimeiri's restoration did Beijing report it. The putschists were labeled a "coup clique."[23] There was no mention of executions. In October Zhou Enlai congratulated Nimeiri on his "election" as president, and in December Zhou congratulated the Sudan for having successfully smashed a "foreign subversive plot."[24]

The Sudan has never been an area of traditional concern for Vietnamese diplomacy. But North Vietnam followed the Soviet position there. It recognized the Sudanese government of Nimeiri shortly after his 1969 coup, but it showed little interest in the region prior to the coup and the countercoup of 1971. After Nimeiri's restoration and the first repressions, a *Nhan Dan* article denounced "the massacre and persecution of leaders of the Communist Party and trade unions, and other patriots in Sudan."[25] A *Nhan Dan* editorial expressed sympathy for the putschists.[26] The army paper and other party-run organizations issued similar protests.[27]

Military Coup and Revolution in Portugal, 1974–75

In early 1974 Portugal experienced political upheaval that thrust it into the world spotlight. On April 25, 1974, a group of Portuguese military officers, who were members of an underground political organization known as the Armed Forces Movement (AFM), overthrew the dictatorship of Marcelo Caetano. An AFM junta subsequently assumed power. The uneasy AFM coalition soon split into a conservative-to-liberal coalition and a radical coalition, which included supporters of the Moscow-aligned Portuguese Communist Party (PCP).[28] But as the totalitarian ambitions of the PCP became more obvious, many AFM members changed their ideology and their political alliances over the next year and a half, as did many civilian politicians. During this time Portugal was in the grip of an intense power struggle between the factions of the AFM and their civilian political party allies. Its NATO membership and the outcome of its colonial wars in three African countries were at stake.

The Soviet Union in 1974 endorsed the alliance that united the Portuguese Socialist Party (PSP) and other left parties against the right.[29] But by February 1975 the Soviets were concerned about the Socialist Party's split with the PCP. *Pravda* attributed the PSP change to the influence of a "motley coalition" of "militant NATO circles" and Western European Social Democratic figures.[30] Soviet views were always indistinguishable from those of the PCP, which it funded.[31]

After the 1974 coup, China's initial interest was only in Portugal's Africa policy.[32] By June 1975 China began to describe Portugal as a place over which the superpowers were "locked in fierce contention." But it considered "Soviet social imperialism's covetousness for Portugal" the main source of conflict.[33] China supported European unity and independence in the face of "Soviet revisionism's expansionist move in Europe" and favored strengthening both NATO and the European Economic Community.[34]

Traditionally, Portuguese domestic politics had not been of interest to Vietnamese rulers. But North Vietnam developed a relationship with the PCP in the early 1970s. In 1973 a PCP delegation visited North Vietnam for nine days.[35] Hanoi cautiously welcomed the 1974 coup. Hanoi was interested in Lisbon's foreign policy, particularly in whether Lisbon would abandon its colonies and whether it would remain in "the aggressor NATO military bloc."[36] (This description of NATO identified North Vietnam as a supporter of the Warsaw Pact.) The Hanoi media closely followed the Portuguese leaders' statements on the future of its colonies.[37] They also welcomed the formation of a new government, which included the Communists and Socialists, as "a new step forward of the democratic and progressive forces in the country."[38] But as soon as the alliance between the Communists and Socialists had disintegrated, Hanoi rushed to defend the PCP.[39]

With the failure of a November 1975 uprising by radical Portuguese military officers and their subsequent arrests, the Vietnamese army paper, *Quan Doi Nhan Dan*, condemned the "brazen repression of the leftist forces in Portugal."[40] By 1976 Hanoi's commentaries had become even more anxious. The party daily claimed that "bourgeois and feudalist reactionary forces in Portugal" were conspiring to restore a regime even worse than the 50-year-old Salazar-Caetano regime. According to *Nhan Dan*: "To unite with the people and the militant communists of Portugal is our noble international duty."[41] The Vietnamese communist position on Portugal, which was manifested even before the collapse of the ancién regime, was thus unequivocally identical with the position of the Soviet Union.

The Struggle for Angola, 1975

The struggle for Angola provides a useful barometer of alignment in the Soviet-Chinese dispute, since it is one conflict where both the Soviet Union and China were involved in more than a diplomatic and symbolic way. In Angola both the Soviet Union and China were supplying arms and training to rival political forces.

From the early 1960s Portuguese colonial rule was challenged by three separate political movements engaged in a guerrilla insurgency. The Popular Movement for the Liberation of Angola (MPLA), whose leader was Agostino Neto, was the only movement led by Marxists and received military aid from the Soviet Union. The Front for the National Liberation of Angola (FNLA), led by Holden Roberto, was a client of Zaire but was also supported by China and North Korea.[42] The Union for the Total National Liberation of Angola (UNITA), led by Dr. Jonas Savimbi, received little external support before 1975, though Zambia and China initially had supported it.[43] From early 1974 the Organization of African Unity (OAU) supported a coalition government for independence. In January 1975 the three groups negotiated an agreement with Portugal. The Alvor agreement gave all three the status of "sole legitimate representatives of the people of Angola" and set the independence date at November 11, 1975.[44] But unity did not last. Once fighting began, international involvement accelerated, with the Cubans and the Soviets supporting the MPLA.

Angola is further from Vietnam than even the Sudan, and as irrelevant to the security concerns of any Vietnamese regime. Yet even before the outbreak of Angola's civil war, the Vietnamese communists had expressed interest in Angola's struggle. In February 1974 the Hanoi-controlled National Liberation Front of South Vietnam (NLFSV) celebrated the anniversary of the first military action by the MPLA in 1961.[45] With the Alvor agreement in January 1975, NLFSV leader Nguyen Huu Tho sent a message of "warmest greetings" to the leaders of all three parties.[46]

At the end of October 1975, *Nhan Dan* publicly committed itself to the MPLA. It denounced the "imperialist forces and South African racists" for intervention in Angolan affairs, charging them with neocolonialist objectives and with plans to "sow discord among the Angolan people."[47] The army paper ran a similiar editorial.[48] On November 12 Pham Van Dong sent a message to Neto informing him that the DRV recognized the People's Republic of Angola.[49] A week later the army paper denounced the MPLA's Angolan rivals.[50] During December 1975 Hanoi closely followed the debate in the United States over policy toward Angola. Hanoi's denunciations of the FNLA and UNITA were vitriolic.[51]

Issues That Hanoi Took No Stand On

During the time period under examination, the Vietnamese communists failed to attend the Conference of Communist and Workers Parties in Moscow in June 1969. That conference was preparatory for the Soviet announcement of a policy of détente with the West, and was an attempt to marshall support for that policy from the international communist movement. Absent from that conference among Asia's ruling parties were the Chinese and North Koreans, as well as the Vietnamese.[52]

The Vietnamese communists also failed to express support for the Soviet idea of a collective security arrangement in Asia. That proposal, floated by Brezhnev in June 1969, was an attempt by the Soviet Union to enhance its influence in Asia at the expense of China and the United States.[53]

In 1971 the war between India and Pakistan was the most violent international confrontation of the year. The Soviet Union strongly supported India while China strongly supported Pakistan. In the other international events that we have considered so far, the Soviet Union had been far more deeply involved in supporting one contending party than China had been on the other side. However, in the Indo-Pakistan war, the Soviets and Chinese were both heavily involved. For North Vietnam to have taken a side on the Indo-Pakistan war would have insulted and greatly antagonized the patron of the other side.

Finally, the Vietnamese communists took no public position on the ideological disputes raging between the Soviet Union and China. This is despite the fact that in 1963 they had issued proclamations jointly with the Chinese denouncing "revisionism," which was a Chinese code word for Khrushchev's policies.

This suggests that the Vietnamese communists were supporting the Soviet position on international issues where they thought that they were not placing themselves in direct confrontation with China. Hanoi thought that this strategy would not put its Chinese aid in jeopardy. But as we will see, Hanoi was wrong.

The timing of the Vietnamese communist tilt to the Soviet Union, and the rationale that I have suggested, is corroborated by the former justice minister of the Provisional Revolutionary Government of South Vietnam, Truong Nhu Tang:

> I knew that the Party had already decided to ally itself with the Soviets. Movement in that direction had begun as far back as 1969, and Ho's death had opened the way to formalizing the decision. Though nothing like an open declaration could be expected while there was still a need for Chinese aid, in fact, by 1974 the bitter infighting had resulted in a clear victory for the pro-Soviet faction led by Secretary General Le Duan and Paris negotiator Le Duc Tho.[54]

The Tensions of 1972

Although in 1970 the Vietnamese had publicly supported Soviet détente with West Germany, in 1972 and 1973 they expressed a different view about détente between the United States and the major communist powers. According to a November 1973 editorial in *Quan Doi Nhan Dan*:

> Nixon's policy of détente is aimed at achieving the objective of dividing the socialist camp in an attempt to weaken the revolution. In implementing a policy of "détente" with the big countries, the U.S. imperialists are scheming to "con-

trol" the socialist countries in their movement to develop the revolutionary offensive, while the United States is continuing its limited counteroffensives against the revolutionary movement in various areas and small countries.[55]

According to the Soviet embassy in Hanoi, the Vietnamese leaders were most upset by the visit of U.S. President Richard Nixon to Moscow in May 1972. They had been told about the visit as far back as October 1971, during a visit to Hanoi by a Soviet delegation headed by President Nikolai Podgorny. According to the embassy, at that time the Vietnamese did not express any protest against the visit taking place. But as the time for the visit drew closer, the Vietnamese public stance changed.[56]

The Soviet embassy explained Hanoi's anxiety over Nixon's visit to Moscow as a response to the unfavorable consequences of his visit to China for the Vietnamese communists. That is, after Nixon visited Beijing, the United States broke off negotiations in Paris, mined the approaches to North Vietnamese seaports, and strengthened military pressure on Vietnam.[57] In fact, the American actions were a response to the North Vietnamese Easter offensive, not the Nixon visit to China. Nevertheless, Moscow was experiencing a negative reaction from Hanoi, based on Hanoi's fear that it would suffer from friendlier relations between its patrons and its main enemy. This reaction, in spite of being restrained, demanded a response.

Several high-level delegations were exchanged between Moscow and Hanoi in 1972 in order to try and smooth out the differences between the two countries. The most difficult period in the relationship was between April and September (during North Vietnam's Easter offensive). But by late 1972 Hanoi's attitude toward Moscow had improved.[58]

Ultimately it was U.S.-China rapprochement, not U.S.-Soviet détente that was perceived by the Vietnamese as treacherous.

EXPLAINING NORTH VIETNAM'S TILT TOWARD
THE SOVIET UNION

Any explanation of Vietnamese foreign policy behavior must take account of the complete record of the Vietnamese communists in power and, most especially, of their entire foreign policy record. It must also take account of the nature of the policy-making elite.

Until 1976 there had been a remarkable continuity in the Vietnamese communist party's leadership. The people who ruled the country at the time the decision to realign was made—the members of the Politburo—were people who had joined the party in the 1930s and had become members of the Central Executive Committee in the 1940s and 1950s. Except for the deaths of General Nguyen Chi Thanh in 1967 and Ho Chi Minh in 1969, the top leadership of the party from 1968 to 1975 was basically the same as it had been since the 1950s.[59] Thus any explanation of a decision to tilt toward Moscow in 1968–70 must take account of the fact that the decision was made by the same people who had made the decision to tilt toward Beijing in the early 1960s.

A second point that must be emphasized is the relevant time frame for any explanation. In the previous section it was suggested that the initial decision to tilt was made between 1968 and 1970. Thus anything that happened after 1970 could not be an initial cause.

However, we should not be crippled by the search for a single cause of the Vietnamese decision. Multiple causality is a normal feature of social and political action and the motives underlying political decision-making should be evaluated no differently. Moreover, multiple causation need not be simultaneous. Different relevant causes may follow each other over time, in which case they may either consolidate or strengthen the already existing outcome—a political decision.

Finally, a note of scholarly caution. After the open rupture between the Socialist Republic of Vietnam and the People's Republic of China in 1978, culminating in the Chinese invasion of 1979, there had been an outpouring of statements from both sides about the origins of their political dispute.[60] It would be very foolish to accept uncritically the contents of these statements at face value. The primary purpose of these statements is propagandistic—to provide a political justification for the actions of the side that is making the statement. Their factual content may or may not be true. We should have independent evidence before believing any factual claims, unless the factual claim serves no obvious propaganda purpose.

Alternative Explanations of Hanoi's Tilt: A Critique

Since, as was pointed out at the beginning of this chapter, no other Western scholar had discerned the Vietnamese tilt toward the Soviet Union as having taken place during the 1968–70 period, so obviously no Western scholar has ever tried to explain the Vietnamese tilt. Thus, before presenting my own explanation, I wish to consider alternative explanations of Vietnamese behavior that could conceivably be offered. These hypothetical explanations would be: a Vietnamese national security need to counterbalance China, a Vietnamese national security need based upon greater dependency on Soviet aid, and a traditional Vietnamese national antipathy toward China.

National Security: The Need to Counterbalance China

China is a giant neighbor that occupied Vietnam for over a thousand years. China has invaded Vietnam many times in the past. The Soviet Union, by contrast, is a country that is far away, that has never before invaded and occupied Vietnam, and that for purely logistical reasons, could not have done so easily even under a stable expansionist regime. By tilting toward the Soviet Union, it could be argued, the Vietnamese communists were providing a political and military counterweight to Vietnam's northern neighbor, and thus preserving Vietnam's independence.

But the need for a counterbalance does not require a tilt toward another power. All it requires is a comparably close relationship with another power. In fact, even the word "counterbalance" implies a rough equality of relative power relationship of the subject with two other rival powers. But by tilting, Hanoi was abandoning the concept of balance.

Furthermore, during the relevant time period under discussion, 1968–75, China was anything but threatening to North Vietnam. On the contrary, it was very supportive of North Vietnam economically, militarily, and politically. The main threat to North Vietnam came from the United States, and dealing with that real threat, of which Hanoi was well aware, required good relations with China. Tilting toward China's main enemy during those years could have been anticipated as eliciting China's hostility and weakening China's much needed support. In fact, this is precisely what happened.

National Security: Greater Dependency on Soviet Aid

The second of the potential national security arguments would point to the disparity in aid North Vietnam received from the Soviet Union and China after 1965. The argument would be that North Vietnam received greater amounts of aid from the Soviet Union after 1965, including most of its heavy weapons, such as tanks, long-range artillery, and the surface-to-air missiles that ringed Hanoi and Haiphong. Without these Soviet weapons, which China could not supply, North Vietnam would have been unable to resist the United States Air Force, let alone win a total victory over the South Vietnamese army in 1975.

Although the factual points raised here are correct, the argument they are attempting to sustain is not very convincing. For although North Vietnam was dependent upon Soviet supplies, it was dependent upon Chinese supplies as well. China did not supply heavy weapons. But it did supply rice to a food-deficient northern population. Without Chinese rice shipments, the civilian population that undertook Hanoi's logistical and economic support work would have been physically handicapped in its activities and probably its morale. China also supplied agricultural experts, engineers, and road and bridge repair teams; this assistance was vital to the Vietnamese communist war effort. Finally, many of the light weapons that were used by North Vietnam were manufactured and supplied by China.[61] Therefore, while the Vietnamese were more dependent quantitatively upon the Soviet Union than upon the People's Republic of China, it did not mean they were more dependent qualitatively.

Nor should there have been any resentment or ingratitude by the Vietnamese because China was giving quantitatively less aid than the Soviet Union. The Vietnamese communists knew that China was giving within the framework of its economic capacity, which was much smaller than that of the Soviet Union. Furthermore, why should a greater quantitative dependence upon one country rather than upon another translate into political alignment with the former? Rationality suggests that one does not alienate one important source of aid by lining up with that supplier's enemy. The essence of a strategy of maximizing external support is to maintain the competitive interest of all outsiders, playing them off against each other rather than making any of them feel rejected.

Another point worth noting is that in the first years after Hanoi began to tilt toward the Soviet Union, China actually increased its aid. Between 1970 and 1971, according to secret Soviet estimates, Chinese economic and military aid rose from 235 million rubles to 360 million rubles. This was an increase not only in absolute terms but also in proportional terms. Owing to a decrease in the Soviet Union's aid over that period, Chinese aid as a proportion of all aid from socialist countries increased from 34 to 47 percent during those years.[62] In 1972 the amount of Chinese aid rose again to approximately 400 million rubles.[63] Because Soviet aid also rose during that year, the Chinese proportion of all aid from socialist countries may have dropped to around 39 percent, though the Soviets acknowledge that their figures on Chinese aid may be incomplete.[64] But the point is that actual Chinese aid rose and was a highly significant percentage of the total.

The Vietnamese communists admitted these facts in 1979, the year after their relations with China went sour.

> In 1968, protesting Vietnam's negotiation with the United States, the Chinese leaders reduced the amount of aid to Vietnam. In 1971 and 1972, in a bid to drag Vietnam into Beijing's trend of agreement with the United States, they gave Vietnam much larger amounts of aid than in the previous years. This was also a trick to cover their betrayal and soothe the Vietnamese people's indignation.[65]

The aid increase was a sufficiently important fact that the Vietnamese leaders felt the need to explain it away. At the same time they were emphasizing how economic considerations could not determine their foreign policy.

Traditional Nationalism: Antipathy Toward China

The first two arguments assumed that a certain degree of political rationality and strategic calculation influenced North Vietnam's decision to align with the Soviets. A different argument is that as a result of centuries of history, the Vietnamese have a deeply rooted and compulsive desire to be independent of China. This desire, which is the expression of Vietnamese nationalism, operates like all tradition-bound behavior, which is to say, without regard for calculable consequences.

The problem with this argument is that Vietnamese behavior has never been that consistently anti-Chinese. Before the arrival of French colonialism, Vietnamese social and political institutions were modeled upon those of China, even if the tranfer wasn't total and complete.[66] In the rural areas most of these institutions persisted under colonial rule. The Vietnamese communists' main nationalist rival in the late 1920s and early 1930s, the Viet Nam Quoc Dan Dang (VNQDD), was modeled on the Chinese Kuomintang.

As we saw in the previous chapter, the Vietnamese communists were supported for many years in political training and military logistics by the Chinese communists. Furthermore, they were also permanently influenced by the Chinese in their institutional structures and in their initial revolutionary policies, such as the Campaign Against Counterrevolutionaries, the Land Reform campaign, and the Hundred Flowers campaign during the 1950s. Ho Chi Minh wrote of the enormous debt of the Vietnamese communists to Mao Zedong and the Chinese communists.[67]

Of course, it can be argued that Vietnamese nationalism is a nation-state political nationalism rather than a cultural nationalism, and expresses itself in the desire for national political independence from China. But the fact is that for one thousand years after Vietnam's liberation from Chinese occupation, the Vietnamese emperors entered into a tributary relationship of subordination to China.[68] Deference, not overt hostility, was the traditional pattern of Vietnamese diplomatic relations with China. We should remember that both communist parties previously proclaimed their political intimacy as being "like lips and teeth." Moreover, as we have seen, Hanoi and Beijing once pursued an integrated foreign policy, which was opposed to the line of the Soviet Union. Finally, North Vietnam's political independence from China was at risk neither when they were close to China nor when the decision to tilt toward the Soviet Union was made.

In other words, the record of history suggests that the Vietnamese might just as well have aligned themselves with China as against it, and nationalism is either not decisive in determining Vietnamese communist foreign policy, or else is not automatically directed against China. And even if nationalism has been a factor during the time period we are discussing, the North Vietnamese had a quite sufficient enemy to focus on in the form of the United States.

Explaining Vietnam's Decision

There is no single factor that can adequately explain North Vietnam's tilt toward the Soviet Union at the time that it happened. The explanation that I would provide is a multicausal one. It consists of three distinct aspects of China's domestic and foreign policies that had alienated the North Vietnamese leaders during the period 1969–71. These three factors are Vietnamese communism's ideological "centrism," which rejected the radical left policies of China's Cultural Revolution; Vietnamese communist "internationalism," which rejected the schismatic attitude of Mao toward the international communist movement; and Vietnamese communist distrust of China's strategic realignment toward the United States in order to counter what China's communist leaders perceived to be the threat of the Soviet Union. The first two of these three factors can only be understood in the context of Vietnamese political culture.

Vietnamese Communist Ideological "Centrism": Rejecting China's Great Proletarian Cultural Revolution

The foundation of Vietnamese communist ideology is Marxism-Leninism, an ideology that possesses a quasi-religious quality within the party. According to Party Secretary Le Duan:

> The light of our age, the light of Marxism-Leninism, illuminating mankind's path to progress, is becoming increasingly brighter. It reached the working class and working people of Vietnam immediately after the Great October Socialist Revolution. With emotion, enthusiasm, and joy, the dear and much respected leader and teacher of the Vietnamese revolution, Comrade Ho Chi Minh, saw this wonderful light of all conquering Leninism for the first time half a century ago! For many centuries Vietnam was in the gloom of night, and only in our age has it been illuminated by the bright ray of the morning dawn. From this time, advancing along the path of national liberation, the Vietnamese people have believed in Leninism more and more and have understood more clearly with every day that Lenin is eternally alive, not only in the hearts of the Soviet people, but also the peoples of the whole world.[69]

Yet like all great world religions and chiliastic political ideologies, Marxism-Leninism has been subjected to a certain degree of reinterpretation by some of its adherents. In the history of communism there have been two main deviations from orthodoxy in domestic policy. The deviation of the right has been in the direction of allowing cultural pluralism, as exemplified by the Eastern European reforms of the mid-1950s, the Prague Spring in Czechoslovakia in 1968, and Gorbachev's rule in the USSR. Communist critics of this approach condemn it as "revisionism." The deviation of the left has been in the direction of accelerated campaigns for institutional collectivization and cultural monism, which involve a high degree of social violence. This deviation is exemplified by the "high tides" of Maoism in China during the late 1950s and late 1960s and by Pol Pot's rule in Cambodia. Communist critics of this approach dismiss it as "infantile leftism."

The Vietnamese communists have always rejected these right and left deviations and pursued their notion of centrist orthodoxy in their domestic policy. They also have not tolerated the pursuit of ideological deviations by others. This has inflamed their foreign policy, as we saw in the case of Czechoslovakia in 1968. It has also influenced their attitude toward China. In a 1971 secret report to a Vietnamese party plenum, secretariat member Hoang Anh stated: "With regard to China we are in agreement with the necessity of conducting a 'great proletarian cultural revolution,' but we are not in agreement with the methods of carrying it out.[70] Hoang Anh added that there were several Vietnamese party comrades who criticized the leadership for this policy. He was thereby indicating not only the existence of party factions, but also that the issue was a matter of some political gravity.

The Vietnamese leaders' ideological disagreement with Mao's Cultural

Revolution was probably insufficient by itself to have fundamentally changed the DRV's foreign policy course. Rather, it should be considered one element in Hanoi's thinking about Beijing.

Vietnamese Communist Internationalism Versus Maoist Schismatics

Another aspect of the Vietnamese interpretation of Leninism centers around the concept of world revolution, a phenomenon whose defining objective is the struggle against imperialism. The world revolution, according to a 1970 essay by Vietnamese leader Le Duan, consists of three components. The first is the world socialist system. The world socialist system then included China, as well as the Soviet Union and the other "fraternal socialist countries."[71] The second component of the world revolution is the national liberation movement. The third component is "the rapid, uninterrupted, and ubiquitous upsurge of the workers' movement in the developed capitalist countries."[72]

This internationalist ideology is deeply ingrained in the worldview of the Vietnamese communist leadership. According to this worldview, the struggle against imperialism is the primary objective of all true communists. Thus unity is a practical necessity.[73] Disunity within the socialist camp has always been attributed to the plotting of the imperialists, long before the détente era.[74] Ho Chi Minh's will purportedly stressed the need for international communist unity.[75] *Nhan Dan* cited Ho's alleged words: "Having dedicated my whole life to the cause of the revolution, the more I am proud to see the growth of the International Communist and Workers' Movement, the more deeply I am grieved at the current discord between the fraternal parties!"[76]

Given the assumptions behind the Vietnamese worldview, it follows that unity demands a single line for communists in international affairs. If so, then whose line—Moscow's or Beijing's? In 1963 the answer was Beijing. By 1970 it was Moscow. What was the common thread in the earlier pro-Chinese and the later pro-Soviet decisions? The militancy of the "anti-imperialist" posture of the two nations? Certainly in 1963 the Vietnamese saw the Chinese as more militant opponents of imperialism, at a time when Khrushchev was interested in limiting the Soviet global offensive in order to avoid direct confrontation with the United States. But in 1968–70, did the Vietnamese see the Soviets as the more militant opponents of imperialism at a time when China's leaders wanted to diminish their conflicts with the United States?

Probably not. Even as late as 1971, when its decision to tilt had already been made, nothing in Hanoi's public analyses of the global accommodations of 1968–71 intimated that the Chinese had been more profoundly seduced by imperialism than the Soviets. For example, in Hanoi's analysis of Nixon's policy, its concerns seemed equally if not more strongly directed at Soviet behavior than at Chinese behavior.[77] Thus their public analyses provided no reason for Hanoi's distrusting China more than the Soviet Union. But there were reasons. They have to do with the schismatic policy of the Chinese toward the international communist movement, especially during the Cultural Revolution, and the Hanoi leaders' reaction.

The Vietnamese had had their own direct experiences with China's Cultural Revolution. For example, some of the Chinese volunteers engaged in military and economic assistance to North Vietnam during the Cultural Revolution years propagated the gospel of Chairman Mao by handing out the Little Red Book to unreceptive Vietnamese cadres and peasants.[78] Furthermore, Red Guards held demonstrations outside the Vietnamese consulates in Canton, Kunming, and Nanning in 1968 to protest Hanoi's entering into peace negotiations with the United States. The consulate in Kunming was severely damaged.[79] What was important about this incident was not only the physical offense against a Vietnamese legation. Also important was the fact that, in the name of revolutionary purity, Beijing was trying to dissuade Hanoi from a tactical political course that had worked well for the Vietnamese party in the past. Here the two parties' differences over ideology and political tactics were intertwined.

But there was a largely ideological dimension to Vietnamese attitudes. Red Guard behavior in general—which had included physical attacks upon the British and Soviet embassies and the physical abuse of Soviet diplomats in China—was part of a pattern of "leftism" in Chinese foreign policy that must have at least irritated if not frightened the Vietnamese. The Vietnamese would have considered the Chinese as too militant, not too accommodating, in their general foreign policy line.

This amounts to the Vietnamese blaming the Chinese more than the Soviets for splitting the international communist movement and thus violating their "internationalist" values. In a secret report issued in 1971, Hoang Anh, a senior Vietnamese communist official, stated the matter indirectly: "[W]e do not think that the present leaders of the Soviet Union are revisionist and endanger the unity of the international communist and workers' movement."[80]

As has been made clear over and over again by the Vietnamese, they did not want to see a heightened competition between the major communist powers in order to exploit it for their own advantage. Rather, they have always worked toward reconciliation between their two contending patrons. As Hoang Anh stated in 1971: "A purpose of foreign policy activities in our time is to promote the restoration of unity of the international communist and workers' movement."[81] Given its own embrace of the Soviet line in international affairs, Hanoi wished to see China also embrace that Soviet line.

This thinking makes no sense in terms of the assumptions of realist international relations theory. It makes sense only in the context of Vietnamese communist political culture, which consisted of an entrenched Marxist-Leninist internationalist ideology. From the perspective of the Vietnamese communists, the Soviet line with regard to relations with the West ("the camp of war and imperialism") was sophisticated and steady, while the Chinese position was "infantile leftist". This does not mean that the Vietnamese communists were merely fervent ideologues who did not pursue their state interests. It does mean that they pursued their state interests within certain parameters defined by their ideological values.

China's Strategic Realignment

As I have argued earlier, one cannot rely upon the *post facto* statements of either the Vietnamese or Chinese in order to explain their alienation from each other. These statements have the primary function of serving propaganda objectives. Though the claims made may be true, they need to be verified independently. Fortunately, there is some independent evidence of one of the post-1978 claims made by the Vietnamese—the Vietnamese claim to have been unhappy with, in fact to have felt betrayed by, the Chinese rapprochement with the United States.

From 1970 until 1975 Prince Norodom Sihanouk was the chairman of the National United Front of Khmer and president of the Royal Government of National Unity of Cambodia, the political facades behind which the Khmers Rouges insurgency operated. Both of these organizations were supported by the North Vietnamese and the Chinese. Most of Sihanouk's time was spent resident in Beijing, though he also made several visits to Hanoi. Sihanouk met the Vietnamese and the Chinese leaders frequently during those years, as allies. He has recalled the first manifestation that he observed, albeit indirectly, of Vietnamese anger with China:

Zhou Enlai, after signing the Shanghai agreement with Nixon [in 1972] came to Hanoi. And at that time I was in Hanoi also. . . . Zhou Enlai seemed very sad after his discussion with the Hanoi leadership. Because already in 1972 there was a crisis between Hanoi and Beijing, because of the rapprochement of China with the U.S.A. . . . I met Zhou Enlai after lengthy discussions between Zhou Enlai and the leaders of Hanoi. . . . Zhou Enlai was very tense. He used to be very charming, very cheerful. But after [discussions with the North Vietnamese] he told me he had to give explanations about the agreement with the U.S.A. . . . It seemed to me that he was not very successful, that he could not persuade the North Vietnamese to be satisfied.[82]

In 1973 Sihanouk visited Hanoi, where the Vietnamese leaders told him directly of their dismay with Chinese policy:

For instance, Vo Nguyen Giap told me that "the Chinese we cannot trust. . . . [T]hey told us that we have to be hostile to the Japanese militarism, and now the Chinese . . . have decided to be friends with Japan. . . . The Chinese, now they want to have a rapprochement with the West and so on." So they told me they were not very satisfied with the Chinese approach to the West.[83]

Indeed, it was not just China's rapprochement with Hanoi's direct enemy, the United States, but also China's rapprochement with the West in general, which upset the Vietnamese. This supports the view that the Leninist ideological construct of imperialism was central to the Hanoi leaders' values and choices in international affairs. This motivation behind the Vietnamese communist alienation from the Chinese was also asserted by Truong Nhu Tang, former minister of justice of the PRGSV.[84]

The Chinese rapprochement with the West was not the sole or even the initial cause of North Vietnam's alienation from China. Rather, it exacerbated preexisting Hanoi-Beijing tensions that had other causes and reinforced Hanoi's previous decision to tilt toward Moscow.

Yet there is a problem with this explanation as it now stands. For many years already the Soviet Union had enjoyed a closer relationship with the Western powers, including the United States, than China had. The year of the Shanghai communiqué was also the year of the highpoint of the period of détente in the Soviet-U.S. relationship. Major agreements between the United States and the Soviet Union were signed in that year and after. The Vietnamese did express concern about the détente policy at that time.[85]

Also, China's relationship with the United States was at that time much less developed than the Soviet relationship with the United States. China was still moving out of its total diplomatic isolation in the years 1969–72. It was not even granted full diplomatic recognition by the United States until December 1978. Why should the Vietnamese communists have been more worried about the U.S.-China relationship than the U.S.-Soviet relationship?

A partial answer is provided by Truong Nhu Tang. He has pointed to the Vietnamese communists' distinction between "compromise with principles" and "compromise without principles." The distinction will be familiar to readers of Lenin's writings. Vietnamese political theoreticians invoked Lenin's maxims in 1972:

> The revolutionary struggle remains a protracted, difficult, and complicated undertaking. There is a time for us to advance, but there is also a time for us to step backward temporarily in order to advance more steadily later. . . . For this reason . . . sometimes we must accept a certain agreement with the enemy which must be essentially based on a revolutionary stand, that is, aimed at weakening his forces and increasing our forces. Such an agreement is one in principle and it is basically different from the unprincipled agreement of opportunism.[86]

The Vietnamese saw the Soviet relationship with the West as cunning and strategically sound from an orthodox communist perspective. The Vietnamese saw the Chinese rapprochement with the West as motivated by short-term national self-interest (and was thus a "betrayal"). The whole concept of the "Chinese betrayal" makes sense not by reference to North Vietnamese national security, but rather by reference to Vietnamese communist political culture. By 1972 the Chinese leaders regarded Soviet "social imperialism," not American or Western imperialism, as their main enemy. Still, the Beijing leaders were trying to reassure Hanoi of China's continuing support—not only by words but also by actually increasing China's level of material assistance. Yet these actions were insufficient for Hanoi. Their Manicheaen view of the world as being divided between "the camp of peace and socialism" and "the camp of war and imperialism" was fundamental. Thus, engaging in strategic compromises with imperialism amounted to a betrayal of the socialist camp. This was true even if the compromising party was continuing to aid members of the camp, as China was doing amply with Vietnam.

Political Elite Factionalism and Political Culture

None of this reasoning is inconsistent with the notion that the Vietnamese communist leadership contained political factions. There is substantial evidence from secret Vietnamese and Soviet documents contained in the archives of the former Communist Party of the Soviet Union, as well as from Vietnamese defectors, that the Hanoi leadership contained factions opposed on a number of issues, including Vietnamese relations with the Soviet Union and China. We have already noted how a shift in Vietnamese policy toward China during 1963 subsequently resulted in a purge of pro-Soviet North Vietnamese cadres and military officers.

During the 1970s Soviet analysts identified a pro-Chinese minority faction within the Hanoi leadership. The existence of such a faction, insofar as it represented an ethos and a worldview (tied to the political subculture of Maoism), may be considered as constituting an elite subculture.

The dissident faction within the Vietnamese communist party wanted an end to the Vietnamese leadership's criticism of the methods of the Chinese Cultural Revolution. They also wanted to see North Vietnam ask China to introduce its troops directly into the war against the United States and South Vietnam.[87] Interestingly, their line was not for a genuine neutrality between the Soviets and Chinese, but for a clear alignment with China.

Although this view was a minority view within the party, it was held by a sufficiently significant number of communist party leaders to incur the wrath of the party majority's spokesman. What this implies once again is that shared experience of history in the broadest sense (i.e., knowledge of centuries of Chinese-Vietnamese relations) and shared experience of geopolitical power realities does not result in a uniform reaction. This is contrary to what realists and exponents of "Vietnamese nationalism" as an explanatory key to Vietnamese foreign policy seem to believe. History, geography, and objective power realities are always filtered through the prisms of cultural and subcultural identities, as well as through prejudices created by the impact of personal experiences. That is why one group of Vietnamese communists could interpret the same international events and power arrangements during the 1960s and 1970s differently from another group, and could propose an alternative foreign policy.

The origins of each faction within the Vietnamese communist party and the reasons why one faction prevailed over another are puzzles that remain to be solved.[88] My own view, based upon secret Vietnamese documents, is that pro-Soviet and pro-Chinese factions competed for support from a neutral group by arguing over the "evidence" in terms of the common values of the leadership. But solving these puzzles goes beyond our task. Our main point is that the same situation can be interpreted differently by different members of a nation's political elite.

CONCLUSIONS

North Vietnam's tilt toward the Soviet Union makes little sense from the sole perspective of national security. China was not applying pressures that Hanoi needed to counter by tilting toward the Soviets. Simply by having a political, military, and economic relationship with the Soviet Union, Hanoi was countering Chinese pressures to conform to Beijing's wishes. By tilting, Hanoi was abandoning political balance. Nor did a greater volume of aid from the Soviet Union in the mid-1960s explain Hanoi's tilt. The Vietnamese communist war effort was dependent upon sizeable amounts of Chinese aid. From the standpoint of maximizing external aid, a deliberate Vietnamese policy of ideological-strategic neutrality between the Soviet Union and China made the best sense, while tilting to one side made no sense. Nor did Vietnamese nationalism dictate the tilt toward the Soviet Union. Vietnamese nationalism has never consistently determined a particular policy toward China. The Vietnamese communists, like other Vietnamese political leaders, have had politically intimate relations with the Chinese in the past. They have copied many aspects of Chinese political practice, even though they have rejected others. The tilt was the expression of a political alignment with one of two intensely rival powers, thus manifesting a global strategic preference.

As part of their decision to tilt toward the Soviet Union, the Vietnamese leaders had decided not to alienate the Chinese completely. They maintained formally correct relations not only on a government-to-government level but also on a party-to-party basis. This shows that the Vietnamese valued their ties with China.

But Hanoi's decision had dire consequences for what it judged to be its own vital interests. It dampened Beijing's enthusiasm for Hanoi's then primary strategic objective—the conquest of South Vietnam. And it ensured that Beijing would later view with suspicion and resolutely oppose another of Hanoi's long-term primary strategic objectives—the political domination of Cambodia.

Hanoi's decisions can best be explained with reference to its ideological values. Under pressure from both the Soviets and the Chinese to take sides in their doctrinal dispute, Hanoi's ideological repudiation of aspects of Maoist radicalism—in particular Mao's Cultural Revolutionary policies within China and abroad—caused an initial estrangement of Hanoi from Beijing. Hanoi's dismay with Beijing's later policy reversal toward rapprochement with the West consolidated its shift. Hanoi's interpretation of Chinese foreign policy as a malevolent betrayal of the "anti-imperialist struggle" came despite Beijing's promise of continued support and the delivery of increased material assistance to its desperate southern neighbor. Hanoi's criticism of Chinese foreign policy was also made in the context of an already established and more extensive Soviet détente with the West, and the United States in particular.

Thus Hanoi's decisions can best be explained with reference to the political culture of its political elite. Both the formal aspects of this revolutionary culture (its ideological precepts) and its informal aspects (its paranoid worldview) are vital to an understanding of the perceptions and values that guided Hanoi's foreign policy. They provided the cognitive and evaluative prisms that filtered and structured elite reactions to the objective political, military, and economic environment.

The existence of factionalism within the Vietnamese elite and the espousal of alternative foreign policy positions by these factions provides evidence of elite subcultures. It also provides additional evidence of the subjective nature of foreign policy judgment, in that different elite groups can interpret the same objective situation differently and make different policy choices.

This does not mean that Hanoi's leadership made policy without regard for considerations of national security, power, material well-being, and nationalist impulse. Rather, insofar as this leadership pursued such goals, it did so only without sacrificing its pursuit of other political values. Thus a broader concept of political culture, which includes but goes far beyond commonly employed explanatory concepts, is essential for explaining Vietnamese foreign policy.

CHAPTER SEVEN

The Collapse of Vietnamese-Chinese Relations

An examination of the objective military and economic situations of China and Vietnam in mid-1975 would not have led one to predict that either nation was interested in becoming embroiled in any further conflicts in Indochina. But as we have seen earlier, political decisions do not necessarily reflect objective military or economic conditions.

Vietnam's leaders did not want to be embroiled in conflict with China. Having just attained its final and most decisive military victory after thirty years of war, the Vietnamese leadership had decided to turn its attention to economic development. Long-standing border disputes were matters that should have been resolvable through peaceful negotiations between the two governments.

But there was a complicating factor in Vietnam's foreign policy. As we have seen earlier (Chapter 6), the Vietnamese communists had clearly indicated by the early 1970s that they were tilting toward the Soviet Union in their foreign policy "general line." This tilt persisted throughout the last five years of the Vietnam war. It involved many issues of foreign policy that were matters of contention between the Soviet Union and China. Although the tilt did not involve Hanoi's direct involvement with Moscow in its polemics against Beijing, nor Hanoi's open alignment with Moscow on the most incendiary issues of the Sino-Soviet dispute, it did involve alignment in several areas of contention in Western Europe and the Third World. Moreover, the Vietnamese had abandoned their former partial adherence to elements of Chinese military doctrine in favor of Soviet doctrine, and reequipped much of their armed forces from the Soviet arsenal. These were matters about which China could not have been expected to be indifferent.

Despite its unhappiness with the pro-Soviet drift of Vietnamese foreign policy, the Chinese leadership had reason to believe that, given the Vietnamese leadership's clearly stated desire for economic development, the carrot of Chinese economic assistance would be sufficient incentive to bring Vietnam back to its earlier position of neutrality in the Sino-Soviet dispute. Yet economic considerations would not determine the foreign policy of Vietnam or China.

China was traditionally the suzerain power in mainland Southeast Asia. It was geographically adjacent to Indochina, and had traditionally been treated deferentially by the rulers of the Indochinese states. China had supported North Vietnamese, Laotian, and Cambodian independence in 1954. Following the Phnom Penh coup d'état in March 1970, China had become the principle supplier of military, economic, and diplomatic aid to the Cambodian communist insurgency, initially in harmonious conjunction with the Vietnamese communists.

But since 1975 China had publicly thrown its support behind Democratic Kampuchea, which was independent of and increasingly in a self-initiated conflict with Vietnam. Although China was not inciting the Khmers Rouges' aggressiveness, it could not back away from its commitment to Cambodian independence without a loss of face. From the perspective of traditional Chinese culture this would be unacceptable.

Traditional status considerations were reinforced by very contemporary national security considerations. The enemy of Cambodian independence, Vietnam, was under the influence of China's main enemy, the Soviet Union. Thus the elimination of Cambodian independence would not only likely result in a complete loss of Chinese political influence in Indochina, it would also lead to the enhanced influence of China's main enemy.

Prior to 1978 there was nothing in the public statements of Vietnamese and Chinese leaders that indicated a serious and insoluble problem in relations between the two nations and their leaders. This is not to say that there were no public signs of underlying problems in the relationship, nor that the issues of contention between Vietnam and China were not serious. But the various underlying conflicts between the two nations were kept under control and not trumpeted about publicly, until the complex intertwining of events and issues further exacerbated relations, leading to a political and eventually a military confrontation.

INCIPIENT TENSIONS BETWEEN NORTH VIETNAM
AND CHINA: 1970

The expansion of the Vietnam War into Cambodia in 1970 presented an op-portunity for China to assert its leadership role vis-à-vis the Indochinese rev-olutionary movements through its patronage of the Cambodian insurgency. But any such Chinese ambition competed with Vietnamese ambitions, which by then operated within the perspective of Hanoi's recent reorientation away from Beijing and toward Moscow.

During Sihanouk's rule, China's relationship with Cambodia was always much warmer than Vietnam's. China, more than the Soviet Union, was seen by the Cambodian head of state as the guarantor of Cambodian indepen-dence against the pro-American Thais, and against Vietnamese of all politi-cal persuasions. Thus in the immediate postcoup weeks of 1970, when the self-exiled Sihanouk threw in his lot with Beijing, the stage was set for China to play a new leading role in the new Cambodian situation, and an enhanced role in Indochina generally. Yet Beijing was initially hesitant to take a clear stand.

During the weeks following the coup, the Chinese ambassador to Cam-bodia remained in Phnom Penh and the Cambodian ambassador to China, who switched his allegiance to Lon Nol, was allowed to remain in Beijing.[1] The new Cambodian republican leader, Lon Nol, claimed at the time that the Chinese had initially approached him and asked if his government would continue to allow China to use Cambodian territory to aid the North Viet-namese and Viet Cong, would continue to allow the Vietnamese communists to use Cambodia as a sanctuary, and would continue to provide propaganda support for these forces.[2] Only after Lon Nol refused did China break diplo-matic relations with Phnom Penh and give its complete support to Sihanouk.

On April 24, 1970, the Chinese government sponsored an Indochinese People's Summit Conference in Canton, which brought together the leaders of the three Indochinese communist insurgencies, the North Vietnamese, and Prince Sihanouk. The Cambodian prince chaired the meeting. However, no formal body was set up to coordinate the activities of the three revolu-tions. At that time the Chinese also floated the idea of establishing a "United Front of Struggle of the Peoples of China, Korea, Vietnam, Laos, and Cam-bodia." But this balloon never even got off the ground. Hanoi opposed such plans.

According to the Soviet ambassador in Hanoi, this was because the "leadership of the VWP understood in time the plan of Peking," in which "the role of conductor of Chinese interests and counterweight to the Vietnamese was assigned to N. Sihanouk."[3] This may be true, but it may also be a little more complicated than that. For Hanoi was the first advocate of Sihanouk's leadership of the Cambodian insurgency. Also, Hanoi did not know then that the Khmers Rouges leaders were pro-Beijing. And Beijing, in contrast with Moscow, soon began to support Hanoi's position in Cambodia. Thus the Cambodian situation was unlikely to have been a major source of Hanoi-Beijing tension during this period.

THE INITIAL DISCRIMINATION AGAINST ETHNIC CHINESE

The role of the ethnic Chinese residents of Vietnam has been an extremely complex one. As in other countries of Southeast Asia during the immediate postcolonial era, the question of the national loyalties of the ethnic Chinese became an important but controversial political issue. In the northern half of the country, the ethnic Chinese were made naturalized Vietnamese citizens in the mid-1950s, with the approval of the government of the PRC. In the noncommunist south, President Ngo Dinh Diem had forcibly naturalized the hundreds of thousands of ethnic Chinese residents during the late 1950s, without the approval of either the PRC or the Republic of China.

In the northern half of the country, with the completion of "socialist transformation" in the late 1950s, the majority of ethnic Chinese were employed as workers in mines, factories and ports, and as fishermen. A few thousand were engaged in small trade and family handicraft industries in Hanoi and Haiphong. Virtually none of the northern Chinese were peasants. The sociological profile of this group was, in Marxist terminology, primarily "proletarian."[4]

In South Vietnam the ethnic Chinese played a role much like that of their brethren in the rest of Southeast Asia, providing the core of the mercantile and financial capitalism of the nation. Ethnic Chinese controlled southern Vietnam's rice export trade, which flourished until the war expanded in the early 1960s. Many southern ethnic Chinese were small traders and even workers in light industries in Cholon, Saigon's Chinese district. But here the community structure tied them in closely with the Chinese big businessmen.

Back in the 1930s and 1940s, a genuine spirit of internationalism seemed to pervade relations between the Chinese and Vietnamese communist parties, highlighted by the two countries' mutually agreed policies toward ethnic Chinese joining the Vietnamese party.[5] However, the testimony of some who have subsequently defected to the west indicates that a subtle and covert campaign of discrimination was initiated against them in the early 1970s. For example, the wife of an ethnic Chinese artist has stated:

> My husband is Chinese, but I am ethnic Vietnamese. There were never any problems, or any real feeling of difference. Both of our families were happy enough about our marriage. It wasn't until 1970 that a bad feeling began to creep into things. That's when the first anti-Chinese campaign began. Whispering campaigns were started against the Chinese. At soccer games, fights began to break out between Vietnamese and Chinese in the crowds. You could feel the animosity.[6]

The discrimination was also reported by a senior cultural cadre named Han Vi, who was ethnic Chinese:

> After Ho Chi Minh died [September 1969] there were some signs of anti-Chinese feeling. I put them out of my mind, tried to suppress it. Tension between the ethnic Chinese and the government began in 1972. At least that was the year the campaign began. It was done covertly at first, disguised as an opportunity for certain groups of cadres to retire early. Anyone sixty or older was included—that meant all of them who were trained or heavily influenced by the Chinese. After the Paris Peace Agreement [January 27, 1973] they allowed people fifty-four and older to retire. The public rationale was to give them more time to enjoy themselves.[7]

Though these two accounts differ on the exact year that the campaign of discrimination began, they agree that it was in the early 1970s. This period was while North Vietnam was still at war with South Vietnam and the United States—victory in which war the Vietnamese communist leaders considered their most vital policy objective, and for which victory North Vietnam still depended upon China's support. Thus the decision to campaign against Vietnam's ethnic Chinese did not reflect instrumentally rational political judgment. Given what Hanoi regarded as its vital foreign policy goals, the decision was irrational. It is nevertheless intelligible in terms of Hanoi's recent tilt away from Beijing, taken in the context of the paranoid tendencies inherent in Vietnamese communist political culture. Estranged from Beijing over secondary foreign policy matters, Hanoi now imagined that all ethnic Chinese were hostile.

THE TERRITORIAL DISPUTES

There were three components of the territorial dispute between China and Vietnam. The first is the 797-mile-long land border between northern Vietnam and China's two southern provinces (Guangdong and Yunnan) and autonomous region (Guangxi). The second is the division of the water area of the Gulf of Tonkin (Beibu Gulf to China and Bac Bo Gulf to Vietnam), which is enclosed by Vietnam's northern coast and the Chinese island of Hainan. The third is the issue of sovereignty over two offshore island groups in the South China Sea, which are called the Paracels (Xisha in Chinese and Hoang Sa in Vietnamese) and the Spratlys (Nansha in Chinese and Truong Sa in Vietnamese).[8]

Of the three contested territories, the dispute over the offshore islands was the most significant. This was not only because of the two island groups' strategic location abreast the main sea-lanes between the Indian and Pacific Oceans but also because of their location in areas with rich undersea oil deposits. Claims to these islands were made by communist China and Vietnam (the French-created State of Vietnam) in 1951, and later during the 1950s and 1960s. But the two parties did not appear together at any international conference and no international adjudication took place.

In late January 1974 China clashed with South Vietnamese troops over the Paracel Islands and occupied them by force. In early February 1974 South Vietnamese forces occupied six islands of the Spratly group. In the first instance, the North Vietnamese leaders urged negotiation between what was their ostensible ally (China) and their enemy (South Vietnam). In the second instance, Hanoi said nothing, thereby giving tacit support to the action of Saigon.[9] Thus a territorial dispute between Beijing and Hanoi was implicit by 1974.

After the North Vietnamese conquest of South Vietnam in April 1975, the issue of the islands as well as the other territorial issues became matters of explicit contention between Hanoi and Beijing. During the period before and after the September 1975 visit of a high level Vietnamese delegation to China, both countries published maps or photographs that indicated their claims to the disputed islands. But during 1975–76 the disagreements were kept very low key.[10]

The issue of sovereignty over the disputed Spratly and Paracel Islands remained a point of contention between Hanoi and Beijing, as it was between each of those and Taipei and Manila, who also had claims to sovereignty. But there was no evidence that these issues were serious enough to constitute the basis for a fundamental split between Hanoi and Beijing.[11] In February 1977 a senior Hanoi official was reported to have told the *Far Eastern Economic Review* that Vietnam was patiently in waiting until the time when the island sovereignty dispute could ultimately be settled "between brothers."[12]

The way in which the two nations dealt with their territorial disputes was a function of the health of the relationship in general.

CHINA'S DISPLEASURE WITH NORTH VIETNAM'S
   FOREIGN POLICY

The Chinese had subtly indicated their grave displeasure with the Hanoi leaders during their private meetings even before the North Vietnamese victory over South Vietnam.[13] But the most serious private manifestation of tension between Vietnam and China came in a secret meeting between the leaders of the two parties five months after the war's end in September 1975. Details of this meeting and a subsequent report by Le Duan to the Vietnamese Politburo were never published, but an account of both was conveyed to the Soviets in October 1975.[14]

From September 22–28, 1975, a Vietnamese party-government delegation, headed by Le Duan, visited China. The Vietnamese, in their communications with the Soviets, indicated that their goal during the visit was to improve Vietnamese-Chinese relations. In particular, they wanted to assure the Chinese that Vietnamese relations with the Soviet Union and China would remain as before.[15]

This assurance apparently provided little comfort to Beijing. According to Hanoi the Chinese leaders "openly and officially" showed their dissatisfaction with the conduct of Vietnamese foreign policy, in particular in Vietnamese relations with the Soviet Union. Insofar as Vietnam continued this political line, it would not find support from China. Le Duan claimed that the visit enabled the Vietnamese leadership to show the Chinese "officially and openly" that the VWP stood steadfastly by its political platform, regardless of the Chinese reaction. If relations between the two parties should worsen, Le Duan argued, all the fault would lie with the Chinese.[16] At the same time, Le Duan noted, even if relations between the VWP and the CCP were to worsen in the future, the VWP would act in support of the principles of solidarity, mutual support, and unity of the world communist and workers' movement and the "unity of all socialist countries." It would not insult China over its activities.

Yet Le Duan's overall evaluation of the results of the visit was grim. In his own words, a difficult period in relations between the Vietnamese and Chinese parties had set in. Relations between the VWP and the CCP were in an "alarming, critical condition." That is why the VWP had to be careful, vigilant, and patient and do everything to avert a split between the two parties and countries.[17]

Le Duan noted that there was no serious discussion of important political questions of mutual interest. The Chinese indicated that they did not want to discuss such questions and the Vietnamese did not insist on such. Thus there was no published document or communiqué confirming the results of the visit. However, Le Duan reminded the members of the VWP Politburo, Vietnamese-Chinese discussions about the territorial water border of the Tonkin Gulf and the littoral continental shelf were due to commence at the beginning of October. The Vietnamese side intended to continue fishing on the shelf without waiting for the outcome of negotiations. But Le Duan felt that the negotiations would be an important indicator of the intentions of the Chinese leaders to develop relations with the Vietnamese in the future.

Le Duan's report demonstrated an alarm about the decline of relations between the two parties and countries. Despite this concern, the Vietnamese leader opposed making any concession on the issue of most concern to China—Vietnam's relations with the Soviet Union.

China had begun to demonstrate its displeasure in tangible material ways. China's assistance to North Vietnam declined rapidly during the second half of 1975. A number of departments of the DRV reported to the Soviet embassy that the amount of freight being unloaded off Chinese vessels in the port of Haiphong during that half year was only half of what it had been for the same period the previous year. Furthermore, at the beginning of 1976 China recalled several groups of its specialists from Vietnam and delayed work on a number of projects being built with Chinese aid.[18]

By early 1976 the Vietnamese leaders were telling the Soviets that they were very anxious about their relations with China. They particularly cited the lack of an agreement for long-term economic aid from China, and the failure of the Chinese to settle the disputed territorial problems, particularly over the Tonkin Gulf and the Paracel and Spratly Islands. Furthermore,

Hanoi leaders were especially anxious about the influence that Beijing was thought to have over the Chinese community in South Vietnam, whose activities were said to be "in conflict with the line of the revolutionary authorities." The Hanoi leaders claimed that they detected a connection between what they described as "the subversive appearances of the Maoists in Indochina" (a cryptic reference, possibly to the ideological orientation of the Cambodian communist leaders).[19]

These anxieties had led to repeated discussions of Vietnamese-Chinese relations at the highest level in the VWP's Central Committee. Yet in spite of this, the Hanoi leaders expressed to the Soviets their determination "not to withdraw from a principled political position," while at the same time attempting to "normalize relations with the PRC . . . on a state-to-state basis."[20]

How then, given the situation in early 1976, would the VWP repair relations with the Chinese party and avoid a total split? Hanoi's subsequent policies toward its ethnic Chinese minority and the thinking that inspired those policies suggested that the Hanoi leadership did not fully understand how to pursue that stated goal in a realistic or even rational way.

VIETNAM'S RESPONSE TO CHINA'S DISPLEASURE: A NEW
POLICY TOWARD VIETNAM'S ETHNIC CHINESE

According to a report issued by the Soviet embassy in Hanoi, the Soviets regarded the Chinese emigrants as the most important conduit for Chinese influence in Vietnam. And the Chinese embassy in Hanoi was seen by the Soviets as the main instrument for China's contact with the minority community. The Chinese embassy was said to periodically send propaganda literature to the ethnic Chinese community. It also organized "open door days," during which the embassy was said to conduct meetings of a propaganda character. Some of the ethnic Chinese community periodically visited China in order to meet with relatives there. This was said to be another means for the Chinese government to exert influence over the community. However, the Vietnamese authorities did not encourage these contacts and restricted access to the embassy grounds.[21]

In 1976 the Vietnamese government began a series of measures against its ethnic Chinese community. Among these measures was a campaign for substituting a single Vietnamese citizenship in place of the dual citizenship embraced by many ethnic Chinese.[22] By early 1978 those ethnic Chinese who evaded taking up Vietnamese citizenship were said to be subject to administrative measures. This involved deprivation of basic citizenship rights. For example, such people could not become members of the Communist Party of Vietnam, be appointed to high posts, enter the army, undertake private trade, or participate in elections.[23]

In 1976 the Vietnamese authorities also began closing a number of the parochial Chinese schools and prohibiting teaching subjects in the schools in the Chinese language. Chinese was to be taught on an equal footing with other foreign languages.[24] The third measure begun in 1976 was resettling ethnic Chinese among the ethnic Vietnamese population.[25] This included a slow process of evicting ethnic Chinese from the Cholon district of Ho Chi Minh City.[26] It also included evicting ethnic Chinese who lived along the Vietnamese-Chinese border. These were the biggest group of ethnic Chinese having contact, through means of visits or letters, with relatives on the Chinese side of the border. Their deportation to the so-called New Economic Zones deep inside the country seriously limited such contacts.[27] These ethnic Chinese were replaced along the Chinese border by civil and military settlements of Vietnamese.[28]

A report from the Soviet embassy in Hanoi outlined the bureaucratic measures that were also introduced to prevent the movement of ethnic Chinese abroad. In 1977 the Vietnamese authorities reduced the quotas of trips allowed for ethnic Chinese to visit relatives in the PRC. And temporary visits by ethnic Chinese to other countries practically ceased. However, the Vietnamese government was not simultaneously hampering migration of ethnic Chinese to other countries. According to the Soviet embassy, the Vietnamese government was moving toward allowing Chinese emigrants to other countries to transfer their wealth abroad at the time of final departure.[29]

All of these accumulated measures suggest that from 1976 on the Vietnamese communist leaders regarded the entire ethnic Chinese community as potentially disloyal and subversive. This is manifested in the Vietnamese leaders' simultaneous tolerance for some ethnic Chinese migration (a right denied to ordinary ethnic Vietnamese citizens) while restricting ethnic Chinese visits to China. The ethnic Chinese threat to the Vietnamese state was perceived as deriving from their contacts with China and the Chinese authorities. Other measures initiated by Hanoi confirm this interpretation.

The contacts of the Chinese embassy in Hanoi with the ethnic Chinese community in North Vietnam were severely restricted. The Vietnamese authorities also continued to delay a decision on the request of the PRC to open a consulate in Ho Chi Minh City. The Beijing newspaper *Renmin Ribao* was permitted for sale with great delay and only in small quantities. Thus the Soviet embassy, writing in October 1977, concluded that the opportunities for the Chinese embassy to engage in political agitation and propaganda were by then largely restricted to the Chinese embassy's photo window and the work of the Chinese economic and technical specialists in the SRV. However, the Soviet embassy also noted that in Hanoi the ethnic Chinese were still purchasing Chinese books and magazines through specialized bookstores, and that some Chinese diplomats had traveled to southern Vietnam in order to establish contact with the Chinese community in spite of restrictions imposed by the Vietnamese government.[30]

Beginning in 1976 efforts were undertaken by the Vietnamese communists to establish control over the organizational structures of the ethnic Chinese community. First, in the middle of 1976, a department was established within the Central Committee of the Vietnamese Communist Party to "work with the popular masses." Under the direction of the international department's head, Xuan Thuy, one of the new department's specific tasks was to take control of the activities of the ethnic Chinese and the leadership of their associations.[31]

The northern branch of the Association of Chinese Emigrants was already under the control of the party. In August 1976 a joint sitting of its Hanoi and Haiphong branches was held. At this meeting it was decided to attempt to form a unified organization that would merge the associations of the north and the south, and merge the various ethnic Chinese newspapers as well. Initially, the task of taking control of the newspapers made rapid progress. In September 1976 the southern newspaper *Tszefan Zhibao* ceased publication, and in January 1977 the same fate befell the newspaper of the Haiphong society of Chinese emigrants, *Quang Ninh*.

However, the southern Chinese associations were not given any forewarning of the decisions of the northern organizational meeting. This was because it was clear that the northern organizational leadership could not compel the southern Chinese to follow their wishes, and that any voluntary merger between northern and southern organizations would not result in dominance by the northerners. The southerners after all were unified and more numerous, and the existence of clan networks and financial ties enabled the southerners to strengthen the independence of the southern branch of the association. According to the Soviet embassy's October 1977 report, by the end of 1976 the activities of all ethnic Chinese societies and associations had practically ceased. No information was said to be available in newspapers about any measures of the ethnic Chinese societies, nor was there any notification of a planned magazine or newspaper of a combined association of Chinese emigrants.[32] However, an analysis in May 1978 by the Soviet military intelligence directorate, the GRU, described the two main associations—one in the north with a membership of 300,000 and one in the south with a membership of 2.7 million—as still in existence.[33]

Measures were undertaken by the Vietnamese authorities to try to exclude the ethnic Chinese from any political power. The Soviet embassy cited the results of elections to the people's councils in Vietnam during 1977 as evidence that "there is practically no participation of Chinese emigrants in the organs of state power." The only exception was said to be in the cases of district and communal people's councils.[34]

The final set of measures undertaken by the Vietnamese communists were in the economic realm. But they had a dual purpose—not only to break the independent economic power of the ethnic Chinese, but to destroy the institutional structures of capitalism and lay the foundations for a socialist economy in Vietnam. In 1976 the Vietnamese government undertook a series of measures for limiting private trade. This caused an influx of Chinese workers, especially youth, out of the private sector and into the state-controlled sector of the economy, particularly into industrial enterprises, mines, and ports. However, some ethnic Chinese in the north of the country continued to act in the sphere of trade, engaging in the resale of contraband goods from the PRC and in "speculative" trading with scarce goods from the south.[35] And the much stronger economic position of the ethnic Chinese business community in the south was not severely undermined at this stage.

The Vietnamese authorities also resorted to legal measures against the ethnic Chinese community. At the end of 1976, a special People's Tribunal was established to consider "the affairs of the criminal comprador bourgeoisie." It received substantial powers. The tribunal, according to a Soviet embassy analyst, "undertook energetic measures, nearly always unswervingly directed against the most prosperous part (basically Chinese) of the bourgeoisie in the south." Furthermore, as before, the authorities refused to allow the conscription of ethnic Chinese into the Vietnamese army, and refused to allow them to work at important state institutions.[36]

In 1977 the long-preferred term "Chinese emigrants" was being replaced everywhere in Vietnam by the term "Vietnamese of Chinese origin." This was in order to deflect the protests of Beijing against Hanoi's policies, which were traditionally justified as "defense of the Chinese compatriots overseas," and make such protests appear as interference in Vietnam's internal affairs.[37] It is very important to note that the entire gamut of policies against the ethnic Chinese community, outlined above, was undertaken in spite of the negative attitude of the Beijing leaders towards these measures. Moreover, in the opinion of the Soviet embassy analyst, "a harsh approach was revealed in this work, without any half measures or compromises."[38]

What this amounted to was a blatant repudiation of Beijing's concerns about Vietnamese policy. This stance would not be difficult to understand were it not for the stated interest of the Vietnamese communist leaders themselves in maintaining good relations with China and avoiding actions insulting to the Chinese leaders, as Le Duan had urged in late 1975. We should not forget that it was the Vietnamese leaders themselves who were continuing to emphasize the importance of securing a long-term economic aid agreement from China and of resolving the border disputes amicably. The Vietnamese leaders' belief that the entire ethnic Chinese community was a potential threat constituted nothing less than a paranoid attitude toward a highly differentiated and predominantly apolitical community. And the policy responses that this attitude elicited served only to undermine the major foreign policy objectives that the same Vietnamese leaders had determined for themselves. In other words, the policy measures introduced by Hanoi in 1976 toward the ethnic Chinese community, and continued through subsequent years, were objectively irrational from the perspective of Hanoi's fundamental foreign policy goals.

THE FOURTH VIETNAMESE PARTY CONGRESS AND HANOI'S CHINA POLICY

The Vietnamese communists held their Fourth Party Congress—their first after sixteen years of war—in December 1976. As with all party congresses the meeting served to ratify political decisions that had already been made by the higher echelons of the party leadership. The Chinese Communist Party did not break its custom of not sending delegations to foreign party congresses, even though a Chinese delegation had been present at the Vietnam party's Third Congress in 1960, and even though this time the Soviet Union sent a high level delegation led by Politburo member and chief Soviet ideologist Mikhail Suslov.[39] The Chinese informed the SRV Embassy in Beijing of its decision not to attend in advance.

Le Duan, in his conversation with Soviet ambassador Chaplin during November 1976, claimed that there were people in China who "are now expressing opinions against the orientation of the [Chinese ambassadorial] delegation in Hanoi." He noted, as if in support of this point, that the Chinese had sent the Vietnamese Workers' Party Central Committee a "long congratulatory telegram, in which was contained wishes for successes in the work of the Congress."[40]

It seems that Le Duan thought that Vietnam's problems with China were heavily rooted in the political outlook of the Chinese embassy in Hanoi. The Vietnamese leaders were acutely aware of, and deeply interested in the outcome of, the factional struggles in Beijing. But insofar as they thought that their problems with China could be solved by the ascendancy of one Chinese political faction over another, the Vietnamese were greatly misinformed (see next section).

During the Fourth Party Congress, the Hanoi leaders removed the most pro-Chinese elements from the leadership. This included most notably the dropping of Hoang Van Hoan, the former Vietnamese ambassador to China (1950–57) and a founding member of the Indochinese Communist Party, from the Politburo and Central Committee. (Hoan defected to China in 1979.) Among the others dropped from the Central Committee were Ngo Minh Loan, Ngo Thuyen, Nguyen Trong Vinh, and Ly Ban. These individuals also had all served in China, three as the DRV's ambassadors.[41] The demise of these figures could only have been interpreted in Beijing as a further and now overt repudiation of Chinese influence. Notwithstanding the demotion from alternate membership of the Central Committee of one former ambassador to the Soviet Union, the sackings of these prominent former ambassadors to China would have been interpreted as a further affirmation of Hanoi's desire to deepen its already close relations with the Soviet Union. Finally, given Beijing's earlier explicit expressions of concern about the pro-Soviet drift of Vietnamese foreign policy, Beijing may well have considered these new Vietnamese party actions as an insult to China by the Vietnamese leaders. Thus it was no accident that in February 1977 Beijing notified Hanoi that it was unable to provide any new economic aid.[42]

Again, given the importance the Vietnamese leaders attached to economic assistance from China, and their statement of the necessity of avoiding a split with their socialist patron, their behavior at the Fourth Party Congress would appear to be irrational from the perspective of stated material policy goals and national interests. The behavior only becomes intelligible (but not necessarily rational) in the context of an emotional Vietnamese communist assumption that anyone with an explicit connection to China, past or present, was potentially an enemy and potentially disloyal to the party.

HANOI'S VIEW OF CHINA'S POLITICAL SUCCESSION STRUGGLE

The Vietnamese leaders were not only aware of but also paid great attention to the conflict among the political factions in China. Their interest was linked to a belief that one faction rather than another would be more considerate of Vietnam's foreign policy positions.

During a conversation with the Soviet ambassador in Hanoi in April 1976, Vietnamese Foreign Minister Nguyen Duy Trinh spoke of the struggle within China as one between "moderates" and "young activists." The moderates, who included Deng Xiaoping, impressed Trinh with their apparent strength because they dared to criticize Mao's wife, Jiang Qing. He believed that their popularity derived from their having worked with Zhou Enlai.[43]

Later that year Pham Van Dong spoke favorably of the Gang of Four's fall from power. While he felt then that it was too early to draw conclusions about the situation in the PRC, he felt that so far "little had changed" in the PRC's foreign policy. The only signs of possible improvement in Vietnam-China relations were more friendly Chinese attitudes at meetings with Vietnamese representatives.[44]

During 1977 the Vietnamese leadership was still uncertain about the evolution of the political situation in China, but expressed concern about its outcome. In October 1977 Le Duan told the Soviet ambassador in Hanoi that some of the Chinese leaders, especially Hua Guofeng and Ye Jianying, "do not understand us," whereas Deng Xiaoping "treats Vietnam with great understanding." Le Duan predicted that if Deng Xiaoping were to win the power struggle then changes in Chinese policy could be expected because Deng Xiaoping did not follow in Mao Zedong's path and even expressed opposition to several of Mao's ideas. Le Duan stated that Deng's attitude toward the Soviet Union was "well known" and that Deng's "words in connection with the USSR show that . . . he is convinced that the Soviet Union is a socialist country." This, together with the restoration in key posts of repressed former activists like Lo Xitsin, who had earlier expressed himself in favor of rapprochement with the Soviet Union, was treated hopefully by Le Duan.[45]

This interest by Le Duan in whether or not Chinese leaders favored a foreign policy of rapprochement with the Soviet Union was not merely in response to Soviet inquiries. We have already seen that international solidarity between all of the socialist countries—particularly the Soviet Union, the PRC, and the SRV—had been a long-standing position of the Vietnamese communists' foreign policy. That objective was stated again by the top Vietnamese party leaders in their private meetings with the Chinese in November 1977.[46]

But by late 1978, as their conflict with China deteriorated rapidly, the Vietnamese leaders' attitude toward the Chinese leadership struggle had changed. In September 1978 Le Duan told the Soviet ambassador that while China's leaders seriously disagreed among themselves on domestic policy, in foreign policy they shared a common conception.[47]

THE LAST PHASE OF VIETNAMESE-CHINESE COOPERATION

A new trade agreement between Vietnam and China was signed in Beijing in March 1977.[48] That year China exported goods worth $51.7 million to Vietnam while importing goods worth $27.7 million from that country. In terms of China's general pattern of international trade, Vietnam was not at all significant. Exports to Vietnam represented 0.7 percent of China's total, while imports represented 0.4 percent.[49] Vietnam's trade with the Soviet Union was more than four times the value of its China trade.[50] In 1977 China took just under a quarter of Vietnam's meager exports to countries outside the Soviet bloc.[51] But given the rough estimate that China provided around $300 million in economic aid in 1977, it is safe to say that the economic relationship between Vietnam and China was not primarily one of trading partners, but rather one of aid donor and recipient.[52]

In April 1977 Vietnamese Premier Pham Van Dong undertook an official visit to France, Finland, Norway, and Denmark. On his way he stopped over in Beijing, where a dinner in his honor was given by Chinese Premier Chen Xilian.[53] That month China had proposed to carry out repair work on the

Hanoi-Youyiguan railway in a disputed area of the Sino-Vietnamese border. Hanoi agreed. But on May 4, just after the work started, Hanoi reportedly sent five hundred troops into the area who attacked the Chinese workers, wounding fifty-one Chinese, six of them seriously.[54]

On his return in June, Pham Van Dong again stopped over in Beijing. He met with Chinese Communist Party Chairman Hua Guofeng and other Chinese leaders. According to the official Vietnamese radio account, Pham Van Dong "expressed his immense joy at meeting Chairman Hua Guofeng." However, there was a subtle hint of problems in the relationship: "The two leaders exchanged views on the relations between the two countries in an atmosphere of brotherly friendship and solidarity."[55] Chinese Vice Premier Li Xiannian had just raised with Pham Van Dong China's concern about the Vietnamese claim to the greater part of the Gulf of Tonkin and to the Paracel and Spratly Islands.[56] Later that month Politburo member and Defense Minister Vo Nguyen Giap led a military delegation to China on what the army newspaper, *Quan Doi Nhan Dan*, described as an "official friendship visit." The delegation was received by Chinese Party Chairman Hua Guofeng.[57]

In a secret speech presented on July 30, 1977, the Chinese Foreign Minister Huang Hua made clear that China was happy with the "anti-revisionist" (anti-Soviet) line of the Cambodian communists, as contrasted with the "not anti-revisionist" line of the Vietnamese communists. But China had no interest in a military solution to the Vietnamese-Cambodian conflict. Moreover, China desired to mediate between the two Indochinese states. Huang Hua stated:

> 1) The three states of Indochina should stop all armed conflicts and return to the negotiating table. They should . . . seek to resolve their differences through mutual respect and mutual concession.
>
> 2) All people of the three Indochina states cherish the same wish for solidarity. Having been neighbors for generations, they have no basic conflicts of interest and they should be united as one. If the three states deem it necessary, China is willing to serve as a mediator in order to enable the three states to return to the negotiating table to resolve their problems and promote their solidarity, friendship, and cooperation.[58]

In August 1977 the Central Committee of the Communist Party of Vietnam sent a message of greetings to the Central Committee of the Communist Party of China.[59] On the occasion of China's National Day (October 1),

Vietnamese party and state leaders sent a message of congratulations to Hua Guofeng. It included a general endorsement of Chinese communist domestic developments and the goals of the Eleventh Congress of the CCP. It also thanked the Chinese Communist Party, government, and people for their support during the war against the United States, as well as their support for Vietnam's "socialist construction." It described the solidarity between the two peoples as "indestructible."[60] This would be the last time for over a decade that the Vietnamese Communist Party would send a greeting on the occasion of China's National Day.

Between November 20 and 25, 1977, a high-level delegation of Vietnamese party and government leaders, led by Le Duan, with Economics Minister Le Thanh Nghi and Central Committee Secretary Xuan Thuy among the team, made an unexpected visit to China. No reason for the visit was given. On its completion, *Nhan Dan* editorialized that the "official friendly visit" had ended "successfully."[61]

In his account of the meeting that he provided on December 1 to the Soviet ambassador in Hanoi, Xuan Thuy did his best to paint a picture of the meeting that confirmed this optimistic judgment. However from his account of the details, the opposite seems to have been the case. He claimed that the goals of the visit were to inform each other about the situation in the countries; to exchange opinions about a number of international questions; "to touch upon the question of international solidarity, in particular between the USSR, the PRC and the SRV"; to contribute to the strengthening of friendship between the SRV and the PRC in order that relations between them "are not changed for the worse." Xuan Thuy claimed that, on the whole, these goals were attained.

Much of the meeting, according to the Vietnamese account, was devoted to a discussion of the more general foreign policy theories of both parties. However, in negotiations with the Chinese, the Vietnamese side emphasized that the different points of view of the two countries on a series of international problems must not affect friendly relations between them. The Vietnamese also thanked the Chinese for past aid and for their offer of further aid. Xuan Thuy reported that the Chinese side expressed its willingness to complete construction projects already begun and to initiate several aid programs in the form of rice deliveries.

However, what is most striking was what was not discussed. According to Xuan Thuy, long-term Chinese aid was not discussed because this was not the goal of the visit. Nor did the two sides discuss the problem of the ethnic Chinese in Ho Chi Minh City, the border problems between the PRC and the SRV, nor Vietnam's problems with Democratic Kampuchea. This is especially strange since these were the most important foreign policy issues of mutual concern. Xuan Thuy's explanation for their not being raised was that this would only "complicate negotiations."[62]

This was to be the last friendly direct communication between the communist parties of Vietnam and China. Future messages were to be on a government-to-government basis, rather than party-to-party. Following the break in diplomatic relations between Vietnam and Cambodia, Vietnamese relations with China declined rapidly.

Vietnam's Vice Foreign Minister Phan Hien, reputedly the country's leading expert on border questions, arrived in Beijing on January 9, 1978. Nine days later a high-level Chinese delegation, led by Zhou Enlai's widow, Deng Yingchao, flew to Phnom Penh. It was not known then whether these two events indicated that China might have been trying to play a mediating role between Vietnam and Kampuchea, or whether it was privately expressing its backing for the Cambodian communists.[63] It may have been doing both.

On January 9, 1978, the Vietnamese ambassador in Beijing, Nguyen Truong Vinh, announced that he had previously "drawn the attention" of the Chinese Foreign Ministry to what he termed his "dissatisfaction" with the way the Chinese press had so far reported Hanoi's position in its conflict with Phnom Penh. China had given extensive coverage to the Cambodian viewpoint, but only limited coverage of the Vietnamese position. Then on January 10 the Chinese *People's Daily* quoted two communiqués published by the governments of Cambodia and Vietnam, presenting their respective viewpoints.[64]

Meanwhile the Soviet Union had chimed into the polemics, accusing China of provoking the deterioration in relations between Vietnam and Cambodia. China denounced the charges as "lies and slanders," and accused the Soviet Union of wanting to "get rid of" Democratic Kampuchea in order to realize "its strategic aim of establishing domination over Southeast Asia."[65]

The Vietnamese were not immediately drawn into this exchange. But in late February Hanoi introduced the notion that the Cambodian communists were being assisted by "the imperialists and international reactionaries." The term "imperialists" had always referred to the Western powers, particularly the United States. But reference to a new category of "international reactionaries" was not explained. Hanoi radio charged:

> Assisted and encouraged by the imperialists and international reactionaries, the Kampuchean authorities have turned friends into foes and pointed their guns at their old comrades-in-arms who helped them win victory. . . . Those who have used Kampuchea to attack Vietnam have also made a wrong move and committed a blunder in the choice of allies and objectives.[66]

Here we see the first public sign of Hanoi's view that Khmers Rouges behavior was a function of Chinese policy. In private discussions the Vietnamese were more explicit. In a conversation with a Soviet embassy official, Vietnamese Central Committee member Tran Quyen suggested that by stirring up a conflict between the SRV and the DK, the Chinese wanted to distract Vietnam from the fulfillment of its strategic task of the construction of socialism. China wanted Vietnam to be drawn into conflict in order to weaken Vietnam. However, Quyen insisted, Vietnam would resist any provocations and would concentrate on constructing a powerful state.[67]

On the occasion of the PRC's Fifth National People's Congress, held in Beijing in late February and early March, Hanoi radio gave a brief, terse, and factual account of the proceedings. The congratulatory messages normally associated with such reports were missing.[68] On March 8, Vietnamese Vice-Premier and Defense Minister Vo Nguyen Giap sent a message congratulating Xu Xiangqian on his appointment as vice-premier and minister of national defense of the PRC. The message included the wish for "militant solidarity and fraternal friendship" between the "peoples and armed forces" of the two countries. But no mention was made of relations between the two parties.[69]

Nonetheless, it should be noted that Giap was the only high-ranking Vietnamese leader to send such a friendly message in 1978. In February 1980, Giap, the architect of his party's historic victory at Dien Bien Phu, and one of Ho Chi Minh's closest disciples, lost his post as defense minister. At the Fifth Party Congress, held in March 1982, Giap was officially demoted from the Politburo.[70]

In April 1978 a Swedish radio correspondent returning from Hanoi reported that there had been armed clashes along the Sino-Vietnamese border in February. Foreign travelers were being denied access to the border area.[71] The correspondent quoted a Vietnamese official: "We have claims on their territory. They have claims on our territory. It is not just a matter of the islands [the Spratlys and the Paracels], but also along the land border."[72]

The Vietnamese government attempted to conceal its conflict with China. On April 21, the Vietnamese embassy in Paris denied that there had been military combat between China and Vietnam on their common border.[73] Conflict between Vietnam and China finally came out into the open over the issue of Vietnam's ethnic Chinese minority.

THE EXODUS OF THE ETHNIC CHINESE FROM VIETNAM

In a conversation with the Soviet ambassador in October 1977, General Secretary Le Duan was upbeat, stating that the Hanoi leaders faced "no insoluble problems of any kind." The single complex problem cited was Vietnam's border conflict with Cambodia, which the Soviet ambassador observed was a worry for Hanoi. Turning to domestic affairs, Le Duan expressed confidence that Vietnam's ethnic Chinese community did not pose a serious problem for the Vietnamese leadership. Speaking specifically of the ethnic Chinese population of Ho Chi Minh City, Le Duan stated that this community was not strong enough to prevent the policies of the "people's authority." Le Duan claimed that whereas the Hoa (ethnic Chinese) previously controlled 80 percent of the economic activity in the south, now the basic positions in the industrial sphere were firmly in the hands of the "people's authority." Thus Hanoi had succeeded in taming the power of ethnic Chinese in a way that neither the U.S. nor the "puppet administration of [South Vietnamese President] Nguyen Van Thieu" were able to do.[74]

It would be easy to dismiss this analysis by Le Duan as an attempt to impress his Soviet interlocutor with the political strength of the Vietnamese regime. However, the conversation as a whole is marked by a high degree of candor, which led the Soviet ambassador to note Hanoi's anxiety over the border conflict with Cambodia. In contrast, the Soviet ambassador sensed a genuine confidence on the part of the Vietnamese authorities in their ability to handle any challenge from the ethnic Chinese minority. What eroded this sense of confidence was the breakdown of Vietnamese-Chinese relations at the state and party levels over the Chinese attitude to the conflict between Vietnam and Cambodia.

In March 1978 the government of Vietnam introduced laws abolishing private trade in southern Vietnam. This struck most heavily at the ethnic Chinese capitalists. In May a currency reform reduced the bank savings of most Vietnamese to virtually nothing. In April 1978 thousands of ethnic Chinese began leaving Vietnam for China. By the end of May the number had reached 105,000, according to the Chinese government.[75] The flow continued throughout 1978. More important, it became the focus of conflict between the Vietnamese and Chinese governments, each of which blamed the other for the mass exodus of people.

Initially, the Vietnamese government's explanation was that ethnic Chinese residents of Vietnam had been incited to leave by "bad elements" of the Hoa, who "spread rumors to divide Vietnam and China and to deceive the Chinese people living in Vietnam." According to Xuan Thuy, the Vietnamese official who first publicly propagated this explanation in an interview with the Vietnamese News Agency, the rumors being spread were that the war between Vietnam and Kampuchea would be expanded, and that because China supports Kampuchea, the Chinese in Vietnam would be harmed. Thus, according to Xuan Thuy, the rumormongers had claimed that it was best for Vietnam's ethnic Chinese to find ways of leaving. The Vietnamese official suggested that these rumors were unwarranted, because the Vietnamese and Chinese had always lived together in friendship "in the great socialist family of Vietnam." But then Xuan Thuy concluded his interview with a wish and an offer:

> We hope that these Chinese will not let themselves be duped by by bad elements and will remain in Vietnam to carry out their normal lives. Should anyone want to return to China, let him openly send his application to the Vietnamese administration in his locality. He will be given prompt asssistance in the procedure so that he may go back to his country in accordance with his wishes, through the prescribed border posts.[76]

Several days after the Vietnam News Agency interview, hundreds of Vietnamese of Chinese descent besieged the Chinese embassy in Hanoi to request exit visas from Vietnam.[77]

On May 12, 1978, the foreign ministry of the PRC delivered a note to the SRV embassy in China expressing the Chinese government's views on the situation of the ethnic Chinese within Vietnam. According to the Chinese note, the Vietnamese side was "ostracizing, persecuting, and expelling Chinese residents on an ever-larger scale." The Chinese claimed that the process began in early 1977, when the Vietnamese side began expelling the population who had come from China long ago and settled in the northern border areas. The Vietnamese operation was expanded to three provinces in November 1977 and, according to the Chinese, intensified in April 1978. No mention was made in the Chinese note of the nationalization measures recently undertaken in the south of the country. Most attention was focused on the plight of those in the north, who provided the bulk of those fleeing to China. The note claimed that the persecution of ethnic Chinese had been going on for years. It then spoke of the process of their expulsion from Vietnam:

> Then, the Vietnamese side has in many ways expelled them en masse to China. In many places, Vietnamese security agents, under the pretext of controlling residence registrations, illegally searched their houses, used various means to threaten and intimidate them, and coerced them to leave Vietnam. The expelled Chinese residents are now helpless. They have not enough food and clothes. The greater part of their property, accumulated through so many years of hard work, has been illegally confiscated. The little furniture they can take with them on their way back to China has also been plundered. When they enter China, most of them have nothing left, except for the clothes they are wearing.
>
> The Vietnamese side has been transporting contingents of Chinese residents by train to places near Lao Cai, Hoang Lien Son Province, forcing them to alight and walk tens of kilometers before they can enter China. On their way to the border, they have to experience all kinds of suffering. Some are groundlessly beaten and wounded. Others, old people and children included, are left hungry and sick. Their plight is miserable indeed. Moreover, in Ho Chi Minh City, of late, there have been mass arrests of Chinese residents, some have even been beaten to death or injured.[78]

As for the "bad elements" who, according to the Vietnamese, were spreading rumors, the Chinese had another account. According to the Chinese note, it was "the Vietnamese authorities and security agents themselves who have spread rumors to deceive and intimidate the Chinese residents."

The Chinese note also informed the Vietnamese government that in light of the heavy expenses being incurred to maintain the influx of refugees from Vietnam, China was compelled to cut cut some of its aid to Vietnam, in the form of equipment and money used on a number of projects.[79]

One week later the Vietnamese government sent its own note of reply to the PRC. It expressed regret at the PRC decision to cut off aid to what it listed as twenty-one projects, and it claimed that this was part of a series of episodes beginning in 1975 in which the PRC had begun to renege on or failed to fulfill aid agreements. The note rejected Chinese charges that Vietnam had been "ostracizing, persecuting, and expelling" Hoa people. And the Vietnamese still insisted that "bad elements" among the Hoa had spread rumors that caused the others to flee, whereas the Vietnamese people and local administrations had "advised them to stay on without anxiety, and not listen to the bad elements' rumors." Who these "bad elements" were, and what their underlying motivation was, was not explained at this time. Nor was the apparent impotence of the local administrations in the face of the Hoa refusal to listen to "friendly advice." Over one year later, the official Vietnamese account of these events became more precise in detailing what it now described as a Chinese government conspiracy:

> Early in 1978, the Chinese rulers fabricated the so-called problem of "victim-ized residents" to openly start a large-scale campaign against the Socialist Republic of Vietnam. The activities of the secret Hoa organizations and the intelligence network of the Chinese embassy in Hanoi, closely guided by the Beijing propaganda machine; the brazen allegations accusing Vietnam of "expelling, ostracizing, and persecuting the Hoa people"; together with deception, briberies, enticements, and threats, created a feeling of anxiety and fear of an imminent war and instigated suspicions, even enmity toward the Vietnamese and caused the Hoa people to leave for China en masse. Chinese agents helped the Hoa to cross the border illegally and then held them up at the Vietnam-China border and incited the stranded people to oppose and to assault Vietnamese local officials. When the exodus of the Hoa to China began, Beijing sent two ships to Vietnam to take "the victimized residents," although they had not yet raised this question with the Govern-ment of Vietnam. Within only a few months, 170,000 Hoa people left Vietnam for China. The so-called question of "victimized residents" was only a coer-cion of the Hoa in Vietnam to leave en masse for China. The culprit here was the reactionary group in the Beijing leadership who practiced deception and betrayal in an attempt to provoke political, social, and economic unrest in Vietnam, to subjugate the Vietnamese people and, at the same time, to arouse public opinion in China and to prepare a "fifth column" for an eventual aggression against Vietnam.[80]

We have two competing conspiracy theories set forth by the rival govern-ments to explain the flight of the Hoa. Which one was true?

Unfortunately, neither of the two governments at loggerheads on this issue would allow independent observers to conduct unsupervised interviews with randomly selected refugees, who were either in the process of fleeing Vietnam or else had arrived in China. The Chinese government did allow some for-eign correspondents to interview some selected refugees. But the Vietnamese government would not give independent Western correspondents even that liberty. For example, when the correspondent for *Le Monde*, R. P. Paringaux, who had been allowed to visit areas near Vietnam's border with China, asked permission to go to the border bridge at Mong Cai and to meet some of the Hoa who were stranded on the Vietnamese side of the border, local authorities denied him that permission. The reason given was that the Chinese officials would think he was a Russian, and consider his visit a "provocation." As for the Hoa, he was told: "The Hoas, worked up by the anti-Soviet propaganda of Peking, would make the same mistake and attack you."[81]

It might be tempting to think that no conclusions could be drawn about the truth of either of the competing claims. But that would be an unnecessarily cautious approach to a significant political event. There is other relevant indirect evidence. As we have seen, Soviet sources had described the series of discriminatory policies toward the ethnic Chinese that had begun in 1976. In other words, where there is Soviet evidence relevant to the contending charges—and the Soviet analysts were politically inclined to be sympathetic to the Hanoi regime—it corroborates the Chinese account.

Also relevant is the fact that the Vietnamese communist regime exercised fairly tight control over Vietnamese society. This is especially true of the northern half of the country, where the party has been in power since 1954. The key instrument of control is the party-controlled Cong An, or Public Security Bureau (PSB), which controls on a day-to-day basis the rights of the population to a place of permanent residence and the right to temporary movement between towns and districts within Vietnam. The PSB is also responsible for preventing illegal movement in or out of the country. In these tasks it is aided by local neighborhood committees in every community and a network of secret informers. The PSB also possesses its own armed militia.[82] It is simply implausible to believe that each week in April and May of 1978, and for several months thereafter, tens of thousands of residents of Vietnam could have left their jobs and homes, carrying personal possessions in hand, and traveled hundreds of miles overland to China without the knowledge and approval of the PSB and the central authorities in Hanoi.

Furthermore, we have another more direct form of evidence as to how the exodus of ethnic Chinese from Vietnam took place. That is the account provided by those refugees—the so-called "boat people"—who escaped by sea in 1978 and 1979 to Hong Kong and several countries in Southeast Asia. For while the Chinese government expressed concern at the arrival of so many land refugees at its border, it did not not have to deal with what eventually became the even greater number of ethnic Chinese—mainly residents of southern Vietnam—who departed by boat for other countries in Asia. Their accounts were received by officials of the governments of the United States, Canada, Britain, France, Hong Kong, and Australia in particular, and by journalists from all those countries and more. Most interviews with refugees support the conclusion that, although not officially announced as such, the whole program of expulsion was organized by the Vietnamese Public Security Bureau.[83] Representatives of the governments of Britain and Australia made this charge at a United Nations sponsored conference on Indochinese refugees held in Geneva, Switzerland, in December 1978.[84] It was also confirmed publicly by the former editor of the Vietnamese army newspaper, Colonel Bui Tin.[85]

A special subdivision of the PSB, the political security division known as B-2, was given responsibility for refugees. After China virtually closed its borders to the Hoa in July 1978, the PSB began a program of encouraging departures by boat from the northern part of the country to Hong Kong and Southeast Asia. Though in the north PSB officials took on the task of organizing refugees directly, in the south intermediaries were used to contact the potential refugees, arrange the logistics of their departure by sea, and collect what amounted to an exit tax, usually payable in gold, of several thousand dollars. Part of the exit tax was retained by the government, but another part went into the pockets of PSB officials.

Clearly the deportation of ethnic Chinese was a profitable business for the PSB and the government in Hanoi. But profit was a secondary motive for the Vietnamese Communist Party leadership. Its ultimate purpose was to rid the country of an ethnic minority whose loyalty to the Vietnamese government was felt to be in question.

That the flight of the ethnic Chinese was the result of a deliberate Vietnamese policy is further confirmed by the reaction of Le Duan to a subsequent Chinese proposal to return 100,000 of the ethnic Chinese refugees to Vietnam. In a private conversation with the Soviet ambassador in September 1978, Le Duan stated that in response to China's offer the Vietnamese leaders were carrying out active preparations in order "not to allow the return to Vietnamese territory of a single Chinese."[86]

Did Hanoi have good reason to doubt the loyalty of the Hoa? It is most unlikely that the entire ethnic Chinese community, or even a majority, had any desire to support the People's Republic of China against the Socialist Republic of Vietnam. More important, there was no likelihood that any minority, whatever their sentiments, could act in unison as a fifth column against the SRV, given the pervasive effectiveness of Vietnam's Public Security Bureau.[87]

But we have to remember that the Vietnamese communists had for decades been infiltrating their weaker neighbors with treacherous fifth columns—successfully in the case of Laos, unsuccessfully in the case of Cambodia. Given that fact, and given their political pedigree as former disciples of the Chinese communists, it would not have been a fantastic assumption of the Vietnamese that their more powerful and now embittered former mentors would try to do the same to them. That is why the Vietnamese communists perceived all the Hoa to be potentially disloyal as Vietnam moved into a major military confrontation with Beijing-supported Kampuchea. The paranoia of the Vietnamese communists lay not in their suspicion of some, but rather in their suspicion of all of the ethnic Chinese residents of Vietnam. Hanoi's response may have been unprecedented in the form it took—a pogrom against and mass expulsion of an entire ethnic minority. But the mentality underlying these actions was not new.

We should recall that during the early 1970s, a subtle and covert campaign of discrimination was initiated against North Vietnam's ethnic Chinese.[88] It involved, among other things, a rumor campaign and the early retirement of many Chinese-trained cadres. Again in 1976 the Hanoi leaders initiated policies to control the social, economic, and political activities of the entire ethnic Chinese community.

The post-1975 VCP behavior toward the former military and police officers and civil servants of the defeated Republic of Vietnam—incarcerating them en masse in reeducation camps, regardless of their past behavior as individuals or present protestations of loyalty—also demonstrated a VCP propensity to distrust entire status groups, to hold them collectively guilty, and to punish them collectively on suspicion of potential disloyalty. However, in the case of the deportations of 1978, paranoia had important consequences for international relations.

THE CUTBACK OF CHINESE AID

The PRC's cutback of aid to the SRV should be understood as a calculated reaction to the expulsion of the Hoa, in the broader context of PRC anger over the SRV's war with its eastern neighbor. The aid cutback began with the cancelation of aid to twenty-one projects in May 1978.[89] Chinese aid was cut back even further with the cancelation of fifty-one more projects, including the equipment and money used in them, and the recall of numerous specialists.[90]

On June 7 Deng Xiaoping told a group of visiting Thai journalists in Beijing that China was reducing its assistance to Vietnam because of Hanoi's unfriendly acts. He cited the expulsions of the Hoa from Vietnam and the resettlement of Chinese residents in New Economic Zones. But he also stated that China would continue providing some aid to Vietnam and would exercise "extreme self-restraint in the face of such unfriendly acts from Vietnam."[91]

On June 16 the Chinese Foreign Ministry sent a note to the Vietnamese Foreign Ministry, announcing that in light of the refusal of the Vietnamese side to make arrangements for a Chinese advance party to set up a consulate-general in Ho Chi Minh City, the Chinese government was canceling the appointment of the consul-general. The Chinese government simultaneously notified the Vietnamese government that it should close its consulates-general in Guangzhou, Kunming, and Nanning, China.[92] This move marked a further serious deterioration in relations between the two countries.

On June 29 the SRV announced that it was joining the Soviet-controlled Council of Mutual Economic Assistance, or Comecon (discussed in the next chapter). This indicated Vietnam's economic integration into the Soviet bloc, as well as providing a further gesture of political affinity with Moscow. It was a clear rebuff to China. And it was understood as such by the Vietnamese. For as a Vietnamese diplomat had told the journalist Nayan Chanda in March 1977: "The Soviets insist that all Socialist countries should join the COMECON. But other than Cuba, no other country outside Europe has done it. And we certainly do not want to. If we join, the Chinese won't be happy."[93]

A few days later, on July 3, 1978, China announced the end of all economic aid projects in Vietnam.[94] The reason officially given was Vietnam's treatment of the Hoa.[95] No doubt this was a major factor, but so too was the Vietnamese war with Democratic Kampuchea. And Hanoi's Comecon decision, integrating Vietnam into the Soviet economic bloc, most surely added a third major source of anger for China.

CONCLUSIONS

The available evidence suggests that the Chinese cutoff of aid to Vietnam was, as the Chinese government claimed, a response to the hostile actions of the Vietnamese communist leaders. But it is equally clear that the Vietnamese government's hostility toward China had not come out of thin air. In spite of the political distance between Vietnam and China that had begun a decade earlier, the breakdown of relations took place in two phases. The first began at the end of the Vietnam War and lasted two and a half years. The second began suddenly, and took only six months to complete. These phases happened at specific historical moments, and thus had specific historic causes. The cause of the initial decline in Vietnamese-Chinese relations was Hanoi's political tilt toward the Soviet Union. This was compounded by Vietnam's persecution of its ethnic Chinese minority. The cause of the rapid disintegration of relations was the exacerbation of the conflict between Vietnam and Cambodia.

We must not assume that China's attitude derived from an irrational, traditional nationalist rivalry between the Chinese and Vietnamese. It was, rather, because the Vietnamese had already aligned themselves with the Soviet Union, China's main enemy. Moreover, an extension of Vietnamese power on the Southeast Asian mainland, which would result from a Vietnamese invasion of Cambodia, automatically entailed an expansion of Soviet power there, too. Furthermore, China's long-standing public commitment to the independence of Cambodia, now via the regime called Democratic Kampuchea, meant that Chinese credibility was at stake if its client was toppled by military force, especially pro-Soviet military force. Certainly, the "Chinese threat" to Vietnam was the effect, not the cause, of Hanoi's actions. In its attitude toward Vietnam, China was behaving quite rationally.

In the context of all these issues, Vietnam's behavior toward its ethnic Chinese minority makes no strategic sense. By instigating policies of discrimination and persecution against its ethnic Chinese minority in mid-1976, spiraling in degree and finally culminating in the expulsion of over 100,000 Hoa to China during the first half of 1978, the leadership of Vietnam was exacerbating its already tense and difficult relationship with the Chinese government for no conceivable strategic advantage. By suggesting that these ethnic Chinese were a fifth column, Vietnam was declaring China to be its enemy. The Vietnamese leadership had based this judgment of its citizens, especially of those in the north, on the basis of no reasonable objective evidence.

It might be noted that even democratic governments, such as the United States and Canada during World War II, have persecuted those ethnic minorities whom they suspected of sympathizing with the nation's enemy.

While these actions might also be interpreted as examples of regime paranoia, the contrast between the two cases is more illuminating than the similarities. For when the Western democracies rounded up all of their ethnic Japanese citizens on unfounded suspicion of potential hostile intent, the democracies and Japan were actually in an official state of war. In the Vietnamese example, not only were China and Vietnam not at war, officially or unofficially, when Hanoi began its persecution in the early 1970s, but they were de jure and de facto allies. And when Hanoi accelerated its persecution in 1976, it was still the recipient of Chinese economic aid, which it desperately hoped would continue. Yet Hanoi was acting toward the Hoa as if the two nations were at war.

This behavior indicates that Hanoi assumed that Beijing would be upset with its foreign policy and would react in a hostile manner, using all the resources at its disposal. It also demonstrates that when chiliastic regimes are the parties to political disputes, even seemingly arcane intramural differences can assume an apocalyptic significance in the minds of their leaders. The concept of a threat is sensed by a chiliastic regime at a conflict threshold that no "normal" state would ever react to.

In this manner we can discern how the objective situation alone did not create a crisis between the regimes. The political cultures of the regimes were crucial.

CHAPTER EIGHT

The Emergence of the Soviet-Vietnamese Alliance

An objective examination of the economic and military positions of the Soviet Union in mid-1975 would not have led one to predict that it, any more than China, would soon be embroiled in conflict in Indochina. But the history of Soviet involvement in Indochina, and the more active Soviet involvement in other Third World conflicts following the American retreat from Indochina, did suggest that Soviet ties with Vietnam were likely to deepen.

In mid-1975 the Soviet Union had many more policy choices open to it than China did in reacting to the evolving new political situation in Indochina. After all, with the complete withdrawal of the United States, the Soviet Union had become the most powerful of the remaining parties to the conflicts in Indochina, and the only one not facing a credible threat of annihilation from its antagonistic neighbors. Of course, any conceivable war in Indochina would have a significant economic cost for the Soviet Union. The drain upon limited Soviet economic resources that supplying a militarized Vietnam would pose was significant. But the cost of supporting a militarized Vietnam at war would not be nearly as economically debilitating for the Soviets as the costs that such a war would pose to the Chinese, Vietnamese, and Cambodians. In any case, the Soviet Union already had committed far greater resources to supporting Cuban forces intervening in Africa and to subsidizing the militarized Cuban economy. Moreover, the political advantages that would most likely accrue to the Soviet Union as a result of increased tension in Indochina—a greater dependency of the Vietnamese and Laotians upon it, with the prospect of access to strategically significant air and naval bases in Vietnam—must surely have exerted a strong appeal to the Brezhnev-led Politburo in Moscow. In other words, the Soviet Union was the only party to the tense situation in Indochina for whom heightened conflict offered political and strategic advantages not outweighed by the economic and political costs.

In contrast with China, the Soviet Union was geographically distant from Indochina, and was less deeply committed to Vietnam than China was to Democratic Kampuchea. It was not compelled to deepen its commitment, especially since the SRV was not threatened with annihilation by its weaker neighbor. Only if China became more deeply involved would the Soviet Union face any pressure to deepen its commitment. Nonetheless, the Soviet Union had real political options since its national security was not directly threatened by developments in Indochina. The Soviet Union, as the most powerful and least vulnerable actor and Hanoi's arms supplier, was in a position to encourage or discourage those Vietnamese leaders who favored a military solution to their regional political problems. The Soviet Union chose to deepen its commitment. That decision makes sense only in the context of the Soviet elite's political culture, which saw itself engaged in a global struggle against both Western "imperialism" and the Chinese "reactionaries."

This is not to suggest that the Soviet Union manipulated the situation to the point that it determined the ultimate decisions, as the Chinese and Cambodian communists have suggested. The Vietnamese, like the Cambodian communist leaders, though not fully autonomous, were independent actors who made their own decisions. Ultimately, it was decisions by the local Indochinese contenders—the Vietnamese and Cambodian communists—that enticed the external communist powers to involve themselves further.

But Soviet antagonism toward China and the buildup and projection of Soviet military power were historical facts that provided a political and military context that influenced Vietnam's decisions. As we have already seen, between 1965 and 1968 the Vietnamese communists had maintained equidistance between the Soviet Union and China on matters of foreign policy. But the North Vietnamese leaders decided during the late 1960s to abandon strict neutrality and to tilt their foreign policy toward the Soviet Union. Moreover, after the military defeat of the Tet offensive of 1968, the North Vietnamese leaders decided to reorient their military strategy against the United States and South Vietnam away from their modified version of the Maoist doctrine of "people's war" and toward the Soviet doctrines of conventional war. The Vietnamese army was reequipped with Soviet heavy weaponry. But Vietnamese-Soviet relations were always complex, and Hanoi's diplomatic tilt evolved into a full political and economic alliance, with close military relations, only after the final breakdown of Vietnam's strained relations with China. Yet even after this evolution into a full alliance, the

Vietnamese communist leaders failed to reveal to their patron and protector their real intentions toward Cambodia.

DIVERGENT SOVIET AND NORTH VIETNAMESE STRATEGIES TOWARD CAMBODIA, 1970–75

One of the more unusual aspects of the Indochinese conflict before 1975 is that while the Vietnamese communists were developing a closer relationship with the Soviet Union, these two increasingly amicable parties were pursuing different policies toward Cambodia. Immediately after Cambodia experienced an anticommunist, anti-Vietnamese coup d'état in March 1970, the Vietnamese communists attacked the new republic's army and began to foster a Cambodian communist insurgency nominally headed by Prince Sihanouk. But Hanoi's ally, the Soviet Union, kept an ambiguous distance from the Cambodian insurgents and maintained diplomatic relations with the anticommunist government in Phnom Penh until its very end.

In spite of professions of support, the Soviet Union offered no formal recognition of GRUNK, Sihanouk's government in exile. (China had formally recognised GRUNK on May 5, 1970.) The Soviet Union continued to recognize the Lon Nol government.

Why did the Soviet Union draw the distinction between the insurgent political united front organization, FUNK, whose program it endorsed, and the government, GRUNK, which it failed to recognize? The answer almost certainly lies in the political complexities of the Cambodian insurgency at that time—the fact that during the first two years of the war, FUNK appeared to be under the direct control of the Vietnamese communists, while GRUNK was a Sihanoukist diplomatic entity, resident in Beijing, and under the influence of China. This interpretation of Soviet behavior is given some corroboration by Sihanouk, in his subsequent recollection of the period March 1970 to February 1973:

> At that time I was going frequently to Hanoi where, regularly, the ambassador of the Soviet Union was asking me for an audience. This diplomat did not hide from me the fact that his government keenly wished to see me leave Beijing and return to Cambodia to lead the struggle for national liberation at the head of my people.[1]

For almost the entire duration of the war, the Soviet Union and its Warsaw Pact allies continued to recognize the Lon Nol government, hosting republican diplomats in Eastern Europe and maintaining a Soviet embassy in Phnom Penh. This led to various embarrassing incidents. For example, in August 1970 in Prague, a dissident Cambodian diplomat and several Cambodian students seized control of the Cambodian embassy from the republican representatives accredited there in the name of the GRUNK. Czech authorities surrounded the embassy and forced the defecting diplomat and students to leave.[2]

According to a former participant in the Soviet policy-making discussions on Cambodia, there was a disagreement within the Soviet decision making elite over Cambodia policy. The central point of disagreement was over whether or not the Cambodian insurgents would win. The "pragmatic" group did not believe that a victory by the Cambodian communists and Sihanouk was possible. The "radical" group believed that the insurgents would win in the context of the likely victory of the Vietnamese and Laotian communists. The pragmatic group prevailed at the critical meeting in 1970, even though the debate within the Soviet political elite continued with some intensity for five years.[3]

Open polemics with Sihanouk in early 1972 apparently convinced the Soviets that they had to work toward another political solution. In early 1972 the Soviets began to initiate contacts with the Lon Nol government with a view to creating a "Third Force" that would include a legal communist party free to participate in elections. The communists Moscow wanted to participate in this legal "Third Force" would be led by Hang Tun Hak, director of Phnom Penh's University des Beaux-Arts. It was reported that cadres would be recruited from the same university, the Soviet Institute of Technology in Phnom Penh, and from among Cambodians trained at the Patrice Lumumba University in Moscow.[4] The Soviets also proposed a de facto partitioning of Cambodia to allow Hanoi the free use of sanctuaries east of the Mekong. But the plan was unacceptable to the Lon Nol government because it could not accept the idea of allowing Hanoi's troops to remain on Cambodian soil. And the plan was totally rejected by Sihanouk and the Chinese—understandably, given the fact that it was clearly aimed at limiting their influence.[5] But it never could have been realized because obviously the pro-Chinese Khmers Rouges, who by now controlled the insurgency, were also totally opposed to the concept.

Another remarkable aspect of the Soviet policy is the fact that they continued to repudiate GRUNK, which had always been political window-dressing, while giving limited political support to FUNK, which was by 1972 controlled by anti-Soviet ultra-Maoists. Why did the Soviets misjudge the situation? The Soviets, who had less intelligence on the Cambodian insurgency than Hanoi, clearly were not alerted to the Maoist and anti-Vietnamese attitudes of the Khmers Rouges and overestimated the strength of pro-Soviet and pro-Hanoi elements within the insurgency.[6]

But a turning point in Soviet policy came with the end of United States bombing in August 1973. The Soviet press paid close attention during the spring and summer of 1973 to the effects of American bombing and attempts within the U.S. Congress to have it terminated. Once it was clear that the bombing was to come to an end, the Soviet Union began moving to restore some legitimacy to Prince Sihanouk and his Royal Government. In late July *Pravda* noted Prince Sihanouk's visit to North Korea, though it identified him as FUNK chairman (his secondary title from the perspective of diplomacy).[7] In August, the day after the end of U.S. bombing, *Pravda* reported Prince Sihanouk's statement on this occasion, read by Penn Nouth, identifying both of them as leaders of the government in exile. Three days later *Pravda* reported a Royal Government statement.[8] Other statements by Sihanouk were reported during August. Then in October *Pravda* reported that the Soviet ambassador had met with Sihanouk in Beijing.[9]

In the context of the 1973 U.N. General Assembly debate over the credentials of the Lon Nol government versus the Sihanouk Royal Government, Sihanouk's statement was reported.[10] In the U.N. debate, the Soviet Union voted to seat the GRUNK, but that motion was narrowly defeated. The previous month the Soviet Union had withdrawn its charge d'affaires and most of its diplomats from Phnom Penh, leaving only a small staff to guard the embassy. It seemed to be approaching something like a dual recognition.

The end of American bombing seems to have caused the Soviets to reappraise the insurgency's prospects. But with characteristic caution, the Soviet Union did not yet sever all connections with Phnom Penh. It was not until March 28, 1975, that the Soviet Union decided to expel all diplomats and other officials of the Lon Nol government accredited in Moscow and announced that it would recognize GRUNK as the legitimate government of Cambodia.[11] Yet the Soviet Union never actually closed its embassy in Phnom Penh.

That change of policy during the very last weeks of the Lon Nol government was not fully appreciated by the insurgent leaders. When the Khmers Rouges marched into Phnom Penh in April 1975, they arrested the Soviet diplomatic personnel still there and transported them to the French embassy to await their deportation from what had become Democratic Kampuchea. According to Sihanouk:

> [W]hen the Khmers Rouges . . . entered Phnom Penh . . . a unit of the Khmers Rouges went straight to the embassy of the Soviet Union . . . let down the Soviet flag [and] burned it. They burned it as a revenge. They told the Russians: "You were with Lon Nol, you were with the American imperialists, and now we have to punish you, to humiliate you." So they tied the hands of the Soviet diplomats with rope, and they sent them on a jeep to the French embassy. . . . It was a terrible humiliation for the Russians![12]

Why did the Soviet Union fail to give full diplomatic support to the anti-American forces in Cambodia until the final weeks of the war? Obviously the Soviets recognized a preponderant Chinese influence over both the Khmers Rouges and Sihanouk. They probably did not want to commit themselves to a Chinese client.

But this explanation is not fully satisfactory, in that the Soviets supported the North Vietnamese, who in turn gave full, public diplomatic support to the Cambodian guerrillas and also funneled Chinese arms to them until 1975. Why was the Soviet Union out of step with its client? According to a former participant in Soviet policy debates, the Vietnamese leaders never insisted that the USSR recognize the Sihanouk government. Had they done so, he contends, the Soviet leaders would have complied.[13]

The Soviets were playing a cautious political game. Until an uncertain military situation finally became clear, they chose to leave the North Vietnamese to make all the decisive moves in Cambodia, thereby reaping the benefits if Hanoi succeeded, while incurring no costs if Hanoi failed.

There was undoubtedly more than one reason for the Moscow-Hanoi divergence over Cambodia, but the differing attitudes of the Soviet Union and North Vietnam toward China constituted another powerful factor. As we have seen in the previous chapter, by 1970 the Vietnamese communists did have important political and ideological differences with China, differences that had developed during the previous decade. But even as late as 1975, the Vietnamese did not yet share the Soviets' intense hatred of the Chinese, and they did not yet allow the existing differences that they had with China to play the dominant role in their Cambodia policy.[14]

SOVIET ATTITUDES TOWARD VIETNAMESE FOREIGN
POLICY, 1970–75

One important dimension of Soviet thinking about Vietnam was the evaluation of Hanoi's policy provided by the Soviet embassy in Hanoi. At the end of 1970, the Soviet embassy in Hanoi showed little acknowledgment of Hanoi's foreign policy tilt toward the Soviet Union. The exception was their reference to a change in the structure of Vietnamese communist strategic thinking in 1968. In that year the Vietnamese began to speak of three types of combat—military, political, and diplomatic—which the Soviets interpreted as a departure from the Chinese position and "an acceptance of our views."[15] However, the embassy still perceived Hanoi as following a policy of balancing between Moscow and Beijing.[16]

But the bulk of the Soviet embassy's evaluation of Vietnamese foreign policy was highly critical. In the first place, the Soviet Union was eager to coordinate the two nations' foreign policies. By contrast, the Vietnamese were not only resistant to such an idea, but indicated explicitly that they would not tell the Soviets in advance about tactical aspects of specific foreign policy moves that they were undertaking, and that they would not consult on specific issues. This upset the Soviets, who had been providing the Vietnamese with information and advice about internal and foreign policy matters. But the lack of reciprocity by the Vietnamese had to be accepted, the Soviets felt, because the Chinese were also providing the Vietnamese with information and advice.[17] Yet some bitterness seemed to remain:

> [O]n account of the DRV's narrow national interests, which continue to exist among the Vietnamese leadership in relations with the Soviet Union and socialist countries of Eastern Europe, they are not to this day sufficiently sincere and trustworthy; they are not truly brotherly. Our friends were not adequately sincere with these countries concerning their plans for solving the Indochina problem. They have evaded agreeing and coordinating their actions with them.[18]

The Soviet embassy analysts were also upset that the Vietnamese approached the Soviet and Eastern European allies separately, secretly making similar requests for assistance to more than one of these countries with the view to creating what the Soviets called "an unhealthy competition of a sort between socialist countries." The Soviets also felt that the DRV maintained closer relations with East Germany, Bulgaria, Hungary, North Korea, and Cuba than it did with the USSR.[19]

Despite substantial Soviet military aid, which was reequipping and providing training, repair, and maintenance support for the Vietnam People's Army, the 250 to 300 Soviet military specialists in the DRV faced difficulties. The Soviet embassy complained that the Vietnamese army command tried to limit the Soviet specialists' activity in every possible way to technical assistance only. Decisions on the combat use of military equipment and combat action tactics were said to be zealously guarded from the influence of the Soviet specialists.[20]

But a special distress was expressed for the conditions of work of Soviet diplomats, who were said to be subjected to a system of bans and restrictions. Despite the fact that the Soviet Union was undertaking great efforts in support of the DRV, and that hundreds of Soviet specialists were working for "the Vietnamese people," nevertheless, "the Soviet embassy has been placed under unjust and severe conditions; it is under surveillance and suspicion."[21]

By the middle of 1971, the Soviet embassy had come to recognize a significant shift in Hanoi's foreign policy, which was favorable to Moscow. In a political letter written to Moscow in May, Ambassador Shcherbakov analyzed the shift as having two indices. First was the decision of the Vietnamese in 1968 to broaden their strategic approach to the war to incorporate military, political, and diplomatic forms of struggle. This was apparently connected with Hanoi's decision to enter into negotiations with the United States in Paris. Second was the fact that the Vietnam Workers' Party "understands and apprehends more the policy of the CPSU."[22] Later in his report the Soviet ambassador noted that "by leaning to the Soviet Union, the VWP has endured the crude pressure of the Chinese leaders."[23]

The ambassador's main grievance with Hanoi was its failure to exchange opinions and information on a future settlement for Indochina, and its refusal to arrange with the socialist countries "a fully valuable coordination of actions, especially in the foreign policy sphere." The Hanoi leadership was accused of "trying to preserve for itself the exclusive right to a solution of the Vietnamese and Indochinese problems" and of "trying to impede, at least at the present stage, the broad involvement of the socialist countries on the matter."[24]

By the end of 1972 the Soviet embassy was reporting extensively on the tensions that had arisen between the Soviet Union and the DRV because of the visit of Richard Nixon to Moscow (see Chapter 6), and on the efforts of the Soviet side to diminish those tensions. The Soviets also spoke of their dissatisfaction with the alleged Vietnam Workers' Party policy of maintaining equally friendly relations with the USSR and the PRC. The Soviets spoke of how news of polemics between the USSR and the PRC was prohibited in the DRV, while news of each country was presented evenly. This had restrained the deepening of Soviet-Vietnamese relations. Interestingly, the embassy also remarked that "objectively one should recognize that the VWP for the present cannot foresee a single alternative to this policy." Soviet tolerance for Hanoi's situation is justified so far, the report noted. Yet the Maoists were said to be abusing this policy by trying to drive a wedge between the VWP and the CPSU. "One must hope that the VWP is aware of this."[25]

But as in previous years, the embassy was most dismayed by what it described as the distrustful and deceitful behavior of the Vietnamese communist leaders toward the Soviet Union. It was noted that unofficial contacts by Vietnamese with foreigners were not permitted, even with Soviet people. But even in their official contacts, Vietnamese officials were said to be "insufficiently frank, they conceal a lot, they dissemble, etc." In spite of the fact that the Soviet Union's leaders kept the Vietnamese leaders informed on many political issues, the Vietnamese were accused of holding back information on their foreign and internal policies. For example, the Vietnamese were said to inform the Soviets more candidly about developments at the Paris peace negotiations only when they needed the assistance and support of the Soviet Union. Information provided about party building, about the economic situation of the country, about losses incurred from American bombing, and about ties of the DRV with other countries, was said to be of poor quality and acquired by the Soviets only with great difficulty.[26]

But the most telling example was provided by the experience of a Soviet delegation headed by Marshall P. F. Batitski (commander-in-chief of the Soviet Air Defense Forces) that visited North Vietnam in March 1972. According to the Soviet embassy, when the Vietnamese leaders requested the provision of new arms from Batitski, they said nothing about the fact that they were planning to launch the biggest military offensive of the war immediately after his delegation's departure.[27] This incident is a stunning reflection on the Vietnamese distrust of their main patron at that time.

Referring to these events, the Soviet embassy report concluded its evaluation of Soviet-Vietnamese relations for the year 1972:

> These and similar negative moments are gradually being overcome, but they are leaving certain impressions in our relations. However, on the whole, we

repeat that the leadership of the DRV continued on the course of strengthening ties with the Soviet Union, seeing in that the main buttress of its struggle and of peaceful construction.[28]

No doubt this sometimes rather jaundiced report reflected the tensions of 1972. A year later the Soviet embassy's view of the relationship was more upbeat. The embassy's annual report for 1973 spoke of the aspiration of "the Vietnamese comrades" to rely upon the Soviet Union in deciding the most important questions of domestic and foreign policy, during what was called the transformative period from war to peace after the signing of the Paris peace agreement.[29] The report claimed that the visit of a high-level Vietnamese party and government delegation to the USSR in 1973 helped to weaken Chinese influence in the DRV, in particular undermining its anti-Soviet propaganda.[30] The report explained only indirectly what might have been the decisive factor in this matter when it specified the details of the agreement on new Soviet aid unveiled in August. The most significant feature of this agreement was the section in which the Soviet Union forgave the DRV a debt of more than $1 billion from earlier credit deliveries.[31] Trade relations involved the USSR providing goods worth nearly 133 million rubles, of which 108 million rubles was on credit and more than 7 million rubles was an outright gift. Besides this, social organizations in the USSR sent gratuitous aid worth 10 million rubles.[32]

The embassy saw 1973 as the year in which the Vietnamese leaders "began to take a significantly critical approach to several steps of the Maoists." In so doing it was breaking from the previous VWP line of standing aside from the "hostile, anti-Soviet line of Peking" and promoting "externally identical friendly relations with the Soviet Union and the DRV."[33]

By the beginning of 1975, the Soviet embassy could speak of "the further closeness of the positions of both of our parties and countries on a whole series of important international problems." However, the embassy noted the continuing existence of "specific negative phenomena" in the policy of the Vietnamese friends. One of these was the aspiration of the VWP leadership to remain "aloof from the struggle of the CPSU and other fraternal parties against Maoism." Moreover, the Vietnamese were not interested in establishing broad ties with the Council for Mutual Economic Assistance although they had told the USSR representatives in meetings that they were studying the question of their participation in this organization.[34]

The report recognized that the China factor was exercising a restraining influence on the cooperation of the DRV with the socialist countries. But so too was "the narrowly nationalistic path of the Vietnamese comrades," which caused them to form their attitude to the most important international problems "through the prism of the solution of the Vietnamese question." That is why the Vietnamese leaders remained skeptical of Soviet-American dialogue. Yet, the report noted, their reaction to the 1974 Brezhnev-Nixon meeting was calmer than before, because the Vietnamese leaders "are certain of the Soviet Union's position in relation to the Vietnamese people's struggle" and they regard the meetings as "an internal affair."[35]

VIETNAM'S POSTWAR INTERACTION WITH THE SOVIET UNION

Clearly, the Soviet Union was not completely satisfied with the Vietnamese taking a pro-Soviet position "on a whole series of important international problems." As genuine Marxist-Leninists, they wanted complete unanimity on all questions, including support for the CPSU in its struggle against Maoism. These Soviet complaints, and their desire for the Vietnamese to join Comecon, would require the Vietnamese to further alienate the Chinese. It would not be until 1978 that the Vietnamese would be prepared to do this.

In the wake of the North Vietnamese conquest of South Vietnam, the Hanoi leadership was already involved politically in support of Soviet objectives in western Europe (especially Portugal) and the Third World (especially Angola). The military relationship between the two countries was close; it involved by 1972 the Vietnamese army abandoning Maoist military doctrines in favor of Soviet military doctrines and almost totally reequipping itself with Soviet weaponry. These developments had greatly upset the Chinese, as we have seen in the previous chapter. By the second half of 1975, the warming Soviet-Vietnamese relationship had become the central point of tension between China and Vietnam.

There were other more concrete ways in which the Vietnamese leaders were now working in support of Soviet foreign policy goals. In late 1975 the Soviet KGB appealed to the Vietnamese Interior Ministry for the provision of 10,000 captured American automatic rifles and 10 million rounds of ammunition. The KGB normally supplied specific foreign communist parties and "national liberation movements" with Western-produced weaponry.[36] (This was obviously to conceal the Soviet Union's role as supplier.) But at that time the KGB was in short stock of such weapons. In December the

Vietnamese minister of Internal Affairs, Tran Quoc Hoan, confidentially informed Soviet KGB representatives that the VWP Politburo had agreed to satisfy that Soviet request. However, because such captured arms were located under the control of the DRV Defense Ministry, Hoan advised the KGB to request that Vietnamese Defense Minister Vo Nguyen Giap provide the arms for free. KGB Chairman Yuri Andropov, in a report to the Soviet Central Committee in December 1975, agreed with that procedure and advised that the Soviet request to Giap be accompanied by an offer of a similar number of Soviet-produced arms in exchange.[37]

The increased closeness of Soviet-Vietnamese relations by the mid-1970s was also reflected in the kinds of candid, confidential political conversations the Vietnamese party leaders would have with the Soviet ambassador. The kinds of conversations held during the 1976–78 period (discussed in Chapters 4 and 7), in which Le Duan and other leaders outlined Hanoi's strategic goals in the region and their political assessments of the international situation, had not taken place during the early 1970s, let alone during the 1960s.

The Vietnamese attitude toward the Soviet Union during the period from 1975 until Vietnam's open break with China was summed up by Secretariat member To Huu in early 1978, in a meeting with a Soviet propaganda department delegation. The Soviet delegation reported To Huu stating that although at that time there was no leading center of the world communist movement, every true communist, internationalist, and patriot knew that all the best of them in the contemporary world were concentrating around the CPSU and the USSR. Moreover, the CPV was constantly orienting itself to the experience of the CPSU.[38]

While this statement was partly intramural diplomacy among fellow propagandists, it did have some political meaning. To Huu was simultaneously conceding that there were genuine communist power centers independent of the Soviet Union, but that the Vietnamese felt that the CPSU and the USSR provided the most worthy center of support and inspiration for other communists.

The Soviet Union had been the major supplier of economic aid to Vietnam since the 1960s. But as China's support diminished at the end of the Vietnam war, aid from the Soviet bloc continued to increase. The economic relationship with the Soviet bloc was by the mid to late 1970s vital for the Vietnamese. According to Le Duan, as of February 1978 there were 245 projects that had been completed or were being built with Soviet economic assistance. He cited Soviet involvement in the construction of Vietnam's power, machine, and coal industries.[39] According to the Soviets, as of January 1, 1978, 185 major projects had been put into operation. A most important component of these projects were factories that were said to generate 25 percent of Vietnam's electricity; the total volume of its tin, sulphuric acid, apatite, and superphosphate; nearly all of Vietnam's coal; and nearly two-thirds of its machine tools and metal-cutting machines.[40]

According to the Soviets, from 1975 to 1977 more than 6,000 Soviet technical experts worked in Vietnam. During the same period more than 15,000 Vietnamese graduated from "advanced Soviet schools" and about 3,000 Vietnamese received advanced science degrees in the Soviet Union. It was also claimed that during the same period nearly 9,000 Vietnamese engineers and workers underwent practical training at various enterprises and construction sites in the Soviet Union.[41]

The trade turnover between Vietnam and the Soviet Union was said to have constituted over 400 million rubles in 1977, making it the highest in all the years of Soviet-Vietnamese cooperation.[42] These statistics were touted by the Soviet Union at that particular time as a political preparation for the entry of Vietnam into Comecon. Yet they provide no real explanation as to why Vietnam should have wanted to join Comecon. After all, if this was the help Vietnam was receiving while it was outside the organization, what extra benefits was it likely to receive once it was inside? This question was especially pertinent because of the fact that by joining Comecon Vietnam would predictably antagonize its second major aid donor, China, and probably provoke the termination of China's aid. The Vietnamese leaders were only prepared to do that when their relationship with China had deteriorated for other political reasons.

VIETNAM'S DECISION TO JOIN COMECON

The Vietnamese decision to join Comecon and the Soviet decision to admit Vietnam were not made overnight. Vietnam had already been given observer status in Comecon, a status it shared with Laos, Angola, and Ethiopia. In May 1977, Hanoi became a member of the International Bank for Economic Cooperation (IBEC) and the Soviet-sponsored International Investment Bank.[43]

But in mid-1977 the Vietnamese indicated to the Soviet leaders their interest in acquiring full membership in Comecon. The Vietnamese were told that they had to make a written request for such membership. Then at the beginning of 1978 a formal letter was sent to the Comecon organization requesting Vietnam's admission as a full member.[44] At some point—probably no later than early April 1978—a "Vietnam working group" was formed within the Comecon (also known as CEMA) framework to study the coordination of economic aid to Vietnam.[45] Thus we can see that Vietnam had decided to move into closer alignment with the Soviet Union during the year of its open warfare with Democratic Kampuchea, but before its public polemics with China, and before its final break with the Khmers Rouges.

On June 15 Vietnamese Foreign Minister Nguyen Duy Trinh invited the Soviet embassy's charge d'affaires Igor Ognetov to a meeting in the Vietnamese Ministry of Foreign Affairs. There Trinh conveyed a message from the Vietnamese Politburo stating that Party General Secretary Le Duan wished to visit Moscow in June to meet with Leonid Brezhnev and other Soviet leaders. The purpose was said to be "to exchange opinions about the situation in Vietnam and also about a series of important international questions" involving conditions in Southeast Asia. More to the point, Le Duan also intended "to express several requests to the leadership of the CPSU in Moscow."[46] Nguyen Duy Trinh hoped for a favorable response to this initiative of the CPV and emphasized that the Vietnamese wanted the meeting to be held secretly.

We do not have the records of what transpired at the Moscow meeting in late June. However, we do know some details of a follow-up meeting held in Hanoi in late July between Vietnamese Economics Minister Le Thanh Nghi with the Soviet charge d'affaires Igor Ognetov. In that meeting, Nghi referred to the many requests that he had previously addressed to "the Soviet comrades" in Moscow. However, Nghi stated that on instructions from the SRV government he had additional requests for economic raw materials—coal, sulphuric pyrites, and sulphate ammonia. The supply of these commodities had been terminated by China, and Vietnam needed them to be replaced by the Soviet Union.[47] Thus it is likely that this request for replacement of Chinese supplies was typical of one aspect of the discussions that took place in Moscow. Vietnam would have regarded that meeting as preparation for its entry into Comecon.

During the session of the Council for Mutual Economic Assistance, held in Bucharest June 27–29, 1978, Vietnam was admitted to that organization. According to *Nhan Dan*, Vietnam's admission was "a logical development of our motherland on the road to socialism."[48]

The admission of Vietnam to Comecon was worked out between the Vietnamese and Soviet leaders in advance. But according to Yugoslav observers at the Bucharest summit, a majority of Comecon members were not informed in advance of the Vietnamese application. It was clear that some East European members resented Vietnam's entry because it would mean a further drain on their own resources.[49] Among the tasks that the Comecon countries were liable to have to undertake was the completion of at least some, if not all, of the eighty projects that the Chinese had abandoned.

The eighty-seventh session of the Comecon Executive Committee, held in Ulan Bator, Mongolia, at the end of September, was the first to be attended by Vietnam. There it was announced that "necessary measures" would be taken by the organization to help Vietnam carry on projects abandoned by China.[50] Specifically, the committee discussed providing assistance for the completion of the Hanoi–Ho Chi Minh City railway, resumption of other projects abandoned by China, and filling in the gaps caused by the withdrawal of Chinese experts and technical assistance.[51] In the light of these decisions, one suspects that Hanoi's decision to join Comecon was not made in order to acquire major new economic advantages, but rather merely to make up for recent economic losses. Naturally, the Vietnamese leadership did not explain it in these terms. According to *Nhan Dan*:

> Expanding economic cooperation with fraternal countries means enhancing our country's strength and at the same time contributing to beefing up the forces of the community of socialist countries and strengthening the bastions of world peace and world revolution.[52]

Whatever the relative economic advantages to Vietnam of joining Comecon, it is clear that Vietnam's entry, in the context of Vietnam's loss of Chinese aid, posed an enormous economic burden upon the Soviet bloc. The dissatisfaction of Eastern European members of the bloc at having to share the economic burden of Vietnam is reflected in the willingness of East European officials to provide details of their burden to the Western press.[53] The advantage to the Soviet Union and its like-minded allies within Comecon of having Vietnam's membership was clearly not economic but political. It was a step in bringing Hanoi closer to Moscow's political control.

VIETNAM'S DECISION TO FULLY ALIGN WITH
THE SOVIET UNION

The June 1978 meeting in Moscow undoubtedly dealt with more than economic matters. This is corroborated by the presence in Le Duan's delegation of the deputy chief of staff of the Vietnam People's Army, Le Truong Tan. Also, as we have discussed earlier (Chapter 4), Vietnamese cadres were told in June 1978 that Vietnam was planning to invade Cambodia.[54] Soviet military support would have been regarded by the Vietnamese as vital for the success of such an operation. The provision of such support was probably on the agenda, even though all of Vietnam's purposes were not.

In June reports began emanating from China that the Soviet Union had established guided missile bases in Vietnam stocked with missiles directed at China. The first such report claimed that a base had been established at Huong Khe in north central Vietnam. The source of the story was the Hong Kong pro-Chinese communist newspaper *Wen Wei Pao*.[55] At the end of June, AFP reported that a former Vietnamese Communist Party cadre of ethnic Chinese origin, who had recently returned to China, had claimed that the Soviet Union had set up a long-range missile base, directed at China, at Cam Ranh Bay on the south Vietnam coast.[56] Another ethnic Chinese, a former captain in the Vietnamese army, made a similar claim from China about a missile base being established near Hon Gai port, east of Hanoi.[57] These reports, sponsored by the Chinese government, could not be independently corroborated. But Beijing was projecting the view that the closer ties between Hanoi and Moscow were of military significance.

Soon reports of increased Soviet military activity were being disseminated by Western sources. In August it was reported by Western diplomats in Singapore that the Soviet Union was shipping significant quantities of military equipment to Hanoi for the first time since the Vietnam War ended in 1975.[58] According to U.S. officials, during August 1978 the Soviet Union also undertook a major airlift of military and civilian supplies to Hanoi.[59]

All of these events were taking place in the context of heightened tensions on the Cambodian-Vietnamese and the Sino-Vietnamese borders. These behind-the-scenes military events were to be given a public political climax that would at last clear up any residual ambiguities in the minds of observers about Asia's new political realignments.

THE TREATY OF FRIENDSHIP AND COOPERATION

In November, on the occasion of the sixty-first anniversary of the Great October Revolution, a high-level Vietnamese delegation, led by Party Secretary General Le Duan and Prime Minister Pham Van Dong, arrived in Moscow. The visit was previewed by Moscow Radio, which spoke glowingly of the importance of the Soviet Union's support in the realization of successive victories by "the Vietnamese people."[60] Other Moscow Radio broadcasts denounced China as the cause of the SRV-PRC conflict.[61]

The Vietnamese delegation was welcomed at Moscow's Vnukovo Airport on November 1 by Leonid Brezhnev, Alexei Kosygin, Andrei Gromyko, Viktor Grishin, Dmitri Ustinov, Rusakov and other officials.[62] These top Soviet leaders all participated in talks in the Kremlin with the Vietnamese delegation.

On the Vietnamese side were not only Le Duan and Pham Van Dong, but also Politburo member and SRV vice premier, Le Thanh Nghi, the SRV ambassador to the USSR, Nguyen Huu Khieu (also a Central Committee member), and chairman of the SRV State Planning Committee (and VCP Central Committee candidate member), Le Khac. Most interesting were the other two members of the delegation—Van Tien Dung, a Politburo member and chief of staff of the Vietnam People's Army, and Nguyen Co Thach, a Central Committee member and deputy minister of Foreign Affairs. Dung's presence (like that of Ustinov from the Soviet side) was an indication that military matters were under discussion. But there was a second reason why Dung and Thach's presence was of interest. Both of these individuals were outranked, in party and government protocol terms, by the two Politburo members who theoretically were in charge of the same functional areas—Defense Minister Vo Nguyen Giap and Foreign Minister Nguyen Duy Trinh. Both Giap and Trinh were replaced in their ministerial portfolios by Dung and Thach in February 1980, and officially removed from the Politburo at the Fifth Party Congress in 1982. Obviously, they were out of favor already by November 1978. Vietnam's realignment with the Soviet Union and the decision to invade Cambodia were probably connected to their demise[63]—a demise manifested by their absence from the November 1978 delegation to Moscow.

On November 3 the Soviet Union and Vietnam signed a Treaty of Friendship and Cooperation. The key elements of the treaty were to be found in three places. In Article 2:

> The two parties shall continue to coordinate their long-term national economic plans, agree upon long-term measures aimed at developing the most important sectors of the economy, science, and technology and exchange knowledge and experience accumulated in the building of socialism and communism.

In Article 4:

> The two parties shall do their utmost to consolidate the world socialist system and actively contribute to the development and defense of the socialist gains.

In Article 6:

> In case either party is attacked or threatened with attack, the two parties signatory to the treaty shall immediately consult each other with a view to eliminating that threat, and shall take appropriate and effective measures to safeguard peace and the security of the two countries.[64]

The treaty amounted to a statement of economic and political alliance, and almost but not quite a military alliance. It was the formal climax of a process that had been taking place since 1970. Yet, as the Vietnamese themselves pointed out, the signing of the treaty "opened a new stage in the relationship between the Vietnamese and Soviet parties and countries."[65]

What was the purpose of the treaty? Perhaps Vietnamese motives can be discerned in an article in the V.C.P.'s theoretical journal, *Tap Chi Cong San.* In the course of extolling the inspirational success of the Soviet Union since 1917, the article made a most telling claim:

> Today, there is one fact that no one can deny: in the face of the invincible strength of the USSR and the fraternal socialist countries, the imperialists and international reactionaries, regardless of how bellicose they might be, think twice before recklessly unleashing a war against the world socialist system. They realize that the inevitable outcome of a military attack upon the USSR and the fraternal socialist countries closely linked to it by means of a bond of great friendship would be heavy retaliation. This situation has increased the bravery and confidence of the fighters for the revolution and peace in the world.[66]

What this passage suggests is that the Vietnamese communists thought that by formally tying themselves to the "world socialist system" led by the Soviet Union, they would be compelling the Soviet Union into providing a protective shield for Vietnam against the possible attacks of the "imperialists" and "international reactionaries." The need for such a shield was becoming more apparent as the tensions with China were exacerbated over the related issues of the Hoa and the independence of Cambodia. In effect, the treaty was perceived as a minimal insurance policy by the Vietnamese communists, who had already decided to launch a full-scale invasion of Cambodia at the beginning of the next dry season, only a few weeks later.

But the Soviets seem to have perceived the treaty differently. According to Article 6, the obligatory reaction for each party to any military attack on one party was for each to "consult" with a view to taking "effective measures" to "eliminate the threat." No obligation for direct military intervention was required. According to a former senior Soviet official, Mikhail Kapitsa, it was a political treaty only. The Vietnamese had wanted a clear formulation of military assistance, but the Soviets refused. The Soviet Union had no intention of going to war with China over Vietnam.[67]

THE SOVIET UNION AND VIETNAM'S DECISION TO INVADE CAMBODIA

The Chinese government, and many western leaders and political analysts, have always assumed that Vietnam's decision to invade Cambodia was at the urging of the Soviet Union. But there is no direct evidence of any such Soviet role. On the contrary, although the evidence available to us is incomplete, all of that available evidence suggests that the Soviet leaders were not informed of Vietnam's plans until after the event.

The transcripts of the secret conversations between the leaders of the Soviet Union and Vietnam, conducted in June and November 1978 in Moscow, have never been made available to anyone outside the former Soviet leadership. But one leading China expert in the former Soviet Foreign Ministry (who is still an employee of the Russian Foreign Ministry), and the two principal experts on Vietnam and Cambodia in the former Soviet Central Committee during the latter half of 1978 (both of whom are now retired from Russian government service), all now emphatically deny that the Vietnamese had informed the Soviets in advance of their plans to invade.[68]

There are two pieces of evidence that tend to support this claim. One is the official secret record of conversation between the Vietnamese general Secretary Le Duan and Soviet Ambassador Igor Sherbakov, which took place in Hanoi in September 1978, and which I have read. During their meeting, Le Duan spoke in vague terms of how the Vietnamese Communist Party Politburo had set as its goal "to solve fully this question [of Kampuchea] by the beginning of 1979." He also indicated that Vietnamese calculations about the possible military reaction of China had now changed. More ominously, Le Duan also emphasized that it was impossible for Vietnam to wait until Beijing "consolidates itself in Kampuchea."[69] But in terms of practical solutions, Le Duan spoke only of the efforts that Vietnam had undertaken in promoting a Cambodian resistance, making claims that there were nine battalions of Khmers trained by the Vietnamese in operation and twenty leaders of provincial districts "coming out against the Phnom Penh regime and sympathizing with Vietnam." Though Le Duan's talk of how the Vietnamese Politburo had decided "to solve fully this question [of Cambodia] by the beginning of 1979" can be interpreted by us in hindsight, when taken in conjunction with other evidence, as evidence of Hanoi's plan to invade, it would not have been crystal clear to the Soviets at that time that the Vietnamese had abandoned the idea of overthrowing the Khmers Rouges only by the more limited means of sponsoring an internal insurrection. No mention was made in the Soviet ambassador's official report of the conversation of any Vietnamese plan to invade and occupy Cambodia.

The second piece of evidence that tends to suggest that the former Soviet functionaries' recent accounts are credible is the confirmed fact, mentioned earlier in this chapter, that the Vietnamese communist leaders had failed to inform the Soviets in advance of their plans to launch the 1972 Easter offensive—the biggest military offensive of the Vietnam war. This deception was perpetrated despite the fact that the Vietnamese had asked a Soviet delegation headed by Marshall P. F. Batitski (the commander-in-chief of the Soviet Air Defense Forces), for the provision of new arms during his visit to Hanoi just prior to the launching of the offensive.[70]

Of course one cannot prove a negative. It is possible, for example, that Le Duan did inform Brezhnev or Kosygin secretly, in an unrecorded conversation, of Vietnamese plans to invade Cambodia. But though such a conversation is possible, it is inconceivable that Brezhnev, Kosygin, or any Politburo member would have had any reason to keep such important information secret from other Soviet Politburo members and thereby have concealed the information from the Central Committee's foreign policy specialists.

If the invasion plans were not discussed, then what could have been the

Vietnamese agenda at its June and November 1978 meetings with the Soviet leaders? It was most likely what the Hanoi leaders would have described as the Chinese threat to Vietnam's independence. As we have seen, Chinese-Vietnamese polemics over Vietnam's expulsion of its ethnic Chinese citizens and the cutoff of Chinese aid to Vietnam were the main public issues between those two neighbors. We know that the Vietnamese desperately needed Soviet bloc economic assistance to replace Chinese aid. Undoubtedly, they could play to a more sympathetic Soviet ear the need to contain a Chinese threat rather than a Cambodian threat.

One former Soviet official today attempts to explain Vietnamese behavior by suggesting that Hanoi may have believed that Moscow would have opposed the planned invasion.[71] Even so, the basic norms of alliance protocol would have suggested that the Vietnamese inform the Soviets just prior to the event, when it would have been too late for Moscow to leverage Hanoi by withholding supplies, but when there would have been enough time for the Soviets to prepare themselves politically and diplomatically. Hanoi's deception shows the limits of the Soviet-Vietnamese relationship, even at its zenith. The Vietnamese communist leaders were not willing to be candid with their patrons about their most important political and military plans even after fully committing themselves to a political alliance with the Soviets, at a time when Vietnam needed Soviet material and diplomatic support for its regional adventures, and when it needed Soviet protection against a possible Chinese retaliation. Yet, given the international perceptions of Soviet responsibility for Vietnamese foreign policy behavior, Hanoi's deceptions would have dire political consequences for the international reputation and hence national security of the Soviet Union.

CONCLUSIONS

The internationalization of the struggle for Cambodia was not the result of events ultimately set in motion by the two major communist powers, the Soviet Union and China. Both major powers were brought into the conflict by the actions of their clients, who were the actual instigators of the hostilities.

But there was still a certain asymmetry in the role of the Soviets and Chinese in the conflict. Only China had been a direct participant in the fighting. The Soviet Union had the good fortune to be needed only as a supplier of arms and economic aid. Its client was able to take care of its own wars. In contrast with China, the Soviet Union had no direct security threats posed to it by the outcome of the struggle for Cambodia, though it did face other political and diplomatic costs.

It is worth noting from an earlier period, before the end of the Vietnam War, the extent to which the Vietnamese communist leadership was unable to fully trust the Soviet Union. Hanoi even failed to inform the Soviet leaders of its plan to launch the 1972 Easter offensive. This was in spite of the fact that it was heavily dependent upon Soviet aid and had tilted away from China and toward the USSR in the Sino-Soviet conflict.

The apparent failure of the Hanoi leaders to share information with Moscow about impending plans to invade Cambodia is an even more striking manifestation of their congenital suspiciousness.

Hanoi may have concluded that Moscow was boxed into supporting whatever Vietnam did by virtue of its now shared antipathy toward Beijing. If this was its calculation, then Hanoi was correct. Nevertheless, Hanoi's deceit on this occasion could not avoid tempering Soviet-Vietnamese relations. If fear of betrayal was at the root of Hanoi's deceit, then its insult to its patron would ensure that in any future crisis, if Soviet and Vietnamese state interests were ever in conflict, the Soviet Union would have that much less sentiment for the Vietnamese to be swayed by.

CHAPTER NINE

The Consequences of the Vietnamese Invasion

The Vietnamese invasion and subsequent ten-year military occupation of Cambodia was a disaster for both of the local belligerent states and for the local populations. Neither of the two local regimes saw their objectives fully realized. The Khmers Rouges, and especially Pol Pot and his inner circle, were the biggest losers. They had anticipated that they would defeat the Vietnamese army. Instead, they lost all political and military power and eventually, after fifteen years spent literally in the wilderness, suffered political and military disintegration through defections.

The consequences of the invasion for the Vietnamese communists are mixed. They did eventually achieve their initial goal of destroying the Khmers Rouges regime. But they had expected a quick victory and the acceptance of a fait accompli by the international community. Instead, there was no quick victory and the Vietnamese suffered for over ten years from Chinese military pressure and international diplomatic and economic isolation, which retarded the economic growth of the country. The Vietnamese were forced to withdraw their military forces from Cambodia and accept the temporary reconstitution of the Cambodian polity under U.N. supervision. However, Vietnam's Cambodian clients were able to retain power.

The Soviet Union initially made great strategic gains from the Vietnamese invasion. It gained naval and air bases in Vietnam for the first time. But the Soviet Union collapsed from within in 1991, and the successor Russian state has shown little interest in the benefits of alliance with Vietnam. Russia's main concern now is to recoup some of its billions of dollars squandered in aid to Vietnam.

Of all of the involved states, only China seems to have emerged from the conflict with great success. Initially it too paid a price in manpower and prestige as a result of the failure of its February 1979 invasion to pressure a Vietnamese withdrawal from Cambodia. Yet China eventually succeeded in its goal of removing Vietnamese forces from Cambodia. China is now the dominant military and political force in the region, and its political and human losses over standing tough on Cambodia seem inconsequential in light of its dynamic economic growth and global political influence.

THE KHMERS ROUGES LEADERSHIP'S LOSS OF POWER

The first and most immediate consequence of the invasion was the toppling of Pol Pot's regime from power in the capital, Phnom Penh, and throughout most of the country. In the initial weeks of the invasion, Pol Pot and his inner circle adopted a strategy of full-scale, main-force unit confrontation with the invading army. This strategy was based upon the Cambodian regime's assumption of the ideological superiority of the Cambodian "people's army" as contrast with the "revisionist" Vietnamese. This assumption proved to be as false after the Vietnamese invasion as it had been before. Against the numerically superior and much better-armed Vietnamese, this strategy was a recipe for military disaster. The Vietnamese forces annihilated entire units of the revolutionary army of Democratic Kampuchea, reducing the defending force to perhaps half of its preinvasion size. Eventually the rump armed forces of Democratic Kampuchea broke up into smaller units and reverted to guerrilla warfare. They were soon forced to retreat to bases in the jungle areas in the west and north of Cambodia, adjacent to Thailand and Laos, from which they launched attacks against the Vietnamese army.

On January 9, 1979, the Vietnamese army reached the capital, Phnom Penh, and installed in power the leaders of the National Salvation Front, which became known as the People's Republic of Kampuchea (PRK). Its leadership consisted in part of former members of the Khmer Viet Minh, who had been trained and kept under wraps in Hanoi for years. But most PRK leaders were former Khmers Rouges commanders from Cambodia's eastern provinces, most notably Heng Samrin, Chea Sim, and Hun Sen.[1] They had fled to Vietnam in order to escape Pol Pot's terror. The organizational vanguard of this government was the Kampuchean People's Revolutionary Party, which, as we saw in Chapter 1, had been created by the Vietnamese communists back in 1951.[2]

VIETNAM'S WAR WITH CHINA

In a statement before the U.N. Security Council in January 1979, the Chinese government condemned the Vietnamese invasion of Cambodia as "a major step in pushing its own regional hegemony and an important part of the Soviet drive for hegemony in Asia and the Far East."[3] No doubt China believed this and was worried about this. But it also had reason to fear that Vietnamese success over its client regime in Cambodia would be seen as a humiliation for China. Thus it was inevitable, even if only for the purpose of saving face, that China had to retaliate against Vietnam militarily.

On February 17, 1979, Chinese armed forces invaded northern Vietnam in order "to teach Vietnam a lesson." After three weeks of heavy fighting in the northern provinces bordering China, the Chinese forces withdrew, having suffered tens of thousands of casualties. The Vietnamese also suffered heavy losses, although they never used their regular forces in the fighting. The reports of Western correspondents indicated devastation of the border towns of Lao Cai, Lang Son, and Cao Bang.[4] The Chinese invasion failed to force the Vietnamese to withdraw from Cambodia. But it did compel Hanoi to maintain a large portion of its army in the northern part of Vietnam and thereby prevented those troops from being deployed in Cambodia. The threat of a second Chinese invasion meant that Vietnam had to continue to keep a large portion of its forces in this location indefinitely.

China responded to the Vietnamese invasion in a second important way. It maintained aid to the forces of the Khmers Rouges, which had abandoned Phnom Penh and retreated to the western and northern portions of the country, enabling itself to carry on the struggle by guerrilla warfare. China also subsequently provided military aid to emergent noncommunist resistance forces led by Prince Sihanouk and former Prime Minister Son Sann.[5] Eventually, the Vietnamese inability to eliminate the Cambodian resistance, combined with the drying up of Soviet aid, forced an end of the direct Vietnamese military presence in Cambodia. At this point, China had won its confrontation with Vietnam.

VIETNAM'S ALIENATION OF INTERNATIONAL SUPPORT

Prior to its invasion of Cambodia, Hanoi was making feverish efforts to win over the United States to political normalization, which it was hoped would soon be followed by reconstruction aid from the United States and international lending agencies. The Vietnamese prospects had been thwarted prior to 1978 by Hanoi's insistence that aid be provided as "reparations." This precondition was clearly an unacceptable assault upon American pride, which made it impossible for even those U.S. officials sympathetic to normalization to pursue that objective.[6]

The Vietnamese leaders were confident that their invasion and continuing occupation of Cambodia would be quickly forgotten.[7] But they were wrong. Their actions precluded any prospects of imminent normalization with the United States. In addition, it turned most of the Western and Third World nations against any cooperation with Vietnam. The European community cut off its food aid to Vietnam. Only Sweden and France were left as aid donors from that important part of the world.

Furthermore, the international community, expressing itself through the annual meetings of the United Nations General Assembly, failed to recognize the Vietnamese-installed government. Instead a majority at first recognised the Khmers Rouges government of Democratic Kampuchea. Then, after a coalition government was formed in 1982 between the Khmers Rouges forces and the two noncommunist resistance groups headed by Prince Sihanouk and Son Sann, that entity—the Coalition Government of Democratic Kampuchea (CGDK)—began to receive greater and greater majorities at the annual meetings of the United Nations committee on credentials. When Vietnam and the Soviet bloc posed their final challenge to the CGDK credentials for the Kampuchea seat at the U.N. in 1983, a record 90 countries voted to recognize the CGDK. In 1984 and 1985, in a concession of political defeat, the Vietnamese failed to challenge the CGDK credentials. Moreover, in the annual U.N. General Assembly resolution on withdrawal of foreign troops from Cambodia, the number voting in favor rose from 91 in 1979 to 97 in 1980, and reached 100 in 1981. In 1982 and 1983 the General Assembly vote had climbed to 105 in favor and 23 against, and in 1984, 110 nations voted for withdrawal of Vietnamese troops.[8]

Thus a major consequence of Hanoi's decision to invade Cambodia was Vietnam's international isolation, diplomatically and economically. Only the Soviet bloc nations and India recognized the Vietnamese-installed government in Phnom Penh, and it is these nations that provided almost all of Vietnam's foreign aid until 1991. With the ascension of Mikhail Gorbachev in the Soviet Union, and the emergence of "New Thinking" in Soviet foreign policy, the Vietnamese were pressured to withdraw most of their occupation forces from Cambodia.[9] Finally in 1991, following the collapse of communism in Eastern Europe and the Soviet Union and the ending of Soviet economic aid, Vietnam was forced to accept a United Nations-sponsored peace plan which would lead to the holding of free elections and the creation of an independent Cambodian government.

Even after the invasion, seeing the international consequences of their decision, the Vietnamese leaders could still easily have found a way out. They could have arranged a "neutralization" political solution, which would have involved a role for the noncommunist Cambodians, and excluded the Khmers Rouges. ASEAN and the United States would have settled eagerly for that. Given China's dependence upon ASEAN member Thailand as a conduit for Chinese arms supplies to the Khmers Rouges, China would have been compelled to accept such a solution. This alternative Vietnamese strategy was conceivable for Western analysts. It certainly could have been conceived by the Hanoi leadership. (According to a former Vietnamese communist official, this solution was actually proposed by former defense minister Vo Nguyen Giap in 1982.)[10] But the Hanoi leadership chose another course.

THE SOVIET POLITICAL AND MILITARY PRESENCE IN VIETNAM

The Soviet military presence in Vietnam was drastically increased as a result of the train of events set in motion by the Vietnamese invasion of Cambodia. After the Chinese invasion of Vietnam, the Soviet navy began to use Vietnamese ports for the first time. According to Singaporean intelligence, a Soviet cruiser moved into Cam Ranh Bay in March 1979, while some fifteen warships were operating in the South China Sea along with four submarines.[11] In mid-April TU-95 Bear strategic reconnaisance aircraft were deployed to Vietnam. It was in September 1979 that the first contingent of Soviet forces was believed to have landed at Cam Ranh Bay. In early 1980 most Vietnamese military forces were moved out. Though some security was provided by Vietnamese army units, throughout the 1980s the base had been for the exclusive use of the Soviet Union.

But the foreign and defense policy reforms instituted by Mikhail Gorbachev in the late 1980s had a powerful impact upon the Soviet-Vietnamese relationship. With the general cutback of Soviet forward air and naval deployments beginning in 1989, Soviet use of Cam Ranh began to decline. Vietnam became gradually less important for the USSR.

DIMENSIONS OF VIETNAMESE COLONIZATION OF CAMBODIA

Prior to their acceptance of the U.N. peace plan, the Vietnamese communists seemed likely to accrue one major gain from their decision to invade Cambodia. They had installed in Phnom Penh what was a fragile regime, but nevertheless their colonial regime, which was administering the "Vietnamization" of Cambodia. There were two dimensions of the colonial relationship.

First there was the direct political control of the Phnom Penh administration—the People's Republic of Kampuchea (PRK), later renamed the State of Cambodia (SOC) in 1989—by the Vietnamese. According to the accounts of numerous defectors from the regime, the PRK operated under the tutelage of Vietnamese advisers at all levels. Western aid workers in Cambodia agreed that the most important Vietnamese adviser was the Vietnamese ambassador to the PRK.[12] According to two senior defectors from the PRK Foreign Ministry, each morning the ambassador met with the foreign minister of the PRK, Hun Sen, and Hun Sen's senior subordinates, to outline the proper response to the events they would be dealing with that day. The ambassador himself acted upon the instructions cabled daily from Hanoi. The ambassador's instructions were passed down from Hun Sen and his aides to the heads of the fourteen departments of the Foreign Ministry. In these departments there were another fifteen to seventeen Vietnamese advisers supervising the day-to-day activities of the Ministry. All the Vietnamese advisers were under the control of an office in Hanoi, attached to the party apparatus, identified as B-68. Whenever a Cambodian Foreign Ministry official traveled abroad, he was armed with position papers written by the Vietnamese in French or English. According to the former head of the political indoctrination department of the Central Committee of the Kampuchean People's Revolutionary Party, Mun Sek Yen, this was the pattern for all government departments.[13] Numerous other defectors from the PRK have confirmed this. Yen also claimed that most SOK Cabinet members were married to Vietnamese women who met regularly with Vietnamese officials to report on their husbands.[14]

Officials of the PRK/SOK were compelled to study the Vietnamese language. The highest posts were allegedly given to those with the best command of Vietnamese. High level PRK officials were sent to Vietnam for several months for "political education."[15] The whole political relationship was given a formal gloss from the very beginning with the signing of a Treaty of Peace and Friendship between the SRV and the PRK in February 1979. That treaty gave Vietnam the right to station "advisers" in Cambodia.[16]

The second dimension of the colonial relationship was the arrival from 1979 onwards of hundreds of thousands of Vietnamese civilians. The Vietnamese government has claimed that these Vietnamese settlers are people who lived in Cambodia before 1975, and either fled during the Lon Nol pogroms of 1970 or were expelled by the Khmers Rouges after 1975. But the observations of Western correspondents inside Cambodia and interviews with refugees on the Thai-Cambodian border demonstrate that many of these Vietnamese settlers were newcomers.[17] French ethnographer Marie Alexandrine Martin's estimate is that between 400,000 and 600,000 Vietnamese civilians had settled in Cambodia since 1979. A decree of September 1983 specified that the Khmers had to share their land with the Vietnamese civilians and to help them to set themselves up and construct their houses. Also, each rural commune was obliged to receive a certain number of Vietnamese families.[18] As a further sign of Vietnam's colonial power, the Vietnamese army conscripted Cambodian civilians as corvée labor on military projects, such as mining and ditch-digging along the Thai-Cambodian border.[19]

In spite of their claim to have come to Cambodia to liberate the people from the tyranny of Pol Pot, the Vietnamese were for twelve years adamant that there could be no system of government in Cambodia other than the communist one that they had imposed, staffed as it was by unrepentant former Khmers Rouges. During this time the political consequences of their invasion were said to be "irreversible." This meant that any authentic noncommunist political leaders—most notably Prince Norodom Sihanouk, Son Sann, and their prominent followers—could not play a genuinely independent role in the political life of Cambodia. Until their acceptance of the United Nations peace plan in 1991, the Vietnamese attitude toward Sihanouk and Son Sann was that if these Cambodian resistance leaders dissociated themselves from Pol Pot and "the genocidal clique," they could play a role in the SOC as figureheads.

Although the Vietnamese were eventually forced to abandon their direct occupation of the country, their client communist party, led by Hun Sen, was able to retain power in the country for many years. This was formalized by Hun Sen's coup d'état of July 1997. Hun Sen's political endurance ensured a continuing Vietnamese influence over Cambodia.

THE FAILURE OF THE KHMERS ROUGES SURVIVAL STRATEGY

In 1982, under advice if not pressure from their only military and diplomatic lifelines, China and Thailand, the Khmers Rouges formally entered into an alliance with two noncommunist factions—the Khmer People's National Liberation Front led by former prime minister Son Sann and the FUNCINPEC partly led by supporters of Prince Norodom Sihanouk. Together they formed the Coalition Government of Democratic Kampuchea. This entity held Cambodia's seat at the United Nations. From Thai sanctuaries and Cambodian jungle redoubts, the Khmers Rouges and their allies undertook a decade-long guerrilla war against the armies of Vietnam and the Cambodian communist faction that Vietnam had installed in Phnom Penh.

That guerrilla insurgency achieved little success until the Gorbachev era in the Soviet Union and the subsequent collapse of communism in Eastern Europe and the USSR. The withdrawal of Soviet support forced a Vietnamese military withdrawal and forced all the Cambodian factions to accept a peace settlement involving elections under U.N. supervision. The Khmers Rouges initially agreed to the U.N. plan, which its leaders signed in Paris in October 1991. But after the first deployment of the United Nations Temporary Administration in Cambodia (UNTAC), it came to believe that the implementation was favoring the Vietnamese and their Cambodian clients in the State of Cambodia. At this point the Khmers Rouges withdrew their cooperation from UNTAC.

The elections were held without the participation of Pol Pot's forces. A majority of the large Cambodian voting turnout chose the noncommunist parties, especially the royalist FUNCINPEC party led by Sihanouk's son, Prince Norodom Ranariddh. Despite substantial intimidation conducted by the pro-Hanoi State of Cambodia faction, only 38 percent of the voters supported its candidates. But the losers, who controlled the police and the armed forces despite the specific provisions of the U.N. plan for their effective neutralization under U.N. supervision, refused to accept the electoral verdict. Hun Sen threatened civil war. In an attempt to avoid a renewal of the civil war, Prince Sihanouk agreed to allow the KPRP/SOC apparatus to retain control of key ministries, including police and defense, and their leaders to enter a coalition government of "national reconciliation" with the winners.[20]

Although the new Cambodian government was no more successful than its predecessor in defeating Pol Pot's forces militarily and ending the stalemate, it was able to persuade a large percentage of them to defect. In this sense, the electoral process helped the process of dismantling the Khmers Rouges forces under Pol Pot's leadership. Thousands of Khmers Rouges troops defected between 1993 and 1996, culminating in the defection of Standing Committee member and former Foreign Minister Ieng Sary to the government in September 1996.

By late 1996 the Khmers Rouges army under Pol Pot was but a shadow of its former self and utterly incapable of ever again seizing power by force. Factional strife within the Khmers Rouges leadership, revolving around what strategy to adopt toward the Phnom Penh government, led to Pol Pot ordering the assassination of his senior aide, former defense minister Son Sen, and all of Son Sen's family. In subsequent infighting, Pol Pot himself was arrested by other aides and removed from his leadership position.[21]

For over a year Pol Pot was held under house arrest in a remote jungle base by his remaining senior comrades, led by Ta Mok and Nuon Chea. But the disintegration of the movement and the defections to the Phnom Penh regime continued. Shortly after hearing a radio report of U.S. plans to have him arrested and brought before an international tribunal, Pol Pot died on April 15, 1998.[22] Thus Pol Pot, the instigator of armed defiance of Vietnam, had become irrelevant to Cambodian political life.

CONCLUSIONS

The final political consequences of the Vietnamese invasion of Cambodia have yet to be realized and thus a definitive final evaluation of that invasion is premature. But one can say that most of the central political leaders of the Khmers Rouges, most notably Pol Pot, lost almost everything. The weakest power of the four belligerents had suffered the most.

The Vietnamese communists are undoubtedly pleased that their Cambodian clients' resort after 1991 to Eastern European communist methods for regaining political power has paid off. But it is unclear whether the gains of both the 1993–97 "silent coup d'état," and the overt coup of July 1997, will be consolidated in the long run. These actions, in the context of the election results of 1993 and the partially rigged elections of 1998,[23] have demonstrated the domestic illegitimacy of Hun Sen's rule.

What is clear is that the invasion and occuption of Cambodia cost Vietnam much blood and resources and retarded its economic development for over a decade. Ultimately, after the collapse of communism in Eastern Europe and the Soviet Union compelled the Vietnamese leaders into a reconciliation with China, the tensions between the two neighbors were greatly diminished. But the reconciliation was achieved on China's terms, and it provided some loss of face for the smaller dragon.

Conclusion: History and Theory

This study has woven together the complex series of events and evolving international political relations that led to the Vietnamese decision to invade Cambodia. We began our analysis with a discussion of the problems this history posed to the prevailing academic theories of international relations and to foreign policy analysis more generally. The assumptions of academic theories were said to be overly rationalistic, betraying a very narrow conception of human psychology and a flawed understanding of the actual behavior of states in twentieth-century world politics. It was argued that the concept of political culture was a necessary intellectual tool for the analysis of international relations and the foundation for any attempts at building general theories.

The logical test for any viable theory of political science is its consistency with the empirical events that it purports to explain, and its ability to explain more than alternative competing theories. Let us then recapitulate the key elements in the causal chain of historical events that led to the Vietnamese invasion of Cambodia. After undertaking that task we can proceed to consider the theoretical implications of this historical process.

HISTORY

In summary we can say that Vietnam invaded Cambodia because it saw the action as a means of simultaneously achieving two purposes: ending the military attacks begun by the Khmers Rouges and satisfying a long-standing ambition to dominate its weaker neighbor. The first purpose, were it the only purpose, could have been achieved by actions short of full-scale invasion and occupation. An alternative response might have included an intensification of the counterattacks inside Cambodia's eastern provinces, which would have quickly destroyed Khmers Rouges offensive capabilities; the creation of a coordinated indigenous Cambodian armed resistance; and the temporary seizing of several eastern Cambodian provinces in conjunction with the pursuit of a sincere negotiation strategy to secure peace, involving China as an intermediary (which China had briefly tried of its own volition in 1977). That Vietnamese response would have avoided the severe political and economic costs that Vietnam suffered for over a decade as a result of the negative international reaction to its invasion and occupation of Cambodia.

On the other hand, without Khmers Rouges provocations, the Vietnamese would probably not have invaded, since they would have lacked a legitimizing public rationale. In other words, Khmers Rouges provocations provided a convenient pretext for a Vietnamese action that also had other less easily legitimizable purposes. But this does not tell us the whole story. For the behavior of the two local belligerents was affected by their relations with the two major communist powers, the Soviet Union and China.

It is customary for historians to distinguish between long-term, medium-term, and short-term or triggering causes. The long-term cause of Vietnam's invasion was Vietnamese imperial ambitions. Vietnamese political elites have aspired for centuries to dominate their weaker neighbors. This ambition was first displayed by the Vietnamese emperors, who modeled their courts on the political culture of the Chinese imperial court. Although Vietnam did not possess the relative preponderance of material power that had enabled China to dominate all of its immediate neighbors, Vietnam did possess sufficient power to dominate at least its immediate western and southwestern neighbors—the nations that are now known as Laos and Cambodia. That traditional imperial ambition was realized briefly in Cambodia in the nineteenth century before the arrival of the French colonialists. It was given both an additional impulse and a legitimacy by the appearance in the early twentieth century of the Communist International (Comintern), to which the Vietnamese communist political elites were then attached both organizationally and ideologically. The Comintern specified that the former colonies of what was then known as French Indochina should be unified in a political federation under de facto Vietnamese control.

The imperial ambitions of the Vietnamese communists were realized in Laos, where Vietnamese armed forces installed a client regime in 1975. They were thwarted in Cambodia by a combination of the resilience of Cambodian nationalism, the desire of the external powers at Geneva in 1954 to guarantee Cambodian sovereignty, and the political skills and international prestige of Cambodia's first post-independence leader, Prince Norodom Sihanouk. The eventual ascension to power in 1975 of a communist movement not under Vietnamese control seemed to ensure the security of Cambodia from Vietnamese domination. Yet this newly victorious communist movement soon began to act in such a provocatively aggressive way as to provide a pretext for the Vietnamese to justify their invasion and occupation of Cambodia. This was the immediate or triggering cause.

The Khmers Rouges, who emerged from an organizational embryo created by the Vietnamese communists, were not always hostile to their fellow revolutionaries. A genuine solidarity based upon Marxist-Leninist "proletarian internationalism" existed during the early years of the movement. But it did not last. The divergence of Vietnamese and Cambodian communist political interests during the 1960s, and the clear manifestation of Vietnamese ambition to control the Cambodian revolution during the early 1970s, slowly turned the Khmers Rouges leaders against their former mentors. At some stage in this political metamorphosis the Khmers Rouges leaders became ideological disciples of Mao Zedong. They pursued Mao's ideological precept of "self-reliance" only up to a point. They more consistently acted in accordance with the Maoist precept of the priority of subjective factors such as willpower and ideological purity over objective material factors such as military power and economic and manpower resources. This explains the Khmers Rouges' decision to confront the Vietnamese communists militarily, first over the Vietnamese communist presence in Cambodia during the 1970–75 war against South Vietnam and then, at war's end, over the borders and territory in dispute between Vietnam and Cambodia.

But the Khmers Rouges decision for military confrontation was irrational and counterproductive for a variety of reasons. It was a challenge to Vietnamese "face" and a provocation of the Vietnamese communists to take military countermeasures. It was a decision taken without consulting Cambodia's external patron, the People's Republic of China. It was a decision that did not betray any serious concern for the massively disproportionate military and manpower resources that Vietnam could array against Cambodia. It was a decision that was being applied by late 1977 in tandem with another decision to launch military attacks against Thai civilian settlements across Cambodia's western border. This final action further dispersed the Khmers

Rouges' military forces and even further increased the overwhelming number of military forces against which it had to contend. Then in 1978 Pol Pot began a purge of the political and military leadership of the Eastern Zone of the country, killing many experienced officers and cadres and causing others to flee to Vietnam. He thereby further weakened his own capacity to challenge Vietnam. These purges, and the Khmers Rouges attacks against Thailand, must have convinced the Vietnamese communists of the political and military irrationality of their antagonists, and thus of the likelihood of Vietnam prevailing in any major military conflict. Thus Pol Pot both provoked and enticed Vietnam to invade.

The intermediate causes of the invasion and war were the attitudes and policies of the external communist powers in relation to each other and in relation to the two local Indochinese nations. To understand why the major communist powers became involved in the conflict, making full-scale war between Vietnam and Cambodia more likely, one has to consider the foreign policies of Cambodia, Vietnam, the Soviet Union, and China.

As we have seen, the Khmers Rouges were ideological disciples of Mao Zedong. Because of this ideological affinity, the Khmers Rouges were natural allies of the Chinese communist regime until Mao's death in September 1976, and the arrest of his ultraleft allies, the Gang of Four, the following month. The shift by Mao's successor, Deng Xiaoping, toward more moderate domestic policies weakened Chinese authority in the minds of the Khmers Rouges. But the Deng regime was able to temper some, if not all, of the extreme aspects of Khmers Rouges foreign policy. For to the limited extent that the Khmers Rouges did think in traditional realpolitik terms, those thoughts compelled them to align with China against Vietnam.

This shift by the Khmers Rouges leaders from the original alliance with China based upon both an ideological inspiration and common political and military strategic interests to a more complex and less harmonious alliance based upon limited political and military strategic mutual interests was not understood by the Vietnamese leaders. Hanoi continued to see the China-Cambodia relationship as one of master and servant, in which Khmers Rouges aggressiveness was merely the acting out of a script that had been written in Beijing. Cambodia was described as a Chinese dagger pointed at the heart of Vietnam.

The Vietnamese leaders' flawed vision of the China-Cambodia relationship prevented them from responding to apparently genuine mediation attempts by China in 1977. Moreover, in accordance with their fears of China's hostility over their tilt toward Moscow, the Vietnamese had begun purging their own party of ethnic Chinese and Chinese-trained cadres in the early 1970s, and in 1976 they began a repressive policy against the entire ethnic Chinese population of Vietnam. In 1978 when the Vietnamese leaders' anxiety over their pro-Soviet policy fused with their fear of a Chinese–Khmers Rouges conspiracy, their persecutory policy climaxed. Hundreds of thousands of ethnic Chinese residents of northern Vietnam were expelled to China. This policy had the serious consequence of intensifying Beijing's anger with Hanoi. It caused cutbacks of Chinese aid to Vietnam in 1977 and 1978 and full aid termination in June 1978. It also consolidated the previously ambivalent Beijing–Phnom Penh alliance.

Hanoi's own earlier behavior had also triggered responses from Beijing that were detrimental to Hanoi's interests. China's traditional desire for a weak collection of tributary states on her borders would have ensured post-Mao China's continuing support for Cambodian independence. But Vietnamese actions in the context of the Sino-Soviet conflict provided a new security dimension to Chinese attitudes toward Cambodia. Vietnam's decision in the late 1960s to tilt toward the Soviet Union in its foreign policy line—in particular on many foreign policy issues that were irrelevant to Vietnamese national security but were matters of contention between the Soviet Union and China—angered Beijing. Given the massive assistance that Beijing had been providing the Hanoi leaders for over 20 years, Beijing came to regard Hanoi's pro-Moscow tilt as insulting in its ungratefulness. More ominously, Beijing came to perceive Hanoi as a mere servant of Soviet foreign policy. This was an exaggeration of the closeness of the Soviet-Vietnamese relationship at that time. But China's anger at the ostensible insult was genuine, as was its deep fear of Soviet military encirclement. Thus when the Vietnamese subsequently clashed with the Khmers Rouges (in events that followed and were causally unconnected to Hanoi's tilt toward the USSR), China came to see the struggle for Cambodia as a struggle for or against Soviet "social imperialist" expansion. China redefined what was originally a local issue into an issue of great global significance.

Finally, one has to consider the role of the Soviet Union. Without the political, military, and economic support of the Soviet Union and its East European satellites, the Vietnamese communists would not have even contemplated challenging China's political preferences in Southeast Asia. Of course, the Soviet Union did not determine Vietnamese imperial ambition, but it made the realization of that ambition at least plausible. That Soviet policy in Indochina after 1970 was as much concerned with curbing Chinese influence as it was in undermining American power can be seen in the Soviets' Cambodia policy. Instead of supporting the communist FUNK insurgency's Beijing-based front government, nominally headed by Prince Sihanouk, the Soviets continued to recognize the pro-American, anticommunist government of Lon Nol until the last weeks of the 1970–75 war. This Soviet policy had a clear albeit unintended consequence: it confirmed the Khmers Rouges' sense that the Soviet Union was their enemy and that the subsequent Soviet-Vietnamese alliance was a conspiracy aimed at Cambodia.

In reality, the Soviet-Vietnamese alliance, by the time it was formalized in 1978, was a conspiracy aimed at China. The Vietnamese communists, distrustful of even their most powerful sponsor, had failed to tell the Soviet Union of their plan to invade and occupy Cambodia until after the event. Nevertheless, subsequent Soviet willingness to assist the Vietnamese in establishing what amounted to a regional hegemony under Soviet auspices exacerbated China's concern for the threat to its own security. Soviet policy thereby produced more important unintended consequences in that it accelerated the process of Chinese-American rapprochement, and it resulted in the formation of a unified international coalition (led by China, the Association of Southeast Asian Nations, and the United States) opposed to Soviet foreign policy throughout the region. This in turn ensured China's ability to revitalize the Khmers Rouges from bases in Thailand, and thereby guaranteed that the Vietnamese invasion would result not in a swift military victory but instead in a protracted war.

THEORY

Both the long-term cause and the short-term cause of the conflict cannot be explained by the concepts generated by the dominant academic schools of international relations theory. They are, however, explicable in terms of the role of political culture.

Vietnamese ambition for direct imperial domination did not derive simply from the fact that it was more powerful than Cambodia. After all, other major states in the region could have been expected to unite to resist Vietnamese expansionism. Moreover, Thailand was also more powerful than

Cambodia but was satisfied with an independent regime in Phnom Penh that was politically deferential to Bangkok. The Vietnamese desire for direct control over Cambodia can be explained only insofar as it has been derived from two cultural impulses: the traditional nationalist belief that it was morally superior to the "barbarians" in the west who needed to be civilized; and the nontraditional Comintern-inspired belief that Marxist-Leninist revolution throughout Indochina was a desirable goal that could only be realized under the leadership of a "federal" vanguard movement led by the Vietnamese communists. Broadly speaking, a particular historically unique and complex political culture, not any purportedly universal motives of states, determined the objectives of Vietnamese state policy.

The immediate, triggering cause of the Vietnamese invasion—the Cambodian attacks upon Vietnamese border villages and outposts—was obviously not derived from an enticing power vacuum or even a power imbalance in Cambodia's favor, nor from any objectively realistic prospect of rectifying an unfavorable power imbalance. It was only intelligible in terms of explicit cultural values. Although some of those values—such as the Cambodian desire for national status restoration—were traditional, others were not. They were instead the values of a nontraditional millenarian ideology that led the Khmers Rouges to believe that "subjective" factors, especially revolutionary purity and willpower, could compensate for an otherwise unfavorable "objective" balance of military and other material forces. But even the traditional Cambodian desire for national status restoration was magnified in its urgency by the voluntaristic and apocalyptic temper of the millenarian ideology. For while most Cambodians accepted their unjust borders as divine fate, many communist Cambodians could not.

China's decisions to become involved in the chain of events that ultimately led to the Vietnamese invasion of Cambodia are only intelligible, at least in part, with reference to Chinese political culture. After all, it was the traditional Chinese elites' view of China's neighbors that they should be politically fragmented and deferential to China. Vietnam, by attempting to dominate Indochina despite China's explicit disapproval, was behaving with enormous disrespect. It was discarding its traditional tributary status.

But at the same time, China's decision to involve itself was also derived from the fact that it faced a real security threat from the Soviet Union, and Vietnam's alignment with the Soviet Union enhanced that security threat now on China's southern border. Vietnamese imperial expansion was not only insolent, it also entailed expansion of the influence of the only power that really threatened Chinese security.

The decision of the Soviet Union to support Vietnamese objectives only makes sense in the context of its values, particularly its profound preexisiting hostility toward the Chinese regime. Admittedly, Vietnam being geographically bigger, more populous, and better endowed with strategic assets like deep warm water ports, made it a more attractive client than Cambodia from a strictly power perspective. But on that line of argument, China should have been more attractive as a client of the Soviet Union than Vietnam. The fact that China could not be considered as a client by the Soviet Union had to do with preexisting antipathies, derived at least in part from ideological differences, in part from the Soviet tendency to dominate clients and have no real allies, and in part from China's culturally rooted refusal to be a client, as opposed to an ally, of any other power. Thus the Soviet Union's decision to back and thereby encourage Vietnamese ambitions is a direct by-product of the political cultures of the communist world in the 1960s and 1970s.

That political culture was a factor in Soviet behavior was seen in subsequent events—specifically, the policy effects of the ascension to power of Mikhail Gorbachev in 1985. The Gorbachev-Shevardnadze "New Thinking" constituted a profound alteration in the political ethos and worldview of some of the Soviet political elites. "Universal human values" replaced Leninist "class struggle." By early 1989 it had led the Soviet Union to abandon much of its imperial ambition in the Third World and its domineering approach to its clients, including the Eastern Europeans. Most important, it had led the Soviet Union to prefer improving its relations with China at the expense of Vietnam.

So far we have pointed to the inadequacies of orthodox international relations theory in explaining the *purposes* of the foreign policies of the major actors. Neither power nor economic interests alone determined the ultimate goals of foreign policy, nor the judgment of who were to be considered friends or who were to be considered enemies. Ultimate values did, and these were to be found in the political culture of each of the political elites.

But the historical developments we have examined here also point to an unusual series of judgments by all of the actors about the motives of their adversaries and the methods to be used against them. This history is riddled with examples of misperceptions of reality on the part of all of the actors—misperceptions that had serious effects upon the historical process. This is not to deny a germ of truth in some of these misperceptions. But it was the distortions, not the germs of truth, that created policy.

The most extreme example is Pol Pot's secret report to a party meeting in 1976 in which he stated that Cambodia was being attacked by both Thailand and Vietnam. This claim was pure fiction. In the context of other statements and actions by him, the statement manifested completely delusional thinking and placed Pol Pot's level of paranoia further along the continuum of pathology than that of most chiliastic leaders. Such thinking appears to have motivated Pol Pot to order the "retaliatory" attacks upon Vietnam and Thailand that eventually incited the Vietnamese invasion.

The Khmers Rouges' fear that the Vietnamese wished to seize control of Cambodia by means of a coup d'état within the Kampuchean Communist Party was justified at the beginning of Khmers Rouges rule. But Pol Pot's power within his party was never seriously challenged after 1972, and by 1977 his preemptive purges of the party and military had eliminated any possibility of a coup. Pol Pot's purges against nonexistent enemies during 1978 further weakened his already weak political and military position in relation to his foreign enemies. Although self-destructive, these policies had precedents in the acts of other chiliastic regimes.[1]

The faith of the Khmers Rouges leaders in the superiority of subjective factors like will and ideological purity over objective factors like military technology, firepower, and manpower constituted an ideological dogma that was destructive to Democratic Kampuchea's national security. It provided the spirit of optimism that propelled the DK armed forces to undertake an unrealizable task, the pursuit of which would ultimately destroy the state that they were trying to defend.

The Vietnamese belief in the early 1970s that China's rapprochement with the United States violated Marxist-Leninist "internationalism" was justified. But the added fear that China's rapprochement necessarily entailed a betrayal of the Vietnamese communist revolution was not justified. Only Hanoi's response to its false suspicions—to align more closely with the Soviet Union—ensured that eventually its fears of betrayal would be realized.

Hanoi's judgments in the early to mid-1970s that all ethnic Chinese members of the Vietnamese Communist Party (VCP)[2] and that all ethnic Chinese living in Vietnam were a fifth column for Beijing constituted unfounded fears. But the delusions resulted in a purging of the VCP and a pogrom against all ethnic Chinese. As a consequence of these policies, China became more hostile toward Vietnam and hardened its opposition to Hanoi's Cambodia policy.

The Vietnamese leaders held a false belief that Khmers Rouges behavior was at the behest of the Chinese leaders, and that the Beijing–Phnom Penh conspiracy meant that Cambodia was a dagger pointed at the heart of Vietnam. This very distorted view of what were in reality complicated Chinese-Cambodian relations constituted a paradigm case of the "paranoid pseudo-community" construction. It also influenced Vietnam's eventual decision to invade Cambodia.

These misperceptions affected the chain of events that led to the outbreak of war. And they were not random misperceptions of atypical individuals, but rather misperceptions rooted in paranoid tendencies of the ruling elite culture. Yet, in spite of their frequent delusionary thinking about the intentions and capabilities of others, these Marxist-Leninists have demonstrated that like others they are usually capable of calculating, rational reactions. So paranoia is relevant to irrationality insofar as the behavior of the rulers of a state creates an active hostility on the part of formerly nonhostile or inactively hostile states that sabotages the "victim's" objectives. Instead of warding off the dangers they think they face, paranoid rulers may instead magnify or even create that danger. Paranoid regimes, like paranoid individuals, not only often have real enemies, they often also create real enemies.

There are clear patterns of behavior in this historical case study with significant theoretical implications for the structure of the purported "international system." They directly contradict the dominant rationalistic approach to international affairs.

The "rational actor" theorists of international relations, both Realist and non-Realist, would have us believe that the absence of power is a constraint upon freedom of action. According to this view, the weaker a state is, the less freedom of maneuver and the less policy choices of action it possesses. Small states behave predictably, in accordance with their greater need for security. Large and powerful states are less predictable, since their security is less challenged and their options are greater. The primacy of the need to survive, and the assumption of rationality in pursuit of that primary goal, drive the theory of relative power as an overriding constraint. Yet while such assumptions may be wise in many historical instances, the cases we have considered here inform us otherwise.

It is interesting to see how the Khmers Rouges acted irrationally toward

Vietnam and the Vietnamese acted irrationally toward China. But the Soviets were carefully calculating with regard to China. The Chinese were measured and coolly calculating in their response to Vietnamese hostile actions, and the Vietnamese likewise in their response to Khmers Rouges aggressive actions. In other words, irrational action was directed from the weaker against the stronger powers, while these same powers acted carefully and rationally against their weaker adversaries. In situations of policy choice, these powers acted rationally. But under conditions of overwhelming lack of objective options, they acted irrationally. Furthermore, of the four states, it was the weakest—Democratic Kampuchea—that was most inclined toward irrational action. It was also the one most influenced by ideological precepts and the one that had the least contact with reality.

The conclusion is that we have a connection between powerlessness and irrational action. But since hitherto we have many, perhaps most examples of international relations between strong and weak states characterized by rational, constrained behavior on the part of the weak, it would seem that the atypical behavior that we have analyzed here has something to do with the nature of the state.

As I have asserted in the first chapter, the Marxist-Leninist ideology is characterized by a Manicheaen worldview that is inherently paranoid. The ideology attracts adherents who are already quite paranoid or else susceptible to embracing paranoid thinking. Marxist-Leninists reject the role of accident in history and instead tend to view history as a conspiracy. They often project their own conspiratorial thinking and action upon their opponents.

Given the evidence we have of paranoid personality disorder among the decision-making elites, we may turn to the theories of psychiatry and abnormal psychology to provide us with a possible explanation.

For this study, we need to understand the relationship between paranoia and aggression. Of course, aggression can have many causes, many of them based upon rational calculation of material self-interest. But the paranoid personality has a desperate need for preservation of the subjective self. The paranoid person sees its persecutor as powerful and destructive. Not anger alone, but anxiousness, helplessness, and powerlessness cause the paranoid person to act sometimes in a simultaneously destructive and self-destructive way. As W. W. Meissner explains:

> The normal person is able to feel and exploit anger in the interests of obtaining objectives or in righting wrongs. But where the operation of the paranoid

process becomes too overwhelming, the need to lash out blindly and destroy the enemy becomes overpowering.[3]

In this psychological context, it is not rational cost-benefit analysis, but emotional impulse under the strain of delusional thinking that precipitates aggression. This suggests an answer to the main theoretical puzzle posed by our study: Why do chiliastic regimes sometimes act very irrationally? The hypothesis that this study suggests is that chiliastic regimes may behave irrationally when in conflict with a materially more powerful regime of a common ideological background. The combination of extreme anxiousness—caused by disagreements among fellow ideologues—and powerlessness, causes emotional "lashing out" by the weaker against the stronger. The sense of moral virtue, with which all of these regimes are imbued, especially in their early decades in power, gives psychological comfort to, and reinforces the emotional impulses of, the regime leaders. That sense of moral virtue is derived from adherence to the revolutionary ideology.

CONCLUSIONS

One of the most important political features of the twentieth century has been the appearance and proliferation of regimes committed to the total transformation of man and society, in accordance with a utopian ideological program. The most common form of this revolutionary millenarian impulse has been communism. The most common kind of political system created in pursuit of this chiliastic agenda has been totalitarian dictatorship. Such dictatorships are characterized not only by the pursuit of ideological objectives but also by a paranoid pattern of thinking about the state and its relations with society that is suffused with images of conflict, conspiracy, and betrayal.

Although the distinctiveness and relevance of a chiliastic political culture has been fairly widely accepted with regard to understanding the domestic structures and policies of such regimes, its relevance to the study of international relations has been far less widely appreciated. The assumptions that all states always primarily pursue universal objectives, such as national security, power, and prosperity, and that all states always pursue their political objectives rationally have persisted in shaping Western academic and nonacademic discourse on international relations. This work has challenged those assumptions.

The behavior of major states in the events leading up to the Third Indochina War suggests that the international environment of military power and economic resources is not always the determining factor in the behavior of states on the brink of war. Furthermore, states are not necessarily either passive or rational choice actors responding to an objective balance of power in their environment.

To understand better the diversity of the behavior of states in international affairs we would do well to reconsider the conceptual insights of classical sociological thought. Max Weber is often remembered for his analysis of the rise of rationality in the modern world. But the concept of instrumental rationality was only one of several ideal types of social action that he formulated. Irrational action in the case of the weaker Marxist-Leninist states against the stronger provides an example of an alternative Weberian sociological category—emotional action. Those events we have discussed that are examples of ideologically motivated behavior by the Vietnamese and the Khmers Rouges are intelligible in terms of another Weberian ideal type—value-rational action.

The main theoretical thrust of this study has concerned the role of revolutionary culture in the foreign policy decision making of chiliastic regimes. But it has not ignored the role of traditional culture. We have seen that when chiliastic regimes have suffered major fallings out with each other, traditional antipathies have usually surfaced publicly in propaganda abuse expressed in their original atavistic forms. On the other hand, we have also seen how sometimes traditional cultural values, attitudes, and perceptions are transmuted into a revolutionary form. Traditional values, attitudes, and perceptions express themselves in a complex symbiosis with revolutionary ones. But each are independently significant.

The study of political culture will not result in the development of any grand new theoretical framework, which so much contemporary academic social science considers the highest form and ultimate vindication of true scientific work. The aspiration for universal theory in the study of international relations—as for any of the social sciences—will inevitably founder on the diversity of human culture. But the study of political culture does have great scientific value. It encourages an appreciation of the complexity of human behavior and a more modest scientific agenda that seeks to discover true generalizations restricted to the specific places and times where particular cultures are found.

Reference Material

The following abbreviations are used in the notes:

AFP	Agence France-Presse
AOM	Archives Outre-Mer
CC	Central Committee
CDEC	Combined Documentation Exploitation Center
CDSP	Current Digest of the Soviet Press
CPV	Communist Party of Vietnam
DSM IV	Diagnostic and Statistical Manual of Mental Disorders
FBIS	Foreign Broadcast Information Service
HPR	Hungarian People's Republic
JPRS	Joint Publications Research Service
KCNA	Korean Communist News Agency
LPA	Liberation Press Agency (Hanoi)
NCNA	New China News Agency
PRC	People's Republic of China
RTsKhIDNI	Rossiiskii tsentr khranyeniya i izuchniya dokumentov noveishi istorii (Russian Center for the Preservation and Study of Documents of Modern History)
SRV	Socialist Republic of Vietnam
TsKhSD	Tsentr khranyeniya sovremennoi dokumentatsii (Center for the Preservation of Contemporary Documents)
UCB	University of California, Berkeley
VNA	Vietnam News Agency
VCP	Vietnamese Communist Party
VWP	Vietnam Workers' Party

Introduction: International Relations, Rationality, and Marxist-Leninist Political Cultures

1. Waltz, "Anarchic Orders," in Keohane, ed., *Neorealism*, p. 117.

2. Two notable exceptions are Wolfers, *Discord and Collaboration*, pp. 89–91, and Hoffmann, *Contemporary Theory in International Relations* and *Janus and Minerva*. Wolfers and Hoffmann, though often partial to realist assumptions, are too eclectic to be classified as rigid followers of any particular school.

3. Waltz, *Theory of International Relations*; Gilpin, *War and International Change*.

4. Huntington, *Clash of Civilizations*. See Katzenstein, ed., *Culture of National Security*, for examples of some of the newer approaches to international relations. For further discussion, see Desch, "Culture Clash"; Hopf, "The Promise of Constructivism"; and Lapid and Kratochwil, eds., *Return of Culture*.

5. Weber, *Economy and Society*, vol. 1, pp. 24–26.

6. Geertz, *Interpretation of Cultures*, pp. 126–27.

7. I am referring to the method of *verstehen*, whose most famous exponent was Max Weber. It has been more recently argued for in "Thick Description: Toward an Interpretive Theory of Culture," in Geertz, *Interpretation of Cultures*, chap. 1.

8. Cohn, *Pursuit of the Millenium*, p. 281.

9. See especially Friedrich, ed., *Totalitarianism*; Arendt, *Origins of Totalitarianism*; Friedrich and Brzezinski, *Totalitarianism, Dictatorship, and Autocracy*.

10. One previous attempt to apply the concept of political culture to the study of the foreign policies of Marxist-Leninist regimes was the reformulation of the writings of Nathan Leites by Alexander George. But George was concerned with the content of the culture, not with the causal impact of the culture upon specific historical events. See George, "The 'Operational Code'," pp. 190–222.

11. This was true until the emergence of Mikhail Gorbachev as leader of the Communist Party of the Soviet Union. But he and those of his colleagues who advocated "New Thinking" were, by instituting these heresies, personally responsible for the collapse of communism in the Soviet Union and Eastern Europe. See George, "Operational Code"; Leonhard, *Three Faces of Marxism*; Smith, *Thinking Like a Communist*.

12. Schram, *The Thought of Mao Tse-tung*, and Zhang, *Mao's Military Romanticism*, chaps. 1 and 2.

13. There is reason to believe that had it not been for the Chinese backing down, the Soviet leaders would have reacted to Mao's taunting and military provocations in 1969 with a nuclear attack upon Chinese military installations. This would have been analogous, though on a more massive scale, with the consequences of Pol Pot's provocations against the Vietnamese. On the Soviet threat to attack China, see Kissinger, *White House Years*, pp. 183–86.

14. See American Psychiatric Association, *Diagnostic and Statistical Manual*, p. 634 (hereafter referred to as DSM IV). For a set of diagnostic criteria for analyzing the paranoid personality disorder, see pp. 637–38.

15. Of course, many individuals join the chiliastic party for selfish reasons. These

individuals, whom the ideologically motivated members usually label "opportunists," often have no emotional bond to the party, and cynically go through public motions of obeisance to an ideology that they do not believe.

16. Tucker explains:

> Hitler and Stalin turn out to have been . . . autocrats who at many crucial points individually dominated the decision-making process and behavior of their governments. The factual evidence likewise supports the further conclusions that 1) in both instances we have to do with individuals whose personalities would be classified somewhere on the continuum of psychiatric conditions designated as paranoid; and 2) in both instances the needs of the paranoidal personality were a powerful motivating factor in the dictatorial decision-making. The dictator did not, so to speak, confine the expression of his psychopathological needs to his private life while functioning "normally" in his public political capacity. Rather, he found a prime outlet for those needs in political ideology and political activity.

Tucker, *Soviet Political Mind*, p. 30

17. "[D]omestic terror, which may be viewed under the aspect of 'internal aggression' against elements of the population, was followed by foreign aggression, which may be viewed as a turning of the terror outward upon the world." Quoted in ibid., p. 33.

18. Bullock, *Hitler and Stalin*, especially pp. 11–13, 355–60; Waite, *Psychopathic God*.

19. For evidence of Mao Zedong's paranoid personality, see Li Zhisui, *Private Life of Chairman Mao*.

20. The most popularly cited case of recent times is that of former U.S. president Richard Nixon.

21. See Meissner, *The Paranoid Process*, p. 37.

22. Ibid., p. 107.

23. Ibid., pp. 39–40.; The concept was originally formulated by N. A. Cameron in "The Paranoid Pseudocommunity," pp. 32–38.

24. Recall a most bizarre example of this mode of thinking: Stalin's description of his party enemies during the late 1930s as "Trotskyite-Bukharinite agents of German and Japanese fascism." For this and other examples, see Conquest, *Great Terror*.

25. Examples of highly disordered personalities include Idi Amin of Uganda and Jean-Bedel Bokassa of the Central African Republic. For a description of the Paranoid Type of Schizophrenia, see American Psychiatric Association, *DSM IV*, p. 287.

Chapter 1: Roots of a Conflict

1. Hall, *History of Southeast Asia*, p. 439.

2. Cotter, "Vietnamese Southward Movement," p. 17.

3. Woodside, *Vietnam and the Chinese Model*, p. 234. Most of the discussion that follows in this section is derived from Woodside's analysis.

4. Ibid., p. 235.   5. Ibid., pp. 235–36.

6. Ibid., p. 239.   7. Ibid., p. 247.

8. Ibid., pp. 248–50.   9. Ibid., p. 254.

10. See Hall, *History of Southeast Asia*, chap. 24.

11. For more detail, see Chandler, *History of Cambodia*, chaps. 5–7. Also see Chandler, "Cambodia Before the French."

12. In May 1924 Nguyen Ai Quoc wrote a letter to the Eastern Department of the Executive Committee of the Communist International with a proposal to establish a separate group of students from Asia in the Communist University for the Toilers of the East. The university, he wrote, "must become a base for the establishment in the future of a Communist Federation of the East." This letter is cited in Afonin and Kobelev, *Tovarishch kho shi min*, p. 55.

13. "The Communist International and the Indochinese Revolution," *Vietnam Courier*, no. 2, 1984, p. 8.

14. V. I. Lenin, "Theses on the National and Colonial Questions" (1920), in Tucker, ed., *Lenin Anthology*, pp. 621–22.

15. McKenzie, *Comintern and World Revolution*, pp. 243–45.

16. "Lettre ouverte du Comite Central du Parti Communiste de Chine aux membres du Parti Communiste d'Indochine," April 15, 1934. This document is located in the archives of the Communist International in Rossiiskii tsentr khranyeniya i izuchyeniya dokumentov noveishei istorii (Russian Center for the Preservation and Study of Contemporary Historical Documents; hereafter RTsKhIDNI), Fond 495, Opis 154, Delo 678.

17. See Pipes, *Formation of the Soviet Union*. It was only after the collapse of the Communist Party of the Soviet Union in 1991 that such rights to self-determination were actually respected by the Russian authorities in Moscow. This point must be kept in mind in evaluating the Vietnamese communist promises of respect for the right to national self-determination, as cited in the tendentious argument of Gareth Porter, "Vietnamese Communist Policy Towards Kampuchea, 1930–1970," in Chandler and Kiernan, *Revolution and Its Aftermath in Kampuchea*. The article is seriously flawed, in part due to Porter's reliance on unreliable documentation. For example, in his endnotes, Porter mostly cites Vietnamese communist documents not in the original, but either as reported by French writer Pierre Rousset or, more frequently, as cited by an official Vietnamese communist party history published in Hanoi in 1958. Porter seems oblivious to the possibility that these latter documents were selected or even tampered with to conform to the Vietnamese Workers' (Communist) Party line of the later time. By contrast, most of the documents that I have used and cited in this work are originals (sometimes handwritten by the Vietnamese communist leaders) located in the archives of the former Communist Party of the Soviet Union in Moscow.

18. Letter of Nguyen Ai Quoc to the Comintern, February 18, 1930, RTsKhIDNI, Fond 495, Opis 154, Delo 615.

19. "INDOKITAI" ("Indochina"; a summary statement of Indochinese communist party history written by the Comintern's Eastern Bureau official Vassilieva), n.d. (probably 1932), RTsKhIDNI, Fond 495, Opis 154, Delo 577.

20. Untitled typescript, n.d., RTsKhIDNI, Fond 495, Opis 154, Delo 615.

21. "La structure organisationelle et la composition sociale du P.C.I.C," RTsKhIDNI, Fond 495, Opis 154, Delo 615.

22. Duncanson, *Government and Revolution in Vietnam*, p. 144. This number is based upon a published Vietnamese communist party source. We can now say that in the beginning, the majority of members were not even ethnic Vietnamese. In secret correspondence with Nguyen Ai Quoc, passed on to the Comintern, dated October 28, 1930, the Vietnamese leadership cited the number of party members in February 1930 as 250, of which 190 were Chinese. But by October the party leaders claimed to have 1,740 members, of whom only the original number of 190 were Chinese. RTsKhIDNI, Fond 5, Opis 154, Delo 615.

23. "The Lao People's Revolutionary Party is 30 Years Old," *Tap Chi Cong San*, no. 3, March 1985, JPRS-SEA-85-058, April 8, 1985, p. 1.

24. On the variety of noncommunist nationalist groups, see Buttinger, *Vietnam*; Duiker, *Rise of Nationalism in Vietnam*. There are several studies of the differences between Marxist anticolonial movements. One of the best is Hemery, *Revolutionnaires vietnamiens*. See also Sacks, "Marxism in Vietnam," in Trager, ed., *Marxism in Southeast Asia*.

25. Letter to the Central Committee of the Communist International from the Central Committee of the Indochinese Communist Party, April 6, 1938, RTsKhIDNI, Fond 495, Opis 10a, Delo 140.

26. "Letter No. 8, 22/9/30," RTsKhIDNI, Fond 495, Opis 154, Delo 615, p. 10.

27. "Taches actuelles du Parti Communiste Indochinois," RTsKhIDNI, Fond 495, Opis 154, Delo 577.

28. RTsKhIDNI, Fond 495, Opis 154, Delo 688.

29. RTsKhIDNI, Fond 495, Opis 10a, Delo 139a.

30. Letter to the Central Committee of the Communist International from the Central Committee of the Indochinese Communist Party. April 6, 1938, RTsKhIDNI, Fond 495, Opis 10a, Delo 140.

31. RTsKhIDNI, Fond 495, Opis 154, Delo 688.

32. Turner, *Vietnamese Communism*, p. 31.

33. In order to conceal the communist role in the Viet Minh from potential supporters, in May 1945 the ICP was formally "dissolved." As Ho Chi Minh admitted later, in reality it went underground. See Ho Chi Minh, "Political Report Read at the Second National Congress of the Vietnam Workers' Party, Held in February 1951," in Fall, ed., *Ho Chi Minh*, p. 196.

34. See Heder, "Kampuchea's Armed Struggle"; Kiernan, "Origins of Khmer Communism;" Langer and Zasloff, *North Vietnam*; Brown and Zasloff, *Apprentice Revolutionaries*, chap. 2; Uthit Pasakhom, "Beyond A Soviet-Vietnamese Condominium."

35. This issue is discussed in detail, based upon research in the French archives, in Martin, *Le Mal Cambodgien*, pp. 52–56.

36. Migozzi, *Cambodge*, p. 45, n. 1.

37. Haut-Commissariat de France en Indochine: Affaires économiques, *Annuaire statistique de l'Indochine, douzième volume: 1947–1948*, chap. II, p. 19. The statement that the overwhelming majority of the "other Indochinese" population of Phnom Penh was Vietnamese is inferred from the fact that, apart from the Vietnamese, the Indochinese peoples—the Lao and the various hilltribes—were not migratory.

38. See Migozzi, *Cambodge*, pp. 42–46.

39. Fall, *Vietminh Regime*, pp. 61–63. Fall, at that time, believed incorrectly that Son Ngoc Minh and Son Ngoc Thanh, another Cambodian of mixed ancestry, were one and the same person. But Thanh, an anti-communist who operated the Khmer Serei nationalist insurgency out of Thailand, first against the French and later against the Sihanouk government in the post-Geneva years, became part of the Lon Nol government in the 1970s. The ICP communist Son Ngoc Minh died in North Vietnam in 1972.

40. Notice technique de contre-ingérence politique, "Indochine: Les menées antifrançaises au Cambodge," mars 1945 a fin juin 1946, Archives d'Outre-Mer (hereafter AOM), Indochine, Nouveaux fonds, Cartons 138–39, Dossier 1245, pp. 6–8.

41. The details are found in a declassified French intelligence report: Direction des Services de Securite du H.C. en Indochine, "Note sur l'organisation politique et administrative Viet-Minh au Cambodge," December 1952, hereafter referred to as "Note sur l'organisation," AOM, 7F29, pp. 1–3.

42. Ibid., p. 7.

43. "Rapport d'activités en 1948 et programme pour 1949 du parti communiste Indochinois," AOM, Slotfom XIV, Carton 13, p. 14.

44. Fall, *Vietminh Regime*, p. 62.

45. Ibid.

46. Interestingly, Son conceded the telling fact that by contrast with the revolutionary forces, the great majority of the enemy (that is, anti–Viet Minh/Issarak) troops in Cambodia consisted not of Vietnamese but of natives of Cambodia or Cambodians native to southern Vietnam. The speech is found in "Exposé relatif à la situation et à la mission de la révolution Khmere. (Presente par le camarade Thanh Son)," *Société Historique de l'Armée de Terre* (SHAT), 10 H 284, Divers Cambodge, 1949–50, pp. 12, 16, 26, 39. I am grateful to Stephen Heder for providing me with a copy of this document.

47. "Note sur l'organisation," AOM, 7F29(2), pp. 8–9.

48. Turner, *Vietnamese Communism*, pp. 75–77.

49. Fall, *Vietminh Regime*, pp. 62–63.

50. For example:

The Vietnamese Party reserves the right to supervise the activities of its brother parties in Cambodia and Laos. . . . Later, however, if conditions permit, the three revolutionary parties of Vietnam, Cambodia, and Laos will be able to unite to form a single party: the Party of the Vietnam-Khmer-Laotian Federation.

Captured document, "Instructions on conditions of adherence of the Chinese members of the Party," June 24, 1952. Official U.S. Telegram no. 749, S.D.C.S., available at the Wasson-Echols Collection, Cornell University. Cited in Becker, *When the War Was Over*, p. 88. See also Turner, *Vietnamese Communism*, pp. 78–79.

51. "Summary of Annotated Party History" (Copy of the original text, by Eastern Region military political service), in Jackson, ed., *Cambodia*, p. 254.

52. "Note sur l'organisation," p. 21.

53. Ibid.

54. Service de Securité du Haut Commissariat au Cambodge, "Etude sur les activités Viet-Minh dans la ville de Phnom Penh," Phnom Penh, March 14, 1952, AOM, 7F 29 (5), p. 14.

55. As the later party history conceded:

During this period we accomplished the utmost in the areas of ideology and politics. However, the accomplishment remained minimal; it was like a shadow. . . . From the ideological point of view, we had not yet won the support of the revolutionary class, which is the real master of the country and the perpetrator of the revolution.

"Summary of Annotated Party History," in Jackson, ed., *Cambodia*, p. 255.

56. According to Francois Ponchaud, writing of the Khmer Viet Minh: "About half of the five thousand men who constituted its military strength went to Hanoi, the remainder stayed underground in Cambodia." See Ponchaud, *Cambodia*, p. 157. According to Prince Norodom Sihanouk:

There were about 5,000 Khmer Viet Minh in Cambodia—not 5,000 armed Khmer Viet Minh, but 5,000 Khmer Viet Minh civilians and armed soldiers, with the Viet Minh. . . . So came in July 1954 the Geneva Conference in Switzerland . . . the Viet Minh agreed to withdraw their troops and their puppets from Cambodia. So 5,000 Khmer Viet Minh went up to Hanoi with the Viet Minh troops.

Interview with Prince Norodom Sihanouk by the author, Ban Saen Thailand, March 8, 1985. Hereafter referred to as Sihanouk interview.

57. Preschez, *Essai sur la démocratie au Cambodge*, p. 62.

58. Chandler, *Tragedy of Cambodian History*, pp. 81–84.

59. Carney, *Communist Party Power*, pp. 6–7, 62–64.

60. Martin, *Le Mal Cambodgien*, p. 160.

61. Naranhkiri Tith, interview by author, Washington, D.C., June 5, 1984. Hereafter referred to as Naranhkiri Tith interview. Also see Marie Alexandrine Martin, *Cambodia: A Shattered Society*, pp. 101–102.

62. Hanoi VNA, in English, July 17, 1984, in the Foreign Broadcast Information

Service, *Daily Report: Asia and Pacific* (hereafter FBIS-APA), FBIS-APA-84-140, July 19, 1984, H1.

63. Steve Heder, "Racism, Marxism, Labelling, and Genocide in Ben Kiernan's *The Pol Pot Regime,*" pp. 124–25.

64. Chandler, *Tragedy of Cambodian History,* pp. 109–11.

65. Becker, *When the War Was Over,* p. 97; "Summary of Annotated Party History," in Jackson, ed., *Cambodia.*

66. For a discussion of the new leadership appointments, see Chandler, *Tragedy of Cambodian History,* pp. 114–15.

67. See the speech by Pol Pot on September 27, 1977, in Phnom Penh, as reported by Phnom Penh Radio, in FBIS-APA-77-189, September 29, 1977, H2.

68. Chandler, *Tragedy of Cambodian History,* p. 149.

69. Ith Sarin, "Nine Months With the Maquis," in Carney, *Communist Party Power,* p. 37. Also see "Summary of Annotated Party History," in Jackson, ed., *Cambodia.*

70. See Chandler, "Revising the Past in Democratic Kampuchea: When Was the Birthday of the Party?"

71. Sihanouk, *War and Hope,* p. xxix. This is confirmed by Pol Pot in his March 17, 1978, interview with a Yugoslav press delegation in Phnom Penh. "In the countryside I stayed mainly in the most remote areas. . . . Our base area was in the minority region of northeastern Cambodia." Phnom Penh Domestic Service, March 20, 1978, in FBIS-APA-78-56, March 22, 1978, H1.

72. Martin, *Le Mal Cambodgien,* p. 164.

73. See Chandler, *Tragedy of Cambodian History,* p. 128.

74. Thomas Engelbert and Christopher E. Goscha, *Falling Out of Touch,* pp. 70–77.

75. Ibid., pp. 84–88.

76. Hanoi Radio VNA, in English, July 17, 1984, in FBIS-APA-84-140, July 19, 1984, H1.

77. Ibid.

78. Prince Norodom Sihanouk, *War and Hope,* p. 7.

79. Engelbert and Goscha, *Falling Out of Touch,* pp. 77–81. See also Appendix 2 of this work.

80. *Cambodian News,* January 1963, p. 4, quoted in Leifer, *Cambodia,* p. 142.

81. Norodom Sihanouk, *Souvenirs,* p. 344.

82. Ibid.

83. Sihanouk interview.

84. Smith, *Cambodia's Foreign Policy,* pp. 73–74.

85. According to Sihanouk, it was at Bandung that he first met a Vietnamese communist leader, Pham Van Dong. "And then, in Bandung, Pham Van Dong took the initiative to shake hands with me, and to ask for friendship. . . . I could not afford to refuse the hands of friendship on behalf of Vietnam, so I shook hands with

him and became friends. And Ho Chi Minh invited me then to make a state visit in Hanoi." Sihanouk interview. On Sihanouk's decision not to join SEATO, see Shaplen, *Time Out Of Hand*, pp. 314–15.

86. Leifer, *Cambodia*, pp. 133–35.

87. Smith, *Cambodia's Foreign Policy*, pp. 199–200.

88. Kirk, *Wider War*, p. 51.

89. Ibid., p. 52.

90. *New York Times*, May 4, 1965.

91. Sihanouk, *War and Hope*, pp. 12–13. Denis Warner, the Australian journalist, wrote about this:

> Under an agreement with China, Peking supplied the Cambodian army and the North Vietnamese and Viet Cong forces operating in the southern provinces of South Vietnam with almost all their munitions and other military material. To confuse American and South Vietnamese agents, all the supplies came through the port of Sihanoukville into the Royal Cambodian Army's storage depots outside Phnom Penh. There the consignments intended for the communists were picked up by a trucking company, operated by Hak Ly, a Vietnamese-born Chinese with close relations with Peking's embassy in Phnom Penh.
>
> Hak Ly was the middle man. He ran the supplies south along the Bassac river and across the Mekong ferries, at points close to the Vietnam border. There the North Vietnamese took delivery and carted them off to their own depots, or to the forces in the field.

Warner, *Certain Victory*, p. 159.

92. Leifer, *Cambodia*, p. 175.

93. *Vietnam Courier*, no. 54, April 14, 1966.

94. Hanoi VNA Radio International Service, in English, March 25, 1967, Indochina Archive, UCB, File: DRV/FOR RELS./CAMBODIA.

95. *Vietnam Courier*, no. 54, April 14, 1966.

96. *Vietnam Courier*, June 19, 1967.

97. Phnom Penh Radio, June 17, 1967, in FBIS-APA-67-118, June 19, 1967, KKK1.

98. Hanoi VNA Radio International Service, in English, June 24, 1967, in FBIS-APA-67-123, June 26, 1967, jjj9.

99. See *South China Morning Post*, April 5, 1967.

100. Local grievances stemmed from the fact that corrupt officials had been manipulating government land policies for their own personal enrichment. Interview with Ieng Mouly, then a leader of the Khmer People's National Liberation Front (KPNLF) at Ampil, Cambodia, September 1983. Mouly had interviewed former residents of the Samlaut area in camps run by the KPNLF.

101. Martin, *Cambodia: A Shattered Society*, pp. 112–14.

102. For a limited, and slightly confused account of the communist-led Khmer

Loeu insurgency, see T. D. Allman, "Hanoi Eggs on a Revolt," *Washington Post,* February 1, 1970. Better is Martin, *Cambodia: A Shattered Society,* pp. 114, 209.

103. In September 1977, Pol Pot claimed that the figure was four thousand. See FBIS-APA-77-189, September 29, 1977, H3.

104. Interrogation Report Number 058/74, March 21, 1974, source: Phan Van Tay, North Vietnamese *hoi chanh* ("political returnees"). Copy in Indochina Archive, UCB, File: Cambodia, 1974.

105. Ibid.

106. Sihanouk interview.

107. See Sihanouk's speech in Battambang, May 2, 1967. Phnom Penh Radio, May 3, 1967, in FBIS-APA-67-94, May 15, 1967, 000 2.

108. *Washington Post,* November 20, 1967.

109. U.S. Information Service, Press Branch, "Text of the December 4 United States Note to Cambodia Expressing Concern Over Viet Cong–North Vietnamese Use of Cambodian Territory in the Vietnam Conflict," December 27, 1967.

110. *New York Times,* December 29, 1967.

111. *Washington Post,* December 29, 1967.

112. Sihanouk interview.

113. Phnom Penh Radio Domestic Service, August 27, 1968, in FBIS-APA-68-169, August 28, 1968, H1.

114. Phnom Penh Radio Domestic Service, May 17, 1969, in FBIS-APA-69-96, May 19, 1969.

115. Phnom Penh Domestic Service, March 10, 1970, in FBIS-APA-70-48, March 11, 1970.

116. AFP (Paris) report quoted in ibid.

117. For example, Stanley Karnow, *Washington Post,* March 12, 1970.

118. *New York Times,* March 14, 1970. See Sihanouk's statement of purpose on French television, reported by AFP (Paris), March 12, 1970, in FBIS-APA-70-50, March 13, 1970.

119. As Sihanouk later recalled:

I was negotiating with Moscow not only the giving by the USSR of new aid to Cambodia, but I was telling the Russians to advise the Viet Cong and the North Vietnamese not to use any more the territory of Cambodia to operate against the Americans in South Vietnam and the South Vietnamese. Why? Because I told the Russians: "Lon Nol and Sirik Matak they are very pro-American and anti-communist, and if you don't prevent the Viet Cong and the North Vietnamese— your allies—from using my territory as sanctuaries . . . the group of Lon Nol and Sirik Matak could then prepare a coup against me. And if I am deposed . . . you the communists will see Cambodia no more neutral, no more nonaligned, no more friendly to the communist bloc, but align itself to the United States of America. . . .

I had lengthy discussions with Kosygin, and Kosygin did not promise any-thing. But he told me: "Please advise Lon Nol and Sirik Matak not to try to strike our allies the Viet Cong and the North Vietnamese in the back." He told me that. So my negotiations with Kosygin were not successful.

Sihanouk interview.

120. Reuters, March 13, 1970, in FBIS-APA-70-50, March 13, 1970.

Chapter 2: *The Public Rise and Secret Fall of "Militant Solidarity"*

1. Nixon, *Memoirs*, p. 433; Kissinger, *White House Years*, p. 463.

2. Shawcross, *Sideshow*, p. 112. Despite Shawcross's investigation, many still contend, without any supporting evidence, that the United States was involved in the coup. For instance, in a chronology on history of the Khmers Rouges, the *New York Times* wrote on June 14, 1997: "1970—Right-wing coup supported by the United States and led by Prime Minister Lon Nol, topples Sihanouk . . . "

3. General'nii shtab vooruzhennikh sil SSSR, Glavnoye razvedivatel'noye upravleniye, "Doklad sekretarya TsK PTV Khoang Anya na XX plenume TsK PTV sostoyavshemsya v kontse dekabrya 1970 goda—na nachale yanvarya 1971 goda" (General Staff of the Armed Forces of the USSR, Main Intelligence Administration, "Report of the VWP Central Committee Secretary Hoang Anh to the Twentieth Plenum of the VWP Central Committee, held at the end of December 1970/beginning of January 1971"), Moscow 1971. In Tsentr khraneniya sovremennoi dokumentatsii [TsKhSD], Fond 89, Opis 54, Delo 8, p. 20. Hereafter referred to as Hoang Anh Report.

4. For the DRV's denunciation, see Hanoi Radio Domestic Service, March 21, 1970, in FBIS-APA-70-56, March 23, 1970. On the DRV's support for Sihanouk, see the *Washington Post,* March 26, 1970; Hanoi Radio Domestic Service, March 24, 1970, in FBIS-APA-70-57, March 24, 1970.

5. Hanoi Radio VNA, May 26, 1970, in FBIS-APA-70, May 27, 1970, K2.

6. See the announcement of Phnom Penh Radio on March 31, 1970, in FBIS-APA-70-63, April 1, 1970, H1. Henry Kissinger dates the beginning of the North Vietnamese attacks at April 3. See Kissinger, *White House Years*, pp. 467, 471.

7. Chandler, *Tragedy of Cambodian History*, pp. 209–10; Sihanouk interview.

8. For evidence of an important impact in South Vietnam, see George McArthur, "Cambodia Attack Hurt Pro-Red Viet Province," *Los Angeles Times*, July 9, 1970; Peter Osnos, "Cambodia Action Helps Delta Security, But Terrorism Is Up," *Washington Post*, May 28, 1970.

9. Deac, *Road to the Killing Fields*, p. 87.

10. The capacity of the Cambodian government's armed forces is described by the Australian journalist Denis Warner:

The thirteen Russian MIGs in the Cambodian Air Force had so little hydraulic fluid for their landing gear that when the war began the planes were flying only three hours each month. Of the six T28s, only five were serviceable. Green recruits, shovelled into uniforms, commandeered civilian buses and trucks and fanned out from Phnom Penh to meet every new threat. They had spirit on the way to the front, but they were like boy scouts when it came to war. One day, south of Phnom Penh, I saw the road jammed for hundreds of yards with buses. Cambodian government troops, six batallions of them, were spread out along the road, making no attempt to guard their flanks. The head of the column had been pushed back by mortar fire, and here the troops were following their natural and correct instincts to dig in. Over each foxhole they had erected shelters of banana fronds which they covered patiently with half an inch of earth—not to protect them from heat but from North Vietnamese mortars! At Kompong Cham the troops used park benches as barricades to block the road. Outside Phnom Penh they relied on earthenware jars filled with stones.

Warner, *Certain Victory*, p. 163.

11. Deac, *Road to the Killing Fields*, p. 92.

12. Hoang Anh Report, p. 21, TsKhSD, p. 205.

13. The document continued:

We must help them:
   Organize a complete Party network.
   Organize a Front.
   Establish a system of government from central down to province levels.
   Activate an armed force which is to be controlled by TW.

Captured Enemy Document, CDEC document log no. 06-1647-70, copy in Indochina Archive, UCB (File: Cambodia, 1970). It is not clear what "TW" referred to, but it was probably the Central Office for South Vietnam (COSVN).

14. Hoang Anh Report, p. 21, in TsKhSD, p. 205.

15. Captured Enemy Document, CDEC document log no. 06-2884-70, copy in Indochina Archive, UCB (File: Cambodia, 1970).

16. Posol'stvo SSSR v DRV, "O politike partii trudyashchikhsya v'etnama v reshenii problem indokitaya i nashikh zadachakh, vitekayushchikh iz reshenii XXIV s'ezda KPSS" [Politicheskoye pis'mo] (Embassy of the USSR in the DRV, "About the Policy of the Vietnam Workers' Party Toward a Solution of the Problem of Indochina and Our Tasks, Flowing From the Decisions of the 24th Congress of the CPSU" [Political Letter]), May 25, 1971, p. 14. Located in TsKhSD, Fond 89, Opis 54, Delo 10, p. 36.

17. Ibid., p. 5, TsKhSD, p. 27.

18. Captured Enemy Document, CDEC document log no. 08-1250-70, copy in Indochina Archive, UCB (File: Cambodia, 1970).

19. Interrogation Report no. 058/74. March 21, 1974. Source: Phan Van Tay, North Vietnamese hoi chanh [rallier]. Copy in Indochina Archive, UCB (File: Cambodia, 1974).

20. Circular Number 6 of the Eastern Region, National United Front of Cambodia, March 19, 1971, CDEC document log no. 06-1339-71. Copy in Indochina Archive, UCB (File: Cambodia, 1971).

21. Norodom Sihanouk, *Le Calice*, deuxième partie, chapitre XIII.

22. In his study of the revolution in southern Cambodia, Kenneth Quinn found that the Khmers Rouges began their campaign in May 1973. See Quinn, "Political Change in Wartime," pp. 9–10.

23. Kissinger, *Years of Upheaval*, p. 36. Kissinger falsely identifies the meeting as taking place during February 1973, in the course of his futile attempt to bring the Vietnamese communists to an agreement on Cambodia. Sihanouk did not visit Cambodia until March of that year.

24. Carney, *Communist Party Power*, p. 7; Unpublished interviews by Stephen Heder with former Khmers Rouges in 1981 (no. 18). Hereafter referred to as Heder interviews.

25. See Interrogation Report no. 283, December 29, 1973, Republic of Vietnam, Presidential Palace, Central Intelligence Agency. Source: war prisoner Hoang Van Lam. Copy in Indochina Archive, UCB (File: Cambodia, 1973).

26. Interrogation Report no. 062/74, March 27, 1974. Source: Phan Van Tay, North Vietnamese hoi chanh. Copy in Indochina Archive, UCB (File: Cambodia, 1974).

27. Interrogation Report no. 6 029 0067 71, January 27, 1971. Source: Vu Van Quang, North Vietnamese hoi chanh. Copy in Indochina Archive, UCB (File: Cambodia, 1970).

28. Ibid.

29. Quinn, "Political Change in Wartime," p. 8.

30. As discussed in the last chapter. For an example, see Heder interview no. 28.

31. Heder, "Kampuchea: From Pol Pot to Pen Sovan," in Khien Theeravit and Brown, eds., *Indochina*, p. 19; Democratic Kampuchea, *Biography of Comrade Pol Pot*, p. 5.

32. Deac, *Road to the Killing Fields*, p. 112.

33. "Directive of the Political Staff Department, HQ, South Vietnam People's Liberation Army," October 8, 1971. Copy in Indochina Archive, UCB (File: DRV/ Foreign Relations/Kampuchea, October 1971).

34. Circular, National United Front of the Khmer Republic Special Region, 25th Sector (Kandal), number 37, January 18, 1972 and January 31, 1972. CDEC document log no. 04-1408-72. Copy in Indochina Archive, UCB (File: Cambodia, 1972).

35. Interrogation Report, ARVN no. 1635/TTTVHH/BT, August 22, 1972. Source: Le Van Dung, Viet Cong hoi chanh. Copy in Indochina Archive, UCB (File: Cambodia, 1972); Heder interviews.

36. Letter from the secretary of the Red Khmer Region Party Committee, 1971. CDEC document log no. 12-1213-71. Copy in Indochina Archive, UCB (File: Cambodia, 1971).

37. Beijing Radio NCNA, December 9, 1972, in FBIS-CHI-72-240, December 12, 1972, A6; Beijing Radio NCNA, January 12, 1973, in FBIS-CHI-73-9, January 12, 1973, A11.

38. Beijing Radio NCNA, January 30, 1973, in FBIS-APA-73-21, 31 January, 1973, A1.

39. AFP (Paris), February 1, 1973, in FBIS-APA-73-22, February 1, 1973, K8–K9

40. Beijing Radio, NCNA, February 2, 1973, in FBIS-APA-73-24, February 5, 1973, A13.

41. Department of Press and Information of the Ministry of Foreign Affairs of Democratic Kampuchea, "Black Paper: Facts and Evidences of the Acts of Aggression and Annexation of Vietnam Against Kampuchea," September 1978, pp. 66–70.

42. General John Vogt, head of the U.S. Support Activities Group (USSAG) in a letter included in a 1979 memorandum by Henry Kissinger to the State Department historian. Cited in Deac, *Road to the Killing Fields*, p. 171.

43. Heder, "Kampuchea: From Pol Pot to Pen Sovan," p. 20.

44. Sihanouk interview; Heder interviews, no. 18 and no. 23.

45. Heder, "Kampuchea: From Pol Pot to Pen Sovan," p. 20.

46. Ith Sarin, in Carney, *Communist Party Power*, p. 39.

47. Hanoi VNA International Service in English, November 16, 1971.

48. Hanoi Radio Domestic Service in Vietnamese, November 17, 1971, Indochina Archive, UCB (DRV/FOR RELS/INDO/11-71).

49. Truong Nhu Tang, interview by author, Washington, D.C., September 1981.

50. Timothy Carney, "The Unexpected Victory," in Jackson, ed., *Cambodia*, p. 26.

51. Kissinger, *Years of Upheaval*, p. 16.

52. Interrogation Report no. 109/74, June 11, 1974. Source: Nguyen Ngoc Phuong, North Vietnamese hoi chanh. Copy in Indochina Archive, UCB (File: Cambodia, 1974).

53. Interrogation Report, FVP-4736, June 5, 1974. Source: Cao Van Thanh, Viet Cong hoi chanh. Copy in Indochina Archive, UCB (File: Cambodia, 1974).

54. See the AFP interview with two "Hanoi-Khmer" who defected in 1974 in FBIS-APA-74-66, April 4, 1974.

55. Interrogation Report no. 087/74, May 11, 1974. Source: Pham Huy Bau, North Vietnamese hoi chanh. Copy in Indochina Archive, UCB (File: Cambodia, 1974); also Interrogation Report no. 058/74. Source: Phan Van Tay.

56. Interrogation Report no. 087/74.

57. Interrogation Report no. 058/74.

58. Deac, *Road to the Killing Fields*, p. 165.

59. AFP (Hong Kong) in English, September 20, 1973, in FBIS-APA-73-2[TO COME], September 21, 1973, H1.

60. *Far Eastern Economic Review*, January 7, 1974, p. 59.

61. Carney, "The Unexpected Victory," in Jackson, ed., *Cambodia*, p. 21.

62. "We avail ourselves of this occasion to reaffirm to you the firm determination of the Cambodian people to work constantly for the strengthening of the militant solidarity and fraternal friendship with the fraternal Vietnamese people against U.S. imperialism and its henchmen, in accordance with the spirit of the joint declaration of the Indochinese people's summit conference."
Hanoi Radio VNA, January 31, 1973, in FBIS-APA-73-22, February 1, 1973, K8.

63. Pham Van Dong Speech, Hanoi Radio VNA, April 10, 1973, in FBIS-APA-73, April 10, 1973, K10.

64. Hanoi Radio VNA in English, November 12, 1973, in FBIS-APA-73-219, November 1, 1973, K14.

65. Hanoi Radio VNA in English, March 28, 1974, in FBIS-APA-74-62, March 29, 1974, K6.

66. Hanoi Radio VNA in English, May 29, 1974, in FBIS-APA-74-105, May 30, 1974, K7.

67. Pos'olstva SSSR v DRV, "O politike" p. 6, in TsKhSD, p. 28.

68. Posol'stvo SSSR v DRV, "Politicheskii otchet posol'stva SSSR v Demokraticheskoi Respublike V'etnama za 1972 god" (Embassy of the USSR in the DRV, "Political Report of the Embassy of the USSR in the Democratic Republic of Vietnam for 1972") Hanoi, February 1973, p. 11, in TsKhSD, Fond 5, Opis 64, Delo 472, p. 13.

Chapter 3: The Foreign Policy of Democratic Kampuchea, 1975–78

1. This started in 1977. Chandler, *Brother Number One*, p. 118.

2. Francois Ponchaud, "Social Change in the Vortex of Revolution," in Jackson, ed., *Cambodia*, p. 165.

3. Charles Twining, "The Economy," in Jackson, ed., *Cambodia*, p. 150.

4. Phnom Penh Radio Domestic Service, September 18, 1976, in FBIS-APA-76-183, September 20, 1976, H2.

5. Ibid., H4–H5.

6. Beijing NCNA, September 28, 1977, in FBIS-PRC-77-189, September 29, 1977, A19.

7. Interview with Ieng Sary by author, Phum Tmey, Cambodia, September 1983. Hereafter referred to as *Ieng Sary interview*.

8. Sihanouk interview.

9. "Excerpted Report on the Leading Views of the Comrade Representing the Party Organization at a Zone Assembly," *Tung Padevat*, June 1976, in Chandler, Kiernan, and Boua, eds., *Pol Pot Plans the Future*, p. 29.

10. "Preliminary Explanation Before Reading the Plan, by the Party Secretary" (Party Center, August 21, 1976), in ibid., p. 128. See also Karl D. Jackson, "The Ideology of Total Revolution," in Jackson, ed., *Cambodia*, chap. 2.

11. "Report of Activities of the Party Center According to the General Political Tasks of 1976," in Chandler, Kiernan, and Boua, eds., *Pol Pot Plans the Future*, p. 204.

12. Phnom Penh Radio Domestic Service, September 27, 1977, in FBIS-APA-77-188, September 28, 1977, H1.

13. "Report of Activities of the Party Center According to the General Political Tasks of 1976" (Party Center, December 20, 1976), in Chandler, Kiernan, and Boua, eds., *Pol Pot Plans the Future*, p. 182.

14. "Preliminary Explanation Before Reading the Plan, by the Party Secretary" (Party Center, August 21, 1976), in ibid., p. 126.

15. "Report of Activities of the Party Center According to the General Political Tasks of 1976" (Party Center, December 20, 1976), in ibid., p. 185.

16. Ibid., p. 183.

17. AFP (Hong Kong), July 12, 1977, in FBIS-APA-77-133, July 12, 1977.

18. Ibid., August 19, 1977, in FBIS-APA-77-162, August 22, 1977.

19. Chandler, *Brother Number One*, p. 121.

20. Ibid., p. 124.

21.

B. SUBSTANCE OF THE SUMMARY.

1. The Soviets are the head of the treasonous machination. The Vietnamese were the implementers.

2. The U.S. imperialists collude with the Soviets by compelling the Thais to provide supplies to the Khmer Serei in Thailand.

3. Inside the country, the CIA agents and particularly the Vietnamese expansionists cooperated to implement the same scheme in constant contact with outside.

Cited in Jackson, ed., *Cambodia*, p. 299.

22. FBIS, Daily Report, IV, July 1, 1975, H1, cited in ibid., p. 44.

23. "The Party's Four-Year Plan to Build Socialism in All Fields, 1977–1980" (Party Center, July–August 1976), in Chandler, Kiernan, and Boua, eds., *Pol Pot Plans the Future*, p. 47.

24. FBIS-APA, June 3, 1975, H2, cited in Jackson, ed., *Cambodia*, p. 74.

25. "The Party's Four-Year Plan to Build Socialism in All Fields, 1977–1980" (Party Center, July–August 1976), in Chandler, Kiernan, and Boua, eds., *Pol Pot Plans the Future*, p. 48.

26. "Excerpted Report on the Leading Views of the Comrade Representing the Party Organization at a Zone Assembly," *Tung Padevat*, June 1976, cited in ibid., p. 16.

27. The experience of the expelled Westerners is recounted by Sydney Schanberg in "The Death and Life of Dith Pran," *New York Times Magazine*, January 20, 1980.

28. *New York Times*, January 23, 1978.

29. FBIS-APA-76-85, April 30, 1976, H1.

30. See *Time*, October 24, 1977.

31. FBIS-APA-76-85, April 30, 1976, H1.

32. See Khieu Samphan's message to Francisco Xavier de Amaral, chairman of Fretilin and president of the Democratic Republic of East Timor. Phnom Penh Radio, November 27, 1976, in FBIS-APA-76-231, November 30, 1976, H1–H2.

33. Phnom Penh Radio Domestic Service, January 3, 1977, in FBIS-APA-77-1, January 3, 1977, H12.

34. Ibid., February 5, 1977, in FBIS-APA-77-25, February 7, 1977, H1–H3.

35. Rangoon Domestic Service, March 7, 1977, in FBIS-APA-77-44, March 8, 1977, G1.

36. AFP (Hong Kong), March 24, 1977, in FBIS-APA-77-57, March 24, 1977, O2.

37. *Japan Times*, June 20, 1977, in FBIS-APA-77-120, June 22, 1977, Annex 4.

38. *Ashahi Shimbun*, June 18, 1977, in FBIS.

39. *Far Eastern Economic Review*, October 7, 1977.

40. *New York Times*, March 30, 1977.

41. Phnom Penh Radio Domestic Service, September 27, 1977, and September 28, 1977, in FBIS-APA-77-188, September 28, 1977, H1.

42. Ibid., September 28, 1977, in FBIS-APA-77-188, September 28, 1977, H1; *New York Times*, September 29, 1977.

43. *New York Times*, September 29, 1977.

44. Pyongyang Domestic Service, October 8, 1977, in FBIS-APA-77-196, October 11, 1977, D15.

45. Pyonyang KCNA, October 7, 1977, in FBIS-APA-77-196, October 11, 1977, D7.

46. Phnom Penh Radio Domestic Service, November 15, 1977, in FBIS-APA-77-221, November 16, 1977, H1; ibid., November 24, 1977, in FBIS-APA-77-228, November 25, 1977, H1.

47. *New York Times*, February 1, 1977.

48. *Daily Telegraph* (London), February 17, 1977.

49. *Bangkok Post*, February 27, 1977; ibid., April 30, 1977.

50. Ibid., June 20, 1977.

51. *New York Times*, July 22, 1977; *Washington Post*, July 22, 1977.

52. *The Times* (London), August 15, 1977.

53. AFP (Hong Kong), August 6, 1977, in FBIS-APA-77-152, August 8, 1977, J1.

54. *Bangkok Post*, November 1, 1977, in FBIS-APA-77-210, November 1, 1977, J7.

55. Ibid., November 3, 1977, in FBIS-APA-77-212, November 3, 1977, J1.

56. Ibid., November 5, 1977, in FBIS-APA-77-214, November 7, 1977, J1; *Bangkok World*, November 10, 1977, in FBIS-APA-77-218, November 11, 1977, J7.

57. Phnom Penh Radio Domestic Service, November 10, 1977, in FBIS-APA-77-218, November 11, 1977, H1.

58. *Bangkok Post*, December 17, 1977, in FBIS-APA-77-243, December 19, 1977, J6.

59. *Siam Rat* (Bangkok), December 19, 1977, in FBIS-APA-77-243, J1.

60. *Bangkok Post*, December 21, 1977, in FBIS-APA-77-245, December 21, 1977, J1.

61. Phnom Penh Radio Domestic Service, November 25, 1977, in FBIS-APA-77-228, November 28, 1977, H1.

62. Beijing NCNA, December 3 and 4, 1977, in FBIS-PRC-77-233, December 5, 1977, A4–A5.

63. Kuala Lumpur Domestic Service, December 8, 1977, in FBIS-APA-77-237, December 9, 1977, H1.

64. Ibid., December 9, 1977, in FBIS-APA-77-238, December 12, 1977, H4.

65. *Bangkok Post*, December 23, 1977; *Nation Review* (Bangkok), December 24, 1977, in FBIS-APA-77-249, December 28, 1977, J2–J3.

66. *New York Times*, January 15, 1978.

67. *Bangkok Post*, January 19, 1978, in FBIS-APA-78-13, January 19, 1978, J1; ibid., January 23, 1978, in FBIS-APA-78-16, January 24, 1978, J2.

68. *Nation Review* (Bangkok), January 20, 1978, in FBIS-APA-78-14, January 20, 1978, J2.

69. Phnom Penh Radio Domestic Service, January 30, 1978, in FBIS-APA-78-21, January 31, 1978, H4.

70. *New York Times*, February 3, 1978; Bangkok Domestic Service, February 2, 1978, in FBIS-APA-78-23, February 2, 1978, J1.

71. *World* (Bangkok), February 7, 1978, in FBIS-APA-78-26, February 7, 1978, J1.

72. Bangkok Domestic Service, February 14, 1978, in FBIS-APA-78-31, February 14, 1978, J1.

73. AFP (Hong Kong), February 15, 1978, in FBIS-APA-78-32, February 15, 1978.

74. *Nation Review* (Bangkok), February 16, 1978, in FBIS-APA-78-33, February 16, 1978, J1.

75. Ibid., February 17, 1978, in FBIS-APA-78-34, February 17, 1978, J1.

76. *Bangkok Post*, February 20, 1978, in FBIS-APA-78-35, February 21, 1978, J2.

77. Ibid., February 25, 1978, in FBIS-APA-78-39, February 27, 1978, J1.

78. *New York Times*, February 21, 1978.

79. Bangkok Domestic Service, March 4, 1978, in FBIS-APA-78-44, March 6, 1978, J1.

80. *Bangkok Post*, March 29, 1978, in FBIS-APA-78-62, March 30, 1978, J2.

81. Ibid., April 2, 1978, in FBIS-APA-78-64, April 3, 1978, J1.

82. Ibid., April 10, 1978, in FBIS-APA-78-69, April 10, 1978, J1.

83. *World* (Bangkok), April 10, 1978, in FBIS, ibid.

84. *Bangkok Post*, April 30, 1978, in FBIS-APA-78-84, May 1, 1978, J1.

85. *Washington Post*, June 7, 1978.

86. "Preliminary Explanation Before Reading the Plan, by the Party Secretary," (Party Center, December 20, 1976), in Chandler, Kiernan, and Boua, eds., *Pol Pot Plans the Future*, p. 126.

87. The story is related by Henry Kamm, in an interview with Thai Prime Minister Chatichai in the *New York Times*, July 15, 1978. A shorter version is contained in *Nation Review* (Bangkok), July 22, 1978, in FBIS-APA-78-142, July 24, 1978.

88. See the *New York Times*, July 18, 1978.

89. *Nation Review* (Bangkok), September 14, 1978, in FBIS-APA-78-180, September 15, 1978, J4.

90. Phnom Penh Radio Domestic Service, September 16, 1978, in FBIS-APA-78-181, September 18, 1978, H9.

91. Ibid., September 21, 1978, in FBIS-APA-78-185, September 22, 1978, H1.

92. Ibid., August 6, 1978, in FBIS-APA-78-1 [TO COME], August 7, 1978, H1.

93. AFP (Hong Kong), October 19, 1978, in FBIS-APA-78-204, October 20, 1978, H1.

94. Radio Djakarta, October 20, 1978, in FBIS-APA-78-205, October 23, 1978, N1.

95. "The Cambodian People Firmly Adhere to the Stands of Independence, Mastery, and Self-Reliance, and Clearly Distinguish Friends and Foes the World Over," Phnom Penh Radio Domestic Service, January 20, 1978, in FBIS-APA-78-14, January 20, 1978, H2.

96. Nayan Chanda, *Brother Enemy*, p. 210.

97. The Chinese leader Geng Biao continued:

In the first place they failed to treat Sihanouk well, this made the old soldiers recalcitrant; nor did they evince the correct attitude in treating these soldiers, as they did not proceed to transform this contingent of old soldiers with rich fighting experience like we did to the troops of Wu Huawen, Dong Qiwu, and others. In certain districts they did especially badly, as they even treated them and their families as reactionary troops and reactionary families, who were subject to either persecution, or the fate of disbandment or disarmament. This way of doing things inadvertently forced a part of the forces previously in support of the Communist Party to revolt and turn around to merge with those remnant units of Lon Nol who had become bandits in the hills and change into counter-revolutionary armed guerrillas. In handling the pro-Vietnam faction, the commanding officers also failed to make a distinction between the question of stand and the question of ideology, grabbing all at once more than 4,000 of them, who were either put to death or imprisoned; thus everybody felt threatened and ultimately ended up in open revolt. This greatly affected the morale and inclination of those units that were originally loyal to the party.

Chinese Communist Party Central Political Bureau Member Comrade Geng Biao's "Report on the Situation in the Indochinese Peninsula," January 16, 1979, in *Chung-Kung Yen-Chiu (Studies on Chinese Communism)* (in Chinese), vol. 14, no. 10, October 15, 1980, pp. 141–62. Translated in JPRS-SEA, 77,074, December 29, 1980, p. 7.

98. Laurence Picq, *Beyond the Horizon*, p. 46.

99. Ibid., p. 101.

100. Ibid., p. 125.

Chapter 4: The Public Disintegration of "Militant Solidarity" in Indochina

1. At the end of the Vietnam War in 1975, the Chinese told the Hanoi leaders that they were ending all military assistance to Vietnam, but economic assistance was at this time not affected.

2. See Hoang Van Chi, *From Colonialism to Communism*; Turner, *Vietnamese Communism*, pp. 130–46; Bui Tin, *Following Ho Chi Minh*, pp. 24–30.

3. Especially on the question of whether or not there would be a bloodbath after their victory, as had been predicted by Presidents Nixon and Ford. See, for example, FBIS-APA, March 25, 1977, K2.

4. The former editor of the Vietnamese army daily, Bui Tin, suggests that 100,000 were sent for long-term reeducation. Bui Tin, *Following Ho Chi Minh*, p. 91. Another source, Nguyen Cong Hoan—a former appointed representative in the "rubber stamp" National Assembly in postwar Vietnam—estimated that there were at a minimum 200,000 prisoners in 1977. See "Statement of Nguyen Cong Hoan, former member of the National Assembly, representing Phu Khanh province." Hearings Before the Subcommittee on International Organizations, Committee on International Relations, House of Representatives, Ninety-Fifth Congress, First Session, July 26, 1977, p. 153. Washington, D.C.: U.S. Government Printing Office, 1977.

5. Including, to take just one striking example, An Quang Buddhist monks and nuns who had been opposed to the previous anticommunist governments and to United States policy in South Vietnam. See Jacqueney, "Human Rights in Vietnam." Also Forest, *The Unified Buddhist Church of Vietnam*.

6. For more details on the political influence of Stalin and Mao on the Vietnamese communists, see Chapter 5. The Vietnamese communists were the most orthodox adherents of Marxism-Leninism in Asia. They were politically educated under the tutelage of the parties of both Joseph Stalin and Mao Zedong. But while they adopted many of the terroristic methods of each of the great communist tyrants against their own society, they eschewed directing the terror against the party itself. By treating the party, or at least its upper echelons, as a sacred brotherhood, in their domestic policies they were emulating the behavior of Lenin and his comrades before the ascension of Stalin.

7. Martin, *Le Mal Cambodgien*, p. 55.

8. In an interview with Marie Alexandrine Martin, cited in ibid.

9. Timothy Carney, "The Unexpected Victory," in Karl D. Jackson, ed., *Cambodia*, p. 26.

10. International Institute of Strategic Studies, *The Military Balance, 1975–1976*.

11. Chanda, *Brother Enemy*, pp. 12–13.

12. From a Vietnamese Foreign Ministry document, Hanoi VNA, in English, April 7, 1978, in FBIS-APA-78-68, April 7, 1978, K5.

13. Statement by Khieu Samphan on behalf of the government of Democratic Kampuchea. Phnom Penh Radio Domestic Service, December 30, 1977, in FBIS-APA-78-1, January 3, 1978, H4.

14. Chanda, *Brother Enemy*, pp. 14–15.

15. *Vietnam Courier*, no. 40, September 1975, p. 3.

16. Huang Hua, "Huang Hua's 42,000 Word Foreign Policy Address," in Chen, ed., *China and the Three Worlds*, p. 269.

17. *Vietnam Courier*, no. 45, February 1976, p. 3.

18. Hanoi Radio VNA, April 14, 1976, in FBIS-APA-76-74, April 15, 1976.

19. Ibid.

20. Phnom Penh Radio Domestic Service, June 14, 1976, in FBIS-APA-76-116, June 15, 1976, H1.

21. In the broadcast it was stated:

[T]he Cambodian people take the greatest pleasure in welcoming the founding of the SRV and express warmest congratulations to the Vietnamese state leaders and Vietnamese people—their comrades-in-arms—and most ardent wishes to the SRV and the Vietnamese people for brilliant successes in their task of strengthening socialism throughout the territory of unified Vietnam.

Ibid., July 7, 1976, in FBIS-APA-76-132, July 8, 1976, H3.

22. Ibid., July 21, 1976, in FBIS-APA-76-143.

23. Ibid., July 26, 1976, in FBIS-APA-76-146, July 28, 1976, H1.

24. *Vietnam Courier*, no. 52, September 1976, p. 7.

25. Hanoi Radio VNA, September 22, 1976, in FBIS-APA-76-186, September 23, 1976, K2.

26. "Zapis' besedi s chlenom Politburo TsK PTV, prem'er-ministrom SRV Pham Van Dongom" ("Report of the conversation with member of the Politburo of the VWP Central Committee, prime minister of the SRV Pham Van Dong"), November 6, 1976, TsKhSD, Fond No. 5, Opis 69, Delo 2314, p. 101.

27. "Zapis besedi s pervim sekretarem TsK PTV Le Zuanom" (Report of a conversation with First Secretary of the VWP Central Committee Le Duan"), November 16, 1976. TsKhSD, Fond No. 5, Opis 73, Delo 2314, p. 113.

28. Ibid.

29. Ibid.

30. Ibid., pp. 113–14.

31. Radio Phnom Penh Domestic Service, September 28–29, 1977, in FBIS-APA-77-189, September 29, 1977.

32. See Barry Kramer, "Cambodia's Communist Regime Begins to Purge Its Own Ranks While Continuing a Crackdown," *Wall Street Journal*, October 19, 1977; Michael Chinoy, "Killings Mark Cambodia Power Struggle," *Los Angeles Times*, November 16, 1977.

33. *Nhan Dan*, April 17, 1977, p. 6, quoted in FBIS-APA-77-95, May 17, 1977, K3.

34. It included:

[u]nder the leadership of the Cambodian Revolutionary Organization . . . the heroic people of Cambodia over the past two years have upheld the spirit of self-reliance and have overcome many difficulties in their resolve to heal the wounds of war, restore the economy, and stabilize their living conditions. They have also thwarted various schemes of sabotage by the imperialists and their henchmen.

Hanoi Radio VNA, in English, April 16, 1977, in FBIS-APA-77-74, April 18, 1977, K9.

35. Chanda, *Brother Enemy*, p. 87. According to Colonel Bui Tin, the now-exiled former editor of the Vietnamese communist army newspaper *Quang Doi Nhan Dan*, 800 civilians were killed in the attack on villages in Chau Doc. Bui Tin, interview by author, Boston, October 22, 1991. Hereafter referred to as Bui Tin interview.

36. According to Colonel Bui Tin, who was traveling at the time with Vietnamese Defense Minister Vo Nguyen Giap on a scheduled visit to China and the Soviet Union. Bui Tin interview.

37. Khmers Rouges attacks and Vietnamese retaliation were first reported in the West only three and a half months later. See AFP (Hong Kong), August 15, 1977, in FBIS-APA-77-158, August 16, 1977. Also *New York Times*, August 9, 1977. Nayan Chanda has speculated that the visit to Moscow at that time by Le Duc Tho—the Vietnamese Politburo member with responsibility for Cambodia—was for secret meetings with the Soviets in response to this attack. In fact, secret Soviet Communist Party Secretariat minutes show that the Vietnamese leader had already requested a visit for medical treatment, approved by the Soviet party on April 27, *before* the Khmers Rouges attack. See TsKhSD.

38. "Spravka posola VNR v SRV L. Karshai o neskol'ko voprosov vietnamskikh-kampuchianskikh otnoshenakh" ("Information from the Ambassador of the HPR in the SRV L. Karshai about several questions of Vietnamese-Kampuchean relations"), November 1, 1977, TsKhSD, Fond 5, Opis 73, Delo 1407, p. 98.

39. (AFP) Hong Kong, August 15, 1977, in FBIS-APA-77-158, August 16, 1977; *New York Times*, August 9, 1977.

40. FBIS-APA-77-124, June 28, 1977.

41. Radio Phnom Penh Domestic Service, July 30, 1977, in FBIS-APA-77-149, August 3, 1977.

42. Ibid., August 8, 1977, in FBIS-APA-77-153, August 9, 1977.

43. *Bangkok Post*, September 1, 1977.

44. Radio Phnom Penh Domestic Service, September 17, 1977, in FBIS-APA-77-182, September 20, 1977.

45. Hanoi Radio VNA, in English, September 29, 1977, in FBIS-APA-77-190, September 30, 1977, K3–K4.

46. "Spravka posola VNR v SRV L. Karshai o neskol'ko voprosov vietnamskikh-kampuchianskikh otnoshenakh," November 1, 1977, TsKhSD, Fond 5, Opis 73, Delo 1407, p. 99.

47. Ibid., p. 100.

48. Ibid., p. 98.

49. See the account in Chanda, *Brother Enemy*, pp. 192–95.

50. Bui Tin emphasizes the leadership's preoccupation with internal problems. Bui Tin interview.

51. "Zapis' besedi s general'nim sekretarem TsK KPV Le Zuanom" (Report of a conversation with General Secretary of the VWP Central Committee, Le Duan"), October 6, 1977, TsKhSD, Fond No. 5, Opis 73, Delo 1409, p. 123.

52. Ibid., pp. 123–24.

53. Becker, *When the War Was Over*, p. 318.

54. Phnom Penh Domestic Service, in Cambodian, November 21, 1977, in FBIS-APA-77-225, November 22, 1977, H1.

55. *New York Times*, January 7, 1978.

56. Radio Hanoi Domestic Service, December 31, 1977, in FBIS-APA-78-1, January 3, 1978.

57. Ibid.

58. Radio Hanoi VNA, December 31, 1977, in FBIS-APA-78-1, January 3, 1978.

59. *New York Times*, January 12, 1978, and January 13, 1978.

60. Chandler, *Brother Number One*, p. 138.

61. "Zapis' besedi s korrespondentom BTA I. Gaitandzhiev" ("Report of a conversation with the correspondent of BTA I. Gaitandzhiev"), April 4, 1978, Embassy of the USSR in the PRC. From the diary of V. P. Fedotov, TsKhSD, Fond 5, Opis 75, Delo 1062, p. 23.

62. Phnom Penh Domestic Service, January 8, 1978, in FBIS-APA-78-5, January 9, 1978, H6.

63. *New York Times*, March 8, 1978.

64. These figures are taken from International Institute for Strategic Studies, *The Military Balance, 1978–1979*, pp. 63.

65. Phnom Penh Radio Domestic Service, May 10, 1978, in FBIS-APA-78-93, May 12, 1978, H2.

66. Ibid., H3.

67. Cited in David P. Chandler, "An Anti-Vietnamese Rebellion in Early Nineteenth Century Cambodia," p. 21.

68. Hanoi Radio VNA, June 20, 1978, in FBIS-APA-78-119, June 20, 1978.

69. Chanda, *Brother Enemy*, p. 218.

70. Like Pol Pot and Nuon Chea, Sao Pheum had joined the ICP-led forces in Cambodia in the early 1950s. (I am using Heder's English transliteration of the name.) Another political figure, Heng Samrin, was secretary of the East Zone Division 4, which was a key unit involved in the September 1977 attacks on Vietnamese civilians. Heng Samrin was promoted in November 1977 by Pol Pot. In 1979 Heng Samrin became the first president of the regime that was installed and sponsored by Hanoi after the Vietnamese invading army reached Phnom Penh. Steve Heder, "Racism, Marxism, Labelling, and Genocide in Ben Kiernan's *The Pol Pot Regime*," pp. 140, 142–45.

71. "Zapis' besedi s chlenom TsK KPV, predsedatelem gosudarstvennovo komiteta nauki i tekhniki SRV Chan Kuinem" ("Report of a conversation with member of the CPV Central Committee, Chairman of the SRV State Committee on Science and Technology, Tran Quyen"), TsKhSD, Fond 5, Opis 75, Delo 1061, p. 38.

72. Ibid.

73. Ibid.

74. *New York Times*, May 18, 1978.

75. *Far Eastern Economic Review*, September 1, 1978, pp. 11–12.

76. "Zapis'besedi s chlenom politburo TsK KPV, ministr inostrannikh del Nguyen Duy Trinh" ("Report of a meeting with member of the CPV Central Committee Politburo, Minister of Foreign Affairs Nguyen Duy Trinh"), June 15, 1978, in TsKhSD, Fond 5, Opis 75, Delo 1062, p. 25.

77. Bui Tin interview.

78. Former Soviet Deputy Foreign Minister, M. S. Kapitsa, interview by author, Moscow, March 27, 1992.

79. "Zapis' besedi s pukovoditel'om otdela SSSR v MID SRV Nguyen Huu Ngo" ("Report of a meeting with the director of the department of USSR in the MFA of the SRV Nguyen Huu Ngo") TsKhSD, Fond 5, Opis 75, Delo 1062, p. 56.

80. "Zapis' besedi s general'nim sekretarem TsK KPV Le Zuanom" ("Report of a conversation with General Secretary of the CPV Central Committee Le Duan"), September 5, 1978, TsKhSD, Fond 5, Opis 75, Delo 1061, p. 101.

81. Ibid., p. 100.

82. See the *Far Eastern Economic Review*, August 7, 1997.

83. Chandler, *Brother Number One*, p. 155.

84. *Quan Doi Nhan Dan*, n.d. Hanoi Radio Domestic Service, in Vietnamese, October 13, 1978, in FBIS-APA-78-200, October 16, 1978, K8, contains a report by Hun Sen, deputy commander of a regiment stationed in Region 21 of Military Zone 203. Hun Sen later became foreign minister of the Vietnamese-installed government of the People's Republic of Kampuchea. *Quan Doi Nhan Dan*, October 20, 1978, in FBIS-APA-78-205, October 23, 1978, K11.

85. Hanoi Radio International Service, in Cambodian, October 21, 1978, in FBIS-APA-78-205, October 23, 1978, K10–K11.

86. (AFP) Hong Kong, October 22, 1978, in FBIS-APA-78-205, October 23, 1978, H4.

87. Hanoi Radio International Service, in English, December 3, 1978, in FBIS-APA-78-233, December 4, 1978, K1.

88. *New York Times*, December 15, 1978.

89. *New York Times*, January 8, 1979.

90. On the "paranoid pseudocommunity" concept, see the Introduction.

Chapter 5: Vietnam and the Communist World, 1930–68

1. King C. Chen, *Vietnam and China*, pp. 8–9.

2. Afonin and Kobelev, *Tovarishch Kho Shi Min*.

3. Duiker, *Comintern*, p. 5.

4. Ibid., p. 7.

5. Huynh Kim Khanh, *Vietnamese Communism*, p. 63. There is some confusion between Khanh and Duiker about the precise name of the organization. I have used the name identified by Khanh.

6.

The word fatherland, *to quoc*, was created by the politicians to make the people conform to their laws and to constrain the proletariat to take arms to defend the properties of the landowners and the interests of the capitalists.

In reality there is neither fatherland nor frontiers. All revolutionaries who devote their forces to improve the quality of human life are friends and the earth is their only country. What this proves is that our French comrades would fight on our side against their imperialist compatriots who have seized our country.

Thanh Nien, December 20, 1926, quoted in ibid., p. 81.

7. *Thanh Nien*, July 26, 1925, quoted in ibid., pp. 87–88.

8. Duiker, *Comintern*, p. 19.

9. Ibid., p. 20.

10. Ognetov, "The Comintern and the Revolutionary Movement in Vietnam," in Ulyanovsky, ed., *Comintern and the East*, p. 467.

11. Duiker, *Comintern*, p. 21.

12. Huynh Kim Khanh, *Vietnamese Communism*, p. 171.

13. Duiker, *Comintern*, p. 28.   14. Ibid.

15. Ibid., p. 29.   16. Ibid., p. 31.

17. See Conquest, *Great Terror*, pp. 574–88.

18. Ibid., p. 581.

19. The evidence is contained in the archives of the Comintern in Moscow. RTsKhIDNI, Fond 495, Opis 10a.

20. Resolution of the Ninth Conference of the Central Executive Committee of the Lao Dong Party of Vietnam, December 1963, "World Situation and Our Party's International Mission," *Vietnam Documents and Research Notes*, Document No. 98, September 1971, p. 107.

21. Moscow TASS Radio, in English, December 20, 1979, in FBIS-SOV-79-24, December 21, 1979, R8.

22. Hanoi Radio VNA, December 21, 1979, in FBIS-APA-79-24, December 21, 1979, K1.

23. "About I. V. Stalin on the 100th Anniversary of His Birth," *Nepszabadsag*, December 21, 1979, pp. 6–7, in FBIS-EEU-79-24, December 28, 1979, F4.

24. King C. Chen, *Vietnam and China*, p. 23.

25. Ibid., p. 34.

26. RTsKhIDNI, Fond 495, Opis 154, Delo 585.

27. See endnote 19.

28. King C. Chen, *Vietnam and China*, pp. 38, 40–41.

29. Huynh Kim Khanh, *Vietnamese Communism*, p. 282.

30. Ibid., pp. 188–89.

31. Hoang Van Hoan, "Distortion of Facts," p. 12. The French report of March 1950 is cited by King C. Chen, *Vietnam and China*, p. 261.

32. Chen Jian, "China and the First Indo-China War," p. 91.

33. Ibid., p. 93.

34. King C. Chen, *Vietnam and China*, pp. 261–63.

35. Chen Jian, "China and the First Indo-China War," pp. 92–93.

36. These major campaigns are the Border Campaign of 1950, the Northwest Campaign of 1952, and the siege of Dien Bien Phu in 1954. They are discussed in Qiang Zhai, "Transplanting the Chinese Model," passim; and in Chen Jian, "China and the First Indo-China War," passim.

37. Qiang Zhai, "Transplanting the Chinese Model," p. 705.

38. Chen Jian, "China and the First Indo-China War," p. 97.

39. Chen Jian, "China and the First Indo-China War," p. 101–102; King S. Chen, *Vietnam and China*, pp. 296–97

40. Chen Jian, "China and the First Indo-China War," passim. and especially pp. 105–110; Qiang Zhai, "Transplanting the Chinese Model," p. 713.

41. Nikita S. Khrushchev, *Khrushchev Remembers*, p. 533.

42. "Political Report at the Second National Congress of the Viet-Nam Workers' Party, Held in February 1951," in Fall, ed., *Ho Chi Minh*, pp. 207–8.

43. King C. Chen, *Vietnam and China*, p. 240.

44. Ibid., pp. 257–58. On the Chinese campaigns, see Vogel, *Canton Under Communism*, chap. 2.

45. On the Chinese campaign, see ibid., chap. 3, and the unofficial regime perspective by Hinton, *Fanshen*. On the Vietnamese campaign, see Hoang Van Chi, *From Colonialism to Communism*, and also Turner, *Vietnamese Communism*, pp. 130–46.

46. On the Chinese system, see Whyte, *Small Groups*. Unfortunately, there is no comparable work on the Vietnamese institution.

47. Turner, *Vietnamese Communism*, p. 282.

48. *Nhan Dan*, November 5, 1956, quoted in ibid., p. 150.

49. For a periodization of the Yugoslav relations with the Soviets and Chinese, see Johnson, "Yugoslavia and the Sino-Soviet Conflict."

50. Smyser, *Independent Vietnamese*, p. 17.

51. "Vietnam: The Anti-U.S. Resistance War for National Salvation, 1954–1975: Military Events," JPRS 80968, June 3, 1982.

52. Bui Tin, interview by author, Boston, October 1991. Bui Tin is the former editor of the North Vietnamese army newspaper, *Quan Doi Nhan Dan*. Hereafter referred to as Bui Tin interview.

53. Radvanyi, *Delusion and Reality*; Maneli, *War of the Vanquished*.

54. Khrushchev, *Khrushchev Remembers*, p. 535.

55. On the Albanian issue, see Griffith, *Albania*.

56. Smyser, *Independent Vietnamese*, p. 48.

57. *Hoc Tap*, November 1961, reproduced in Dallin, ed., *Diversity in International Communism*, p. 399.

58. Smyser, *Independent Vietnamese*, p. 49.

59. Ibid., pp. 49–50; King C. Chen, "North Vietnam," p. 1028.

60. *Hoc Tap*, November 1962, cited in Smyser, *Independent Vietnamese*, p. 53.

61. Radvanyi, *Delusion and Reality*, pp. 25–26.

62. Smyser, *Independent Vietnamese*, p. 62.

63. "Joint Statement of Chairman Liu Shao-chi and President Ho Chi Minh," Beijing, 1963, reprinted in *Vietnam Documents and Research Notes*, Document No. 98, September 1971, p. 66.

64. Ibid., pp. 64–65.

65. "Let Us Hold High the Banner of Nuclear Weapons Ban and Spearhead Our Struggle Against U.S. Imperialism," *Hoc Tap*, September 1963, quoted in King C. Chen, "North Vietnam," pp. 1030–31.

66. Khrushchev, *Khrushchev Remembers*, p. 536.

67. Resolution of the Ninth Conference of the Central Committee, Vietnam Workers' Party, December 1963, "World Situation and Our Party's International Mission," *Vietnam Documents and Research Notes*, Document No. 98, September 1971, pp. 103–4.

68. The war resolution stated:

> The revisionists are of the opinion that because of the appearance of nuclear weapons, the nature of imperialism has or may be changed. Therefore, world peace can be protected only through all-out cooperation, mutual confidence, and economic competition between the socialist countries and capitalist countries, especially between the big powers having the most powerful nuclear weapons. The modern revisionists dare not unmask the true nature of imperialism; but they have praised the so-called "good will for peace" of the leaders of imperialist countries. They dare not mobilize the forces of peace to struggle against the imperialists. On the contrary, they have done their best to collaborate with them. They dare not encourage and support the revolutionary wars aimed at weakening the imperialists. On the contrary, they have tried to hinder the world revolutionary movement.

Ibid., p. 85.

69. Ibid., p. 86.

70. Ibid., p. 108.

71. Maneli, *War of the Vanquished*, pp. 174–75.

72. The information on the purge of Giap's aides is based on Bui Tin interview.

73. M. S. Kapitsa, interview by author, Moscow, March 27, 1992. Kapitsa was former deputy foreign minister of the Soviet Union and former head of the Asian division of the Soviet Foreign Ministry.

74. Smyser, *Independent Vietnamese*, pp. 76–78; Griffith, *Sino-Soviet Relations*, p. 68.

75. Radvanyi, *Delusion and Reality*, p. 38. See also Ilya V. Gaiduk, *The Soviet Union and the Vietnam War*, chap. 2.

76. Radvanyi, *Delusion and Reality*, p. 40.

77. Smyser, *Independent Vietnamese*, p. 89.

78. Radvanyi, *Delusion and Reality*, p. 41.

79. Van Der Kroef, "Interpretations of the 1965 Coup in Indonesia," pp. 277–98.

80. Kraslow and Loory, *Secret Search for Peace.*

81. Radvanyi, *Delusion and Reality*, pp. 165–66.

82.

President Ho is the leader of our country's working class and the leader of all our people. Thanks to President Ho, the working class and our people have had a correct political line to make their struggle a success. President Ho is the banner of our entire party and all of our people. We respect and love our leader, but we do not deify him. Deification of a leader will lower the position of the masses of people and even the leader himself.

Hong Chuong, "Leaders and Masses," *Hoc Tap*, no. 5, May 1967, in *JPRS* 41,648, pp. 78, 80.

83. Truong Chinh, "Let Us Be Grateful to Karl Marx and Follow the Path Traced by Him," Hanoi Domestic Service, September 16, 1968, in FBIS-APA-68-193, *Supplement 45*, October 2, 1968, p. 27.

84. Smyser, *Independent Vietnamese*, pp. 98–99.

85. This is an important theme in the *Hoc Tap* article cited in note 82.

86. Consider, for example, Truong Chinh's October 1967 statement. Two years later, on the occasion of the twentieth anniversary of the PRC, Truong Chinh made a virtually identical statement. Hanoi Radio Domestic Service, October 1, 1967, in FBIS-APA-67-191, October 2, 1967, JJJ6; Hanoi Radio VNA International Service, October 1, 1969, in FBIS-APA-69-190, October 1, 1969, K10.

87. Truong Chinh in 1968 wrote with this emphasis. Truong Chinh, "Let Us Be Grateful," Hanoi Domestic Service, September 16, 1968, in FBIS-APA-68-193, Supplement 45, October 2, 1968, p. 49.

88. Foreign Ministry of the Socialist Republic of Vietnam, *Truth About Vietnam-China Relations*, Hanoi Radio, October 4, 1979, in FBIS-APA-79-204, October 19, 1979, p. 19.

89. Hoang Van Hoan, "Distortion of Facts," p. 18.

90. Foreign Ministry of the People's Republic of China, *Vietnamese Foreign Ministry's White Book*, pp. 24–25.

91. Radvanyi, *Delusion and Reality*, p. 220.

92.

We propose the restoration and strengthening of the solidarity within the socialist camp and the international communist and workers' movement on the basis of Marxism-Leninism and proletarian internationalism, so as to increase further our strength to resist the imperialists and their henchmen and to thwart all their schemes and acts of military aggression or of "peace" maneuvers vis-à-vis the socialist countries.

Truong Chinh, "Let Us Be Grateful," Hanoi Domestic Service, September 16, 1968, in FBIS-APA-68-193, Supplement 45, October 2, 1968, p. 50.

Chapter 6: North Vietnam's Tilt Toward the Soviet Union, 1968–75

1. For example, Robert Turner, who has written an empirically sound history of Vietnamese communism, wrote in 1974: "By 1973 North Vietnam was in a position approximately midway between China and the Soviet Union in the Sino-Soviet dispute, experiencing cooler relations with both than had been common during the previous decade." See Turner, *Vietnamese Communism*, p. 304.

Ellen J. Hammer, author of a reputable history of French Indochina for the period 1940 to 1955, wrote in early 1976: "In early 1975, Ho Chi Minh's dictum that Vietnam should steer a middle course between the Soviet Union and China, accepting aid from both and alienating neither, was still the basis of Hanoi's foreign policy." See Hammer, "Indochina: Communist But Nonaligned," p. 7.

Two years later, only months before the Vietnamese conflicts with China became highly visible, Carlyle Thayer wrote: "As a member of the socialist bloc Viet Nam has avoided taking sides in the Sino-Soviet dispute. Indeed the imperatives of Vietnamese nationalism dictate balancing Soviet and Chinese power." See Thayer, "Vietnam's External Relations," p. 230.

2. There is an extensive literature on the Czechoslovakian events of 1968. See especially Zeman, *Prague Spring*; Remington, *Winter in Prague*; Skilling, *Czechoslovakia's Interrupted Revolution*; and Mlynar, *Nightfrost in Prague*, which is the best insider's account, written by a former member of the Secretariat of the Central Committee. The best short history of Czechoslovakian communism is Zdenek Suda, *Zealots and Rebels*.

3. Mlynar, *Nightfrost in Prague*, p. 153.

4. *Beijing Review*, 11, no. 34, August 23, 1968, pp. III–VIII.

5. Hanoi Radio VNA Domestic Service, August 21, 1968, in FBIS-APA-68-164, August 21, 1968, K5.

6. Hanoi Radio VNA International Service, August 22, 1968, in FBIS-APA-68-165, August 22, 1968, K1.

7. Moscow TASS International Service, August 26, 1968, in FBIS-APA-68-171, August 30, 1968, K8.

8. Rubinstein, *Soviet Foreign Policy Since World War II*, p. 99.

9. *Pravda*, August 13, 1970, p. 1, in FBIS-SOV-70-160, A16–17.

10. *Izvestiya*, August 13, 1970, p. 1, in FBIS-SOV-70-159, A15.

11. *Peking Review*, September 18, 1970, p. 7.

12. Hanoi Radio VNA International Service, in English, March 26, 1970, in FBIS-APA-70-60, March 27, 1970, K2.

13. Hanoi Radio VNA International Service, in English, August 14, 1970, in FBIS-APA-70-159, K1.

14. "Fully aware of the West German imperialists' perfidious schemes and maneuvers, the press and public opinion in the Soviet Union and the East European socialist countries have, in the past four days, reminded everyone of the need for contin-

ued vigilance against West German revanchist ambitions." Hanoi Radio VNA International Service, in English, August 14, 1970, in FBIS-APA-70-159, August 17, 1970.

15. Eprile, *War and Peace in the Sudan*, p. 126; Bechtold, *Politics in the Sudan*, p. 261.

16. In 1970 Nimeiri dismissed some of his pro-communist officials, and in 1971 he dissolved some penetrated organizations, Bechtold, *Politics in the Sudan*, pp. 266–67.

17. FBIS-SOV-71-139, July 20, 1971; FBIS-SOV-71-140, July 21, 1971.

18. FBIS-SOV-71-141, July 22, 1971

19. FBIS-SOV-71-142, July 23, 1971.

20. FBIS-SOV-71-147, July 30, 1971.

21. Sylvester, *Sudan Under Nimeiri*, pp. 69–70.

22. Bechtold, *Politics in the Sand*, p. 317.

23. Beijing Radio NCNA International Service, July 27, 1971, in FBIS-CHI-71-145.

24. Beijing Radio NCNA International Service, October 13, 1971, in FBIS-CHI-71-199, October 14, 1971, A10. Zhou's congratulations came during a Sudanese delegation's visit to China. Beijing Radio NCNA International Service, December 16, 1971, in FBIS-CHI-71-243, December 17, 1971, A16. The speech in reply given by the Sudanese leader was broadcast in full by Beijing Radio. In it, Major General Abbas thanked the Chinese for their support during the coup, while implicitly criticizing the Soviet Union for its involvement. Beijing Radio NCNA International Service, December 17, 1971, in FBIS-CHI-71-244, December 20, 1971, A12.

25. Hanoi Radio VNA International Service, in English, July 29, 1971, in FBIS-APA-71-146, July 29, 1971, K9.

26. The paper continued: "These acts and the hysterical witch-hunt currently taking place in Sudan have completely brought to light the intervention of imperialism and other reactionary forces in various countries in Africa and the Middle and Near East." Ibid.

27. "We Vehemently Protest the Brutal Terrorist Acts of the Sudanese Authorities," Hanoi Radio Domestic Service, July 30, 1971, in FBIS-APA-71-152, August 6, 1971, K22; Hanoi Radio VNA International Service, in English, July 30, 1971, in FBIS-APA-71-152, August 6, 1971, K21–22.

28. See McCleod, "Portrait of A Model Ally," pp. 31–52; Cabral, "The Portugese Communist Party."

29. *Pravda*, May 25, 1974, p. 4, *CDSP* XXVI, no. 21, p. 22.

30. *Pravda*, February 22, 1975, p. 4, *CDSP*, XXVII, no. 8.

31. Rubenstein, *Soviet Foreign Policy*, p. 107.

32. Beijing Radio NCNA, May 18, 1974, in FBIS-CHI-74-100, May 22, 1974, A25; Beijing Radio NCNA, May 26, 1974, in FBIS-CHI-74-111, June 7, 1974.

33. Beijing Radio NCNA, June 15, 1975, in FBIS-CHI-75-116, June 16, 1975, A1–A2.

34. Beijing Radio Domestic Service, June 16, 1975, in FBIS-CHI-75-119, June 19, 1975, A1.

35. Hanoi Radio VNA, August 4, 1973, in FBIS-APA-73-153, August 8, 1973, K8–K9.

36. Hanoi Radio Domestic Service, April 28, 1974, in FBIS-APA-74-84, April 30, 1974, K2. Hanoi's caution also derived partly from uncertainty over the future domestic policies of the new regime.

37. Hanoi VNA Radio, May 8, 1974, in FBIS-APA-74-91, May 9, 1974, K4.

38. Hanoi VNA Radio, in English, May 17, 1974, in FBIS-APA-74-97, May 17, 1974, K4.

39. Hanoi Radio stated: "The struggle for the solution of the problem of "who will win?" is taking place in a very complex and fierce manner in Portugal between the correct revolutionary path advocated by the Communist Party, the armed forces movement, and other progressive political organizations and also the bourgeois way of which the Socialist Party is the proponent." Hanoi Radio VNA, in English, June 13, 1975, in FBIS-APA-75-100, June 17, 1975, K3–K4.

40. Hanoi conceded that "the revolution of Portugal is going through difficult hours." Hanoi Radio VNA, December 3, 1975, in FBIS-APA-75-233, December 3, 1975, K3.

41. Hanoi Radio VNA, January 28, 1976, in FBIS-APA-76-20, January 29, 1976, K2.

42. Legum, "Angola and the Horn of Africa," pp. 573–75.

43. Marcum, *The Angolan Revolution*, pp. 160–61.

44. Ibid., p. 255.

45. Liberation Press Agency (Hanoi), February 4, 1974, in FBIS-APA-74-28, February 8, 1974, L7.

46. Liberation Press Agency (Hanoi), January 23, 1975, in FBIS-APA-75-17, January 24, 1975, L8.

47. Hanoi VNA, October 30, 1975, in FBIS-APA-75-212, November 3, 1975, K17.

48. Hanoi VNA, November 9, 1975, in FBIS-APA-75-218, November 11, 1975, K9.

49. Hanoi VNA, November 12, 1975, in FBIS-APA-75-220, November 13, 1975, K2.

50. *Quan Doi Nhan Dan*, November 21, 1975, Hanoi Radio VNA Domestic Service, November 21, 1975, in FBIS-APA-75-229, November 26, 1975, K5.

51. The conclusion was that U.S. intervention plans would inevitably be defeated. *Quan Doi Nhan Dan*, "The Angolan Revolution Is Steadily Advancing" (commentary), December 24, 1975, in FBIS-APA-75-250, December 29, 1975, K6.

52. Buszynski, *Soviet Foreign Policy and Southeast Asia*, p. 42

53. Ibid., chap. 2, especially pp. 67–69.

54. Truong Nhu Tang, *Viet Cong Memoir*, p. 248.

55. *Quan Doi Nhan Dan*, November 24, 1973, p. 1, in FBIS-APA-73-234, December 5, 1973, K2.

56. "Politicheskii otchet posol'stva SSSR v demokraticheskoi respublike v'etnam

za 1972 god" ("Political Report of the Embassy of the USSR in the Democratic Republic of Vietnam for 1972"), TsKhSD, Fond 5, Opis 64, Delo 472, p. 17.

57. Ibid.

58. Ibid.

59. There has been change in the top leadership since 1975. Most notably, the demotion of Hoang Van Hoan from the Politburo at the Fourth Party Congress in 1976, and the removal of Vo Nguyen Giap from the Defense Ministry in 1980 and from the Politburo in 1982, along with former Foreign Minister Nguyen Duy Trinh, former Economics Minister Le Thanh Nghi, and former Interior Minister Tran Quoc Hoan. But these demotions represented the consequences of events in 1978 and after.

60. From the Vietnamese side, see especially, Foreign Ministry of the Socialist Republic of Vietnam, "The Truth About Vietnam-China Relations Over the Last 30 Years," Hanoi Radio, October 4, 1979, in FBIS-APA-79-204, October 19, 1979 (supplement).

61. There are no reliable figures on the amounts of Soviet and Chinese aid. But one estimate for the relevant years 1966–69 puts Soviet economic aid at $210 million annually and Chinese economic aid at $85 million annually. Military aid levels are just as uncertain, but the same source claims that from 1955 to 1971 the Soviet Union supplied $1.7 billion and China $750 million in military aid. See U.S. Congress, *People's Republic of China. An Economic Assessment: A Compendium of Papers Submitted to the Joint Economic Committee*, May 18, 1972, pp. 378–79.

62. "Politicheskii otchet posol'stvo SSSR v Demokraticheskoi Respublike V'etnama za 1970 god" ("Political Report of the the Embassy of the USSR in the Democratic Republic of Vietnam for the year 1970"), TsKhSD, Fond 5, Opis 62, Delo 495, p. 165.

63. "Politicheskii otchet posol'stvo SSSR v Demokraticheskii Respublike V'etname za 1972 god," TsKhSD, Fond 5, Opis 64, Delo 472, p. 49.

64. Ibid., pp. 24–25, 49.

65. Foreign Ministry of the Socialist Republic of Vietnam, "The Truth About Vietnam-China Relations Over the Last 30 Years," FBIS-APA-79-204, October 19, 1979, p. 22.

66. See Woodside, *Vietnam and the Chinese Model*.

67. "Political Report Read At the Second National Congress of the Viet-Nam Workers' Party, Held in February 1951," in Fall, ed., *Ho Chi Minh*, pp. 207–8.

68. King C. Chen *Vietnam and China*, pp. 8–9.

69. Le Duan, "Leninism Illuminates the Revolutionary Aims of the Present Age," *Kommunist*, no. 7, April 30, 1970, in FBIS-APA-70-107, June 3, 1970, K20.

70. Hoang Anh Report, p. 26. TskSD, Fond 89, Opis 54, Delo 8, p. 210.

71. Le Duan, "Leninism Illuminates the Revolutionary Aims of the Present Age," *Kommunist*, no. 7, April 30, 1970, in FBIS-APA-70-107, June 3, 1970, pp. K13, K21.

72. Ibid., K13.

73. Le Duan, *The Vietnamese Revolution*, pp. 147–48.

74. For example, in 1963 the Vietnamese communists issued a resolution that included the following:

Now the imperialists—headed by the U.S. imperialists—are mustering the reactionary forces and are using the modern revisionists to sow discord in the socialist camp, oppose the international communist movement, undermine the revolutionary movement of world people, and sabotage peace. Thus strengthening solidarity in the socialist camp and the international communist movement is of very great significance. This will increase manifoldly the forces of the world revolution and ensure ever greater victories for the world revolution and the protection of peace.

"World Situation and Our Party's International Mission," Resolution of the Ninth Conference of the Central Committee of the Lao Dong Party of Viet Nam (December 1963), *Vietnam Documents and Research Notes*, no. 98, September 1971, p. 125.

75. The authenticity of Ho's published will is uncertain. See Bui Tin, *Following Ho Chi Minh*, pp. 67–68. However, this quote is conistent with other public statements.

76. *Nhan Dan* continued its editorial:

The imperialist circles and all the reactionary forces in the world, headed by the U.S., are exalting at that and feverishly proceeding with acts of division and sabotage. The staunch combatants of Marxism-Leninism are grieved and are earnestly doing everything they can to help restore, consolidate, and develop the solidarity and unity of mind of the revolutionary vanguard forces all over the world in accordance with the principles of proletarian internationalism.

Hanoi VNA, September 15, 1969, in FBIS-APA-69-178, September 15, 1969, K15–K16.

77. With regard to the socialist camp, the basic policy of the Nixon doctrine consists in "dividing, holding, and repelling." When analyzing the socialist countries, Nixon must admit their economic and military growth, especially that of the Soviet Union and China (which Nixon names "two communist powers"). However, he has inflated the differences and division within the communist world, considering this as a new condition and new opportunity for the U.S. to realize its scheme of countering the world's revolutionary movement in a more perfidious and frenzied manner. The Nixon doctrine undertakes to lay "half a bridge," i.e., to expand economic, scientific, technical, and cultural contacts with a view to infiltrating and sabotaging the socialist countries and materializing a counterrevolutionary peace evolution when possible. Nixon also undertakes to stir up nationalism, uphold the signboards of "negotiation" and "East-West détente," realize the policy of making friends with every country with the aim of sowing division among the socialist countries and drawing one country against another. *Quan Doi Nhan Dan* (Hanoi), August 3, 1971, pp. 2–3, in FBIS-APA-71-156, August 12, 1971, K10.

78. Interview by author with Hoang Huu Quynh, a Soviet-trained Vietnamese

engineer who defected to the West, Paris 1981. He claims that the Vietnamese peasants used the Little Red Book as toilet paper.

79. Robinson, "China Confronts the Soviet Union," in MacFarquar and Fairbank, eds., *The Cambridge History of China*, p. 249.

80. Hoang Anh Report, p. 26, TsKhSD, Fond 89, Opis 54, Delo 8, p. 210.

81. Ibid., p. 25, TsKhSD, p. 209.

82. Prince Norodom Sihanouk, interview by the author, Ban Saen, Thailand, March 6, 1985.

83. Ibid.

84. Truong Nhu Tang, interview with the author, Washington, D.C., October 1981.

85. *Quan Doi Nhan Dan*, November 24, 1973, p. 1, in FBIS-APA-73-234, December 5, 1973, K2.

86. Nguyen Khanh Hoan, "President Ho and International Solidarity," *Hoc Tap*, no. 11, November 1972, in FBIS-APA-72-239, December 11, 1972, K15.

87. Hoang Anh Report, pp. 10, 23, 25–30, TsKhSD, Fond 89, Opis 54, Delo 8.

88. For factional analyses of Vietnamese politics dealing with earlier periods, see Honey, *Communism in North Vietnam*; Smith, *An International History of the Vietnam War*.

Chapter 7: The Collapse of Vietnamese-Chinese Relations

1. Duiker, *China and Vietnam*, p. 56.

2. Phnom Penh Radio, May 11, 1970. Cited in Taylor, *China and Southeast Asia*, p. 152.

3. Posol'stvo SSSR v DRV, "O politike partii trudyashchikhsya v'etnama v reshenii problem indokitaya i nashikh zadachakh, vitekayushchikh iz reshenii XXIV s'ezda kpss" (Politicheskoye pis'mo). (Embassy of the USSR in the DRV, "About the Policy of the Vietnam Workers' Party Toward a Solution of the Problem of Indochina and Our Tasks, Flowing from the Decisions of the Twenty-fourth Congress of the CPSU" [Political Letter]), May 25, 1971, p. 7, TsKhSD, Fond 89, Opis 54, Delo 10, p. 28.

4. Chang, *Beijing, Hanoi, and the Overseas Chinese*, p. 10.

5. Recall, from our discussion in chapter 2, that in the first decade of the Indochinese Communist Party (ICP), ethnic Chinese were actively recruited for and were an important component of the ICP membership, especially in Cambodia. See also "Rapport d'Activite en 1948 et programme pour 1949 du parti comuniste Indochinois," November 8, 1949, AOM, Slotfom XIV, Carton 13, p. 9.

6. Mrs. Huynh quoted in Chanoff and Doan Van Toai, *Portrait of the Enemy*, p. 125.

7. Han Vi, quoted in ibid., p. 121.

8. The most comprehensive explanation of the dispute available in English is Chang, *The Sino-Vietnamese Territorial Dispute*.

9. Ibid., p. 25.

10. Ibid., pp. 28–30.

11. For a detailed discussion of this question, see ibid.

12. *Far Eastern Economic Review*, February 25, 1977.

13. Truong Nhu Tang, *Viet Cong Memoir*, pp. 248–49.

14. The contents of the Vietnamese report to the Soviets on the details of this meeting are contained in "Results of the Visit of the Vietnamese Party-Government Delegation to China (1975)," TsKhSD, Fond 5, Opis 73, Delo 1933. It is likely that this account was passed to the Soviets through an informal channel, probably an agent of the Soviet military intelligence directorate, the GRU.

15. Ibid., p. 31.

16. Ibid., pp. 31–32.

17. Ibid.

18. V. Sviridov, second secretary of the Embassy of the USSR in the SRV, "O nekotorikh aspektakh v'etnamo-kitaiskikh otnoshenii" ("About Several Aspects of Vietnamese-Chinese Relations"), April 1976, TsKhSD, Fond 5, Opis 69, Delo 2313, p. 18.

19. Ibid., pp. 18–19.

20. Ibid., p. 19.

21. V. Kuzmin, attaché of the Embassy of the USSR in the SRV, "O nekotorikh momentakh deyatel'nosti posol'stva KNR v SRV" ("About Several Features of the Activities of the PRC Embassy in the SRV"), September 21,1976, TsKhSD, Fond 5, Opis 69, Delo 2313, p. 72.

22. V. Pushnin, second secretary of the Embassy of the USSR in the SRV, "O kitaiskoi kolonii v SRV" ("About the Chinese Colony in the SRV"), October 18, 1977, TsKhSD, Fond 5, Opis 73, Delo 1406, p. 50.

23. Nachal'nik glavnovo razvedivatelnovo upravleniya general'novo shtaba VS SSSR ("Head of the Main Intelligence Directorate of the General Staff of the AF USSR"), "O polozhenii kitaiskikh emigrantov v sotsialisticheskoi respublike v'etnama" ("About the Situation of the Chinese Emigrants in the Socialist Republic of Vietnam"), May 19, 1978, TsKhSD, Fond 5, Opis 75, Delo 1459, p. 5.

24. "O kitaiskoi kolonii v SRV," p. 50

25. Ibid.

26. "O polozhenii kitaiskikh emigrantov v sotsialisticheskoi respublike v'etnama," p. 5.

27. "O kitaiskoi kolonii v SRV," p. 49.

28. "O polozhenii kitaiskikh emigrantov v sotsialisticheskoi respublike v'etnama," p. 5.

29. "O kitaiskoi kolonii v SRV," p. 53.

30. Ibid., pp. 54–55.

31. "O polozhenii kitaiskikh emigrantov v sotsialisticheskoi respublike v'etnama," p. 4.

32. "O kitaiskoi kolonii v SRV," pp. 51–52.

33. The figures probably represent the numbers of people whom the associations would claim to represent, rather than active members. "O polozhenii kitaiskikh emigrantov v sotsialisticheskoi respublike v'etnama," p. 3.

34. "O kitaiskoi kolonii v SRV," p. 53.

35. Ibid., p. 50.   36. Ibid., p. 53.

37. Ibid., p. 52.   38. Ibid.

39. For the best informed and detailed analysis of the Congress, see Honey, "Fourth Congress of the Lao Dong Party." See also Turley, "Vietnam Since Reunification," pp. 36–54.

40. B. Chaplin, "Record of Conversation with the First Secretary of the CC of the VWP, Le Duan," November 16, 1976, TsKhSD, Fond 5, Opis 69, Delo 2314, pp. 112–13.

41. Honey, "Fourth Congress of the Lao Dong Party," p. 4.

42. *Beijing Review*, March 30, 1979, p. 22. Cited in Chang, *Beijing, Hanoi, and the Overseas Chinese*, p. 21.

43. "Zapis' besedi s chlenom politburo TsK PTV, zam, prem'er-ministrom, ministrom inostrannikh del DRV Nguen Zui Chinem" (Report of a Conversation with a Member of the Politburo of the VWP CC, Deputy Prime Minister, Minister of Foreign Affairs of the DRV, Nguyen Duy Trinh), April 6, 1976, TsKhSD, Fond 5, Opis 69, Delo 2314, pp. 46–47.

44. "Zapis' besedi s chlenom Politburo TsK PTV, Prem'er-ministrom SRV Pham Van Dongom" ("Report of a Conversation with a Member of the Politburo of the VWP CC, Prime Minister Pham Van Dong"), November 6, 1976, TsKhSD, Fond 5, Opis 69, Delo 2314, p. 100.

45. "Zapis' besedi s generalnim sekretarom TsK VKP Le Zuanom" ("Report of a Conversation with the General Secretary of the VCP CC Le Duan"), October 6, 1977, TsKhSD, Fond 5, Opis 73, Delo 1409, pp. 122–23.

46. "Zapis' besedi s sekretarim TsK KPV, nachalnik otdela inostrannikh otnoshenakh Tsk KPV, Zuan Tuinom" ("Report of a Conversation with Secretary of the CPV CC, Director of the Department of Foreign Relations of the CPV CC, Xuan Thuy"), TsKhSD, Fond 5, Opis 73, Delo 1409, p. 133.

47. "Zapis' besedi s generalnim sekretarom TsK Kpv Le Zuanom" ("Report of a Conversation with General Secretary of the CPV CC, Le Duan"), September 5, 1978, TsKhSD, Fond 5, Opis 75, Delo 1061, p. 102.

48. Hanoi Radio, VNA, March 19, 1977, in FBIS-APA-77-54, March 21, 1977.

49. The World Bank, *China: Socialist Economic Development*.

50. Figures on Soviet trade with Vietnam were provided by the Soviet Foreign Ministry, in response to a written request, Moscow, April 2, 1992.

51. International Monetary Fund, *Direction of Trade Statistics: Yearbook 1984*.

52. *Far Eastern Economic Review*, July 14, 1978, p. 9.

53. Hanoi Radio, VNA, April 20, 1977, in FBIS-APA-77-76, April 20, 1977.

54. Chang, *Sino-Vietnamese Territorial Dispute*, p. 35.

55. Hanoi Radio, VNA, June 9, 1977, in FBIS-APA-77-112, June 10, 1977.

56. Chang, *Sino-Vietnamese Territorial Dispute*, p. 35.

57. Hanoi Radio, VNA, June 21, 1977, in FBIS-APA-77-120, June 22, 1977.

58. "Huang Hua's 42,000-word Foreign Policy Address," in King C. Chen, ed., *China and the Three Worlds*, pp. 271–72.

59. Hanoi Radio, VNA, August 21, 1977, in FBIS-APA-77-162, August 22, 1977.

60. Hanoi Radio, VNA, September 30, 1977, in FBIS-APA-77-191, October 3, 1977.

61. The *Nhan Dan* editorial of November 26 cited part of the speech given at a banquet on November 20 by Le Duan. Hanoi Radio, VNA, November 25, 1977, in FBIS-APA-77-228, November 28, 1977.

62. "Zapis' besedi s sekretarom TsK KPV, nachal'nik otdela inostranikh otnoshenax TsK KPV Zuan Tuinom" ("Report of a Conversation with Secretary of the CC of the CPV, Director of the Department of Foreign Relations of the CPV CC, Xuan Thuy"), December 1, 1977, TsKhSD, Fond 5, Opis 73, Delo 1409, pp. 133–36.

63. *Washington Post*, January 19, 1978; *New York Times*, February 9, 1978.

64. AFP Radio (Hong Kong), January 10, 1978, in FBIS-APA-78-6, January 10, 1978.

65. *Beijing Review*, vol. 21, no. 4, January 27, 1978, pp. 24–25.

66. Hanoi Radio, VNA, February 21, 1978, in FBIS-APA-78-36, February 22, 1978.

67. "Zapis' besedi s chlenom TsK KPV, predsedatelem gosudarstvennogo komiteta nauki i tekniki SRV Chan Kuiem" ("Report of a Conversation with a Member of CPV CC, Chairman of the State Committee on Science and Technology of the SRV, Tran Quyen"), March 24, 1978, Fond 5, Opis 75, Delo 1061, p. 40.

68. Hanoi Radio, VNA, February 21, 1978, in FBIS-APA-78-36, February 22, 1978.

69. Hanoi Radio, VNA, March 8, 1978, in FBIS-APA-78-47, March 9, 1978, K2.

70. For details of the leadership changes and other aspects of the Congress, see Honey, "Vietnam's Party Congress and After."

71. Rolf Soderberg, AFP Radio (Hong Kong), April 19, 1978, and Stockholm Radio, April 19, 1978, in FBIS-APA-78-76, April 19, 1978.

72. *Christian Science Monitor*, April 21, 1978.

73. AFP (Paris), April 21, 1978, in FBIS-APA-78-79, April 24, 1978.

74. B. Chaplin, "Zapis' besedi s perv'im sekretarem TsK PTV Le Zuanom" ("Report of a Conversation with the First Secretary of the VWP CC, Le Duan"), October 6, 1977, TsKhSD, Fond 5, Opis 73, Delo 1409, pp. 124–25.

75. *Beijing Review*, no. 23, June 9, 1978, p. 16.

76. Hanoi Radio, VNA, May 4, 1978, in FBIS-APA-78-88, May 5, 1978, K2.

77. AFP (Hong Kong), May 9, 1978, in FBIS-APA-78-91, May 10, 1978, K1.

78. Note of the Foreign Ministry of the People's Republic of China to the Embassy of the Socialist Republic of Vietnam in China, May 12, 1978, in FBIS-APA-78-118, June 19, 1978, K14.

79. Ibid.

80. Hanoi Radio, VNA, "*The Truth About Vietnam-China Relations Over the Last Thirty Years*," October 4, 1979, in FBIS-APA-79-204, October 19, 1979, pp. 32–33.

81. *Le Monde*, October 13, 1978, p. 3.

82. The best account of the operations of the PSB and the neighborhood committees is Nguyen Long and Kendall, *After Saigon Fell*.

83. Refugee-based analysis has been used extensively in Wain, *The Refused*, especially chap. 4.

84. *New York Times*, December 13, 1978.

85. Bui Tin, *Following Ho Chi Minh*, pp. 101–102.

86. "Zapis' besedi s generalom sekratarom TsK KPV Le Zuanom" ("Report of a Conversation with General Secretary of the CPV CC, Le Duan"), September 5, 1978, TsKhSD, Fond 5, Opis 75, Delo 1061, p. 102.

87. I am well aware of the longstanding armed resistance of some of the ethnic hill tribes of Vietnam's central highlands against the communist government. But these groups lived in remote jungle regions of the country, were physically outside effective government control, and were not a fifth column in any meaningful sense of the term.

88. Han Vi and Mrs. Huynh quoted in Chanoff and Doan Van Toai, *Portrait of the Enemy*, pp. 121, 125.

89. See FBIS-APA-78-118, June 19, 1978, K7, K15.

90. Hanoi Radio (VNA) International Service, July 5, 1978, in FBIS-APA-78-129, July 5, 1978, K3.

91. *New York Times*, June 9, 1978.

92. *Beijing Review*, June 30, 1978, p. 19.

93. Chanda, *Brother Enemy*, p. 183.

94. *New York Times*, July 4, 1978.

95. For the most extensive Chinese rebuttal of Vietnam's explanation, see "Time Will Tell the True from the False," *Beijing Review*, no. 30, July 28, 1978, pp. 26–29.

Chapter 8: *The Emergence of the Soviet-Vietnamese Alliance*

1. Sihanouk adds: "I answered frankly to the Soviets that the Khmers Rouges were giving me all sorts of reasons and were finding all sorts of pretexts to prevent me from recovering my former ascendancy over the Khmer nation." Norodom Sihanouk, "Le Calice Jusqu'a La Lie," chapter 6.

2. Beijing Radio (NCNA) International Service, in English, August 16, 1970, in FBIS-CHI-70-159, August 17 1970; Beijing Radio (NCNA) International Service, in English, September 5, 1970, in FBIS-CHI-70-174, September 8, 1970.

3. Evgeny Vasil'evich Kobelev, interview with the author, Moscow, March 30, 1992. Hereafter cited as Kobelev interview, 1992.

4. *Far Eastern Economic Review*, April 22, 1972.

5. Radio Beijing, NCNA International Service, March 19, 1972, *Principal Reports from Communist Radio and Press Sources*, March 21, 1972, pp. 1–10.

6. According to former policy consultant Kobelev, all the Soviet Union's information about the "liberated zones"—i.e., those zones controlled by the insurgency—came from the Vietnamese communists. This was because the USSR did not recognize the nominally Sihanoukist government that represented the Cambodian insurgency. Kobelev claims that before 1974 the Soviet Union got little information from Vietnam. Only in 1974 did the Soviet Union start getting information of a general kind. Kobelev interview 1992.

7. *Pravda*, July 23, 1973, p. 3.

8. Ibid., August 16, 1973, p. 5, and August 19, 1973, p. 5.

9. Ibid., October 12, 1973, p. 4.

10. Ibid., October 19, 1973, p. 1.

11. AFP (Hong Kong), March 28, 1975, in FBIS-APA-75-61, March 28, 1975.

12. Prince Norodom Sihanouk, interview with the author, Ban Saen Thailand, March 1985. Hereafter referred to as Sihanouk interview.

13. Kobelev interview, 1992.

14. This is implied by Le Duc Tho in an interview, when he discussed Zhou Enlai, who died in January 1976: "When Mr. Zhou Enlai was prime minister, relations between our party and the Chinese Communist Party were still friendly and he played a part in helping us in our resistance war. In spite of certain differences of views, on the whole he did follow such a course of action. His death did not allow him to see enmity develop after 1975." *Vietnam Courier* 6, 1985, p. 13

15. "Politicheskii otchet posol'stvo SSSR v demokraticheskoi respublike v'etnam za 1970 god" ("Political Report of the Embassy of the USSR in the Democratic Republic of Vietnam for 1970"), TsKhSD, Fond 5, Opis 62, Delo 495, p. 100.

16. Ibid., p. 125.   17. Ibid., pp. 102–3.

18. Ibid., p. 164.   19. Ibid.

20. Ibid., p. 109.   21. Ibid., pp. 190–91.

22. Posol'stvo SSSR v DRV, "O politike partii trudyashchikhsya v'etnama v reshenii problem indokitaya i nashikh zadachakh, vitekayushchikh iz reshenii XXIV s'ezda kpss" [Politicheskoye pis'mo] (Embassy of the USSR in the DRV, "About the Policy of the Vietnam Workers' Party Toward a Solution of the Problem of Indochina and Our Tasks, Flowing from the Decisions of the Twenty-fourth Congress of the CPSU" [Political Letter]), May 25, 1971, p. 2, TsKhSD, Fond 89, Opis 54, Delo 10, p. 24.

23. Ibid., p. 13.

24. Ibid., p. 8, TsKhSD, p. 30.

25. "Politicheskii otchet posol'stva SSSR v demokraticheskoi respublike v'etnam za 1972 god" ("Political Report of the Embassy of the USSR in the Democratic Republic of Vietnam for 1972"), TsKhSD, Fond 5, Opis 64, Delo 472, p. 22.

26. Ibid.

27. Ibid.

28. Ibid., pp. 22–23.

29. "Politicheskii otchet posol'stva SSSR v demokraticheskoi respublike v'etnam za 1973 god" ("Political Report of the Embassy of the USSR in the Democratic Republic of Vietnam for 1973"), TsKhSD, Fond 5, Opis 66, Delo 781, p. 6.

30. Ibid., p. 9.   31. Ibid., p. 12.

32. Ibid., pp. 14–15.   33. Ibid., p. 10.

34. "Politicheskii otchet posol'stva SSSR v demokraticheskoi respublike v'etnam za 1974 god" ("Political Report of the Embassy of the USSR in the Democratic Republic of Vietnam for 1974"), TsKhSD, Fond 5, Opis 67, Delo 655, p. 35.

35. Ibid., pp. 35–36.

36. Komitet gosudarstvennoi bezopasnosti pri sovete ministrov SSSR, "O poluchenii iz DRV amerikanskovo trofeinovo strelkovovo oruzhiya" (Committee of State Security of the Council of Ministers of the USSR, "About the conditions of transfer from the DRV of captured American small arms"), December 31, 1975, TsKhSD, Fond 89.

37. Ibid.

38. "Zapis' besedi kandidata v chleni Politburo, sekratar' TsK CPV, To Huu s delegatsiei otdela propagandi TsK KPSS" ("Report of a Meeting of Candidate Member of the Politburo, Secretary of the VCP CC To Huu with a Delegation of the Propaganda Department of the CPSU Central Committee"), February 17, 1978, TsKhSD, Fond 5, Opis 75, Delo 1062.

39. Moscow Radio, in Vietnamese, 22 February, 1978, in FBIS-SOV-78-36, February 22, 1978, L1.

40. Moscow Radio, in Vietnamese, June 25, 1978, in FBIS-SOV-78-125, June 28, 1978, L3.

41. Ibid.

42. TASS International Service (Moscow), July 3, 1978, in FBIS-SOV-78-130. July 6, 1978, CC5.

43. Chanda, *Brother Enemy*, p. 188.

44. Evgeny Pavlovich Glazunov, interview with the author, Moscow, April 1, 1992.

45. Moscow Radio, in Vietnamese, April 2, 1978, in FBIS-SOV-78-65. April 4, 1978, L1.

46. "Zapis' besedi s chlenom Politburo TsK KPV, ministr inostrannikh del Nguyen Duy Trinh" ("Report of a Meeting with Member of the Politburo of the DRV Central Committee, Minister of Foreign Affairs Nguyen Duy Trinh"), June 15, 1978, TsKhSD, Fond 5, Opis 75, Delo 1062, p. 25.

47. "Zapis' besedi s chlenom Politburo TsK KPV, zam prem'er ministr pravitel'stva SRV, Le Thanh Nghi" ("Report of a Meeting with Member of the Politburo of the CC of the CPV, Deputy Prime Minister of the Government of the SRV Le Thanh Nghi"), July 24, 1978, TsKhSD, Fond 5, Opis 75, Delo 1062, p. 63.

48. Hanoi Radio (VNA), in English, July 2, 1978, in FBIS-APA-78-128, July 3, 1978, K19.

49. *Far Eastern Economic Review*, August 18, 1978.
50. Hanoi Radio (VNA), October 4, 1978, in FBIS-APA-78-195, October 6, 1978, K3.
51. Ibid.
52. Hanoi Radio (VNA), Domestic Service, October 4, 1978, in FBIS-APA-78-195. October 6, 1978, K4.
53. For example, see *Christian Science Monitor*, October 27, 1978, p. 4.
54. Bui Tin interview.
55. *New York Times*, June 1, 1978.
56. AFP (Hong Kong), June 29, 1978, in FBIS-APA-78-127, June 30, 1978, K1.
57. *Tokyo Kyodo*, July 4, 1978, in FBIS-APA-78-129, July 5, 1978, K2.
58. *Los Angeles Times*, August 25, 1978, p. 7.
59. *Washington Post*, September 2, 1978. pp. A1, A14.
60. Moscow Radio, in Vietnamese, October 28, 1978, in FBIS-SOV-78-211, October 31, 1978, L2.
61. Moscow Radio, in Vietnamese, October 31, 1978, in FBIS-SOV-78-213, November 2, 1978, C1.
62. Moscow TASS, November 1, 1978, in FBIS-SOV-78-212, November 1, 1978, L1–L2.
63. Bui Tin claims that Giap opposed the invasion of Cambodia. But he also claims that a deep enmity had long existed between Giap and the dominant factions of Le Duan and Le Duc Tho. See *Following Ho Chi Minh*, pp. 131–35.
64. *Tap Chi Cong San*, no. 11, November 1978, pp. 8–10, in JPRS: 072720.
65. "Great Friendship," *Tap Chi Cong San*, no. 11, November 1978, p. 1, in JPRS: 072720.
66. "The Trustworthy Base and the Hope of the Revolutionary and Peace Forces of the World," *Tap Chi Cong San*, no. 11, November 1978, pp. 11–15, in JPRS: 072720.
67. Mikhail S. Kapitsa, interview with the author, Moscow, March 27, 1992.
68. The China specialist is Evgeny Bazhanov, in an interview with the author in Moscow in June 1996. The Vietnam specialist is Igor Ognetov, in an interview with the author, in Moscow, December 1997. The Cambodia specialist is Evgeny Kobelev, in an interview with the author in Moscow, December 1997. Bazhanov was the original source for this revelation. All three were interviewed alone and without knowing either that I had interviewed or would interview the others.
69. "Zapis' besedi s general'nim sekretarem TsK KPV Le Zuanom" ("Report of a Conversation with General Secretary of the CPV CC Le Duan"), September 5, 1978. TsKhSD, Fond 5, Opis 75, Delo 1061, p. 101.
70. "Politicheskii otchet posol'stva SSSR v demokraticheskoi respublike v'etnam za 1972 god" ("Political Report of the Embassy of the USSR in the Democratic Republic of Vietnam for 1972"), TsKhSD, Fond 5, Opis 64, Delo 472, p. 22.
71. Kobelev interview, 1997.

Chapter 9: *The Consequences of the Vietnamese Invasion*

1. A list of the original 14-member Kampuchean National United Front for National Salvation and their brief biographical sketches were provided by clandestine radio broadcast Sapordamean Kampuchea to Cambodia on December 4 and 5, 1978. See FBIS, *Daily Report: Asia and Pacific*, December 4, 1978, and December 5, 1978.

2. The only difference in the name was the use of "Kampuchean" instead of "Cambodian" by the post-1979 party, thereby indicating its continuity with the Khmers Rouges movement as well as links with the Vietnamese communists.

3. *New York Times*, January 8, 1979.

4. For example, Jean Thoraval of AFP, cited in *New York Times*, March 27, 1979.

5. For more detail, see Morris, "Vietnam's Vietnam."

6. For example, Secretary of State Cyrus Vance and Assistant Secretary Richard Holbrooke. See Vance, *Hard Choices*, pp. 122–23; Brzezinski, *Power and Principle*, pp. 228–29.

7. Mahbubani, "The Kampuchean Problem," p. 407.

8. *Far Eastern Economic Review*, November 5, 1982.

9. For an extensive examination of this matter, see Buszynski, *Gorbachev and Southeast Asia*.

10. Bui Tin interview.

11. Bao Quoc, "The Cam Ranh Syndrome."

12. *Los Angeles Times*, April 24, 1983.

13. *Far Eastern Economic Review*, October 15, 1982; *New York Times*, October 9, 1982.

14. *New York Times*, May 7, 1984.

15. Martin, "Le Processus De Vietnamisation," p. 185.

16. *New York Times*, February 21, 1979.

17. Paul Quinn-Judge, *Far Eastern Economic Review*, May 26, 1983; Martin, "Le Processus De Vietnamisation."

18. Martin, ibid.

19. Martin, "Cambodge: Une Nouvelle Colonie D'Exploitation;" Luciolli, *Le Mur de bambou*.

20. For a generally optimistic account of the UNTAC efforts and the aftermath of the elections, see Shawcross, *Cambodia's New Deal*. For a more pessimistic evaluation of the electoral process see the chapter entitled "Cambodia" in *Lost Agenda*, from Human Rights Watch.

21. *Far Eastern Economic Review*, July 17, 1997.

22. *New York Times*, April 17, 1998; *Far Eastern Economic Review*, April 30, 1998.

23. On these issues, see Morris, "Our Failure in Cambodia" and "Brutocracy Wins."

Conclusion

1. Stalin's terror within the Soviet Union during 1936–38, especially the purges of his military officer corps, seriously weakened his regime and encouraged his real enemies, the Germans, to believe that he could be overthrown. It also contributed to the severe setbacks suffered by the Soviet Union in the early days of World War II. In China, the chaos caused by Mao's Great Proletarian Cultural Revolution encouraged Maos' real enemy, the Soviet Union, to believe that China's nuclear forces could be preemptively destroyed in a Soviet nuclear strike without effective Chinese military retaliation. The unexpectedly negative reaction of the Americans helped to prevent the Soviet strike from happening.

2. In 1976 the Vietnamese Workers' party was renamed the Vietnamese Communist party.

3. Meissner, *The Paranoid Process*, p. 655.

Primary Sources

Archives

Archives d'Outre-Mer, Aix-En-Provence, France.
Indochina Archive, University of California, Berkeley.
Rossiiskii tsentr khranyeniya i izuchyeniya dokumentov noveishei istorii
    [RTsKhIDNI] (Russian Center for the Preservation and Study of Documents
    of Modern History), Moscow.
Tsentr khranyeniya sovremennoi dokumentatsii [TsKhSD] (Center for the Preserva-
    tion of Contemporary Documents), Moscow.

Published Documents and Radio Broadcasts

Foreign Broadcast Information Service (FBIS), *Daily Report*, U.S. Government,
    Washington, D.C.
Vietnam Documents and Research Notes. Saigon, Republic of Vietnam: United
    States Mission in Vietnam.

Interviews

Hoang Huu Quynh, Soviet-trained Vietnamese engineer, Paris, July 1981.
Truong Nhu Tang, former minister of justice of the Provisional Revolutionary
    Government of South Vietnam, Washington, D.C., October 1981.
Ieng Sary, foreign minister of Democratic Kampuchea, 1975–78, Phum Tmey,
    Cambodia, September 1983.
Prince Norodom Sihanouk, former and current chief of state of Cambodia, Ban
    Saen, Thailand, February 6, 1985.
Bui Tin, former editor of the Vietnamese People's Army newspaper, *Quan Doi
    Nhan Dan*, Boston, October 1991.
Naranhkiri Tith, former student at Lycee Sisowath in Phnom Penh and the Univer-
    sity of Montpelier, Washington, D.C., June 5, 1984.
Mikhail S. Kapitsa, former deputy foreign minister of the Soviet Union and former

head of the Asian division of the Soviet Foreign Ministry, Moscow, March 27, 1992.

Evgeny V. Kobelev, Senior Scholar at the Institute of Oriental Studies, Moscow, and former consultant to the International Department of the Central Committee of the Communist Party of the Soviet Union, Moscow, March 30, 1992, and December 17, 1997.

Evgeny P. Glazunov, former head of the Vietnam Section, International Department of the Central Committee of the Communist Party of the Soviet Union, Moscow, April 1, 1992.

Igor A. Ognetov, former head of the Vietnam Section, International Department of the Central Committee of the Communist Party of the Soviet Union, Moscow, December 10, 1997.

Secondary Sources

Afonin, S. N., and Y. V. Kobelev. *Tovarishch Kho Shi Min* (Comrade Ho Chi Minh). Moscow: Izdatel'stvo politicheskoi literaturi, 1980.

American Psychiatric Association. *Diagnostic and Statistical Manual of Mental Disorders: DSM IV*. Washington, D.C.: APA, 1994.

Arendt, Hannah. *The Origins of Totalitarianism*. Second edition. New York: Harcourt, Brace and Co., 1958.

Armstrong, J. D. *Revolutionary Diplomacy:·Chinese Foreign Policy and the United Front Doctrine*. Berkeley: University of California Press, 1977.

Aron, Raymond. *The Opium of the Intellectuals*. New York: W. W. Norton, 1962.

———. *Peace and War*. London: Weidenfeld and Nicolson, 1966.

Bao Quoc. "The Cam Ranh Syndrome: The Threat of Sovietnamisation." *Asean Forecast* 4, no. 6 (June 1984).

Barron, John, and Anthony Paul. *Murder of a Gentle Land*. New York: Reader's Digest Press, 1977.

Bechtold, Peter K. *Politics in the Sudan: Parliamentary and Military Rule in an Emerging African Nation*. New York: Praeger, 1976.

Becker, Elizabeth. *When the War Was Over: The Voices of Cambodia's Revolution and Its People*. New York: Simon & Schuster, 1985.

Borkenau, Franz. *World Communism: A History of the Communist International*. Ann Arbor: University of Michigan Press, 1962.

Boudarel, Georges, ed. *La Bureaucratie au Vietnam: Vietnam-Asie-Débat-1*. Paris: L'Harmattan, 1983.

Brimmel, J. H. *Communism in Southeast Asia: A Political Analysis*. Oxford: Oxford University Press, 1959.

Brown, Frederick Z., and David B. Timberman, eds. *Cambodia and the International Community: The Quest for Peace, Development and Democracy*. New York: Asia Society, 1998.

Brown, MacAlister, and Joseph J. Zasloff, *Apprentice Revolutionaries: The Communist Movement in Laos, 1930–1985*. Stanford: Hoover Institution Press, 1986.

———. *Cambodia Confounds the Peacemakers*. Ithaca, New York: Cornell University Press, 1998.

Brzezinski, Zbigniew. *Power and Principle: Memoirs of the National Security Adviser, 1977–1981*. New York: Farrar, Straus, Giroux, 1983.

———. *The Soviet Bloc: Unity and Conflict*. Revised edition. Cambridge, Mass.: Harvard University Press, 1967.

Bueno de Mesquita, Bruce. *The War Trap*. New Haven, Conn.: Yale University Press, 1981.

Bui Tin. *Following Ho Chi Minh: Memoirs of a North Vietnamese Colonel*. Honolulu: University of Hawaii Press, 1995.

Bull, Hedley. *The Anarchical Society: A Study of Order in World Politics*. New York: Columbia University Press, 1977.

Bullock, Allan. *Hitler and Stalin: Parallel Lives*. New York: Vintage, 1993.

Buszynski, Leszek. *Gorbachev and Southeast Asia*. New York: Routledge, 1992.

———. *Soviet Foreign Policy and Southeast Asia*. London: Croom Helm, 1986.

Buttinger, Joseph. Vietnam: *A Dragon Embattled*. 2 volumes. New York: Praeger, 1967.

Cabral, Manuel Villaverde. "The Portuguese Communist Party: The Weight of Fifty Years of History." In Howard Machin, ed., *National Communism in Western Europe: A Third Way to Socialism?* London and New York: Methuen, 1983.

Cady, John F. *Southeast Asia: Its Historical Development*. New York: McGraw Hill, 1964.

———. *Thailand, Burma, Laos, and Cambodia*. Englewoood Cliffs, N.J.: Prentice Hall, 1966.

Cameron, N. A. "The Paranoid Pseudocommunity." *American Journal of Sociology* 49, no. 1 (July 1943): 32–38.

Carney, Timothy M. *Communist Party Power in Kampuchea: Documents and Discussion*. Ithaca, N.Y.: Cornell University, Southeast Asia Program, Data Paper: number 106.

Carr, Edward Hallett. *The Twenty Years' Crisis, 1919–1939*. New York: Harper & Row, 1946.

Chanda, Nayan. *Brother Enemy: The War After the War*. San Diego: Harcourt Brace Jovanovich, 1986.

Chandler, David P. "An Anti-Vietnamese Rebellion in Early Nineteenth Century Cambodia: Pre-Colonial Imperialism and a Pre-Nationalist Response." *Journal of Southeast Asian Studies* 6, no. 1 (March 1975).

———. *Brother Number One: A Political Biography of Pol Pot*. Boulder: Westview Press, 1992.

———. *A History of Cambodia*. Boulder: Westview Press, 1983.

———. *The Tragedy of Cambodian History: Politics, War, and Revolution Since 1945*. New Haven, Conn.: Yale University Press, 1991.

———. "Revising the Past in Democratic Kampuchea: When Was the Birthday of the Party?" *Pacific Affairs* 56, no. 2 (summer 1983).

———. "Cambodia Before the French. Politics in a Tributary Kingdom," Ph.D. diss., University of Michigan, 1973. Ann Arbor, Mich.: University Microfilms, 1974.

Chandler, David P., and Ben Kiernan. *Revolution and Its Aftermath in Kampuchea: Eight Essays.* New Haven, Conn.: Yale University Southeast Asian Studies, 1983.

Chandler, David P., Ben Kiernan, and Chanthou Boua, eds. *Pol Pot Plans the Future: Confidential Leadership Documents from Democratic Kampuchea, 1976–1977.* New Haven, Conn.: Yale University Southeast Asia Studies, 1988.

Chang, Pao-min. *Beijing, Hanoi, and the Overseas Chinese.* Berkeley: Institute of East Asian Studies, University of California, 1982.

———. *Kampuchea Between China and Vietnam.* Singapore: Singapore University Press, 1985.

———. *The Sino-Vietnamese Territorial Dispute.* The Washington Papers, Center for Strategic and International Studies. New York: Praeger, 1986.

Chanoff, David, and Doan Van Toai. *Portrait of the Enemy.* New York: Random House, 1986.

Chen, Jian. *China's Road to the Korean War.* New York: Columbia University Press, 1994.

———. *The Sino-Soviet Alliance.* The Cold War International History Project, Woodrow Wilson International Center for Scholars, Washington, D.C., 1992.

———. "China's Involvement in the Vietnam War, 1964–1969." *The China Quarterly* 142 (June 1995): 357–87.

———. "China and the First Indochina War, 1950–1954." *The China Quarterly* 133 (March 1993).

Chen, King C. *Vietnam and China, 1938–1954.* Princeton, N.J.: Princeton University Press, 1969.

———. "Hanoi Versus Peking: Policy and Relations, a Survey." *Asian Survey* 12, no. 9 (September 1972).

———. "North Vietnam in the Sino-Soviet Dispute, 1962–1964." *Asian Survey* 4, no. 9 (September 1964).

———, ed. *China and the Three Worlds.* New York: M. E. Sharpe, 1979.

Chen, Theodore H. E., ed. *The Chinese Communist Regime: Documents and Commentary.* New York: Praeger, 1967.

Coedes, Georges. *The Making of South East Asia.* Berkeley: University of California Press, 1967.

———. *Les Peuples de la peninsule indochinoise.* Paris: Dunod, 1962.

Cohn, Norman. *The Pursuit of the Millennium.* New York: Oxford University Press, 1970.

Congress of the United States. *People's Republic of China: An Economic Assessment. A Compendium of Papers Submitted to the Joint Economic Committee,* May 18, 1972.

Conquest, Robert. *The Great Terror*. London: Penguin, 1971.

———. *Harvest of Sorrow*. New York: Oxford University Press, 1986.

Cotter, Michael G. "Towards a Social History of the Vietnamese Southward Movement." *Journal of Southeast Asian History* 9, no. 1 (March 1968).

Crossman, R. H., ed. *The God That Failed*. New York: Harper & Row, 1950.

Dallin, Alexander, ed. *Diversity in International Communism*. New York: Columbia University Press, 1963.

Deac, Wilfred P. *Road to the Killing Fields: The Cambodian War of 1970–1975*. College Station: Texas A&M University Press, 1997.

Desch, Michael C. "Culture Clash: Assessing the Importance of Ideas in Security Studies." *International Security* 23, no. 1 (summer 1998): 141–70.

Dommen, Arthur J. *Conflict in Laos: The Politics of Neutralization*. New York: Praeger, 1964.

———. *Laos: Keystone of Indochina*. Boulder: Westview Press, 1985.

Doyle, Michael W., and G. John Ikenberry, eds. *New Thinking in International Relations Theory*. Boulder, Colo.: Westview, 1997.

Duiker, William J. *China and Vietnam: The Roots of Conflict*. Berkeley: Institute of East Asian Studies, University of California, 1985.

———. *The Comintern and Vietnamese Communism*. Athens, Ohio: Ohio University, Center For International Studies, Papers in International Studies, Southeast Asia Series, no. 37.

———. *The Communist Road to Power in Vietnam*. Revised edition. Boulder: Westview Press, 1996.

———. *The Rise of Nationalism in Vietnam, 1900–1941*. Ithaca, N.Y.: Cornell University Press, 1976.

Duncanson, Dennis J. *Government and Revolution in Vietnam*. London: Oxford University Press, 1968.

———. "Ho Chi Minh in Hong Kong, 1931–1932." *China Quarterly*, no. 57 (January–March 1974): 84–100.

———. "Revolutionary Wars in Theory and Practice." *Problems of Communism* 21, no. 2 (March-April 1972).

Elliot, David W. P., ed. *The Third Indochina War*. Boulder: Westview Press, 1981.

Elster, Jon, ed. *Rational Choice*. New York: New York University Press, 1986.

Engelbert, Thomas, and Christopher E. Goscha. *Falling Out of Touch: A Study on Vietnamese Communist Policy Towards an Emerging Cambodian Communist Movement, 1930–1975*. Monash Paper no. 35, Clayton, Victoria, Australia: Center of Southeast Asia Studies, Monash Asia Institute, Monash University, 1995.

Eprile, Cecile. *War and Peace in the Sudan, 1955–1972*. London: David and Charles, 1974.

Etcheson, Craig. *The Rise and Decline of Democratic Kampuchea*. Boulder: Westview Press, 1985.

Evans, Grant, and Kelvin Rowley. *Red Brotherhood At War: Indochina Since the Fall of Saigon*. London: Verso, 1984.

Fall, Bernard B. *Le Viet-Minh: La République Démocratique du Viet-Nam, 1945–1960.* Paris: Librairie Armand Colin, 1960.

———. *The Vietminh Regime.* New York: Institute of Pacific Relations, 1956.

———, ed. *Ho Chi Minh on Revolution.* New York: Random House, 1967.

Foreign Ministry of the People's Republic of China. *On the Vietnamese Foreign Ministry's White Book Concerning Viet Nam–China Relations.* Beijing: Foreign Languages Press, 1979.

Foreign Ministry of the Socialist Republic of Vietnam. *The Truth About Vietnam-China Relations Over the Last 30 Years.* Hanoi: Foreign Languages Publishing House, 1979.

Forest, James H. *The Unified Buddhist Church of Vietnam: Fifteen Years for Reconciliation.* Alkmaar, The Netherlands: International Fellowship of Reconciliation, 1978.

Frankel, Joseph. *National Interest.* London: Pall Mall, 1970.

Friedrich, Carl J., ed. *Totalitarianism.* Cambridge, Mass.: Harvard University Press, 1954.

Friedrich, Carl J., and Zbigniew K. Brzezinski. *Totalitarianism, Dictatorship, and Autocracy.* Second edition. Cambridge, Mass.: Harvard University Press, 1965.

Frieson, Kate G. "The Cambodian Elections of 1993: A Case of Power to the People?" in R. H. Taylor, ed. *The Politics of Elections in Southeast Asia.* Washington, D.C.: Woodrow Wilson Center Press, 1996.

Funnell, Victor C. "Vietnam and the Sino-Soviet Conflict." *Studies in Comparative Communism* 11, nos. 1 and 2 (spring-summer 1978): 142–69.

Gaiduk, Ilya. *The Soviet Union and the Vietnam War.* Chicago: Ivan R. Dee, 1996.

———. "The Vietnam War and Soviet-American Relations, 1964–1973: New Russian Evidence." *Cold War International History Project Bulletin*, issues 6–7 (winter 1995/1996).

Geertz, Clifford. *The Interpretation of Cultures.* New York: Basic Books, 1973.

George, Alexander. "The 'Operational Code': A Neglected Approach to the Study of Political Leaders and Decision-making." *International Studies Quarterly* 13, no. 2 (June 1969): 190–222.

Gerth, Hans, and C. Wright Mills, eds. *From Max Weber: Essays in Sociology.* London: Routledge and Keagan Paul, 1970.

Gilpin, Robert. *War and International Change.* New York: Cambridge University Press, 1981.

Goldstein, Judith, and Robert O. Keohane, eds. *Ideas and Foreign Policy.* Ithaca, N.Y.: Cornell University Press, 1993.

Gourevitch, Philip. "Letter from Cambodia: Pol Pot's Children." *The New Yorker*, August 10, 1998.

Greenstein, Fred I. *Personality and Politics.* New York: W. W. Norton, 1975.

Griffith, William E. *Albania and the Sino-Soviet Rift.* Cambridge, Mass.: MIT Press, 1963.

———. *Sino-Soviet Relations, 1964–1965.* Cambridge, Mass.: The MIT Press, 1967.

Halberstam, David. *Ho.* New York: Random House, 1971.

Hall, D. G. E. *A History of Southeast Asia.* Third edition. London: Macmillan, 1970.

Hammer, Ellen J. *The Struggle for Indochina, 1940–1955.* Stanford: Stanford University Press, 1955.

———. "Indochina: Communist But Nonaligned." *Problems of Communism* 25, no. 3 (May–June 1976).

Heder, Stephen. "Kampuchea: From Pol Pot to Pen Sovan to the Villages." In Khien Theeravit and Brown, eds. *Indochina and Problems of Security and Stability in Southeast Asia.* Bangkok, Thailand: Chulalongkorn University Press, 1983.

———. "Kampuchea's Armed Struggle: The Origins of An Independent Revolution." *Bulletin of Concerned Asian Scholars* 11, no. 1 (Jan.–Mar. 1979).

———. "Racism, Marxism, Labelling, and Genocide in Ben Kiernan's *The Pol Pot Regime.*" *South East Asia Research* 5, no. 2, 101–53.

Hémery, Daniel. *Révolutionnaires vietnamiens et pouvoir colonial en Indochine.* Paris: Maspero, 1975.

Herz, Martin F. *A Short History of Cambodia: From the Days of Angkor to the Present.* New York: Praeger, 1958.

Hinton, Harold C. *An Introduction to Chinese Politics.* New York: Praeger, 1973.

Hinton, William. *Fanshen: A Documentary of Revolution in a Chinese Village.* New York: Vintage, 1966.

Hoang Van Chi. *From Colonialism to Communism.* New York: Popular Library, 1964.

Hoang Van Hoan. *A Drop in the Ocean: Hoang Van Hoan's Revolutionary Reminiscences.* Beijing: Foreign Languages Press, 1988.

———. "Distortion of Facts About Militant Friendship Is Impermissible." *Beijing Review,* no. 49 (December 7, 1979).

Hoffmann, Stanley. *Contemporary Theory in International Relations.* Englewood Cliffs, N.J.: Prentice-Hall, 1960.

———. *Janus and Minerva: Essays in the Theory and Practice of International Politics.* Boulder: Westview Press, 1987.

Honey, P. J. *Communism in North Vietnam.* Cambridge, Mass.: MIT Press, 1963.

———. "The Fourth Congress of the Lao Dong Party." *China News Analysis,* no. 1072 (March 11, 1977).

———. "Vietnam's Party Congress and After." *China News Analysis,* no. 1235 (June 18, 1982).

Hood, Steven J. *Dragons Entangled: Indochina and the China-Vietnam War.* Armonk, N.Y.: M. E. Sharpe, 1992.

Hopf, Ted. "The Promise of Constructivism in International Relaitons Theory." *International Security* 23, no. 1 (summer 1998): 171–200.

Howard, Michael. *The Causes of Wars.* Second edition. Cambridge, Mass.: Harvard University Press, 1983.

Human Rights Watch. *The Lost Agenda: Human Rights and U.N. Field Operations.* New York: Human Rights Watch, 1993.

Huntington, Samuel P. *The Clash of Civilizations and the Remaking of the World Order*. New York: Simon & Schuster, 1996.

Huynh Kim Khanh, *Vietnamese Communism, 1925–1945*. Ithaca, N.Y.: Cornell University Press, 1982.

International Institute of Strategic Studies. *The Military Balance, 1975–1976*. London: IISS, 1975.

———. *The Military Balance, 1978–1979*. London: IISS, 1978.

International Monetary Fund. *Direction of Trade Statistics: Yearbook 1984*. Washington, D.C., 1984.

Jackson, Karl D., ed. *Cambodia, 1975–1978: Rendezvous with Death*. Princeton, N.J.: Princeton University Press, 1989.

Jacqueney, Theodore. "Human Rights in Vietnam." *Free Trade Union News* 32, no. 9 (September 1977).

Jervis, Robert K. *Perception and Misperception in International Politics*. Princeton, N.J.: Princeton University Press, 1976.

Johnson, A. Ross. *The Transformation of Communist Ideology: The Yugoslav Case, 1945–1953*. Cambridge, Mass.: M.I.T. Press, 1972.

———. "Yugoslavia and the Sino-Soviet Conflict: The Shifting Triangle, 1948–1974." *Studies in Comparative Communism* 7, nos. 1 and 2 (spring-summer 1974): 184–203.

Joyaux, Francois. *La Chine et le règlement du premier conflit d'Indochine* (Geneva 1954). Paris: Publications de la Sorbonne, 1979.

Jukes, Geoffrey. *The Soviet Union in Asia*. Berkeley: University of California Press, 1973.

Kagan, Donald. *On the Origins of War and the Preservation of Peace*. New York: Doubleday, 1995.

Kamm, Henry. *Cambodia*. Boston: Little, Brown, 1998.

Kapitsa, M. C. *Na raznikh parallelyakh: Zapiski diplomata*. (On Different Parallels: Notes of a Diplomat). Moscow: kniga i biznes, 1996.

Katzenstein, Peter J., ed. *The Culture of National Security: Norms and Identity in World Politics*. New York: Columbia University Press, 1996.

Keohane, Robert O., ed. *Neorealism and Its Critics*. New York: Columbia University Press, 1986.

Keohane, Robert O., and Joseph S. Nye, eds. *Transnational Relations and World Politics*. Cambridge, Mass.: Harvard University Press, 1970.

Khrushchev, Nikita. *Khrushchev Remembers*. With an Introduction, Commentary, and Notes by Edward Crankshaw. New York: Little, Brown, 1970.

Kiernan, Ben. *How Pol Pot Came to Power*. London: Verso, 1985.

———. *The Pol Pot Regime*. New Haven, Conn.: Yale University Press, 1996.

———. "Origins of Khmer Communism." *Southeast Asian Affairs, 1981*. Singapore: Institute of Southeast Asian Studies, 1981.

Kiernan, Ben, and Chanthou Boua. *Peasants and Politics in Kampuchea, 1942–1981*. Armonk, N.Y.: M. E. Sharpe, 1982.

Kirk, Donald. *Wider War*. New York: Praeger, 1971.

Kissinger, Henry A. *Diplomacy*. Boston: Little, Brown, 1995.

———. *White House Years*. Boston: Little, Brown, 1979.

———. *Years of Upheaval*. Boston: Little, Brown, 1982.

Kolakowski, Leszek. *Main Currents of Marxism*. 3 vols. New York: Oxford University Press, 1968.

Knopfelmacher, Frank. *Intellectuals and Politics*. Melbourne, Australia: Thomas Nelson, 1968.

Kobelev, Yevgeny. *Ho Chi Minh*. Moscow: Progress Publishers, 1989.

Kraslow, David, and Stuart H. Loory. *The Secret Search for Peace in Vietnam*. New York: Vintage Books, 1968.

Kyemba, Henry. *A State of Blood*. New York: Ace Books, 1977.

Labedz, Leopold. *Revisionism: Essays on the History of Marxist Ideas*. New York: Praeger, 1962.

Lafont, P. B., ed. *Les Frontieres Du Vietnam: Histoire des frontieres de la peninsule indochinoise*. Paris: L'Harmattan, 1989.

Lamant, Pierre. "Le Cambodge et la décolonisation de L'Indochine: Le caractère particulieré du nationalisme khmer de 1936 à 1945." In *Les chemins de la décolonisation de l'empire coloniale Française*. Paris: Centre National de la Recherche Scientifique, 1986.

———. "Les partis politiques et les mouvements de résistance khmere vus par les services renseignements françaises (1945–1952)." *Guerres mondiales et conflits contemporains*, no. 148 (1987): 79–96.

Langer, Paul F., and Joseph J. Zasloff. *North Vietnam and the Pathet Lao*. Cambridge, Mass.: Harvard University Press, 1970.

Lapid, Yosef, and Friedrich V. Kratochwil, eds. *The Return of Culture and Identity in IR Theory*. Boulder, Colo.: Lynne Rienner, 1996.

Laqueur, Walter, and Leopold Labedz. *Polycentrism: The New Factor in International Communism*. New York: Praeger, 1962.

Lawson, Eugene K. *The Sino-Vietnamese Conflict*. New York: Praeger, 1984.

Le Duan. "Leninism Illuminates the Revolutionary Aims of the Present Age." *Kommunist*, no. 7 (April 30, 1970).

———. *The Vietnamese Revolution: Fundamental Problems and Essential Tasks*. New York: International Publishers, 1971.

Legum, Colin. "Angola and the Horn of Africa." In Stephen S. Kaplan, ed., *Diplomacy of Power: Soviet Armed Forces as a Political Instrument*. Washington, D.C.: The Brookings Institution, 1981.

Leifer, Michael. *Cambodia: The Search for Security*. New York: Praeger, 1967.

Leonhard, Wolfgang. *Three Faces of Marxism: The Political Concepts of Soviet Ideology, Maoism, and Humanistic Marxism*. New York: Paragon, 1979.

Li Zhisui. *The Private Life of Chairman Mao*. New York: Random House, 1994.

Lowenthal, Richard. *Model or Ally? The Communist Powers and the Developing Countries*. New York: Oxford University Press, 1977.

————. *World Communism: Disintegration of a Secular Faith.* New York: Frederick A. Praeger, 1962.

Luciolli, Esmerelda. *Le Mur de bambou: Le Cambodge aprés Pol Pot.* Paris: Règine Deforges–Médecins sans Frontières, 1988.

MacFarquhar, Roderick. *The Origins of the Cultural Revolution, Volume 2: The Great Leap Forward, 1958–1960.* New York: Columbia University Press, 1983.

Mahbubani, Kishore. "The Kampuchean Problem: A Southeast Asian Perception." *Foreign Affairs* 62, no. 2 (winter 1983–84): 407–425.

Mak Phoeun and Po Dharma. "La première intervention militaire vietnamienne au Cambodge (1658–1659)." *Bulletin de l'Ecole française d'Extrème-Orient,* 73 (1984): 285–318.

Maneli, Mieczyslaw. *War of the Vanquished.* New York: Harper & Row, 1971.

Mannheim, Karl. *Ideology and Utopia.* London: Routledge, 1960.

Marcum, John A. *The Angolan Revolution: Exile Politics and Guerrilla Warfare, 1962–1976.* Cambridge, Mass.: The MIT Press, 1978.

Marr, David. *Vietnam, 1945.* Berkeley: University of California Press, 1995.

————. *Vietnamese Anticolonialism, 1885–1925.* Berkeley: University of California Press, 1971.

————. *Vietnamese Tradition on Trial, 1920–1945.* Berkeley: University of California Press, 1981.

Martin, Marie Alexandrine. *Cambodia: A Shattered Society.* Berkeley: University of California Press, 1994.

————. *Le Mal Cambodgien.* Paris: Hachette, 1989.

————. "Cambodge: Une Nouvelle Colonie d'Exploitation." *Politique Internationale,* no. 28 (ete 1985).

————. "Le Processus de Vietnamisation au Cambodge." *Politique Internationale,* no. 24 (ete 1984).

McCleod, Alex. "Portrait of a Model Ally: The Portuguese Communist Party and the International Communist Movement, 1968–1983." *Studies in Comparative Communism* 17, no. 1 (spring 1984): 31–52.

McKenzie, Kermit E. *Comintern and World Revolution, 1928–1943.* New York: Columbia University Press, 1964.

McLane, Charles B. *Soviet Strategies in Southeast Asia: An Exploration of Eastern Policy Under Lenin and Stalin.* Princeton: Princeton University Press, 1966.

Meissner, W. W. *The Paranoid Process.* New York: Jason Aronson, 1978.

Merton, Robert K. *Social Theory and Social Structure.* Glencoe, Illinois: The Free Press, 1949.

Meyer, Charles. *Derrière le sourire khmer.* Paris: Plon, 1971.

Migozzi, Jacques. *Cambodge: Faits et Problemes de Population.* Paris: Editions du Centre National de la Recherche Scientifique, 1973.

Mlynar, Zdenek. *Nightfrost in Prague: The End of Humane Socialism.* New York: Karz Publishers, 1980.

Moise, Edwin E. *Land Reform in China and North Vietnam: Consolidating the*

Revolution at the Village Level. Chapel Hill: University of North Carolina Press, 1983.

Morgenthau, Hans J. *Politics Among Nations: The Struggle for Power and Peace.* Fourth edition. New York: Knopf, 1966.

Morris, Bernard S. *International Communism and American Policy.* New York: Atherton Press, 1966.

Morris, Stephen J. "Brutocracy Wins." *Washington Post Outlook,* August 9, 1998.

———. "Our Failure in Cambodia." *The Wall Street Journal,* July 16, 1997.

———. "Vietnam's Vietnam." *The Atlantic Monthly,* January 1985.

Nguyen Long and Harry Kendall. *After Saigon Fell: Everyday Life Under the Vietnamese Communists.* Berkeley: Institute of East Asian Studies, University of California, 1981.

Nicholi, Armand M., Jr., ed. *The New Harvard Guide to Psychiatry.* Cambridge, Mass.: Harvard University Press, 1988.

Nixon, Richard M. *The Memoirs of Richard Nixon.* New York: Warner Books, 1978.

Ognetov, I. A. "The Comintern and the Revolutionary Movement in Vietnam." In R. A. Ulyanovsky, ed., *The Comintern and the East.* Moscow: Progress Publishers, 1979.

Osborne, Milton. *The French Presence in Cochinchina and Cambodia.* Ithaca, N.Y.: Cornell University Press, 1969.

———. *Sihanouk: Prince of Light, Prince of Darkness.* Honolulu: University of Hawaii Press, 1994.

Peschoux, Christophe. *Les "Nouveaux" Khmers Rouges.* Paris: L'Harmattan, 1992.

Picq, Laurence. *Beyond the Horizon: Five Years with the Khmer Rouge.* New York: St. Martin's Press.

Pike, Douglas. *Vietnam and the Soviet Union: Anatomy of an Alliance.* Boulder: Westview Press, 1987.

———. "Communist Versus Communist in Southeast Asia." *International Security* 4, no. 1 (summer 1979).

Pipes, Richard. *The Formation of the Soviet Union: Communism and Nationalism, 1917–1923.* Revised edition. Cambridge, Mass.: Harvard University Press, 1964.

Ponchaud, Francois. *Cambodia: Year Zero.* New York: Holt, Rinehart, and Winston, 1978.

Porter, Bruce. *The USSR in Third World Conflicts: Soviet Arms and Diplomacy in Local Wars 1945–1980.* New York: Cambridge University Press, 1984.

Porter, Gareth. "Hanoi's Strategic Perspective and the Sino-Vietnamese Conflict." *Pacific Affairs* 57, no. 1 (spring 1984).

Preschez, Philippe. *Essai sur la democratie au Cambodge.* Paris: Fondation Nationale des Sciences Politiques, Centre d'Etude des Relations Internationales, 1961.

Pye, Lucian W. *Asian Power and Politics: The Cultural Dimensions of Authority.* Cambridge, Mass.: Harvard University Press, 1985.

Qiang Zhai. "China and the Geneva Conference of 1954." *The China Quarterly*, no. 129 (March 1992): 103–22.

———. "Transplanting the Chinese Model: Chinese Military Advisers and the First Vietnam War, 1950–1954." *The Journal of Military History*, no. 57 (October 1993): 698–715.

Quinn, Kenneth M. "Political Change in Wartime: The Khmer Krahom Revolution in Southern Cambodia, 1970–1974." *Naval War College Review* 28, no. 4 (spring 1976).

Radvanyi, Janos. *Delusion and Reality: Gambits, Hoaxes, and Diplomatic One-Upmanship in Vietnam*. South Bend, Indiana: Gateway Editions, 1978.

Randle, Robert F. *Geneva 1954: The Settlement of the Indochinese War*. Princeton: Princeton University Press, 1969.

Regaud, Nicolas. *Le Cambodge dans la tourmente: Le troisième conflit indochinois, 1978–1991*. Paris: L'Harmattan, 1992.

Remington, Robin A. *Winter in Prague: Documents on Czechoslovak Communism in Crisis*. Cambridge, Mass.: MIT Press, 1969.

Robinson, Thomas. "China Confronts the Soviet Union: Warfare and Diplomacy on China's Inner Asian Frontiers." In Roderick MacFarquhar and John K. Fairbank, eds., *The Cambridge History of China*, Volume 15. Cambridge: Cambridge University Press, 1991.

Ros Chatrabot. *La République Khmere*. Paris: L'Harmattan, 1993.

Rosenberg, Tina. "Hun Sen Stages an Election." *The New York Times Magazine*, August 30, 1998.

Ross, Robert. *The Indochina Tangle: China's Vietnam Policy, 1975–1979*. New York: Columbia University Press, 1988.

Rotberg, Robert I., and Theodore K. Rabb, eds. *The Origin and Prevention of Major Wars*. Cambridge: Cambridge University Press, 1989.

Rubinstein, Alvin Z. *Soviet Foreign Policy Since World War II: Imperial and Global*. Cambridge, Mass.: Winthrop Publishers, 1981.

Rupen, Robert, and R. Barry Farrell, eds. *Vietnam and the Sino-Soviet Dispute*. New York: Praeger, 1967.

Sacks, I. Milton. "Marxism in Vietnam." In Frank N. Trager, ed., *Marxism in Southeast Asia*. Stanford: Stanford University Press, 1959.

Scalapino, Robert A. *The Communist Revolution in Asia: Tactics, Goals, and Achievements*. Englewood Cliffs, N.J: Prentice Hall, 1969.

———. "Moscow, Peking, and the Communist Parties of Asia." *Foreign Affairs* 41, no. 2 (January 1963).

Schram, Stuart. *The Thought of Mao Tse-tung*. New York: Cambridge University Press, 1989.

Shaplen, Robert. *Time Out of Hand: Revolution and Reaction in Southeast Asia*. New York: Harper & Row, 1970.

Shawcross, William. *Cambodia's New Deal*. Washington, D.C.: Carnegie Endowment for International Peace, 1994.

———. *The Quality of Mercy.* New York: Simon & Schuster, 1985.

———. *Sideshow: Nixon, Kissinger, and the Destruction of Cambodia.* New York: Simon & Schuster, 1979.

———. "The Burial of Cambodia." *The New York Review of Books* 31, no. 8 (May 10, 1984).

———. "The End of Cambodia?" *The New York Review of Books* 26, nos. 21 and 22 (January 24, 1980).

———. "In a Grim Country." *The New York Review of Books* 28, no. 14 (September 24, 1981).

———. "The Third Indochina War." *The New York Review of Books,* April 6, 1978.

Shils, Edward. "The Concept and Function of Ideology." *The International Encyclopedia of the Social Sciences,* vol. 2. New York: The Free Press, 1968.

Shiraishi, Takashi, and Motoo Furuta, eds. *Indochina in the 1940s and 1950s: Translation of Contemporary Japanese Scholarship on Southeast Asia.* Volume 2. Ithaca, N.Y.: Cornell University Southeast Asia Program, 1992.

Sihanouk, Norodom. "Le Calice Jusqu'a la Lie." Unpublished mimeograph.

———. *Prisonnier des Khmers Rouges.* Paris: Hachette, 1986.

———. *Souvenirs doux et amers.* Paris: Hachette, 1981.

———. *War and Hope: The Case For Cambodia.* New York: Pantheon, 1980.

Skilling, H. Gordon. *Czechoslovakia's Interrupted Revolution.* Princeton, N.J.: Princeton University Press, 1976.

Smith, R. B. *An International History of the Vietnam War,* 3 vols. New York: St. Martin's Press, 1981–1990.

Smith, Roger M. *Cambodia's Foreign Policy.* Ithaca, N.Y.: Cornell University Press, 1965.

Smith, Tony. *Thinking Like a Communist: State and Legitimacy in the Soviet Union, China, and Cuba.* New York: W. W. Norton, 1987.

Smyser, W. R. *The Independent Vietnamese: Vietnamese Communism Between Russia and China, 1956–1969.* Athens, Ohio: Ohio University, Center for International Studies, Papers in International Studies, Southeast Asia, no. 55, 1980.

Steinberg, David J. *Cambodia: Its People, Its Society, Its Culture.* New Haven: Human Relations Area Files, 1957.

Suda, Zdenek. *Zealots and Rebels: A History of the Ruling Communist Party of Czechoslovakia.* Stanford: Hoover Institution Press, 1980.

Summers, Laura. "The CPK: Secret Vanguard of Pol Pot's Revolution." *Journal of Communist Studies,* no. 3 (March 1987).

Sylvester, Anthony. *Sudan Under Nimeiri.* London: Bodley Head, 1977.

Taylor, Jay. *China and Southeast Asia: China's Relations With Revolutionary Movements.* New York: Praeger, 1976.

Thai Quang Trung. *Collective Leadership and Factionalism: An Essay on Ho Chi Minh's Legacy.* Singapore: Institute of Southeast Asian Studies, 1985.

Thayer, Carlyle A. "Vietnam's External Relations." *Pacific Community* 9, no. 2 (January 1978).

Thien, Ton That. *The Foreign Politics of the Communist Party of Vietnam.* New York: Crane Russak, 1989.

Thierry, Solange. *Les Khmers.* Paris: Seuil, 1964.

Thucydides. *History of the Peloponnesian War.* New York: Viking Penguin, 1972.

Toranska, Teresa. *"Them": Stalin's Polish Puppets.* New York: Harper & Row, 1987.

Truong Nhu Tang. *A Viet Cong Memoir.* With David Chanoff and Doan Van Toai. New York: Harcourt Brace Jovanovich, 1985.

Tucker, Robert C. *The Soviet Political Mind.* New York: W. W. Norton, 1971.

————, ed. *The Lenin Anthology.* New York: W. W. Norton, 1975.

Turley, William S. "Vietnam Since Reunification." *Problems of Communism* 26, no. 2 (March–April 1977).

————, ed. *Vietnamese Communism in Comparative Perspective.* Boulder: Westview Press, 1980.

Turner, Robert F. *Vietnamese Communism: Its Origins and Development.* Stanford: Hoover Institution Press, 1975.

Ulam, Adam. *Dangerous Relations: The Soviet Union in World Politics, 1970–1982.* New York: Oxford University Press, 1983.

————. *Expansion and Coexistence: Soviet Foreign Policy, 1917–1973.* 2d. ed. New York: Praeger, 1974.

————. *Tito and the Cominform.* Cambridge, Mass.: Harvard University Press, 1952.

Uthit Pasakhom. "Beyond a Soviet-Vietnamese Condominium: The Case Of Laos." *Indochina Report.* Singapore: Executive Publications, no. 1 (January–March 1985).

Van Der Kroef, Justus M. *Communism in Southeast Asia.* Berkeley: University of California Press, 1980.

————. "Interpretations of the 1965 Coup in Indonesia: Probabilities and Alternatives." *Journal of Southeast Asian Studies* 3, no. 2 (September 1972): 277–98.

Vance, Cyrus. *Hard Choices: Critical Years in America's Foreign Policy.* New York: Simon & Schuster, 1983.

Vickery, Michael. *Cambodia: 1975–1982.* Boston: South End Press, 1984.

Vogel, Ezra. *Canton Under Communism.* Cambridge, Mass.: Harvard University Press, 1969.

Wain, Barry. *The Refused: The Agony of the Indochina Refugees.* New York: Simon & Schuster, 1981.

Waite, Robert L. G. *The Psychopathic God: Adolf Hitler.* New York: Basic Books, 1977.

Walt, Stephen M. *The Origin of Alliances.* Ithaca, N.Y.: Cornell University Press, 1987.

————. *Revolution and War.* Ithaca, N.Y.: Cornell University Press, 1996.

Waltz, Kenneth N. *Man, the State, and War: A Theoretical Analysis.* New York: Columbia University Press, 1959.

———. *A Theory of International Relations.* Reading, Mass.: Addison-Wesley, 1979.

Warner, Denis. *Certain Victory: How Hanoi Won the War.* Kansas City: Sheed, Andrews and McMeel, 1978.

Weber, Max. *Economy and Society: An Outline of Interpretive Sociology.* Edited by Guenther Roth and Claus Wittich. New York: Bedminster Press, 1968.

———. *The Methodology of the Social Sciences.* New York: Free Press, 1949.

Weinstein, Warren, and Thomas H. Henriksen, eds. *Soviet and Chinese Aid to African Nations.* New York: Praeger, 1980.

Whyte, Martin King. *Small Groups and Political Rituals in China.* Berkeley: University of California Press, 1974.

Willmott, W. *The Chinese in Cambodia.* Vancouver: University of British Columbia Press, 1967.

Wolfers, Arnold. *Discord and Collaboration: Essays on International Politics.* Baltimore: Johns Hopkins University Press, 1962.

Woodside, Alexander B. *Vietnam and the Chinese Model.* Cambridge, Mass.: Harvard University Press, 1971.

The World Bank. *China: Socialist Economic Development*, Volume II. Washington, D.C., 1983.

Y Phandara. *Retour à Phnom Penh: Le Cambodge du génocide à la colonisation.* Paris: Metailie, 1982.

Young, Marilyn B. *The Vietnam Wars, 1945–1990.* New York: Harper & Row, 1991.

Zacher, Mark W., and Stephen R. Milne, eds. *Conflict and Stability in Southeast Asia.* New York: Doubleday, 1974.

Zagoria, Donald. *Vietnam Triangle: Moscow, Peking, Hanoi.* New York: Pegasus, 1967.

———, ed., *Soviet Policy in East Asia.* New Haven: Yale University Press, 1982.

Zeman, Zbynak A. *Prague Spring: A Report on Czechoslovakia.* New York: Hill and Wang, 1969.

Zhang, Shu Guang. *Mao's Military Romanticism.* Lawrence: University Press of Kansas, 1996.

In this index, an "f" after a number indicates a separate reference on the next page, and an "ff" indicates separate references on the next two pages. A continuous discussion over two or more pages is indicated by a span of page numbers, e.g., "57–59." *passim* is used for a cluster of references in close but not consecutive sequence.

Albania, 75, 130–31, 136, 144
Andropov, Yuri, 208
Angka Padevat (Revolutionary Organization), *see* Khmers Rouges
Angkor, 24
Angola, 144, 149–50, 207, 209
Anh, Hoang, 48, 158, 160f
Anti-Rightist campaign, 127
Armed Forces Movement (AFM), 148–49
Association of Southeast Asian Nations (ASEAN), 76, 79, 83–84, 223, 234

Ban, Ly, 180
Batitski, P. F., 205, 216
Biao Geng, 85
Borodin, Mikhail, 120
Bowles, Chester, 44
Brandt, Willy, 146
Brezhnev, Leonid, 13, 108, 136–37, 207, 210, 213, 216
Buddhism, 25, 70
Bui Tin, 192
Bukharin, Nikolai, 240
Bulgaria, 203
Burma, 24, 76, 79

Caetano, Marcelo, 148
Cambodia: French colonial rule in, 32–33, 35, 91, 113; Indochinese Communist Party (ICP) activity in, 29–36, 278n5; Khmer Issarak (KI) activity in, 31–32, 33; relations with ASEAN, 76, 79, 83–84; relations with Burma, 76, 79; relations with China, 16–17, 40–53 *passim*, 58–59, 66f, 71–72, 75, 76–77, 79, 82, 84–87, 88–89, 91–115, 161–62, 168–70, 183, 187f, 195, 197–98, 199, 217–18, 219–20, 230f, 233; relations with Hong Kong, 76; relations with Indonesia, 76, 83–84; relations with Japan, 76, 79; relations with Laos, 75f; relations with Malaysia, 76, 79; relations with North Korea, 71–72, 75ff, 91; relations with North Vietnam, 39–46, 47–68, 88–89, 125–26, 169–70, 199, 202; relations with Philippines, 83; relations with South Vietnam, 39–41; relations with Soviet Union, 44, 75, 88, 97, 197–202, 233–34; relations with Thailand, 24, 25–26, 69, 72, 78–83, 86–87, 223, 231–32, 234–35, 237; relations with United States, 40, 43–44, 48ff, 52, 58f, 63–64, 68, 77, 91, 93–94, 99, 201–2, 223; relations with Vietnam, 1, 5–6, 13, 15–16, 17, 18–19, 23–26, 31–32, 69, 72–73, 76, 80, 82f, 85–86, 91–115, 165, 168, 175, 185–86, 193ff, 210, 212f, 215–23, 224–28, 229–34, 237, 239; relations with Yugoslavia, 75f; traditional attitudes toward Vietnam in, 10, 13, 17, 31–33, 36, 38, 39–40, 113; traditional Vietnamese attitudes toward, 10, 17–18, 24, 35, 45, 65, 230, 235; and United Nations, 201, 219–26 *passim*; and Viet Cong, 40–41, 43, 44, 49, 54, 55, 57, 61–63, 169, 254n119; Viet Minh activity

in, 31–36. *See also* Kampuchean People's
   Revolutionary Party (KPRP); Khmers
   Rouges; Khmer Viet Minh
Cambodian Communist Party, *see* Khmers
   Rouges
Campaign Against Counterrevolutionaries,
   90, 156
Canada, 195–96
capitalism, 11, 86, 178, 187
CCP, *see* Chinese Communist Party
CEMA, *see* Council for Mutual Economic
   Assistance
Central Intelligence Agency, 40
Central Office for South Vietnam, 61–63
CGDK, 222
Chams, 23, 25, 70, 105
Chanda, Nayan, 194
Chea Sim, 220
Chen Xilian, 182
Chen Yonggui, 79
Chhon, Keat, 58
chiliastic political culture, and Marxist-
   Leninist regimes, 9, 10–15, 104–5, 114–
   15, 158, 196, 235, 237, 240–41
China, 30–31, 38–39, 74, 137, 147, 200;
   cuts off aid to Vietnam, 193–94, 208–9,
   210–11, 217, 233; and ethnic Chinese in
   Vietnam, 170–71, 185, 187–91, 194, 215,
   237–38; influences Vietnamese institutions,
   24, 126–27, 156, 165; provides aid to
   Khmers Rouges, 63–64, 65, 68, 76–77,
   84, 88, 221, 223, 234; provides aid to
   North Vietnam, 88–89, 140–41, 151,
   154–56, 163, 165f, 167–68, 174–75, 197–
   98, 208, 276n61; provides aid to Vietnam,
   174, 179, 180–81, 182–83, 184–85, 189,
   196, 211; relations with Albania, 130–31;
   relations with Cambodia, 16–17, 40–53
   passim, 58–59, 66f, 71–72, 75, 76–77, 79,
   82, 84–87, 88–89, 91–115, 161–62, 168–
   70, 183, 187f, 195, 197–98, 199, 217–18,
   219–20, 230f, 233; relations with Khmers
   Rouges, 60, 71–72, 75, 76–77, 82, 84–87,
   88–89, 91–115, 168–70, 183, 195, 202,
   221, 226, 231, 232–33, 234; relations
   with North Vietnam, 6, 16, 18, 65–66,
   88–89, 119, 125–27, 128–42, 154–55,
   161–66, 167–70, 202ff; relations with
   Soviet Union, 6, 16–17, 45, 47, 87, 128–
   31, 133, 135, 140, 143–44, 148, 149–51,
   168, 181–82, 185, 195, 197–98, 202, 212,

215, 218, 233–34, 235–36, 239, 246n13,
   287n1; relations with United States, 18,
   87, 152, 157, 159, 161–63, 166, 234, 237;
   relations with Vietnam, 1, 5, 6, 13, 16–17,
   18–19, 93, 97, 100–101, 107, 108–9, 111ff,
   119, 140–41, 153–54, 156–57, 164, 168–
   96 *passim*, 209–21 *passim*, 228, 230–42
   passim; supports Sihanouk, 49, 51ff, 65–
   66, 67, 169–70, 202. *See also* Chinese
   Communist Party (CCP); Khmers Rouges,
   Maoism among
Chinese, ethnic: in Vietnam, 6, 16, 108, 112,
   133f; Vietnamese Communist Party policies toward, 18, 170–71, 174–79, 185–96
   passim, 215, 217, 233, 237–38, 278n5
Chinese Communist Party, 2, 28, 39, 74,
   87, 90, 144, 145–46, 150; criticized by
   Vietnamese Communist Party, 18, 127,
   138–40, 157–63, 165–66, 206, 241–42;
   domestic policy, 12–13, 70–71, 90, 127,
   138–39, 140, 157–59, 160, 165–67, 182;
   relations with Communist Party of the
   Soviet Union, 128–31, 133–34, 135; relations with Vietnamese Communist Party,
   13, 121, 123–27, 129–36, 138–41, 151,
   165, 170–71, 173–75, 179–80, 181–82,
   183–85, 186, 195–96, 204–5, 206–7.
   See also China
Chinese Military Advisory Group (CMAG),
   124–25
Chinh, Hoang Minh, 135
Chinh, Truong, 64, 93, 135, 139
CIA, 40
Coalition Government of Democratic Kam-
   puchea, 222
Cohn, Norman, 10
colonialism, *see* French colonialism
Comecon, *see* Council for Mutual Economic
   Assistance
Comintern, *see* Communist International
communism, *see* Marxism-Leninism
Communist International, and Vietnamese
   Communist Party, 16, 26–29, 45, 65,
   119–23, 141, 230, 235
Communist Party of the Soviet Union, 1–2,
   74, 108, 164, 198, 200, 246n11; relations
   with Chinese Communist Party, 128–31,
   133–34, 135; relations with Vietnamese
   Communist Party, 127–31, 133–35, 138,
   140–41, 179–80, 204–5, 206–8, 210,
   212–18. *See also* Soviet Union

Communist Party of Thailand (CPT), 35, 80, 81–82, 86, 96–97
Cong An (Public Security Bureau), 191–93
COSVN, 61–63
Council for Mutual Economic Assistance, and Vietnam, 6, 16, 143, 194, 206f, 209–11
CPSU, *see* Communist Party of the Soviet Union
Cuba, 44, 150, 194, 197, 203
Cuban missile crisis of 1962, 132
Cultural Revolution, 46, 70–71, 75, 287n1; criticized by Vietnamese communists, 18, 138–39, 140, 157–59, 160, 164, 165–66
Czechoslovakia, Soviet invasion of, 87, 106, 107–8, 144–45, 158
Czechoslovakian Communist Party, 144–45, 158

Dan Cong San Dong Duong, *see* Indochinese Communist Party
Dang Lao Dong Viet Nam, *see* Vietnamese Communist Party
Democratic Kampuchea, *see* Cambodia
Democratic Republic of Vietnam (DRV), *see* Vietnam, North
Deng Xiaoping, 181–82, 194, 232, 240
Deng Yingchao, 84, 185
détente, 13, 145–46, 150, 151–52, 162–63, 166
Diem, Ngo Dinh, 39, 170
Dien Bien Phu, 125–26, 186
Do Duc Kien, 136, 142
Dong, Pham Van, *see* Pham Van Dong
Duan, Le, *see* Le Duan
Dung, Van Tien, 213
Dura, Kandor, 99–100

Eastern Europe, *see* Warsaw Pact nations
East Timor, 76, 83
Egypt, 75
emotional action, 8, 240–42
Engels, Friedrich, 126
Ethiopia, 209
ethos of culture, 8–9
Europe, Eastern, *see* Warsaw Pact nations
European Economic Community (EEC), 148, 222

Faas, Horst, 43
Fall, Bernard, 33f

FNLA, 149–50
foreign policy: as influenced by political culture, 1, 8–12, 165–66, 229, 234–42; and paranoia, 1, 18, 69–74, 82, 86, 112–13, 166, 239, 240–41; rationality and irrationality in, 1, 7–8, 14, 16, 18–19, 113, 142, 161, 171, 229, 234–42. *See also* Khmers Rouges, irrationality of; Vietnamese Communist Party, irrationality of
France, 222
French colonialism, 32–33, 35, 65, 91, 113, 121, 156, 230
French Communist Party, 27, 35f, 120
Fretilin, 76
Front for the National Liberation of Angola, 149–50
FUNCINPEC, 226
FUNK (National United Front of Cambodia), 56–57, 60, 61, 64, 200–201; and Sihanouk, 49, 51–55, 58, 161, 199, 234

Gang of Four, 66, 84, 181, 232
Geertz, Clifford, 8
Geneva Conference of 1954, 35–36, 40, 41–42, 125–26, 168, 230–31
George, Alexander, 11
German Democratic Republic (GDR), 146, 203
Germany, West, 145–46, 151
Gia Long, 39
Giap, Vo Nguyen, *see* Vo Nguyen Giap
Gorbachev, Mikhail, 158, 222f, 226, 236, 246n11
Great Britain, 133, 160
Great Leap Forward, 18, 70–71, 127, 138, 140
Great Proletarian Cultural Revolution, *see* Cultural Revolution
Grishin, Viktor, 213
Gromyko, Andre, 75, 213
GRUNK (Royal United National Government of Kampuchea), 49, 51–55, 63–64, 161, 199–203
Gulf of Tonkin, 172, 174, 183

Hak, Hang Tun, 200
Hang Tun Hak, 200
Han Vi, 171
Heng, Sieu, 33, 37
Heng Samrin, 110–11, 220, 267n70
Hien, Phan, 185

Hieu, Nguyen, 136, 142
Hitler, Adolph, 13ff, 247n16
Hoa, *see* Chinese, ethnic
Hoan, Hoang Van, 124, 139, 180, 276n59
Hoan, Tran Quoc, 208, 276n59
Hoang Anh, 48, 158, 160f
Hoang Minh Chinh, 135
Hoang Van Hoan, 124, 139, 180, 276n59
Ho Chi Minh, 39, 128, 135–36, 138–39,
   156, 158, 186; on communist internation-
   alism, 130, 132, 159, 273n1; death of,
   151, 153, 171; forms Viet Minh, 31, 123–
   26, 249n33; forms Vietnamese Communist
   Party/Indochinese Communist Party, 27,
   28–29, 30–31, 119–21
Ho Chi Minh City, 176f, 185, 187, 189,
   194
Ho Chi Minh Trail, 40, 42, 50, 63
Hong Kong, 76, 191f
Hou Yuon, 36f, 43, 60
Hoxha, Enver, 130–31
Hua Guofeng, 77, 181, 183f
Huang Hua, 183
Hundred Flowers campaign, 127, 156
Hungary, 123, 128f, 203
Hu Nim, 36f, 43, 58
Hun Sen, 220, 224, 225–27, 228
Huntington, Samuel, 7
Huu, To, 208

ICP, *see* Indochinese Communist Party
ideology: Maoist, 11–12, 14, 17, 18, 38–39,
   47, 60, 70–71, 74–75, 76f, 83f, 86–87,
   89, 91, 97, 103–5, 107, 114, 126–27,
   138–39, 140, 157–61, 164, 165–66, 181,
   200–201, 206f, 231, 235, 237, 241–42;
   Marxist-Leninist, 1, 9–12, 14, 18, 65, 90,
   126–27, 128–29, 138–39, 140–41, 145f,
   157–61, 163, 207, 237, 239, 240. *See also*
   Chinese Communist Party; Communist
   Party of the Soviet Union; Khmers Rouges;
   Marxist-Leninist regimes; Paranoia; Political Culture; Vietnamese Communist Party
Ieng Sary, 37, 53, 58, 60, 64, 105; as Foreign
   Minister, 75f, 80f, 82–83, 85, 92, 95–96;
   and Pol Pot, 77, 106, 109, 227; as pro-
   Chinese, 38, 70, 95–96, 101
imperialism and Marxist-Leninist regimes,
   11, 13, 141f, 159–61, 163, 185–86, 198,
   202, 214–15
India, 129, 150–51, 222

Indochina Federation, 26–29, 34–35, 45,
   65–66, 102, 230
Indochinese Communist Party, 27, 28–36,
   45, 65f, 180, 249n33, 267n70, 278n5;
   and Vietnamese Communist Party, 28–29,
   34–35, 109, 111, 119–23. *See also* Vietnamese Communist Party
Indonesia, 76, 83–84, 137f
Indonesian Communist Party (PKI), 137f
infantile leftism, 54, 158, 160–61, 240
instrumental rationality, *see under* Realist
   theories of international relations, and
   rationality
International Bank for Economic Cooperation (IBEC), 209
International Investment Bank, 209
international relations, realist theories of, *see*
   Realist theories of international relations
irrationality: of Khmers Rouges, 16, 18–19,
   48, 56, 59, 67–68, 78, 86, 89, 103–5,
   113–15, 231–32, 237, 239, 241–42; and
   realist theories of international relations,
   1, 7–8, 14, 16, 18–19, 113, 142, 161, 229,
   234–42; of Vietnamese Communist Party,
   17, 18–19, 171, 179, 181, 195–96, 239,
   241–42
Issarak Front, 34, 36–37
Ith Sarin, 60

Japan, 31, 76, 79, 162, 196
Jiang Qing, 181

Kampuchean Communist Party, *see* Khmers
   Rouges
Kampuchean People's Revolutionary Party,
   111, 220, 224, 225–27. *See also* Khmer
   People's Revolutionary Party
Kampuchean United Front for National
   Salvation, 110–11, 220
Kampuchean Workers' Party, *see* Khmers
   Rouges
Kapitsa, Mikhail, 215
Karnow, Stanley, 43–44
Kaysone Phomvihan, 96
KCP, *see* Khmers Rouges
Keat Chhon, 58
KGB, 207–8
Khac, Le, 213
Khieu, Nguyen Huu, 213
Khieu Samphan, 36f, 43, 58, 64, 93, 102
Khmer Issarak (KI), 31–32, 33f

Khmer Loeu (Khmer Highlanders), 42
Khmer National Liberation Front, 226
Khmer People's Revolutionary Party, 34, 37.
    See also Kampuchean People's Revolution-
    ary Party
Khmer Rumdoah, 54
Khmer Serei (Free Khmer), 40
Khmers Rouges, 2–3, 161; defectors from,
    106f, 109, 110–11, 220, 225, 227; delu-
    sions of grandeur among, 98, 103–4, 114–
    15; domestic policy, 17, 69–70, 74, 81,
    85, 91, 107, 114; foreign policy, 17, 46,
    75–87; irrationality of, 16, 18–19, 48, 56,
    59, 67–68, 78, 86, 89, 103–5, 113–15,
    231–32, 237, 239, 241–42; Maoism
    among, 11–12, 17, 38–39, 47, 60, 70–71,
    74–75, 77, 84, 86–87, 89, 91, 103–5, 114,
    158, 200–201, 231, 235, 237, 242; op-
    pose Sihanouk, 36–39, 41–44, 47, 51–
    54, 55, 58–59, 67; oppose Vietnamese-
    installed Cambodian government, 220,
    223, 226–27, 241; origins of, 36–39; par-
    anoia among, 17, 69–74, 82, 86, 97–98,
    114–15, 237, 240; political culture of, 17,
    54, 69–75, 86, 97–98, 103–4, 114–15,
    235, 237; provided aid by China, 63–64,
    65, 68, 76–77, 84, 88, 221, 223, 234;
    purges among, 16, 54–55, 60, 62, 66, 73–
    74, 82, 98, 106, 107, 114, 220, 232, 237;
    relations with China, 60, 71–72, 75, 76–
    77, 82, 84–87, 88–89, 91–115, 168–70,
    183, 195, 202, 221, 226, 231, 232–33,
    234; relations with Soviet Union, 75, 88,
    201–2, 234; relations with Thai commu-
    nists, 80, 81–82, 86; relations with United
    States, 77, 91, 93–94; relations with Viet-
    namese Communist Party, 6, 13, 36–37,
    38–39, 41–43, 45–46, 47–68, 69, 72–73,
    76, 91–115, 175, 185–86, 193, 200–201,
    210, 229–34, 239. *See also* Cambodia;
    Kampuchean People's Revolutionary
    Party; Khmer Viet Minh
Khmer Viet Minh: suppressed by Pol Pot,
    54–55, 60, 66, 73, 97, 114; and Vietnam-
    ese Communist Party, 35–36, 47, 49,
    54–55, 57, 60, 66f, 73, 97, 220, 251n56.
    See also Khmers Rouges
Khrushchev, Nikita, 45; and China, 13,
    128–29, 130f, 151; and Vietnam, 132,
    133–35, 136, 141, 159
Kien, Do Duc, 136, 142

Kim Il-sung, 77
Kissinger, Henry, 53, 146
Kompong Cham, siege of, 63f
Korea, North, 44, 136–37, 139, 149, 150,
    169, 201, 203; relations with Cambodia,
    71–72, 75ff, 91
Kosygin, Aleksei, 136–37, 213, 216,
    254n119
KPRP, 37, 111, 220, 224, 225–27
Kriangsak Chomanan, 81
Kuomintang (KMT), 121, 123f, 156
KUTV (Communist University for Toilers
    from the East), 120, 122

Land Reform campaign, 90, 127, 156
Lao Dong, *see* Vietnamese Communist Party
Lao Independence Party, 34
Lao People's Revolutionary Party (LPRP), 96
Laos, 33, 169, 197, 200, 209, 220; and
    Geneva Conference of 1954, 40, 125–26,
    168; relations between Vietnamese and
    Laotian communists, 28–30, 31, 34–35,
    45, 51, 66, 88f, 95ff; relations with Cam-
    bodia, 75f; relations with Vietnam, 24,
    26–27, 66, 95f, 107, 230
League of Oppressed Peoples of Asia, 121
Le Duan, 60, 92, 132, 138, 159; and China,
    108–9, 137, 173–74, 179f, 181–82, 184,
    215–16; on ethnic Chinese, 187, 192; as
    General Secretary of Vietnamese Commu-
    nist Party, 135–36, 157–58; on Khmers
    Rouges, 95–96, 100–101, 107, 109–10;
    and Soviet Union, 137, 151, 208–9, 210,
    212f, 215–16
Le Duc Tho, 34, 53, 64, 151
Le Khac, 213
Le Minh Nghia, 136, 142
Lenin, V. I., 13–14, 27–28, 54, 126, 163,
    236, 240, 264n6
Le Thanh Nghi, 184, 210, 213, 276n59
Le Truong Tan, 212
Le Vinh Quoc, 136
Linh, Nguyen Van, 92
Liu Shaoqi, 126–27, 132
Li Xiannian, 183
Loan, Ngo Minh, 180
Long, Gia, 39
Lon Nol, 38, 58, 63, 65, 199–200, 201–2,
    225, 234, 254n119; overthrows Sihanouk,
    44, 47f, 50, 53, 55, 169
Lo Xitsin, 182

Luang Prabang, 24
Ly Ban, 180

Malays, 25
Malaysia, 76, 79
Maoism, 83, 97, 107, 126–27, 138–39, 198,
  207; among Khmers Rouges, 11–12, 17,
  38–39, 47, 60, 70–71, 74–75, 77, 84, 86–
  87, 89, 91, 103–5, 114, 158, 200–201, 231,
  235, 237, 242; criticized by Vietnamese
  communists, 18, 127, 140, 157–61, 164,
  165–66, 181, 206, 241–42; self-reliance
  in, 74ff, 77, 87, 89, 231; subjective factors
  in, 14, 74–75, 86–87, 103–5, 231, 235,
  237, 242. See also Mao Zedong; Marxism-
  Leninism
Mao Zedong, 11–12, 14, 47, 85–86, 87, 90,
  123, 137, 181, 240, 264n6; domestic policies of, 18, 46, 70–71, 75, 90, 127, 138–
  39, 140, 156, 157–59, 160, 164, 165–66,
  287n1; and Khmers Rouges, 38–39, 70–
  71, 75, 77, 84, 231f; as paranoid, 13, 142.
  See also Maoism
Martin, Marie Alexandrine, 225
Marx, Karl, 13–14, 126
Marxism-Leninism: ideology of, 1, 9–12,
  14, 18, 65, 90, 126–27, 128–29, 138–39,
  140–41, 145f, 157–61, 163, 207, 237,
  239, 240; and internationalism, 45, 120,
  123, 127–28, 130ff, 140–41, 142, 231;
  Maoism, 11–12, 14, 17, 18, 38–39, 47,
  60, 70–71, 74–75, 76, 77, 83f, 86–87,
  89, 91, 97, 103–5, 107, 114, 126–27,
  138–39, 140, 157–61, 164, 165–66, 181,
  200–201, 206f, 231, 235, 237, 241–42;
  and revisionism, 132, 134–36, 139, 142,
  145–46, 151, 158, 160, 183, 220. See also
  Chinese Communist Party; Communist
  Party of the Soviet Union; Khmers Rouges;
  Marxist-Leninist regimes; Vietnamese
  Communist Party
Marxist-Leninist regimes: as chiliastic, 9,
  10–15, 104–5, 114–15, 158, 196, 235,
  237, 240–41; collapse of communism in
  Soviet Union/Eastern Europe, 1–2, 223,
  226, 228, 233, 246n11; domestic policies
  of, 10–11, 12–13, 15, 90; and imperialism,
  11, 13, 141f, 159–61, 163, 185–86, 198,
  202, 214–15; and paranoid pseudocommunities, 15, 74, 238; paranoid tendencies
  in, 12–15, 17f, 69–74, 82, 86, 90–91,

97–98, 112–13, 114–15, 142, 166, 171,
  179, 181, 193, 237–38, 239; political cul-
  ture of, 5, 9, 10–15, 104–5, 114–15, 142,
  158, 195–96, 198, 234–36, 237, 240–41.
  See also Chinese Communist Party; Com-
  munist Party of the Soviet Union; Khmers
  Rouges; Marxism-Leninism; Vietnamese
  Communist Party
Mayaguez, seizure of, 91
McArthur, George, 43
Meissner, W. W., 241
Merton, Robert, 240
millenarian political culture, see Chiliastic
  political culture
Minh, Son Ngoc, 33f, 36–37
Mok, Ta, 37, 227
MPLA, 149–50
Mumm, Thiounn, 53
Mun Sek Yen, 224

Nak Ong Chan, 25
National Liberation Front of South Vietnam
  (NLFSV), 150; and Cambodia, 40–41,
  43f, 49, 54f, 57, 60, 61–63, 169, 254n119
NATO, 148, 149
Netherlands, 76
Neto, Agostino, 149f
Ne Win, 79
New People's Army, 83
Nghi, Le Thanh, 184, 210, 213, 276n59
Nghia, Le Minh, 136, 142
Nghia, Nguyen Minh, 136, 142
Ngo Dinh Diem, 39, 170
Ngo Minh Loan, 180
Ngo Thuyen, 180
Nguyen Ai Quoc, see Ho Chi Minh
Nguyen Chi Thanh, 153
Nguyen Co Thach, 213
Nguyen Duy Trinh, 108, 181, 210, 213,
  276n59
Nguyen Hieu, 136, 142
Nguyen Huu Khieu, 213
Nguyen Huu Tho, 41, 150
Nguyen Minh Nghia, 136, 142
Nguyen Sinh Cung, see Ho Chi Minh
Nguyen Thanh Son, 34
Nguyen Trong Vinh, 180
Nguyen Truong Vinh, 185
Nguyen Van Linh, 92
Nguyen Van Thieu, 187
Nim, Hu, 36f, 43, 58

Nimeiri, Ja'afar el-, 147–48
Nixon, Richard M., 144, 151–52, 160, 162, 204, 207
Nol, Lon, *see* Lon Nol
Norodom Ranariddh, 226–27
Norodom Sihanouk, 3, 35–36, 63–64, 70, 84, 91, 230–31; opposed by Khmers Rouges, 36–39, 41–44, 47, 51–54, 55, 58–59, 67; opposes Lon Nol regime, 48–49, 51–54, 199–203, 234; opposes Vietnamese-installed Cambodian government, 221f, 225, 226–27; policies toward China, 40–41, 43f, 46, 169; policies toward Khmers Rouges, 41–44; policies toward North Vietnam, 39–46, 47, 169; policies toward South Vietnam, 39–41, 42, 45–46, 169; policies toward United States, 40, 43–44; and Soviet Union, 44, 169, 254n119; supported by China, 49, 51ff, 65–66, 67, 161–62, 169–70, 202, 221; supported by North Vietnam, 41–42, 47, 48–49, 51–54, 55, 67
North Korea, *see* Korea, North
North Vietnam, *see* Vietnam, North
Nouth, Penn, 40, 201
Nuon Chea, 37, 92, 93, 95–96, 101, 109, 113, 227, 267n70

Oberg, Jean-Christophe, 79–80
Ognetov, Igor, 210
Organization of African Unity (OAU), 149
Ostpolitik, 145, 146

Pakistan, 150–51
Paracel Islands, 172–73, 174, 183, 186
paranoia: among Khmers Rouges, 17, 69–74, 82, 86, 97–98, 114–15, 237, 240; characteristics of, 12–15; and foreign policy, 1, 18, 69–74, 82, 86, 112–13, 166, 239, 240–41; in Marxist-Leninist regimes, 12–15, 17f, 54, 69–74, 82, 86, 90–91, 97–98, 112–13, 114–15, 142, 166, 171, 179, 181, 193, 237–38, 239f; paranoid pseudocommunities, 15, 74, 238; in Vietnamese Communist Party, 18, 90–91, 112–13, 142, 166, 171, 179, 181, 193, 195–96, 237–38. *See also* Ideology; Political culture
paranoid pseudocommunities and Marxist-Leninist regimes, 15, 74, 238
Paringaux, R. P., 190–91

Paris Peace Conference, 58f, 61, 63, 152, 171, 206
Penn Nouth, 40, 201
Pen Sovan, 111
People's Republic of China, *see* China
People's Republic of Kampuchea (PRK), *see* Cambodia
People's Socialist Community, 36
Peru, 76
Pham Van Dong, 128, 135, 150, 213; and Cambodia, 41, 58, 64–65, 83, 95; and China, 124, 181ff
Phan Hien, 185
Pheum, Sao, 106, 109–10, 267n70
Philippines, 83, 173
Phnom Penh, 32
Phu, Tran, 121
Picq, Laurence, 85
Podgorny, Nikolai, 152
Poland, 129
political culture: characteristics of, 8–10, 12; as chiliastic, 9, 10–15, 104–5, 114–15, 158, 195–96, 235, 237, 240–41; as influencing foreign policy, 1, 8–12, 165–66, 229, 234–42; of Khmers Rouges, 17, 54, 69–75, 86, 97–98, 103–4, 114–15, 235, 237; of Marxist-Leninist regimes, 5, 9, 10–15, 104–5, 114–15, 142, 158, 195–96, 198, 234–36, 237, 240–41; of Vietnamese Communist Party, 89–91, 142, 161, 163–66, 171, 195–96. *See also* Ideology; Paranoia
Pol Pot, 13f, 92ff, 99, 105, 240; early communist activities, 36–39, 267n70; identifies Vietnamese and Thailand as enemies, 72, 82, 97–98, 114, 237; and Ieng Sary, 77, 106, 109, 227; Mao's influence on, 38–39, 70, 77, 86–87; as pro-Chinese, 95–96, 101; purges Khmers Rouges, 73–74, 82, 98, 106f, 114, 220, 232, 237; suppresses Khmer Viet Minh, 54–55, 60, 66, 73, 97, 114
Popular Movement for the Liberation of Angola, 149–50
Portugal, 144, 148–49, 150, 207
Portuguese Communist Party (PCP), 148–49
Portuguese Socialist Party, 148–49
Pracheachon (People's) Party, 36
PRC, *see* China
Provisional Revolutionary Government of South Vietnam (PRGSV), 44, 60, 63–64, 94, 151, 162. *See also* Viet Cong
Public Security Bureau (PSB), 191–93

Quyen, Tran, 106–7, 186

Radvanyi, Janos, 132, 136–37, 138
Ranariddh, Norodom, 226–27
rationality, *see under* Realist theories of
    international relations
realist theories of international relations,
    1, 113, 142, 161; and rationality, 7–8,
    14, 16, 18–19, 229, 234–42. *See also*
    Ideology; Khmers Rouges, irrationality
    of; Paranoia; Vietnamese Communist
    Party, irrationality of
Red Guards, 138f, 160
Republic of China, 129, 173
Republic of Vietnam, *see* Vietnam, South
revisionism, *see under* Marxism-Leninism
revolutionary millenarian political culture,
    see Chiliastic political culture
Rithaudeen, Tengku Ahmad, 79
Roberto, Holden, 149
Romania, 75, 144
Russia, 1–2, 219

Saloth Sar, *see* Pol Pot
Samphan, Khieu, *see* Khieu Samphan
Samrin, Heng, 110–11, 220
Sangkum Reastr Niyum, 36
Sann, Son, 221f, 225f
Sao Pheum, 106, 109–10, 267n70
Sarin, Ith, 60
Sary, Ieng, *see* Ieng Sary
Savimbi, Jonas, 149
self-reliance, Maoist doctrine of, 74ff, 77,
    87, 89, 231
Sen, Hun, 220, 224, 225–27, 228
Shawcross, William, 48
Shcherbakov, Ilya, 51, 204
Shelepin, Alexander, 138
Siam, *see* Thailand
Sieu Heng, 33, 37
Sihanouk, Norodom, *see* Norodom Sihanouk
Sim, Chea, 220
Sirik Matak, 43, 254n119
SOC, *see* Cambodia
socialism, *see* Marxism-Leninism
Socialist Republic of Vietnam, *see* Vietnam
Son, Nguyen Thanh, 34
Son Ngoc Minh, 33f, 36–37, 250n39
Son Ngoc Thanh, 40, 250n39
Son Sann, 221f, 225f
Son Sen, 37, 101, 109, 113, 227

Southeast Asia Treaty Organization
    (SEATO), 40
South Vietnam, *see* Vietnam, South
Sovan, Pen, 111
Soviet Union, 5f, 74, 85, 96, 108–9, 169,
    175, 184; collapse of communism in, 223,
    226, 228, 233, 246n11; and détente, 13,
    144–46, 150, 151–52, 162, 166; domestic
    policies in, 12–13, 122, 286–87; influences
    Vietnamese communists, 11–12, 18, 90,
    119–23, 127–29, 140, 142, 167, 264n6;
    invades Czechoslovakia, 87, 106, 107–8,
    144–45, 158; provides aid to North Viet-
    nam, 132, 136–37, 138f, 141–42, 154–56,
    165, 167, 182, 198, 204ff, 207f, 276n61;
    provides aid to Vietnam, 110, 182, 198,
    208–9, 210, 212, 217–18, 222–23, 226;
    relations with Albania, 130–31, 144; rela-
    tions with Cambodia, 44, 75, 88, 97, 197–
    202, 233–34; relations with China, 6, 16–
    17, 45, 47, 87, 97, 128–31, 133, 135, 140,
    143–44, 148, 149–51, 168, 181–82, 185,
    195, 197–98, 202, 212, 215, 218, 233–34,
    235–36, 239, 246n13, 287n1; relations
    with Khmers Rouges, 75, 88, 201–2, 234;
    relations with North Vietnam, 6, 16, 18,
    88, 90, 119, 127–28, 129–30, 133–35,
    141–42, 143–66, 157, 167, 197–98, 202,
    203–7; relations with United States, 132f,
    151–52, 159, 162–63, 166, 207, 234,
    287n1; relations with Vietnam, 1–2, 6,
    16–17, 108–9, 110, 113, 168, 173f, 180,
    197–98, 207–18, 219, 222–24, 233–34,
    236f; relations with West Germany, 145–
    46, 151; relations with Yugoslavia, 13, 45,
    123, 128ff, 132–33, 144; as revolutionary
    model, 26–28, 47, 67, 90, 122–23, 126f,
    130, 140, 142, 144; and Stalin, 11, 13, 15,
    74, 90, 122–23, 126, 129f, 142, 240. *See
    also* Communist Party of the Soviet Union
    (CPSU)
Spratly Islands, 172–73, 174, 183, 186
SRV, *see* Vietnam
Stalin, Joseph, 11, 74, 129f, 142, 286–87; as
    paranoid, 13, 15, 142, 240, 247n16,
    247n24; and Vietnamese Communist
    Party, 90, 122–23, 126, 142, 264n6. *See
    also* Soviet Union
State of Cambodia, *see* Cambodia
subjective factors in Maoism, 11, 14, 74–75,
    86–87, 103–5, 231, 235, 237, 242

Sudan, 144, 147–48
Sudanese Communist Party, 147–48
Suharto, 83
Sukarno, 137
Suslov, Mikhail, 180
Sweden, 79–80, 222

Taiwan, 129, 173
Ta Mok, 37, 227
Tan, Le Trong, 212
Tang, Truong Nhu, 151, 162f
Thach, Nguyen Co, 213
Thai Communist Party, 35, 80, 81–82, 86, 96–97
Thai communists, relations with Vietnamese communists, 96–97
Thailand, 32f, 40, 93–94, 96, 169, 220; relations with Cambodia, 24, 25–26, 69, 72, 78–83, 86–87, 223, 226, 231–32, 234–35, 237
Thang, Ton Duc, 93
Thanh, Nguyen Chi, 153
Thanh, Son Ngoc, 40
Thanh Nien, 120–21
Thieu, Nguyen Van, 187
Thioeunn, Thiounn, 77
Thiounn Mumm, 53
Thiounn Thioeunn, 77
Tho, Le Duc, *see* Le Duc Tho
Tho, Nguyen Huu, 41, 150
Thuy, Xuan, 177, 184–85, 188
Thuyen, Ngo, 180
Timor, East, 76, 83
Tin, Bui, 192
Tito, 13, 128, 140, 142
To Huu, 208
Ton Duc Thang, 93
Tonkin, Gulf of, 172, 174, 183
Tran Phu, 121
Tran Quoc Hoan, 208, 276n59
Tran Quyen, 106–7, 186
Trinh, Nguyen Duy, 108, 181, 210, 213, 276n59
Truong Chinh, 64, 93, 135, 139
Truong Nhu Tang, 151, 162, 163
Tucker, Robert C., 13

Union for the Total National Liberation of Angola (UNITA), 149–50
United Nations and Cambodia, 201, 219, 221

United Nations Temporary Administration in Cambodia (UNTAC), 226
United States, 9, 51, 83, 129, 150, 184, 195–96, 198, 227; relations with Cambodia, 40, 43–44, 48ff, 52, 58f, 63–64, 68, 77, 91, 93–94, 201–2, 223; relations with China, 18, 87, 152, 157, 159, 161–63, 166, 234, 237; relations with Khmers Rouges, 77, 91, 93–94; relations with North Vietnam, 6, 16, 63–64, 65, 138, 139–40, 154, 156f, 160, 171, 204; relations with Soviet Union, 132f, 151–52, 159, 162–63, 166, 207, 234, 287n1; relations with Vietnam, 3, 221–22
Uppadit Pachariyangkun, 78–79, 80f
Ustinov, Dmitri, 213

value-rational action, 8, 241–42
Van Doan, 136
Van Tien Dung, 213
VCP, *see* Vietnamese Communist Party
Vet, Vorn, 77
Vi, Han, *see* Han Vi
Viet Cong, 150; and Cambodia, 40–41, 43f, 49, 54f, 57, 60, 61–63, 169, 254n119
Viet Minh, 31–36, 65, 123–26, 127, 249n33, 251n56
Vietnam: China cuts off aid to, 193–94, 208–9, 210–11, 217, 233; and Council for Mutual Economic Assistance, 6, 16, 143, 194, 206f, 209–11; ethnic Chinese in, 6, 16, 18, 108, 112, 133f, 170–71, 174–79, 185, 187–93, 194, 215, 233, 237–38, 278n5; French colonialism in, 32–33, 35, 91, 113, 121, 156, 230; influence of Chinese institutions on, 24, 126–27, 156, 165, 230; provided aid by China, 174, 179–89 *passim*, 196, 210, 211; provided aid by Soviet Union, 110, 182, 198, 208–9, 210, 212, 217–18, 219, 222–23, 226; relations with Association of Southeast Asian Nations, 83; relations with Cambodia, 1, 5–6, 13–26 *passim*, 31–32, 69–86 *passim*, 91–115, 165, 168, 175, 185–86, 193ff, 210, 212f, 215–23, 224–28, 229–34, 237, 239; relations with China, 1, 5, 6, 13–19 *passim*, 93, 97, 100–101, 107–19 *passim*, 140–41, 153–54, 156–57, 164–96 *passim*, 209–21 *passim*, 228, 230–42 *passim*; relations with Laos, 24, 26–27, 66, 95, 96, 107, 230;

relations with Soviet Union, 1–2, 6, 16–17, 108–9, 110, 113, 168, 173f, 180, 197–98, 207–18, 219, 222–24, 233–34, 236f; relations with Thailand, 24f; relations with United States, 3, 221–22; traditional attitudes toward Cambodia in, 10, 17–18, 24, 35, 45, 65, 230, 235; traditional Cambodian attitudes toward, 10, 17, 31–33, 35, 36, 38, 39–40, 113; traditional imperial ambitions of, 16f, 23–25, 31–32, 45, 65, 112, 230. *See also* Vietnam, North; Vietnam, South; Vietnamese Communist Party

Vietnam, North: provided aid by China, 88–89, 140–41, 151, 154–56, 163, 165f, 167–68, 174–75, 208, 276n61; provided aid by Soviet Union, 132, 136–37, 138f, 141–42, 154–56, 165, 167, 182, 198, 204ff, 207f, 276n61; relations with Cambodia, 39–46, 47–68, 88–89, 125–26, 169–70, 199, 202; relations with China, 6, 16, 18, 65–66, 88–89, 119, 125–27, 128–42, 154–55, 161–66, 167–70, 197–98, 202ff; relations with Soviet Union, 6, 16, 18, 88, 90, 119, 127–28, 129–30, 133–35, 141–42, 143–66, 157, 167, 197–98, 202, 203–7; relations with United States, 6, 16, 63–64, 65, 138, 139–40, 154, 156f, 160, 171, 204; relations with Yugoslavia, 128, 131, 132–33, 142; supports Sihanouk, 41–42, 47, 48–49, 51–54, 55, 67; war with South Vietnam, 6, 16, 42, 49, 51, 60, 63–64, 65ff, 68, 89–90, 101, 129–30, 135ff, 138, 141f, 152, 154–55, 164f, 169, 171ff, 193, 198, 207, 216, 218, 231, 254n119. *See also* Provisional Revolutionary Government of South Vietnam; Vietnam; Vietnam, South; Vietnamese Communist Party

Vietnam, South, 39–41, 56, 61, 62, 94, 170, 187; war with North Vietnam, 6, 16, 42, 49, 51, 60, 63–64, 65ff, 68, 89–90, 101, 129–30, 135ff, 138, 141ff, 152, 154–55, 164f, 169, 171ff, 193, 198, 207, 216, 218, 231, 254n119. *See also* Provisional Revolutionary Government of South Vietnam (PRGSV); Viet Cong; Vietnam; Vietnam, North; Vietnamese Communist Party

Viet Nam Doc Lap Dong Minh Hoi, *see* Viet Minh

Vietnamese Communist Party, 2–3; aligns with Soviet Union, 6, 16–17, 212–18; Chi-nese Communist Party criticized by, 18, 127, 138–40, 157–63, 165–66, 206, 241–42; Chinese Communist Party influence on, 90, 126–27, 138, 140–41, 156, 164, 264n6; and Communist International, 16, 26–29, 45, 65, 119–23, 141, 230, 235; and détente, 146, 150, 151–52, 162, 166; domestic policy, 6, 13–14, 89–91, 108, 126–27, 138–39, 140–41, 156, 157–59, 170–71, 174–79, 185, 187–93, 194, 195–96, 215; as favoring neither Chinese nor Soviets, 130f, 141–42, 143, 151, 203, 204–5, 206, 273n1; founded by Ho Chi Minh, 28–29, 119–21; imperial ambitions of, 6, 16f, 26–29, 45, 65–66, 85–86, 88–89, 102, 112, 204, 224–26, 229–31, 233–36; and Indochina Federation, 26–29, 65–66, 102; and Indochinese Communist Party (ICP), 28–29, 34–35, 109, 111, 119–23; internationalism in, 18, 120, 127–28, 130ff, 140–41, 142, 146, 157, 159–61, 163, 165–66, 173–74, 182, 184, 231, 237; irrationality of, 17, 18–19, 171, 179, 181, 195–96, 239, 241–42; and Khmer Viet Minh, 35–36, 47, 49, 54–55, 57, 60, 66f, 73, 97, 220, 251n56; leadership changes in, 180, 186, 213, 276n59; paranoia in, 18, 90–91, 112–13, 142, 166, 171, 179, 181, 193, 195–96, 237–38; policies toward ethnic Chinese, 18, 108, 170–71, 174–79, 185, 187–93, 194, 195–96, 215, 233, 237–38, 278n5; political culture of, 89–91, 142, 161, 163–66, 171, 195–96; purges in, 135–36, 142, 164, 233, 237–38; relations with Chinese Communist Party (CCP), 13, 121, 123–27, 129–36, 138–41, 151, 165, 170–71, 173–75, 179–80, 181–82, 183–85, 186, 195–96, 204–5, 206–7; relations with Communist Party of the Soviet Union (CPSU), 127–31, 133–35, 138, 140–41, 179–80, 204–5, 206–8, 210, 212–18; relations with Communist Party of Thailand, 96–97; relations with early Cambodian communists, 28–30, 31, 33–37; relations with Khmers Rouges, 6, 13, 36–37, 38–39, 41–43, 45–46, 47–68, 69, 72–73, 76, 91–115, 175, 185–86, 193, 199, 200–201, 202, 210, 229–34, 239; relations with Laotian communists, 28–30, 31, 34–35, 45, 51, 66, 88f, 95ff, 193; Soviet influence on, 11–12, 18, 90, 119–23,

127–29, 140, 142, 167, 198, 207, 264n6; on Soviet invasion of Czechoslovakia, 106, 144–45, 158; and Stalin, 90, 122–23, 126, 142, 254n6; supports Sihanouk, 41–42, 47, 48–49, 51–54, 55, 170; as tilting toward China, 132–36, 141f, 151, 153, 157, 159; as tilting toward Soviet Union, 18, 119, 127–29, 141–42, 143–66, 167–68, 169, 171, 180, 194f, 198, 204, 206, 207–9, 233, 235, 237. *See also* Provisional Revolutionary Government of South Vietnam (PRGSV); Viet Cong; Viet Minh; Vietnam; Vietnam, North; Vietnam, South
Vietnamese Workers' Party (VWP), *see* Vietnamese Communist Party
Viet Nam Quoc Dan Dang (VNQDD), 156
Viet Nam Thanh Nien Kach Menh Hoi (Vietnamese Revolutionary Youth Association), 120–21
Vietnam War, *see under* Vietnam, North, war with South Vietnam
Vinh, Nguyen Trong, *see* Nguyen Trong Vinh
Vinh, Nguyen Truong, 185
Vo Nguyen Giap, 124f, 135–36, 142, 162, 183, 186, 208, 276n59; and Cambodia, 213, 223

Vorn Vet, 77

Warsaw Pact nations, 75, 128, 144–45, 146, 149, 199–200, 211, 222; collapse of communism in, 223, 226, 228, 233, 246n11
Weber, Max, 8, 240, 241–42
Wei Guoqing, 125
West Germany, 145–46
worldview of culture, 8–9

Xuan Thuy, 177, 184–85, 188
Xu Xiangqian, 186

Ye Jianying, 181
Yen, Mun Sek, 224
Yezhov, Nikolai, 122
Yugoslavia, 75f, 134, 140; relations with North Vietnam, 128, 131, 132–33, 142; relations with Soviet Union, 13, 45, 123, 128f, 130, 132–33, 144
Yuon, Hou, 36f, 43, 60

Zaire, 149
Zambia, 149
Zhou Enlai, 58, 84, 131, 147, 162, 185
Zhu De, 126–27

Library of Congress Cataloging-in-Publication Data

Morris, Stephen J.
Why Vietnam invaded Cambodia : political culture and
the causes of war / Stephen J. Morris
    p. cm.
Includes bibliographical references and index.
ISBN 0-8047-3049-0 (cloth : alk. paper)
1. Vietnam—History—20th century. 2. Cambodia—
History—20th century. 3. Vietnam—Foreign relations—
Cambodia. 4. Cambodia—Foreign relations—Vietnam.
5. Cambodian-Vietnamese Conflict, 1977–1991. I. Title.
DS556.8.M69 1999
959.704—dc21   98-53891

Original printing 1999
Last figure below indicates year of this printing:
08 07 06 05 04 03 02 01 00 99

4952